Windows into the Infinite:

A Guide to the Hindu Scriptures

by

Barbara Powell

ASIAN HUMANITIES PRESS
Fremont, California

ASIAN HUMANITIES PRESS

Asian Humanities Press offers to the specialist and the general reader alike the best in new translations of major works and significant original contributions to enhance our understanding of Asian literature, religions, cultures and thought.

Dedication

This Book is dedicated to all students of religion, both spiritual aspirants and secular students. When I was a student, I badly needed a book like this one, but none existed. It gives me great satisfaction to offer one to you.

Library of Congress Cataloging-in-Publication Data

Powell, Barbara, 1962-
Windows into the infinite : a guide to the Hindu scriptures / by Barbara Powell.
p. cm.
Includes bibliographical references and index.
ISBN 0-87573-071-X
1. Hinduism—Sacred books—Introductions. I. Title.
BL1111.5.P86 1996
294.5'92—dc20 96-6826
CIP

Contents

Diagrams

Introduction

There is an incredible thrill, a hybrid of acute anticipation, frustration, fear and euphoria when one awakens to the reality of the spiritual odyssey. On discovering one's own path among the myriad of possibilities, one experiences yet another phase of joy. The Westerner who has found him or herself drawn to Hinduism and has taken up a form of *yoga*— spiritual practice linking one to the Supreme — has no doubt had some contact with a Hindu scripture, perhaps the *Bhagavad-Gītā* or a novelized version of the *Mahābhārata*. So far so good. Intrigued, the aspirant visits the Hinduism section of the metaphysical bookstore or sends for a catalog offering translations of the Hindu scriptures. Suddenly the honeymoon is over. As the stricken innocent's jaw drops, the terrible reality sets in. Volumes and volumes of intimidating books with titles like *Śrī Lalitāmbika Sahasranāma Stotram* suggest, perhaps, that the Hindu canon is an impenetrable fortress, accessible only to scholars and cultured *brāhmaṇas*. The sheer number of titles is so daunting, it's easy to become discouraged. Leave them for the bookish types, the aspirant thinks, I'll listen to my teacher and attend to my practice. Who needs books? Reading is second-hand experience anyway.

Not so. Submerging oneself in the blissful waters of the sacred texts is not only essential to a well-rounded program of spiritual practice, it is extremely pleasurable. Sacred books are qualitatively different from any other literature and they invoke in one a wholly different mode of consciousness. They inform, inspire, purify, and awaken. So powerful are these texts in transforming those who encounter them, the very act of scriptural study, either by reading or by hearing a recital, is considered a yogic discipline. The scriptures themselves attest to their power:

> Whoever fills the cup of his ears with the nectar consisting in the narratives of the excellences of the Lord, the life and soul of devotees, and quaffs the same, such a person, though corrupted by many worldly tendencies, will become purified, and he will attain to the feet of the Lord.
>
> *Śrīmad Bhāgavatam* (2.3.37)[1]

> And anyone who reads this sacred discourse of ours, I shall consider that he has worshipped me (God) in spirit. Even if a man

simply listens to these words with faith, and does not doubt them, he will be freed from sins and reach the heaven of the righteous.

Bhagavad-Gītā (18.70-71)[2]

Relating and hearing this eternal anecdote . . . the intelligent man becomes glorified in the region that is Brahman.

Kaṭha Upaniṣad (1.3.16)[3]

Were scriptures secondhand knowledge, why would the greatest saints, seers and mystics have poured so much into them for so long? The Hindu canon is comprised partly of the distilled essence of an incredibly rich and illumined oral tradition, and partly of the attempts by spiritually realized souls to express their experiences and discoveries in writing for the benefit of other earnest seekers. All spiritual seekers, then, should take advantage of this treasure. The voices of God-realized beings are there to be heard. This amazing literature enhances one's life so much, it's a wonder and a pity that so many sincere aspirants pass them by. What accounts for this?

I have long suspected that the sheer bulk of the Hindu canon along with its diversity might overwhelm the westerner new to the subject. There are so many titles, so many categories and genres. How do we begin to make sense of them? Jews have their Torah and Talmud, Christians their Old and New Testaments, Moslems their Qur'an, but the Hindus have dozens of scriptures. Where do we start? How do we proceed? The aim of this book is to help the seeker in distress.

While it is primarily addressed to readers who are actually participating in spiritual life, this volume should also be useful to the secular student of religion and religious literature. Both varieties of reader want the same thing, a clear, concise introduction to the principal Hindu scriptures and their contents. This book is not meant to replace a reading of the scriptures themselves, but to be used as a study tool to help guide the reader through the major points of each text and to provide clarification for language, metaphors, etc. which are difficult for contemporary westerners to understand.

Mention should be made of what this book is not. It is not a general introduction to Hinduism as a whole. A complete survey of Hinduism is beyond the scope of this work and there are many good ones available already. I assume the reader has a previous knowledge of some of the basic features of Hinduism, such as reincarnation *(saṃsāra)*, karma, Brahman (literally "The Supreme", God), Ātman (the Self or soul), *yoga* and so on. All Sanskrit terms used in this book are included in the glossary, so any unfamiliar concept can be looked up. As we go through each text, the basics are naturally covered, which is another reason I am not setting aside a separate space for an overview. It is my firm belief that a careful reading of the *Bhagavad-Gītā* is the best and most complete introduction to Hinduism one can find anyway. As this is included in these pages, I prefer to let the master, Lord Kṛṣṇa, do the talking.

A possible criticism of this work is that I present the texts with a philosophical bias, namely *advaita vedānta,* or non-dualism. This is worth addressing. Hinduism is an infinitely varied tradition with many different schools of thought which espouse conflicting interpretations of the same scriptures. Some Hindus strongly argue that the scriptures indicate that the Supreme is a personal God, while others stress just as forcefully that the Supreme is impersonal, without form or attributes. Still others say that both are simultaneously true. Similarly, there are those who insist that God and the individual soul are separate and distinct, while others claim the two are one. Both support this view by referring to the authority of the scriptures. Some people say the sacred literature extols *bhakti yoga* as the preeminent discipline, while others say that many methods are presented as equally efficacious. The genius of the Hindu canon is that it lends itself so readily to a range of interpretations. However, I lean here towards *advaita,* non-dualism, and universality in the sense that all divine forms, all paths, all yogas are equally true, because *advaita vedānta* is the closest thing to a mainstream viewpoint. While many Hindus disagree with it, the majority accept it as the central theme of Hinduism. In a work as general as this one, then, it is appropriate to hearken to the consensus view.

With a few exceptions, the translations I've drawn from are consistently those by the Swamis of the Ramakrishna Order. When I began this book (quite a long time ago) I searched for the best English translations I could find and repeatedly discovered them to be by this order of monks. The texts were even-headed, scholarly and open-minded. As much as I recommend these versions, I encourage the reader to explore as many translations as possible and, in subsequent readings, stick with the one you like best. Different styles appeal to different people and, as far as I know, there are no definitive versions. I would steer clear of very old (19th or early 20th century) translations by Westerners as these too often reflect a condescension and misunderstanding typical of colonialism.

The sacred literature of Hinduism is unique in all the world for its color, diversity and dynamism. One finds in them solid, practical instructions for *sādhanā* (spiritual practice), highly intellectual philosophizing, gorgeous hymns and poems, inspiring accounts of saints and *Avatāras,* moral and ethical instructions, epic sagas, virtually anything a spiritual seeker could ever need or want. It is with great pleasure that I share my enthusiasm with people who might otherwise pass by these gifts which India has so graciously given to the world. I devoutly hope others, both spiritual seekers and secular readers, will grow to cherish them as much as I have. The basis of this love, however, is understanding, and it is in pursuit of this that this book has been written.

> May Brahman protect us both. May he nourish us both.
> May we both work together with great energy.
> May our study be vigorous and effective.
> May there be harmony between us.
> Om Peace! Peace! Peace!
>
> Peace Invocation from *Śvetāśvatara Upaniṣad*[4]

NOTES

1. Swāmī Tapasyānanda, *Śrīmad Bhāgavata, the Holy Book of God* (Mylapore: Sri Ramakrishna Math, 1980), pp. 102-103.
2. Swāmī Prabhavananda and Christopher Isherwood, *The Song of God: Bhagavad-Gītā* (New York: New American Library, 1972), p. 130.
3. Swāmī Gambhīrānanda, *Kaṭha Upaniṣad* (Calcutta: Advaita Asrama, 1980), p. 79
4. Adapted from Swāmī Tyāgīśānanda, *Śvetāśvatara Upaniṣad* (Mylapore: Sri Ramakrishna Math, 1979), p. 8.

Part I

Getting Started

CHAPTER ONE

How to Read and Interpret a Sacred Text

When we read a sacred scripture, there are several things we're looking for. One is, of course, factual information. Perhaps we simply want to know how a book is structured and what it contains, or perhaps we want information that the book supplies, such as the nature of the soul, instructions for spiritual practice, or the activities of the Divine Mother Durgā. In this sense, we would read it like any other book.

However, sacred texts are usually written on more than one level. Most of the time they hint at deeper meanings than are apparent on the surface. They often employ symbolism, metaphor, simile and parable to express realities that are too subtle or multifaceted to explain outright. Often more than one meaning is suggested by a single image or passage; this multilayered style of composition is extremely prevalent in Hindu writings and has given rise to a longstanding tradition of lively and penetrating textual interpretation. So the second thing we're looking for is veiled meaning, and this calls for the art of interpretation.

A special function of the sacred scriptures is their power to inspire. Reading religious books is an extremely efficacious discipline, for while it educates us, it also rouses our spiritual fervor. Scriptures ignite the fires of our devotion, give us the courage to step up our efforts, even make us feel closer to the Divine then and there. Reading of the exploits of Kṛṣṇa can be so spiritually delectable one feels a hair's-breadth away from liberation. Pondering an *Upaniṣad* passage deeply, one senses that Brahman realization is extremely close at hand. Sacred literature acts as a fuel to keep our spiritual journey at a steady clip.

Yet there is still another dimension to sacred literature, the mystical dimension. This aspect is not usually perceptible to the casual or academic reader. Some texts flatly state that they ought not to be read by the worldly because such people can never fully understand them. A mystical reading of a piece takes for granted that it is a conductor of spiritual power, that the Divine dwells in the words and may be communed with through them. Kṛṣṇa literally exists in the *Śrīmad Bhāgavatam*; The Divine Mother is actually present in the *Caṇḍi*, and when we read, hear or chant it, we experience union with Her. In this sense, the text is a theophany, a miraculous appearance of the Divine in the mundane world. When we read the piece in this way, it is no longer "reading" in the ordinary sense. A whole new dimension of experience has opened up.

Simply put, there are three ways a piece can be read. One can read for the surface content, like an ordinary book, one can read with an eye to interpretation and analysis, as an exegete (one who "draws out" meaning), or one can read for a religious experience. All three approaches are valid. Which one you take depends entirely on your reasons for delving into the literature. However, a few basic strategies are helpful no matter what you're looking for, and it is to these we now turn.

Getting Started

Before you begin, try to equip yourself with some basic information about your book. This may be provided in its introduction. You should know its general date of composition, its genre, the school of thought it represents and its actual or legendary author(s). This may seem obvious, but all too often students misread a text for lack of basic background information.

While not absolutely necessary, a method I have found helpful is to give each scripture at least two readings. The first is a preliminary run through, where you make your way to the end quickly. The first time out, you might skip the translator's commentary unless you run across a passage or term you genuinely don't understand. This quick reading will give you a general sense of the book's structure, content and viewpoint, all of which, ironically, could be lost in too slow a first reading. When you come back for the second reading, you will be comfortable and familiar with the piece, will know what to expect, and therefore will be more likely to take the time to examine each passage and ponder its meaning. For some texts, such as the shorter *Upaniṣads*, this first reading could take less than an hour.

The second reading is where the real examination begins. Have a pencil and paper handy so you can jot down references, quotations, questions, impressions. Perhaps you run across a passage that seems familiar, that you think you might have seen repeated in another text, or echoed in a scripture from another tradition, such as the Bible, or reminds you of something you read in a secular book. Perhaps you read a statement on one page and ten pages later one that seems to contradict it. Perhaps you find a passage especially beautiful, significant, or worth meditating on. Perhaps you notice recurring themes, images or metaphors. Take note of them.

If a translator's commentary is provided, read it now. Carefully consider his or her opinions. Do they illuminate the meaning of the text or not? What does the translator decide *not* to comment on? In other words, if the commentator has not addressed an aspect of the scripture you think he or she should have, consider why. Consider, too, the author's tone, as this can give an indication of his or her purpose. Is it reverential? Scholarly and detached? Preachy? Beware of the occasional commentary which seems to express a subtle contempt for its subject. Use your own judgement. Commentaries are important additions to scriptures which appear veiled or heavily symbolic, but the reader should attempt to employ his or her own powers of analysis to glean the meaning from a piece. Now we turn to some approaches you might take to do just that.

The Literal Reading

The most natural point of departure is the literal reading. Simply put, it is the study of the direct, surface meaning of the text. The various books in the Hindu canon and apocrypha superficially appear to espouse divergent views on the nature of the Absolute, the individual and the universe, but when taken as a whole, and considered in terms of a whole, the books can be harmonized and a general scheme comes through. Harmonizing the texts through interpretation has been a preoccupation of *vedāntins* and *paṇḍits* throughout the centuries and continues to this day. Nevertheless, when first studying a particular book, take note of its general theological and cosmological features. Only then can you work with the material creatively and determine how it can be worked into your personal spiritual practices, school of thought, and viewpoint in general.

Notice whether the book seems to indicate that the world is real but ultimately insignificant, or whether it views this world merely as a dream perceived as real because of the veil of *māyā*. Is the Absolute, as is indicated in the *Upaniṣads*, without attributes but the reservoir of all attributes in potential? Is It conceived of as principally masculine, as in the *Śrīmad Bhāgavatam*? Feminine, as in the *Śrīmad Devī Bhāgavatam*? Are the gods various aspects of a single, all-encompassing Brahman, are they individual, lesser deities subordinate to the topmost Godhead, or are they purely symbolic? What does the text recommend people do in order to realize Brahman for themselves? Yogic austerities? Selfless service? Devotion to the Deity? Adherence to *dharma* (individual duty and responsibility) in a spirit of detachment? Intellectual introspection? All of these?

When we take this approach, our goal is to determine precisely what the author meant to say. When we examine the substructure of a text, as will be discussed next, we are looking for clues in understanding it on a deeper level, but in the literal approach we are reading for the practical, informative content. We are accepting the text "as it is", and studying its message and relevance at face value. Before we can proceed to any other approach, we must employ this one first, otherwise we may lose sight of the basic purpose of the piece and our whole understanding of it will become distorted. I have seen scholars of great eminence come up with the craziest conclusions because they lost sight of this most basic first step.

The Art of Interpretation

In general, there are two sorts of interpretation. The first is to determine undercurrents of meaning which the author consciously intended. The second is to identify and evaluate elements which are indicative of the author's broader literary, cultural and historical milieu, or indicate psychological or social realities of which the author might not have been consciously aware, or which represent archetypes or ideas which can be traced cross-culturally.

In the case of the first , themes, symbols, metaphors, poetic devices, methods of argument and persuasion, style and so on are analyzed as to how the author employs them and what he intends to convey. For instance, when the author of the *Śvetāśvatara Upaniṣad* says that the universe resembles a wheel with fifty spokes (1.4), we must determine what this simile meant to him. This is where a good commentary comes in, for without one a westerner to whom the meaning of an image like this is completely foreign would be lost. Swāmī Tyāgīśānanda explains that the fifty spokes signify the five misconceptions, the twenty-eight disabilities, the nine satisfactions and the eight perceptions.[1]

But does the analysis end there? Only if you're satisfied with that explanation. Perhaps your next thought would be, "So what? What's the point here?" Now you must bring your own creative powers to bear on this puzzle. Why did the author consider this image important enough to include in his piece; what bearing does it have on our spiritual lives? A wheel, as we know, goes round and round. The universe, too, moves in cycles, as does the journey of the soul fixed to the wheel of birth-death-rebirth (*saṃsāra*). The spokes are what hold the wheel of the rim steady, what allow it to spin. So what keeps the wheel of *saṃsāra* spinning? Misconception, disability, satisfaction (which causes us to crave more of the same and stay here) and perfections (which are as binding as weaknesses). These five influences contribute to our spiritual bondage.

Interpretation requires a degree of courage and adventurousness. You could err. But so what? Most likely you'll unlock wonderful layers of meaning. Deciphering a difficult passage is like turning the light on in a dark room. In addition, you'll derive a sense of connectedness to the *ṛṣis* of old. You are their contemporary progeny. For whom did they compose these texts if not for you?

There is another, deeper mode of interpretation, where we seek what may be referred to as a subtext. The author may or may not have been aware of it. For instance, if we are analyzing a myth from a psychoanalytic perspective, trying to uncover components of the unconscious reflected in the myth, we can assume the author was not aware of these influences as he wrote. That does not mean they aren't there. It means that elements of his own unconscious, or, more likely, the collective consciousness of his culture, were expressed there, as they are expressed in any product of a culture, be it art, literature, religion, customs, or attitudes.

We can take any artifact and ask, "What was this culture telling itself about itself?" or even, "What are we, as a human race, telling ourselves about ourselves?" For example, let's say we want to interpret the meaning of Kṛṣṇa's *rāsa* dance. We know He danced with the *gopīs* (cowherdesses) in a circular formation. A place to start, then is with this idea of a circle. How many meanings are there in a circle? In our quote from the *Upaniṣad*, we saw that the universe is like a wheel, a circle. Right away a pattern emerges. Other religions besides Hinduism see the sacred in a circle. The Native American medicine hoop is a circle. The Buddhist *maṇḍala* is a circle. Pagan rites are performed in a circle. Circles signify wholeness, completion, totality, eternity. Sometimes they represent repetition or cycles, such as in Nature. The natural world is characterized by circles within circles, from the spiral form of the galaxies to the cyclic seasons and ocean currents, the rings of a tree, the spiral in a seashell, our fingerprints, our DNA. The circle is a good emblem for God because it suggests formlessness and limitlessness. Swami Vivekananda once suggested that we can imagine God as a circle with each one of us the center but with no circumference (this idea was echoed by Jung in reference to the Self). The yolk of an egg is circular and eggs are the origin of new life, new creation. In some Hindu texts, the creative aspect of Brahman is symbolized by a primordial cosmic egg. We could go on and on analyzing just this one aspect of the *rāsa* dance.

When we analyze, there are many strategies we can use. In the example above we employed several. One thing we did was make cross-cultural comparisons. When my students first read the *Bhagavad-Gītā*, inevitably someone will remark on how elements from it resemble the New Testament. Because the experience of being human in the world is something we all share, religions and mythologies from around the world share certain themes and images. As we work through the Hindu scriptures, parallels with other traditions become apparent, and it is certainly fruitful to take note of them. Soon we begin to see the basic unity of all spiritual paths, and find that people everywhere are moved by the same things.

Another important strategy is to identify underlying attitudes. The author may or may not have been intending to express an attitude per se, but because every piece of writing that was ever produced unwittingly reflects the culture, historical epoch and world-view in which the author found himself, attitudes creep in. For example, if women are mentioned or represented in a piece, how are they portrayed? Does the portrayal suggest something about their status or resort to stereotypes? If women are *not* mentioned, what does this suggest? What might the text suggest about political issues like the bases of authority and to what extent authoritarianism is espoused, as well as the equality or inequality of people? We can look for unspoken social norms sandwiched between the lines.

If you possess an outside area of expertise or interest, by all means use it as an analytical method. This is what religious studies at the academic level is all about. Your English major equips you with a knowledge of literary-critical approaches that can be applied beautifully to your study of religious scriptures. If you have an interest in psychology, bring it to bear in your analysis. The feminist approach is an excellent tool, as is the scientific. The conclusions of the ancient texts are often dramatically substantiated by the findings of contemporary physics.

Whatever your background, profession, education or station in life, you bring a unique viewpoint to the sacred literature. Your own experiences and insights shed light where someone else's may not, and you may discern things the next person will miss. All people are endowed with intelligence and creativity, and no better use can be found for these gifts than the pursuit of spiritual life. Trust yourself, believe in yourself, and the scriptures will open themselves up to you like flowers.

NOTES

1. Swāmī Tyāgīśānanda, *Śvetāśvatara Upaniṣad* (Mylapore, Sri Ramakrishna Math, 1979), pp. 21-22.

CHAPTER TWO

Are the Deities and Mythologies Real?

When Westerners first explored and colonized India, their initial reaction to Hinduism was one of repulsion. The multitude of gods and goddesses deeply offended their monotheistic sensibilities, and the Hindu use of images in worship and meditation aroused their habitual horror of "idolatry". Yet the Westerners' disgust was unfounded, for Hinduism is neither polytheistic nor idolatrous. In fact, Hinduism is as monotheistic as a religion can get. The apparent contradiction disappears when one understands Hinduism's conception of God.

Who, or what, are the Hindu deities? There are several rival answers to this question. Some Hindus believe they are purely symbolic. Brahman, God, the One without a second, is formless, infinite, without attributes. How, then, do we approach It? How can we come to know and understand It when our minds can only grasp that which possesses qualities? By means of symbol. According to this view, the gods and goddesses are symbolic representations of an abstract Reality, and by meditating upon the symbol, eventually the aspirant will be drawn to the infinite Truth beyond the finite symbol. Different deities have different powers, qualities, appearances, all of which are deeply and richly significant. An aspirant is drawn to one deity or another depending on which attributes he or she finds most indicative of the Divine. It is not the image which the aspirant is worshipping, but the divine Reality behind it.

Another view is that the deities are real, ultimately so, more real even than you or I. They are the divine manifestations of the one, indivisible Brahman. Brahman is both beyond name, form, qualities, distinctions, and at the same time the very source and substance of all names, forms, qualities, etc. If God is infinite, how can He be otherwise? All paradoxes must exist simultaneously because to say that God is one thing and not another is to limit Him, and He is unlimited. Brahman has become all things; there is no difference between Brahman and any object or event. The gods, then, are different dimensions of the one Brahman, nondifferent from It, nondifferent from one another. They are the manifestations of Saguṇa Brahman, Brahman with attributes. By worshipping one deity, the devotee is worshipping all others and, most importantly, the one Brahman which is the unity behind everything.

Some Hindus reject this view in favor of a more sectarian approach. They believe that one god or another — Kālī, for instance, or Kṛṣṇa, or Śiva — is the one supreme God and that all other deities are celestial entities subordinate to Him or Her. Monotheism is not compromised here, for other deities are considered ultimately mortal, though the extent of their life spans and supernatural powers are so mind-boggling, they appear as gods to us. In this case, the different deities are associated with different atmospheric and cosmic powers, such as sky, fire, earth, wind, death, speech, intelligence. They are also associated with important earthly places and things, such as the Himālayas or the Ganges. In this case, they are simultaneously the thing itself, such as the sacred river, and a transcendent power ruling that thing, such the goddess Gaṅgā (Ganges). This view of the deities is closer to that of the ancient Vedic religion.

Another view, inspired by the revelations of Jung, is that the Hindu deities, like the deities and heroes of all the world's cultures, correspond to universal archetypes, deep psychological realities. Archetypes are components of the unconscious which are expressed through the characters and themes upon which mythology is built. This approach explains why the mythologies of highly divergent cultures so often dramatically resemble each other. According to this view, the deities represent aspects of our own selves, mirror our conscious and unconscious drives, fears, ecstasies, transitions. Kṛṣṇa, for instance, is the Divine Child archetype, the unbounded joy and innocence deep within each one of us which is so often buried. Kālī is the Dark Mother archetype, the primal terror within us which, when entered and passed beyond, reveals ultimate wisdom. Śiva in his yogic aspect, seated alone atop Mt. Kailasa, is the Hermit, that glacial, pure peace at the center of our beings that can only be found in solitude and self-denial.

With the exception of the sectarian view, the different ways of thinking about the gods and goddesses are not necessarily exclusive of each other. The Vedāntic doctrine of absolute Oneness allows room for all viewpoints to exist simultaneously. A thing being a symbol doesn't preclude it from being real. What is reality, after all? Is an abstraction real? Is an idea real? When one begins exploring spiritual truths, at first the world seems topsy-turvy. What we originally took to be real we recognize now to be a dream, while that which we never before conceived of we understand to be the only Reality. If everything is one with Brahman, are we any more real than a character in a book? Some fictional characters have become so well-known, so fixed in the collective consciousness, they seem as real, maybe even more real, than people we know. What makes a person real? What makes a story real? Is it literality? Historicity? Again, the answer lies in how we define "real".

Myths are stories which hold meanings so significant they are more real than literal reality. The historicity of a myth isn't particularly important because the myth's meaning is so profound it dwarfs literal events in comparison. What have I ever done that was as significant as the young Prahlāda's calling forth Nṛsiṃha, the glorious half-man, half-lion incarnation of Viṣṇu, from the pillar of his father's palace? Recalling this event, I may experience greater rapture than recalling any event from my own, very ordinary life. Which event, then, is more "real"? Nṛsiṃha is known as a guardian and protector of devotees. If I pray to Him in times of danger and am delivered to safety, have I not "called Him forth from the pillar" myself, thus participating in the "reality" of the story?

In essence, the reader may approach the Hindu deities as part of a mythic reality rooted in, yet transcending, literal reality, or may see them as symbols, or may see them as actual dimensions of the Divine, or may reject them entirely in favor of an abstract concept of God, or may explain them in a way not mentioned here. So, too, may one understand the mythology. It is symbolic, literal, transcendental, psychological, archetypal all at once.

While an exposition of the specific Hindu gods and goddesses is beyond the scope of this book, anyone undertaking a survey of the Hindu scriptures should equip themselves with a good reference book describing the various deities' appearances, attributes, personalities, stories, etc. There are many available, some of which are listed in the bibliography at the back of this book. As we go through the different texts, references to various deities will crop up and, at these points, brief descriptions may be offered when appropriate.

CHAPTER THREE

Welcome to the Hindu Canon: An Overview

This volume only examines the most important and mainstream of the Hindu scriptures, those which are indisputably authoritative and which are most revered and cherished by the greatest number of people. They are the basic texts, the core scriptures to which other writings refer in order to secure their own validity. They are also the ones which spiritual aspirants will find most helpful in their *sādhanā.* I have left many out — the *Dharma Śāstras,* the lesser-known *Upaniṣads,* the *Tantras,* etc. These were difficult decisions, but as this is meant to be an introductory study guide, particularly specialized, obscure, or quasi-canonical texts had to be passed over. Some of these are given mention in the following chart. The entire Hindu canon is so vast (perhaps infinitely so, as new scriptures appear even today) that no single volume can adequately encompass them all.

Hindu scripture is known collectively as *śāstra* ("instructions", "treatises"). It has two main divisions, *śruti* and *smṛti. Śruti* means "heard" and refers to the *Vedas,* the *Upaniṣads,* and priestly handbooks known as the *Brāhmaṇas.* They are "heard" in the sense that they are believed to be the result of direct revelation of the Divine. All other scriptures are known as *smṛti,* "remembered". This means that they are of human origin, based on oral tradition, history, intellectual theory, philosophical speculation, mythology, and so on. While revered as sacred, they are not as supremely sacred as *śruti.*

The following chart categorizes the Hindu scriptural corpus neatly. It is adapted from David S. Noss and John B. Noss, *A History of the World's Religions,* and Troy Wilson Organ, *Hinduism, Its Historical Development.*[1]

Śruti **— "Heard" — Vedic Literature**

Saṃhitās — The Four Vedas

Ṛg Veda

Sacred hymns

Sāma Veda

Hymns from the *Ṛg Veda* rearranged for liturgical purposes

Yajur Veda

Incantations to accompany Vedic rituals

Atharva Veda

Mantras and rituals for pastoral and domestic use

Brāhmaṇas

Priestly handbooks of instructions for ceremonies with theoretical material about them

Upaniṣads

Mystical treatises espousing the oneness of Brahman and Ātman

Smṛti **— "Remembered" — Post-Vedic Literature**

Vedāṅgas

Code books on a range of subjects, such as grammar, astronomy, prosody, medicine, morals, etc.

Dharma Śāstras

Law books, the best known of which is the *Manu-smṛti* or *Laws of Manu*

Darśanas

Texts associated with the six orthodox systems of Hindu philosophy, namely *Mīmāṃsā* (apologists for Vedic religion), *Nyāya* (logical analysis), *Vaiśeṣika* (proto-science), *Sāṃkhya* (discriminative knowledge), *Yoga* (meditation), and *Vedānta* (apologists for upaniṣadic philosophy)

Purāṇas

Mythological literature dedicated to different deities

Śrīmad Bhāgavatam (Bhāgavata Purāṇa)

Viṣṇu Purāṇa

Śiva Purāṇa

Śrīmad Devī Bhāgavatam

etc.

Itihāsas

Epic Poems

Mahābhārata

Bhagavad-Gītā

Rāmāyaṇa

Āgamas

Sectarian works associated with Śaivism, Vaiṣṇavism and Śaktism

Tantra

Scriptures of the Tantric tradition. These are highly esoteric, often focused on Śiva and Śakti and espouse elaborate yogic practices

Mahānirvāṇatantra

etc.

Writings of Revered *Gurus*

Noss and Noss include this category in their outline and it is very appropriate. Surely the literature associated with these great figures is as significant and spiritually potent as the more ancient texts.

Śrī Śaṅkarācārya (788-820)

Vivekacūḍāmaṇi

Pañcīkaraṇam

Upadeśa sāhasrī

etc.

Śrī Rāmānuja (1017-1137)

Śrībhāṣya

etc.

Śrī Ramakrishna (1836-1886)

The Gospel of Sri Ramakrishna

The writings I have included in this book are the *Vedas*, the *Upaniṣads*, the *Purāṇas* and shorter texts derived from them, the *Bhagavad-Gītā*, and the *Itihāsas*. These scriptures stand out from all the others. Anyone familiar with these books can be considered fully conversant in the Hindu scriptures. I have also included brief mention of three scriptures of *Yoga*, *Bhakti* and *Vedānta* which are particularly outstanding.

Less attention has been given to the *Vedas*, and to *Purāṇas* other than the *Śrīmad Bhāgavatam* because most Westerners will devote much less time to these texts. While the *Vedas* contain examples of the highest wisdom here and there, the bulk is far too archaic and indocentric for the average Westerner to find helpful. A serious student of Indology or religious history will, of course, find them invaluable, but for most of us, a general feel for their content and historical context is sufficient. One should have at least a cursory knowledge of the *Vedas* as background to the scriptures one will study more deeply, because later compositions refer to them constantly.

As for the *Purāṇas*, a full treatment is given here of the *Śrīmad Bhāgavatam* because it is the preeminent *Purāṇa*, in a class by itself. The others are discussed more briefly because, while I highly encourage a study of them, a reader is likely to concentrate only on the *Purāṇa* devoted to his or her Chosen Ideal — Divine Mother, Śiva, Viṣṇu, or Kṛṣṇa — and pass over the others. The *Purāṇas* are incredibly long, and to read all of them is almost unheard of. Only the most popular ones are examined here.

The following chapters are not arranged chronologically, but rather in the order which a student or aspirant will probably study scripture on their own. We begin with a look at the *Vedas* to set the scene and background, then launch into the *Bhagavad-Gītā*, the most important Hindu Scripture. The *Gītā* is an all-around guide to spiritual life which covers virtually every one of its aspects. After reading this, all other scriptures can be viewed as elaboration and commentary. Next we look at the *Upaniṣads*, which establish a firm theological and philosophical background to the spiritual search. Many aspirants may want to stop there. The *Upaniṣads* are the highest expression of the path of *jñāna*, direct perception of oneness with the impersonal, attributeless Brahman. The *Purāṇas*, which come next, address the subject of Brahman with attributes. This is the path of *bhakti*, devotional love for God. Brahman, being infinite, has infinite divine manifestations and infinite divine activities, which are exquisitely narrated in the Purāṇic literature. Underlying the mythology, however, is a solid foundation of *jñāna*. There is no contradiction between the truth of the *Upaniṣads* and the truth of the *Purāṇas*. They are complimentary.

The *Rāmāyaṇa* and *Mahābhārata* comprise the genre known as *Itihāsas*, the epic poems. Anyone, *jñāni* or *bhakta*, who wants to enter into the feel, the timbre, the musicality, the imagination of Hinduism must acquaint themselves with these stories and characters, for they are the very heart of Hindu India and its sense of the sacred.

Finally, three important books are discussed in brief, each dealing with a different aspect of the spiritual path. The *Vedānta Sūtras* are a scholarly work expounding the theory of *Vedānta*, the most widely-held philosophical viewpoint in Hinduism. The *Yoga Sūtras* of Patañjali are the classic how-to-do-it manual for spiritual practitioners. And the *Nārada Bhakti Sūtras* are a wonderful meditation on love for God.

NOTES

1. David S. Noss and John B. Noss, *A History of the World's Religions* (New York: MacMillan Publishing Company, 1990), p. 195;
   Troy Wilson Organ, *Hinduism, Its Historical Development* (New York: Barron's Educational Series, Inc., 1974), p. 180.

Part II

The *Vedas*

CHAPTER FOUR

The Vedas

The word *veda* means "knowledge" and the *Vedas* are India's oldest and most revered scriptures. The ancient form of religion associated with them is no longer practiced, though threads of ritual, prayer and philosophy contained in them do survive to the present day in altered forms. Contemporary Hinduism is the great-grandchild of the Vedic religion and bears a family resemblance. It is important to become at least somewhat acquainted with the *Vedas* and Vedic religion because both are referred to often in the great corpus of Hindu scripture. They are its foundation — historically, stylistically and philosophically.

The Dawn of Hinduism

Excavations in the Indus Valley region of Northwest India have revealed a wonderfully complex, sophisticated civilization which flourished over two millennia before the birth of Christ. The site contains remnants of the earliest planned cities yet known, which include waterways and sewage systems. The Indus Valley dwellers were an agrarian people and literate, though their writing remains to be deciphered. Most interesting for us is that a number of unearthed ceramic seals contain clues to the religious life of these brilliant, mysterious people.

The seals are engraved with mythical animals and what appears to be early forms of Hindu gods and goddesses, the most striking of which is a figure now referred to as the Proto-Śiva. It shows a man in a meditation pose, the lotus position in fact, with a trident on his head. The trident is a symbol associated with Lord Śiva, as is the meditation pose, in which he is often depicted. From this seal we can also infer that the Indus Valley people had already developed the techniques of meditation and *yoga*, practices basic to the attainment of Self-realization.

For reasons still unknown, though flooding or a similar natural calamity is suspected, between 1900 and 1600 B.C. the Indus Valley civilization fell into disorder. This exposed them to incomers from the north, the powerful, patriarchal, brilliant Āryans.

The word Āryan is derived from the Sanskrit *ārya*, or "noble", which is how the Āryans thought of and referred to themselves. They were a nomadic race of proto-Europeans who, at approximately 1500 B.C., swept down from the steppes of Russia into India by means of horse-drawn chariot. A branch of this group split off and continued west, some to settle in Iran, others to migrate as far as Ireland (the "ire" of Ireland also means "noble", it being a cognate with *ārya* and derived from a common root). Not surprisingly, some similarities exist between Zoroastrianism (the native religion of Iran), the indigenous religion of Ireland, and the Vedic religion, most notably an emphasis on fire ritual.

The Āryans entered northern India and settled in the Indus Valley. As time went on, they continued to spread south until their influence spanned most of the subcontinent. They spoke Sanskrit, and while they did not write books, they had a rich oral tradition of sacred poetry. Enormous bodies of sacred literature were committed to memory; it was the job of the priests to safeguard this corpus. By 800 B.C. they had gathered this vast amount of poetry into the four *Vedas*.

The Vedic religion was not other-worldly. The Āryans were not as interested in spiritual liberation as in securing the good life here on earth. The universe as they saw it was three-tiered, with the earth at the bottom, the atmosphere in the middle, and the heavenly realm at the top. Hence, it was named *triloka*, the "three abodes". Different elements of the world and the heavens were presided over by divine beings, or *devas*, "shining ones". Thus, fire had a deity, as did the storms, the sun, the dawn, etc. The entire universe was permeated with sacredness; every element was rich with consciousness.

The major form of religious expression and worship was the *agnihotra*, the fire sacrifice. Its principal import lies in the fact that through the ritual observances of the fire sacrifice, forces were created which could compel the deities to act. When elements could be manipulated and controlled, balance could be maintained in the universe. We have in the sacrifice foreshadowings of the concept of *karma* because people's actions were believed to affect the universe directly, and the universe was compelled to respond.

Domestic fires were used for daily rites, while public ceremonies were performed outdoors. There were no temples in the Vedic religion. The sacrifice was presided over by a team of priests, usually for a specific patron. Atop a temporary altar made of earth a large fire was kindled, fire being the medium by which offerings were transported to the deities. As solid objects are of no use to non-corporeal beings, fire was employed to carry the essence of the offerings up to the god being worshipped. The power which ushered the offering along was Agni, the god of fire (as in the English, "ignite"), who acted as an intermediary between heavenly beings and people, much like Hermes of ancient Greece. By feeding and praising the gods, one secured their favor and could appeal for their help.

The *Vedas* are comprised largely of hymns to different deities of the Vedic pantheon. Vedic verses, or *mantras*, were chanted in accompaniment to ritual. Indra, the king of the gods and deity of lightning and storms, is prominent, as is Rudra, a tawny god of the ferocious elements who is also a precursor to Śiva, and Soma, who is associated with an intoxicating nectar ingested as part of the rites.

After invoking Agni, the priests would invoke the particular *deva* to whom the ceremony was dedicated. While chanting Vedic verses, they would feed the god by casting offerings such as clarified butter, grains, cakes or *soma* into the flames. Perhaps an animal was slaughtered and cooked as well. In this way, the gods were propitiated, and harmony was maintained in the universe.

The Four *Vedas*

The oldest and most important of the *Vedas* is the *Ṛg Veda.* While it is the oldest, it is, in a sense, also the newest, because its compilation spanned many centuries, and the poems in its tenth, and final, section are of relatively late composition and begin to include some highly sophisticated philosophy which foreshadows the mystical realizations of the later *Upaniṣads.* The title comes from the word *ṛc*, or "praise stanza", the literary format of the hymns.

A good example of a *Ṛg Veda* hymn is the following prayer to Agni. It includes a description of Agni's function as intermediary and lord of fire, including the domestic fire, (for which he is referred to as the "household priest"), verses praising his wisdom, fame and luminosity, and direct imploring for his favor.

> Agni I praise, the household priest,
> God, minister of sacrifice,
> Invoker, bestower of wealth.
>
> Agni is worthy to be praised,
> By present as by seers of old:
> May he conduct the gods to us.
>
> Through Agni may we riches gain,
> And day by day prosperity
> Replete with fame and manly sons.

The worship and the sacrifice,
Guarded by thee on every side,
Go straight, O Agni, to the gods.

May Agni, the invoker, wise,
And true, of most resplendent fame,
The god, come hither with the gods.

Whatever good thou wilt bestow,
O Agni, on the pious man,
That gift comes true, O Aṅgiras.

To thee, O Agni, day by day,
O thou illuminer of gloom,
With thought we, bearing homage, come:

To thee the lord of sacrifice,
The radiant guardian of the Law,
That growest in thine own abode.

So, like a father to his son,
Be easy of approach to us:
Agni, for weal abide with us.[1]

The *Ṛg Veda* also includes many passages which are utilized by orthodox Hindus in the course of their daily lives. Diligent Hindus structure their activities around ritual; waking, bathing, eating etc. are all attended to with standard prayers and ritualized actions, thus spiritualizing every aspect of what would normally be considered mundane life. Included in a Hindu's daily observances is the repetition of the Vedic *Gāyatrī mantra* three times a day. Notice how it makes mention of the three-tiered Vedic cosmos but also suggests a divine One who transcends it:

Oṃ. Salutations to the Earth. Salutations to the Sky.
    Salutations to Heaven.
We meditate upon the glorious effulgence of the Supreme
    Divine Creator.
May He guide our minds and inspire our understanding.

Of greatest interest to the western aspirant are the philosophical hymns, which move away from the adoration of particular deities and begin to address a more mature theological concept. We see an idea of the Divine being a Oneness which encompasses the material universe yet also transcends it. The following is a beautiful example of late-Vedic philosophizing; notice how much the first two lines resemble the Universal Form described in the *Bhagavad Gītā*.

> The Universal Being has infinite heads, innumerable eyes,
> and innumerable feet.
> Enveloping the universe on every side, he exists
> transcending it.
> All this is he — what has been and what shall be.
> He is the lord of immortality.
> Though he has become all this, in reality he is not all this:
> For verily he is transcendental.
> The whole series of universes — past present and future
> — express his glory and power.
> But he transcends his own glory.
> All beings of the universe form, as it were, a fraction
> of his being;
> The rest of it is self-luminous, and unchangeable.
> He who is beyond all predicates exists as the relative
> universe.
> That part of him which is the relative universe appears
> as sentient and insentient beings.
> From a part of him was born the body of the universe,
> and out of his body were born the gods, the earth
> and man.[2]

The title of the *Sāma Veda* is derived from the word *sāman*, which means "song". This *Veda* is comprised of over a thousand hymns from the *Ṛg Veda* rearranged for liturgical purposes. The *Sāma Veda*, then, was used during the ceremonies themselves.

The *Yajur Veda* is comprised of incantations to accompany the Vedic rituals. While one priest was chanting hymns from the *Ṛg* or *Sāma Veda*, another was handling the utensils and materials. As he performed the rite, he would recite short verbal formulae to intensify the effectiveness of the ritual actions. These formulae were known as *yajus*, "short incantations", hence the name of the *Veda*.

Lastly, there was the *Atharva Veda*, named for the *atharvan*, a particular class of priest who attended to pastoral duties. The *Atharva Veda* contains rituals and *mantras* for domestic use, such as rites of protection, good fortune, overcoming crises, or medicinal purposes.

The *Vedas* contain many spiritually deep and inspiring verses, but the Western seeker will find the majority of this body of literature too archaic and removed to be truly helpful in their *sādhanā*. Their importance for us is to provide a background to the scriptures we will study more seriously. The *Upaniṣads* often make mention of the *Vedas* and Vedic sacrifices, liberally borrowing terminology and imagery and transforming them into metaphor. The sacred fire, for instance, now stands for the luminous Self in the heart, while the offerings symbolize the desires, ego, mind etc. The lower self is offered up into the purifying fires of the Ātman. Similarly, the dismemberment of the sacrificial horse during the *aśvamedha*, or horse sacrifice, comes to stand for the creation of the universe. Brahman created the cosmos merely by dividing Itself; thus everything is a part of God, everything a fragment of a single source, which remains ever nondifferent. Another context in which the *Upaniṣads*, and the *Bhagavad-Gītā*, refer to the Vedic sacrifices is in questioning their relative merit in the larger scheme of things. The sacrifices do bring the desired results, the texts say, but these are mere material rewards brought about by actions, so they karmically bind us to the wheel of birth, death and rebirth. Spiritual realization requires something entirely different.

NOTES

1. Troy Wilson Organ, *Hinduism: Its Historical Development* (Woodbury: Barron's Educational Series, 1974), p. 73.
2. *Vedanta and the West*, January-April; nos. 183-184.

Part III

The *Bhagavad-Gītā*

CHAPTER FIVE

Introduction

The Bhagavad-Gītā is the most beloved scripture in Hinduism. Certainly no other South Asian text has generated such a flood of scholarly and devotional commentaries, been translated into so many languages, or been so widely received in the West. The extraordinary breadth of subjects it covers coupled with the subtlety of its language leaves it especially open to divergent interpretations, hence its mass appeal. Exponents of rival philosophical camps claim it as their own, citing passages to support their own views. That the *Gītā* can uphold such contradictory ideas and yet maintain a conceptual continuity attests to its genius. There is no book like it in the world. It is, perhaps, the greatest piece of literature Asia has ever produced.

Spiritual aspirants are advised to begin their study of divine topics with this book, as it lays down the basic framework of ideas from which the student may build and embellish. Almost any spiritual topic is touched upon, so that a solid knowledge of the *Gītā* results in a solid knowledge of spiritual Truth in its entirety, as well as a knowledge of its attainment. All other scriptures can be viewed as elaboration on some theme or another contained in the *Gītā*. This is not because the *Gītā* gave rise to these other books. On the contrary, it draws together ideas from various sources into a brilliantly harmonious synthesis.

Yet the miracle of the *Gītā* doesn't end there. While it serves as the perfect introduction to spiritual principles, its sophistication is such that the aspirant can never outgrow it. The more one studies the book, the more profound it becomes, as though it grows and changes along with its reader. It is a bottomless well of wisdom, a lifelong guide and *guru*. One can never tire of it, never exhaust its possibilities.

The title, *Bhagavad-Gītā*, means "Song of God" (*bhagavat,* "God", *gītā* "song"), God here being manifested as the divine incarnation, or *Avatāra*, Kṛṣṇa. The poem is comprised of seven hundred stanzas, all concise, metered couplets. The whole piece is but an excerpt from the enormous epic poem, the *Mahābhārata*, but secular scholars speculate that it is of a later composition than the *Mahābhārata* and was eventually inserted at the appropriate point in the narrative. Assigning it a date is difficult, though, and scholarly estimates range from the fifth century B.C. to the second century A.D., a vast stretch.

It takes the form of a dialogue between the incarnate God, Kṛṣṇa, and his friend and disciple, the warrior Arjuna. Dialogue appears to have been a favored literary device of Hindu authors, as it lends itself well to searching inquiry and philosophical exposition (as in the dialogues of Plato). The scene is set on the battlefield of Kurukṣetra, which is located near the present city of Delhi, and opens just before the onset of an immense fratricidal war. The armies are poised for battle, and Arjuna, our hero, asks Kṛṣṇa, his driver, to draw his chariot between the two armies so that he may see those present.

The origin of the conflict can be traced to Dhṛtarāṣṭra and Pāṇḍu, royal brothers descended from the hero-king Bharata, for whom both India (which, within its own borders is called Bhārata) and the epic *Mahābhārata* ("Great [epic of] the Descendants of Bharata") are named. Dhṛtarāṣṭra, though the elder, was born blind, and thus the throne was passed to the younger sibling, Pāṇḍu. Pāṇḍu suffered an early death, however, and his five sons — Yudhiṣṭhira, Bhīma, Arjuna, Nakula and Sahadeva, known collectively as the Pāṇḍavas ("descendants of Pāṇḍu") — came under the care of Dhṛtarāṣṭra. Like the hundred sons of the blind monarch, the boys were raised in the royal household and trained in the military arts that were required of their *kṣatriya* caste. The hundred sons of Dhṛtarāṣṭra, known together as the Kauravas ("descendants of Kuru", an earlier dynastic patriarch), hated and envied the Pāṇḍavas, and on several occasions plotted, unsuccessfully, to have them murdered. The eldest of the Kauravas, Duryodhana, was the cruellest and most driven, his loathing of the Pāṇḍavas inflated to an obsession.

His murder attempts thwarted, Duryodhana challenged the Pāṇḍavas to a dice tournament, an invitation that Yudhiṣṭhira, a compulsive gambler, couldn't resist. With loaded dice, Duryodhana cheated the Pāṇḍavas out of their kingdom and forced them into exile for thirteen years. Upon their return, they rightfully demanded their kingdom back, but were refused. They reduced their request to a mere five villages, only to have Duryodhana sneer that he wouldn't give them enough land in which to drive a pin. War now seemed unavoidable.

Heads of state around the world took sides and sent their armies to join in the ensuing battle. Kṛṣṇa was a member of the Kuru dynasty and a ruler of Dvārakā. As a cousin to both the Pāṇḍavas and Kurus, He could not formally take sides, but instead offered His army to one side, Himself to the other. Duryodhana, in his foolishness, grabbed Kṛṣṇa's army, while the Pāṇḍavas happily snatched Kṛṣṇa. It was a mistake which would cost Duryodhana everything.

Kṛṣṇa

In the context of the *Gītā*, Kṛṣṇa is Arjuna's cousin (He is the nephew of Arjuna's mother, Kuntī), and brother-in-law (Arjuna is married to Kṛṣṇa's sister Subhadrā). More importantly, He is an incarnation of God. Kṛṣṇa's significance in Hinduism cannot be underestimated. He is certainly believed to have been an historical figure, but secular scholars have not managed to assign Him an accurate date. Traditional sources place him anywhere from 3,000 to 1400 B.C..[1] He is believed by some to be among the several incarnations of Viṣṇu, by others to be a divine incarnation of unique and singular importance (as Jesus is to Christians), by others the highest and most perfect manifestation of Brahman, and by still others simply God, the Original and Supreme.

He has very distinct physical characteristics, most notably a breath-taking, unearthly beauty. In popular iconography His complexion is usually depicted as a lustrous blue. The word *kṛṣṇa* means "black" or "dark" or "attractive", and He is described by various sources as blackish, bluish, bluish-black, or the color of a storm cloud. His eyes are luminous and lotus-petal shaped, His jet-black hair shoulder length, His body adorned with jeweled ornaments and flower garlands. His garments are always yellow and His head — whether bare, turbaned, or helmeted — is always decorated with a peacock feather (as is Viṣṇu, with whom He is associated). He is full-bodied, broad-shouldered, and eternally youthful.

Kṛṣṇa has distinct personality characteristics as well, but we notice a sharp break between the boy and the man, so sharp that scholars like to suggest that they represent two unrelated legends which were blended as the various tribal units of the subcontinent gelled into a unified pan-Indian culture. Devotees of Kṛṣṇa dismiss this theory as nonsense and argue that everyone's behavior is dramatically different as children and as adults. It can be further argued that many personality traits *do* carry over from the boy Kṛṣṇa and the man Kṛṣṇa.

The religion surrounding the worship of Kṛṣṇa centers almost entirely on His boyhood years. In this period He is living in the pastoral idyll of Vṛndāvan, tending herds of cows and enjoying romantic dalliance with the *gopīs*, the cowherdesses. This youthful love-play is rich with sacred metaphors, which will be discussed in our chapter on the *Śrīmad Bhāgavatam*. He is never without His flute during this period, as the sound of it acts as an irresistible lure to all living things, just as the Absolute draws all *jīvas* (individual souls) back to It. He is mischievous, charming, funny and sexy. Most telling about the boy Kṛṣṇa is his epithet, Govinda. *Go* means both "cow" and "senses"; *vinda* means "delight" or "enchantment". So Kṛṣṇa is the delight of the cows and the enchanter of our senses. His beauty dazzles us.

The personality break comes quite forcefully at the event of Kṛṣṇa's slaying of his evil and psychotic uncle Kaṃsa, in accord with prophecy. This is the first step in the fulfillment of Kṛṣṇa's destiny to become a king, and He leaves Vṛndāvan forever. He is approximately twelve or thirteen.

As an adult, Kṛṣṇa assumes the role of statesman, family man and *guru*. He is a sober political negotiator as well as a perfect spiritual preceptor, as is illustrated by the *Bhagavad-Gītā* and by the eleventh chapter of the *Śrīmad Bhāgavatam*, where he discourses to his other principal disciple, Uddhava. Yet hints of the old Kṛṣṇa still come through. He teases and flirts with His numerous queens in much the same way he teased the *gopīs*, and He is not adverse to tricks and deception in the cause of what's right.

A.C. Bhaktivedanta Swami has rightly pointed out that most commentators of the *Gītā* have directed their readers' attention away from the person of Kṛṣṇa.[2] This stems from the fact that Kṛṣṇa, as the narrator of the *Gītā*, states outright that He is the absolute, omnipresent, original Brahman, God. Apparently this troubles some people, and suggestions as to His identity include His representing one's "higher Self", while Arjuna represents the mundane self (or the Jungian Self and ego), that He is acting as a symbolic expression of that which is inexpressible, namely the impersonal Brahman, that He is the manifest aspect of Brahman which, when known, the unmanifest also becomes known, and so forth. All explanations of this sort are partly true, but are limiting to such a degree that they ultimately miss the point. Instead of trying to speculate about who or what Kṛṣṇa is, one is wiser to attend to the verses of the poem itself, where it is revealed that there is nothing which Kṛṣṇa is *not*. That is the highest truth contained in the *Gītā*, the same truth expounded in the *Upaniṣads*. Kṛṣṇa is God; that much we know. But what is God? The middle third of the book is devoted to this topic. As there is nothing which God is not, there is no reason to assume He can't be Kṛṣṇa. This subject will be addressed more fully later.

Chapter One: Arjuna's Distress

The armies are poised for battle. When we open the *Gītā*, the first voice we hear is that of the blind king Dhṛtarāṣṭra. He is seated in a tent by the sidelines with Sañjaya, a seer who can perceive events and hear conversations with his inner, psychic sense and will convey the events on the battlefield to the king. The two were in no danger; in those days war was fought according to strict laws of chivalry and only by members of the *kṣatriya* caste. Civilian deaths, destruction of property, rape and demoralization of the enemy — all features of the contemporary model of "total war" — were completely unknown to the ancient *kṣatriyas*, whose martial skills were considered and art form, and whose *dharma* demanded the highest moral and ethical conduct. Dhṛtarāṣṭra requests Sañjaya to describe the events taking place on the battlefield: "O Sañjaya, after my sons and the sons of Pāṇḍu, who desired to fight, assembled on the sacred field of Kurukṣetra, what did they do?" (1.1)[3].

Sañjaya names many of the more notable warriors present, and describes the tumultuous sound of the soldiers' conchshells being blown to herald the commencement of battle. At this point he zeroes in on Kṛṣṇa and Arjuna's chariot in particular, and begins to recount their extraordinary dialogue. So what we are hearing is a conversation within a conversation. From this point on, the focus will remain entirely on Kṛṣṇa and Arjuna.

Arjuna requests this most remarkable charioteer to drive him between the two armies. Seeing his kinsmen arrayed before him, including teachers, uncles, cousins, in-laws — men with whom he'd grown up and for whom he holds admiration and affection, Arjuna is suddenly overwhelmed by grief. "I see only the seeds of misfortune," he says (1.30), "I do not see how any good can come from killing my own kinsmen in this battle, nor can I desire any subsequent victory, kingdom or happiness!" (1.31).

How could he ever enjoy the fruits of victory when they are drenched with the blood of such carnage? The consequences of war, he explains, are socially devastating, and this war is particularly unjust because it is based on greed. No earthly possession, even a kingdom, is worth the taking of lives. Refusing to fight, Arjuna casts his bow aside and collapses.

Chapter Two: The Indestructibility of the Soul

Initially one might expect Kṛṣṇa to applaud Arjuna's decision. After all, by embracing nonviolence he appears to have assumed a morally superior stance. But Kṛṣṇa knows a deeper truth. He will surprise us.

"Coward!" He reprimands. "Such behavior is unfitting to a man of your station. Get out there and fight!"

Is the *Gītā* advocating violence? Of course not. In many other places in the text, Kṛṣṇa will extol gentleness and nonviolence, even passivity. If there's one generalization we can make about the *Gītā*, it's that it embraces diversity. No one occupation, standard of conduct or spiritual path is appropriate for everyone. Different people require different paths. Arjuna is a *kṣatriya*, a soldier by profession, and it is his moral and spiritual imperative to attend to the duties, the *dharma*, of that profession. Were Arjuna a priest, a spice merchant or a housewife, Kṛṣṇa would have given him very different advice, for violence is never acceptable for these people. But the question of war and peace is not the issue here at all. The issue is action and inaction. If Kṛṣṇa were talking to an exhausted mother with five screaming children all needing her attention at once, she might tell Him, "Kṛṣṇa, I can't face it. There's no way I can be a mom today." His reply would be, "Yes you can. In fact, you must. It's your duty. Get in there and fight!" The War of Kurukṣetra merely provides a context in which to examine the subtler truths of life and death, liberation and bondage. The battlefield represents life in the world, with all its perils, temptations and vicissitudes. Each day we have new battles to fight, the greatest of all being the battle against our own lower natures, the struggle for spiritual emancipation.

Now Arjuna is utterly confused. His decision *seemed* so noble. He's forced to admit that his knowledge is flawed and that he needs guidance. With humility, he places himself at Kṛṣṇa's feet, and begs the Lord to become his *guru*: "Tell me for certain what is best for me. Now I am your disciple and a soul surrendered to You. Please instruct me" (2.7). This is a key verse in the scripture, for it illustrates the manner in which a *śiṣya*, disciple, accepts a spiritual master. The *guru-śiṣya* relationship is one of the foundations of spiritual life. In most cases it is essential if one expects to reach the summit of spiritual realization.

Kṛṣṇa smiles (the Beauty of beauties does everything with a smile), and begins the lesson. There is, He says, no such thing as death: "Never was there a time when I did not exist, nor you, nor all these princes, nor in the future shall any of us cease to be. As the embodied soul continually passes, in this body, from boyhood to youth to old age, the soul similarly passes into another body at death. A sober person is not bewildered by such a change" (2.12-13). The first step of the spiritual path is an understanding of *saṃsāra*, reincarnation. Our bodies die, but our bodies are not our true selves. We are spiritual beings, immortal, separate from our bodies but subject to repeated rebirth in the material world. Nothing, Kṛṣṇa says, can obliterate the soul or Self, the Ātman, for it is beginningless and endless. Therefore one cannot actually kill or be killed. Rebirth into a new body is compared to changing clothes; only the outer appearance changes, while the real Self remains the same.

The term Ātman is generally interchangeable with Brahman, literally "the Supreme", the Hindu conception of the Ultimate Truth or God.

Brahman is infinite, all-pervading, the ultimate Reality, the origin of everything. Much of the *Gītā* will be devoted to describing the nature of Brahman (in a sense, every word of the *Gītā* describes Brahman for Brahman is everything). Suffice it to say at this point that our worldly identities are an illusion, *māyā*. Our true nature is spiritual, blissful, serene, unlimitedly aware Ātman.

Arjuna is advised, therefore, to go out and fight, but only in a spirit of detachment from the results. Working without attachment to the fruit of one's labor, caring not whether the outcome is a success or a failure, or results in pleasure or pain, is the basis of *karma yoga*. The word *yoga* literally means "to link" or "to yoke". In yoking an ox to a cart, there is the image of uniting. *Yoga* refers to any method which unites the individual and the Divine. All religious paths are yoga, and within Hinduism there are countless different yogic traditions and disciplines.The word *karma* means "action" or "doing". Any action we perform is *karma*. The *Gītā* frequently uses the term to imply religious ritual, actions performed in a religious context for religious merit (as in the Vedic sacrifices described in the previous chapter). The word also refers to the natural law of cause and effect, where any action we perform — good, bad or neutral — will boomerang back to us either in this life or a future one. Each action spins out karma like an invisible web, and the karmic debts waiting for us in our futures help keep us tethered to the wheel of *saṃsāra*. However, when we perform actions in a spirit of detachment, as *yoga*, they do not generate new karma. This will be a constant theme throughout the *Gītā*. Kṛṣṇa never advocates inactivity. "Never let there be attachment to inaction," He says. "Perform actions while fixed in *yoga*, having abandoned attachment and having become indifferent to success or failure. Indifference, it is said, is *yoga*" (2.47-48).

Some Indophobes like to blame India's enduring social and economic problems to this concept of detached action. This is preposterous. Never does Kṛṣṇa tell Arjuna to give up his work or to apply anything less than his very best to his work. Half-hearted effort is not *yoga*. Furthermore, detached action is very much an ideal, attained in truth by few. Separated from its spiritual implications and viewed simply as an attitude towards work, it makes a great deal of sense, particularly in today's often neurotically high-stress world. We may apply ourselves to our work to the best of our ability, but beyond that point the results are out our control. Worrying about how we will perform will not make us perform any better and may in fact cause us to do worse. Once the deed is done, worrying about the outcome will not alter it one bit. Being too attached to the results of our work can strap us to an emotional roller coaster, devastating to both mental and physical health. Kṛṣṇa tells us to remain equipoised in both success and failure. Our emotional response to a situation does not alter it, but only makes us agitated. Meher Baba echoed this teaching in his famous adage, "Don't worry; be happy."

How can we learn to be unattached? "Be established in the consciousness of the Ātman, always" (2.45). In other words, be ever aware that your true self is unlimited and divine.

Our teacher tells Arjuna to cultivate steadiness of the intelligence and, as a next step, the ability to meditate deeply. The warrior, who is a man of action and not contemplation, asks: What is such a steady-minded person like? How does he speak? How does he sit? How does he move (2.54)?

Verses fifty-five through seventy-two, which describe the characteristics of an illumined soul, comprise what may be the most oft-quoted section of the *Gītā*. It is almost a mini-*Gītā*, delineating incredibly succinctly the basic theory and method of spiritual practice, which can be summed up in one word: renunciation. We are not asked to renounce our possessions or our jobs; such dramatic gestures are fairly easy to do and not particularly meaningful. We must renounce *attachment* and *egotism*. A sage can be surrounded by riches and have no interest in them whatsoever; if tomorrow they should all disappear he would scarcely notice. On the other hand, another man may have only one possession, say a spoon, and be so attached to it that he flies into a possessive rage if someone so much as looks at it. Proximity to material objects does not bind us, but rather our desire for them.

The sage is desireless, Kṛṣṇa says, because he has found contentment and bliss in the Ātman, the Self, alone. He is never agitated by misfortune, is free from passion, fear and anger, and can withdraw his senses from external stimuli, "as a tortoise can draw its limbs into its shell" (2.55-58). There is great danger in dwelling upon the objects of sense pleasure. What may at first appear as innocent desire can in fact drag us down into personal degradation and spiritual blindness. "For a man dwelling on the objects of the senses," Kṛṣṇa explains, "an attachment to them develops. Attachment breeds addiction, and addiction gives rise to anger (when fulfillment is thwarted). From anger springs delusion, and from delusion the failure of memory (forgetfulness of the lessons of experience). From failure of memory comes the destruction of intelligence, and when intelligence is destroyed, one is lost" (2.62-63). Frequently students of mine who are recovering alcoholics or recovering substance abusers are struck by these verses, and attest to their truth. This powerful passage suggests that attachment to sense pleasures not only binds us to the material plane, but, ironically, aggravates our suffering while we're here. The Buddha (whom Hindus believe to be an *Avatāra*) expressed the same thing in His second and third Noble Truths: that suffering is caused by desire, pure and simple, and that suffering can be overcome when desire is extinguished.

Kṛṣṇa agrees that by eliminating desire and practicing self-restraint, one can attain tranquility (2.64). Free from lust and egotism, indifferent to possessions, one experiences peace and, ultimately, Brahman-realization, the summit of spiritual attainment.

Chapter Three: *Karma Yoga*

This chapter contains a more detailed treatment of *karma yoga*, the yoga of action. First, however, Arjuna needs a point clarified. In the last chapter, Kṛṣṇa said that calming and disciplining the mind while stilling the senses is the means of Brahman-realization. But Arjuna recalls Him also saying that detached action, or *karma yoga,* is called for. Which is better? He asks, "If it is your conviction that *buddhi* (the intellect) is better than *karma* (action), then why do You urge me on to this terrible action, O Handsome Haired One (Kṛṣṇa)?" (3.1).

The apparent contradiction is only superficial, and easily dispelled. Kṛṣṇa replies that there are, indeed, two paths available to the aspirant (later He will introduce even more), namely *sāṃkhya*, a yoga process involving intellectual exploration of the nature of reality, physical and metaphysical, and *karma,* the *yoga* of action. But these *yogas* are not mutually exclusive. "Not by abstention from actions," Kṛṣṇa says, "does a man attain the state beyond *karma*, and not by renunciation alone does he approach perfection" (3.4). This is because one cannot avoid action, even for a split second, and those who attempt to are merely deluding themselves because their mind will continue to brood over objects of the senses (3.6). Action is better than inaction, but we must act in a spirit of detachment, and this is effected through the mind. The mind can take hold of senses and bring them under control (3.7). Mind and action, then, are partners.

At this point Kṛṣṇa engages in a discourse on the nature cycle and its dependence on sacrifice to the demigods (the second definition of *karma* stated earlier). To the contemporary western aspirant, these passages are primarily of historical interest, because later Kṛṣṇa will assert that if one surrenders to *Him*, they are no longer obligated to perform these rituals. We westerners never performed them in the first place, but for Hinduism this marks a momentous theological shift away from the Vedic sacrificial system and its worship of a nature-based pantheon to a more introspective, monotheistic, mystical religion.

Kṛṣṇa now directs the conversation away from the question of action and inaction and points instead to an inner path: "He whose delight is only in the Self (Ātman), whose satisfaction is in the Self, and who is content only in the Self, for him the need to act does not exist. He has no purpose at all in action, nor any whatever in non-action" (3.17-18).

The next four verses are particularly intriguing because they hint, for the first time, at Kṛṣṇa's true identity as God. His divinity is not stated outright from the start, but is revealed gradually, building to the climax of the *Gītā* in the eleventh chapter, when Arjuna is shown God's universal form. Whatever great men do, Kṛṣṇa says, lesser men imitate (3.22), therefore He engages in action, though "For Me, there is nothing whatever to be done in the three worlds, nor is there anything to be attained" (3.22). Should Kṛṣṇa give up action, all of humankind would follow, and as a result, "these worlds would perish and a maker of confusion I should be; I would destroy all these creatures" (3.23-24). The subtler implication here is that the world is rooted in, and has its being in, God. God, being complete in Himself, didn't *need* to create and become everything; there is nothing He *needs* to accomplish. But were He to cease "acting", in the sense of maintaining the cosmic manifestation through His own will, everything would vanish, being reabsorbed back into Him.

When we act, it is not really *we* who are acting; in other words, the real Self, the Ātman, does not act. Actions are performed by material nature upon material nature. Here the concept of the three *guṇas*, or modes of material nature, is introduced, though chapter fourteen will provide a fuller treatment of the subject. Briefly, the tangible, material world is the result of the interaction of three principal elements: *rajas*, which is impulse, movement, excitation, passion; *tamas*, which is resistance, inertia, ignorance; and *sattva*, which is continuity, purity, balance, goodness. The science of the *guṇas'* interplay is embodied in the *Sāṃkhya* philosophy, one of the six orthodox philosophical systems of Hinduism. Kṛṣṇa says, "Actions in all cases are performed by the *guṇas* of material nature; he who is confused by egotism imagines, "I am the doer" (3.27). The true I, the Ātman, is transcendent and changeless; it is never affected by matter, thus it cannot be said to act. The soap opera of the physical world is merely *guṇas* acting upon *guṇas*, matter interacting with matter. Keeping this thought in mind would help one to remain aloof from the triumphs and tragedies, pleasures and pains which are inevitable in life, and instead remain fixed in *ānanda*, spiritual bliss. This is the theory behind the *sāṃkhya-yoga* method.

While the sage appears to act, he or she remains unattached to actions because the mind is steady in the Self. But Kṛṣṇa takes it a step further. "Deferring all actions to Me," He says, "meditating on the Supreme Spirit . . . fight." (3.30). Trickster Kṛṣṇa drops this bombshell and at once abandons it for later. So far He has only hinted at His divinity, but later He will expound upon the *yoga* of devotion, which calls for us to lovingly consecrate all of our actions, thoughts, feelings and experiences to Him. Notice how chapter three has introduced brief foreshadowings of three themes which will only be fully developed later — Kṛṣṇa's divinity, the three *guṇas*, and surrendering one's work to God. *Gītā*, remember, means "song", and in its use of thematic presage the *Gītā* resembles a piece of operatic music. It is said that Sanskrit, which is sung, is the language of the gods, so in the celestial realm the *devas* don't talk to each other, but sing! It's like a perpetual grand opera up there.

Resuming the subject of sense restraint, Kṛṣṇa now explains exactly why the senses attach themselves to objects, be they people, flavors, possessions, or whatever. It is passion which serves as the glue. Passion is our enemy, born out of the of mode of *rajas*. "As fire is obscured by smoke, and a mirror by dust, as the embryo is enveloped by the womb, so is the intelligence obscured by passion" (3.38). Passion lodges in the senses, mind and intelligence, resulting in the true self becoming confused and obscured (3.40). One can overcome the enemy passion through self-control and an understanding of the primacy of the pure Ātman over matter, senses, the mind, and the intellect (3.41-42). According to the Hindu model of human consciousness, our minds have two aspects, *manas* and *buddhi*. Though here translated as "intellect" and "mind", there are no direct equivalents in English, which is odd considering that the duality in our heads is so fundamental to our experience. *Manas* is that aspect of mind which is spontaneously, almost independently generating material — images, sounds, memories, rambling, brainless internal monologues, songs you can't make stop. I think of it rather like a radio left on after you leave the room, babbling to itself whether there's an audience or not. *Buddhi*, on the other hand, is the rational, discriminative faculty which is observing the *manas* and making judgements about it. As Kṛṣṇa says, *buddhi* is higher than *manas* and Ātman is higher than *buddhi* (3.42). It is by means of the *buddhi* that the *manas* and the senses are brought under control. We often mistake *buddhi* to be our true selves, our "soul" as it were, but *buddhi* is a mere ephemera, changing and inconstant. It is a tool for disciplining the lower self, but not to be confused with Ātman, which is changeless.

"Kill the enemy, O Mighty Armed One, which has the form of desire and is difficult to approach" (3.43), the chapter concludes. By identifying the enemy with desire, Kṛṣṇa Himself is intimating that the war is a metaphorical one, and that the *Gītā* is an allegory.

Chapter Four: Kṛṣṇa the *Avatāra*; the Inaction Inherent in Action

"I instructed this imperishable *yoga* to the sun god, Vivasvat, and Vivasvat instructed it to Manu, the father of mankind, and Manu in turn instructed it to Ikṣvāku" (4.1).

This transcendental science is of divine origin, ancient and eternally relevant. It was passed down from master to disciple, until at some point the chain was broken and the knowledge lost. Kṛṣṇa is now reviving it for the benefit of everyone. But Arjuna asks, "If Vivasvat was born long before You, how could You have instructed it to him in the beginning?" (4.4).

Now Kṛṣṇa reveals that He is the *Avatāra*, the Incarnation of God. *Avatāra* means "descent", and unlike Christianity, which believes there has only been one, Hinduism holds that there have been many. The reason Kṛṣṇa could instruct Vivasvat is because He is God, and preexists everyone. The paradox of the *Avatāra* is that He seems to take physical birth in this world, assume the limitations of human life, and die. But being pure Brahman, He is eternally changeless, infinite, untouched by material nature. He cannot be "born" in any real sense because He is without boundaries. It is a great mystery, an illusion cast by the power of *māyā*: "Although I am birthless and deathless, the Lord of all beings, I appear to take birth by the magic of My *māyā*. Yet I always remain the Master of *prakṛti* (Nature, substance, primal matter)" (4.6).

He descends when the world is badly in need of Him: "Whenever there is a decline in virtue (*dharma*) . . . and an increase in evil (*adharma*), then I send Myself forth. To protect the pious and vanquish evildoers, to reestablish righteousness, I come back from age to age" (4.7-8).

Those who are fortunate enough to know the truth regarding Kṛṣṇa's divine descent do not go on to rebirth, but attain union with Him (4.9). The *Avatāra* is a sanctifying, saving power; whoever takes refuge in Him, seeks solace in Him, thinks only of Him, will be with Him (4.10-11).

We return to the subject of *karma-yoga* now; in the last chapter we discovered that actions are nothing more than material nature interacting with material nature. Kṛṣṇa resumes the topic, but on an even more subtle and profound level. Using the Vedic fire sacrifice as a metaphor for action and the field upon which action takes place, He states, "Brahman is the sacrifice, Brahman is the oblation, poured out by Brahman into the fire of Brahman; Brahman is attained by one who contemplates the actions of Brahman" (4.24).

One of the key verses in the book, it sums up the philosophy of *advaita vedānta*, non-dualism, the viewpoint espoused by the *Upaniṣads* and their timeless dictum, *tat tvam asi*, "You are That (i.e. Brahman, God). God is the field upon which we act, that is, the material world or plane (symbolized by the fire); God is also the individual (symbolized by the sacrificial priest) and the action performed by the individual (symbolized by the pouring) as well as the means by which action is performed, in other words the body, the senses, and so forth (symbolized by the offering). Everything is God. The actor never really acts; what appears to be action is merely Brahman acting on Brahman. Seen in this light, attachment to actions and their fruits seems absurd.

Having established the sacrificial fire as an apt metaphor for Brahman, Kṛṣṇa enumerates the varieties of sacrifice people offer into the fire, in other words, the practices they embrace as a means of attaining consciousness of God. They include worship of deities (4.25), control of the senses (4.26), *prāṇāyāma* or breath control (4.27, 29), giving up possessions (4.28), scriptural recitation and study (4.28), dietary restrictions (4.30), and so forth. However, the cultivation of knowledge is better than asceticism (4.33). It can be acquired by humbly approaching enlightened teachers, "the knowing ones, the perceivers of truth" (4.34) and, while rendering service to them, enquiring about spiritual life. Once this knowledge is absorbed, the aspirant will see all beings in him or herself and as one with God. He or she will be free of evil (4.36), free of *karma* (4.37), and purified (4.38). "Action", Kṛṣṇa says, "does not bind him who has renounced action through *yoga*, whose doubt is cut away by knowledge and who is possessed of the Self" (4.41).

Chapters Five and Six: The Practice of *Yoga* and Meditation

Relatively short, chapter five primarily reiterates what we have learned so far. We are not the "doer"; with this knowledge we must act without attachment, control the senses, steady the mind, and remain unaffected by external sensations. Brahman is all, so we must absorb our minds in Brahman and see Him equally manifested everywhere — in a learned holy man, a cow, an elephant, a dog, even a "dog-eater", that is, the most abominable of people (5.18).

Kṛṣṇa's discourse has focused on the universal aspect of Brahman, It's being the field upon which we act as well as the divine actor. But there is another way to think about Brahman. It is the radiant, blissful Ātman within us, and we can discover it for ourselves by turning inward: "He whose joy is inward, inward his peace, and his vision inward, shall come know the *nirvāṇa* of Brahman" (5.24). The formal attempt to perceive the inner Ātman is *rāja-yoga*, the path of meditation, which is the primary subject of chapter six. The closing verses of chapter five describe the *rāja-yoga* method in a nutshell: "Shutting off sense from what is outward, fixing the gaze at the root of the eyebrows, checking the breath-stream in and outgoing within the nostrils, holding the senses, holding the intellect, holding the mind fast, he who seeks freedom . . . is made free forever" (5.27-28).

The first principle of *yoga* is renunciation (6.1-2). It is achieved by the power of the mind. The mind can either uplift us, in which case it is our dearest friend, or can drag us down and degrade us like an enemy (6.5-6). When mind has conquered itself, has triumphed over its own lower nature, the *yogī* is dispassionate to both pleasure and pain, praise and insult. A dirt clod, a stone, and gold are all alike (6.7-8), and all people, whether friend or foe, are viewed impartially (6.9).

We can achieve this state through the practical application of *yogic* techniques, which Kṛṣṇa outlines now. The method is surprisingly simple, but its actual practice can be tough. All we are attempting to do is fix the mind on a single point and hold it there, but as Arjuna will remark, "Restraining the mind is like trying to hold back the wind!" The art of meditation is known as *rāja-yoga*, the "king of *yogas*", and it is also a fundamental practice for Buddhists, Sufis, certain Taoists, and Christian mystics.

By holding the mind still, the *rāja-yogī* gradually strips away the layers of physical and psychological edifice which prevents him or her from perceiving Ātman directly. The meditator goes in, in, in, beyond the body, beyond the mind, beyond the intellect, detaching him or herself from each one with the thought, "This is not me, nor is this Ātman." Eventually pure consciousness, serene, limitless, free of dualities, is reached. This is *samādhi*, superconsciousness, Ātman-realization.

To begin, the *yogī* should renounce desire and material possessions (6.10). In a solitary place (forests were favored by *ṛṣis* of old; today a temple, monastic environment, or even a quiet space set apart in one's home is appropriate), level and firm (to provide adequate support for a straight-backed seated posture), the *yogī* should lay down some sort of ground covering (6.11). Kṛṣṇa suggests a cloth, an antelope skin and sacred *kuśa* grass, materials which would have been available to *yogīs* in His day and which, since most *yogīs* would be meditating in the forest, helped keep the bugs off. Today, a mat, a firm, flat pillow, or a folded blanket is just as acceptable. Seated with a straight spine, body and head erect, holding himself motionless, the *yogī* subdues the senses, quiets the mind, and fixes it firmly on a single object — the Self, or Kṛṣṇa (6.10,12-15). The ultimate goal may be called *samādhi*, *nirvāṇa*, or union with Kṛṣṇa; it's all the same thing.

One cannot be a *yogī* who overeats or fasts excessively, who sleeps too much or too little. For one who is moderate in food and recreation, whose actions are disciplined, *yoga* will dispel all sorrow (6.16-17). With constant practice, the mind can be made still "as a lamp-flame in a windless place" (6.19). The *yogī* becomes one with Brahman (6.27), perceives his or her Self present in all other beings and, at the same time, the Selves of all other beings present in him or her (6.29). This extraordinary state is called *samadarśana* ("seeing the same"); while we ordinarily perceive ourselves as distinct individuals, actually we share a common universal Soul which is identical to the Supreme Soul (Kṛṣṇa, or Brahman).

"He who sees Me everywhere, and sees all things in Me, is never lost to Me, and I am never lost to Him" (6.30).

But Arjuna lacks confidence: "The mind, indeed, is unstable, troubling, powerful, intense. The restraining of it, I think, is like restraining the wind, difficult to achieve" (6.34). Kṛṣṇa agrees, but assures Arjuna that with diligent practice the mind can be held steady. The key is perseverance.

What happens, Arjuna wonders, to a person who begins the spiritual path, but does not follow it through to completion? Is he doomed? Not at all, Kṛṣṇa replies; no attempts at spiritual realization are ever futile. The unsuccessful aspirant will take rebirth in a family of wise *yogīs* and pick up where he or she left off (6.37-44). It often takes many births to reach the Supreme Goal (6.45).

Chapter Seven: The Source and Maintenance of the Universe

Here Kṛṣṇa describes how He is the source, foundation, sustainer and destination of the universe. He says that by absorbing one's mind in Him and becoming entirely dependent on Him, one will know Him (7.1). Beyond this, nothing remains to be known. Still, very few people ever strive for spiritual perfection. Out of many thousands, perhaps one will make the attempt, and out of those who try, scarcely anyone knows God in truth (7.3).

In the next eleven verses, Kṛṣṇa discusses *prakṛti*, the material manifestation, and His presence in it. Kṛṣṇa, or Brahman, has a dual nature. On the one hand, He is pure spirit, pure existence-consciousness-bliss (*sat-cit-ānanda*), while on the other, He is substance, matter, the tangible, manifest world. These two aspects are referred to as *puruṣa* and *prakṛti* respectively. *Puruṣa*, literally "male" or "man"[4] (a cognate with the English "person"), is symbolized by the male deities, such as Śiva, or Rāma. *Prakṛti*, literally "the urge to produce"[5] (like the English "procreate"), is, in keeping with the universal archetypes of Mother Earth, the Nature Goddess, Gaia, Divine Mother, etc, represented by the female deities, such as Pārvatī or Sītā (whose name means "furrow", and who arose from the earth). The deities must come in pairs, for without *prakṛti, puruṣa* remains forever static, unmanifest, while without *puruṣa, prakṛti* is inert, lifeless. According to the *Sāṃkhya* philosophy, creation came about when the primordial, then-static principles of *puruṣa* and *prakṛti* united, resulting in a kind of big bang from which the three *guṇas* emerged and, from the interplay of the *guṇas,* the building blocks of creation. In Tantric imagery, the union of *puruṣa* and *prakṛti* is represented by the god and goddess in erotic embrace. Kṛṣṇa says, "My *prakṛti* is of eightfold composition: earth, water, fire, wind, ether, mind, intelligence, and ego. Such is My inferior *prakṛti,* but I also have a higher *prakṛti,* which consists of living beings, by which this universe is sustained" (7.4-5).

In other words, there is a lower *prakṛti,* comprised of matter, and a higher *prakṛti,* comprised of *jīvas* , or living souls, which, by interacting with matter, animate it. Kṛṣṇa is the source and substance of both; "On Me all this universe is strung, like pearls on a thread" (7.6-7). He is the very Being of all beings, the very Reality which lends all phenomena their reality. In some of the most stunning passages of the *Gītā,* Kṛṣṇa tells how all beautiful things derive their beauty from His presence in them, how all extraordinary things derive their magnificence from Him: "I am the liquidity in waters, the radiance in the moon and sun . . . the manhood in men . . . I am the pure fragrance of the earth . . . the life in all beings . . . the intelligence of the intelligent, the splendor of the splendid, the might of the mighty . . . I am love . . ." (7.8-11).

He is also *māyā,* the Grand Illusion which prevents us from perceiving Him (7.12-14). However, one who resorts to Him is brought beyond the veil of *māyā* (7.14). People who are of an evil temperament, are deluded, or are of a low consciousness do not resort to Kṛṣṇa; they are attracted to a demonic existence (7.15). Four types of people do turn to Him — the suffering, the inquisitive, the desirer of wealth (wealth here might refer to the "wealth" of knowledge, for the literal meaning is, perhaps, not in keeping with the rest of the *Gītā's* teachings),[6] and the wise, who are spiritually inclined (7.16). Of the four, the last is preeminent; he is especially dear to Kṛṣṇa and Kṛṣṇa dear to him (7.17). Such a soul is rare (7.19).

Part of the *Gītā's* genius lies in its universality. While some are more direct than others, all religious traditions are recognized as valid paths to God, and since all deities and all religious conceptions are embodiments of a single Divine Truth, one can, by worshipping any god, worship the one God. "Whoever desires to honor with belief this or that worshipped form, I bestow on him unshakable faith. Endowed with the faith I give him, he worships that deity and gets from it everything he prays for. But in actuality these benefits are bestowed by Me alone" (7.21-22).

This is not idolatry. To think that God has taken a divine form, or to worship and meditate upon God through a statue or picture, does not compromise His oneness, nor does it debase Him by associating Him with common matter. God can never be contained, contaminated, or affected by matter. When He takes earthly form as an *Avatāra*, He is by no means bound or conditioned by material nature; similarly, when He is worshipped in a statue, the devotee knows perfectly well that He has not *become* the statue, but that the statue is imbued with His presence, which is all-pervading anyway. To this effect, Kṛṣṇa says, "Though I am unmanifest, the unintelligent think of Me as fallen into manifestation. They do not know My higher nature, which is imperishable and supreme" (7.24).

Kṛṣṇa does not manifest Himself to everybody; we are deluded by *māyā*, which envelops us as soon as we are born (7.25,27). The powers of attraction and aversion seize us right away, for we mistakenly believe the illusion of duality to be real (7.27). We can free ourselves of such delusion, though, and when we do, we will perceive the reality of Brahman, the Supreme, of *adhyātman*, Supreme Self, of *adhibhūta*, Supreme Being, and of *adhidaiva*, Supreme God, all of which are one in the same (7.29-30).

Chapter Eight: Beyond Being and Nonbeing

What, Arjuna asks, is Brahman (the Supreme)? What is *adhyātma* (Supreme Self)? What is *adhibhūta* (Supreme Being)? What is *adhidaiva* (Supreme God)? What is *adhiyajña* (the Supreme Object of Sacrifice)? (8.1-2).

Kṛṣṇa's reply is couched in highly technical and even elusive language. So esoteric are Arjuna's questions and so mysterious Kṛṣṇa's replies, they are appropriate subjects for deep meditation. Brahman, Kṛṣṇa says, is the Supreme Imperishable (8.3). In later verses (8.20-21), He explains further that beyond the manifest state of being exists an unmanifest state of being which is "higher than the primeval unmanifest" (the state of nothingness before the universe comes into being). When all beings perish, It still remains, thus It is known as the Imperishable. It is the Supreme Goal, and when It is attained, one never returns to the embodied state. "This," Kṛṣṇa declares, "is My supreme dwelling place."

The *adhyātma* (Supreme Self, Supreme Soul) is the "inherent nature of the individual" (8.3). In other words, It is the aspect of Brahman which is localized in the individual. It is "the ancient seer" (8.9), and we are called to meditate upon It. It is described as the ruler, smaller than the atom, yet the fundamental support of everything. Its form is unimaginable, but It is "the color of the sun, beyond darkness" (8.9).

"The *adhibhūta* (Supreme Being) is the perishable nature of being" (8.4). In other words, all the worldly ephemera is God too. "Being" refers not just to the abstract, spiritual concept of absolute, limitless *Being* (*sat*), but also to our ordinary state of being creatures, of being ourselves — changeable, mortal, imperfect. All things that exist do so because their individual existences, which are perishable, are rooted in the Supreme Being, *adhibhūta*. Therefore, *adhibhūta* is said to be perishable. So, as *adhyātma* we are eternal and endless, and as *adhibhūta* we are mutable and transitory. Both phenomena are divine, both are Brahman.

"The *adhidaiva* (Supreme God)," Kṛṣṇa says, "is the *puruṣa*" (8.4). Earlier we defined *puruṣa* as the static, unmanifest aspect of Brahman which is pure spirit, pure consciousness, as contrasted with *prakṛti*, the manifest aspect of Brahman which is substance, matter, energy, differentiation, phenomena. *Puruṣa* is represented as masculine, and all of the male deities — Śiva, Brahmā, Rāma, Kṛṣṇa, etc. — are aspects of *puruṣa*. In this sense, *puruṣa* is identified as the archetypal cosmic "male". As an individual figure, He is the cosmogonic Person, a primeval divine man whose body represents the totality and whose energy represents the creative impulse. He is the "seed", the activating force which, when blended with the archetypal "female" field of yet unmanifest material nature, *prakṛti*, gives rise to the material universe with its dualities and variegatedness.

Sometimes *puruṣa* refers to the personal aspect of Brahman, what we would call "God" (hence the term *adhidaiva*, Supreme God). It is also associated with the individual Ātman because it is the spiritual power which animates the material elements. Without the presence of *puruṣa*, there would be nothing but lifeless, inert matter. Because the Ātman which animates matter is, Itself, consciousness, *puruṣa*, too, is identified as consciousness.

Finally, Kṛṣṇa identifies *adhiyajña* (the Supreme Object of Sacrifice) as Himself. All sacrifices, all rituals, all prayers, all meditations go to Him. Later in the Gītā, He will indicate that in this day and age meditation and devotion to God are the most appropriate forms of sacrifice, elaborate rituals being no longer feasible. At this point in the text, though, we are simply told to meditate on Kṛṣṇa, so that at the time of death we may go to Him.

The remainder of the chapter discusses, in highly practical terms, techniques for a conscious death. It is absolutely imperative that at this critical moment of transition we have knowledge of who we really are and control over where we are going. It is a fundamental Hindu doctrine that the state of our consciousness at the moment of death will determine our destination. Kṛṣṇa says, "Whatever state of being one remembers when he quits his body, that state he will attain without fail. Therefore, at all times meditate on Me . . . in this way you shall surely come to Me" (8.6-7). If we think of God at the moment of death, we will be united with Him; if we think of earthly things and people, we will be united with them. This is not an easy "out", an excuse not to attend to spiritual practice while we're here; at the time of death our minds dwell on whatever they dwelled on during our lives. If we doted on our children, they will haunt our last thoughts; if we were obsessed with money, the fate of the estate will consume us; if we thought only of God day and night, God we will think of and to God we will go, never again to experience rebirth. The *Śrīmad Bhāgavatam* contains a cautionary tale about a sage, Bharata, who became intensely fond of a pet deer, so fond, in fact, that at the moment of death he thought only of the deer and hence reincarnated into a deer. Conversely, there is the story of Ajāmila, a hedonist and whoremonger whose only genuine love was for his young son, who happened to be named Nārāyaṇa, a name of God. With his dying breath, Ajāmila called out to his child, "Nārāyaṇa!", and at that moment, the celestial emissaries of Viṣṇu arrived to whisk the man off to spiritual liberation. So potent is the name of God.

One can even die a yogic death, meditating on the Ātman while centering the vital breath between the eyebrows (8.10), controlling the "nine gates of the body" (8.12) namely the eyes, the nostrils, the ears, the mouth, genital organ and anus (women, of course, would have ten "gates"), and chanting Oṃ (8.13).

The cycle of life and death, being and non-being, is common to all levels of reality. Each living thing undergoes life, death and rebirth, as does each day, which revolves from light to dark and back to light, and the seasons of the year. In fact, the universal cosmic manifestation goes through cycles of being and nonbeing. At the beginning of each cosmic cycle, which is known as a *kalpa*, Brahman bursts into manifest being, becoming space, time, matter, phenomenon, and living beings. After an inconceivably huge amount of time, the universe begins to entropy, to break apart and dissolve, until it is eventually reabsorbed back into Brahman, back into a state of non-being. In due time, the process is repeated, with and entirely new creation being born. Each cycle of manifestation is known as a "day of Brahmā", each dissolution a "night of Brahmā", and the spans of time they represent are mind-boggling. According to Bhaktivedanta Prabhupāda:

> One day of Brahmā consists of a thousand cycles of four *yugas* or ages . . . 1,728,000 years . . . 1,296,000 years . . . 864,000 years . . . 432,000 years . . . These four *yugas* rotating a thousand times, comprise one day of Brahmā, and the same number comprise one night. Brahmā lives one hundred of such "years" and then dies. These "hundred years" by earth calculations total to 311 trillion and 40 billion earth years. By these calculations the life of Brahmā seems fantastic and interminable, but from the viewpoint of eternity it is as brief as a lightning flash."[7]

It can be said, then, that Brahman Itself undergoes the cycle of death and rebirth, of being and non-being: "From the unmanifest, all manifestations come forth at the arrival of (Brahmā's) day, and at the arrival of (Brahmā's) night, they are dissolved, once again unmanifest" (8.16). But Brahman has an even higher state of Being, beyond the tumult of being and non-being: "Higher than this state of being is another unmanifest state of being, higher than the primeval unmanifest, which, when all beings perish, does not perish" (8.20).

Returning to the subject of our destinations after death, Kṛṣṇa describes the two possible paths we can take — the path to liberation or the path to rebirth, known respectively as the "bright path" and the "dark path" (8.23-27). An extremely advanced *yogī* can choose the moment of death most conducive to blending back into Brahman and hence embark upon the "bright path", or, if he wishes to be reborn, may exit his body at a moment favorable for rebirth, a journey back down the "dark path". For those of us less adroit at such things, Kṛṣṇa offers an easier solution: "He who thinks of Me constantly, whose mind does not go elsewhere ever, for him . . . I am easy to reach" (8.14). Merely by approaching Kṛṣṇa, one is freed from rebirth (8.15).

Chapter Nine: The Secret Teaching

Recall the *advaita vedāntic* verse in chapter four: "Brahman is the sacrifice, Brahman the oblation, poured out by Brahman into the fire of Brahman; Brahman is attained by one who contemplates the actions of Brahman" (4.24). Compare that to verse 9.16, in which Kṛṣṇa says, "I am the ritual, I am the sacrifice, I am the offering, I am the medicinal herb, the sacred text am I, I am also the clarified butter, I am the fire and I am the pouring out (of the oblation)."

The first verse indicates that everything is Brahman, the second that everything is Kṛṣṇa. There cannot be two everythings, hence Kṛṣṇa and Brahman must be identical. This "royal secret" has been suggested in increments all along, but in chapter nine, and the two succeeding chapters, it will be declared openly and explored in detail.

Kṛṣṇa pervades the whole universe in His unmanifested aspect, and all beings abide in Him. Yet He does not abide in beings (9.4). "Beings" here refers to the physical embodiment. Kṛṣṇa pervades everything but does not *abide* in matter. In other words, while Kṛṣṇa is present in everything, He is not centralized or confined there; His original state remains infinitely full, infinitely unaffected by His contact with matter.

"Behold My majestic power!" He says. "Sustaining beings and not dwelling in beings, I Myself cause beings to be" (9.5). By reposing on His own *prakṛti*, He sends forth the multitude of beings which become "powerless", that is, deluded and ensnared by *prakṛti* and *māyā* (9.8). Yet He remains entirely unaffected by this action (9.9). *Prakṛti* is responsible for actually providing the various forms (9.10).

In reference to His present, human body, Kṛṣṇa remarks, "The deluded despise Me when I assume a human form, not knowing My higher existence as the Great Lord of all Beings" (9.11). The Absolute can assume embodiment in the form of an *Avatāra*, but as indicated above, one must never assume that Brahman is affected in any way by this occurrence. The *Avatāra* only *appears* to live, work suffer, etc. within the constraints of natural laws; in truth, He is never bound, never conditioned, never limited by the forces of *māyā*.

Those who are devoid of knowledge, who don't bother to think, and who pursue vain hopes, abide in *prakṛti* in a deluded, demonic state (9.12). On the other hand, those who are of a great, divine nature worship Kṛṣṇa single-mindedly because they know He is the imperishable Origin of everything (9.13). With firm vows, they perpetually glorify, honor, and worship Him with devotion (9.14). The sacrifice they offer is the "knowledge sacrifice", in other words, meditation, contemplation, the cultivation of knowledge. They worship Kṛṣṇa "as the One and as the manifold (the Many), variously manifested, facing all directions" (9.15).

The concept of "the One and the manifold" is key to understanding the nature of Brahman. The religion of the *Bhagavad-Gītā* is radically monotheistic, yet because God is absolute, all-inclusive and totally unlimited, He assumes an infinite number of forms, such as *Avatāras* and worshipable deities like Śiva, Devī, etc. He also assumes conceptual forms, some of which he lists here. He is the father of the universe, the mother, the grandfather, the object of all knowledge, the syllable Oṃ, the *Ṛg*, *Yajur*, and *Sāma Vedas*, the eyewitness, the abode, the refuge, the friend, the origin, dissolution and continuity, as well as the giver of immortality and death, of being and non-being (9.17-19).

Those who worship the various gods are actually worshipping Kṛṣṇa, for He is the only real recipient of worship. Since the worshipper is not aware of this, however, the results of such devotion are limited (9.23-24). One should bypass lesser manifestations and concentrate on their Source.

"If one offers Me with purity and love a leaf, a flower, fruit, or water, I will accept it" (9.26). Ritual worship, or *pūjā*, can be of extreme simplicity and delicacy, as this famous verse implies. Each morning the practicing Hindu offers the *Iṣṭa-devatā* (chosen deity) various items, such as food, water, incense, flowers, and so forth, with standard prayers and hymns. The same ritual is performed in temples, only on a larger scale. If the worshipper has nothing to offer, he or she may perform *pūjā* mentally and it is equally acceptable to God, some say even more efficacious. The ceremonial movements and words are not the point of *pūjā* at all, but only a means of arousing strong emotions and expressing love, devotion and longing for God. All Kṛṣṇa asks for is a leaf, or a palmful of water. He is not in need of our gifts, rather He wants us to understand that any means by which we express our devotion, no matter how humble, is accepted and cherished by Him.

One may also worship God by consecrating all of one's actions to Him as an offering. Kṛṣṇa says, "Whatever you do, whatever you eat, whatever you offer or give away, do that as an offering to Me" (9.27). This moment-to-moment deliberateness (akin to the Buddhist practice of "mindfulness"), this sanctification of one's actions by constantly remembering God and offering one's life and self as a sacrifice, is one of the most popular, and yet one of the most sublime, forms of *yoga*.

In this day and age, rigorous yogic exercises and austerities are impossible for most people. The "secret" teaching of chapter nine is that one can achieve the same end as the mystic *yogī* simply by fixing the mind on Kṛṣṇa (or any conception of God one finds most relishable) at all times and, with the senses under control and in a spirit of detachment, devote oneself to Him (or Her or It) as the ultimate goal.

"With mind fixed on Me," Kṛṣṇa says, "be devoted to Me. Sacrificing to Me, make reverence to Me. Thus steadfast, with Me as your supreme aim, you shall come to Me" (9.34).

Some of the forms in which we can think of and worship Him are revealed in the next chapter.

Chapter Ten: The Many Manifestations of the Divine

Chapter Ten is one of the most delightful portions of the *Gītā*. Here Kṛṣṇa will enumerate many of His principal manifestations. He has already mentioned a few in previous chapters (7.8; 9.17-19). Besides actual deities, Kṛṣṇa will identify Himself with all wondrous phenomena, anything which displays grandeur, beauty, sublimity, power or ultimacy.

He begins by stating that no one, not even the gods or the great seers, know His origin because He is the origin of the gods, the seers, and everything else (10.2). He has no birth, no beginning (10.3). He is the originator of the earliest human beings, here identified as the seven legendary *ṛṣis* (seers) and the four Manus, who were born of His mind (10.6). The seven *ṛṣis* — Kaśyapa, Atri, Vasiṣṭha, Viśvāmitra, Gotama, Jamadagni and Bharadvāja[8] — are the mythical progenitors of the human race, as are the Manus, the primeval patriarchs.

Those who know that everything proceeds from Kṛṣṇa are united with Him (10.7). They meditate on Him, worship Him, concentrate the vital breath on Him, enlighten one another by speaking of Him constantly, and as a result, Kṛṣṇa, who is present within them, illuminates them with knowledge from within (10.8-11).

Arjuna says, "You are the Supreme Brahman, the Supreme Abode, the Supreme Purifier, the Divine Spirit, the Primal God, birthless and all-pervading . . . God of Gods, O Lord of the Universe!" (10.12, 10.15). Inspired, he requests Kṛṣṇa to describe more completely the manifestations by which He pervades the spiritual and material worlds (10.16). How can He be known? By what various forms may He be thought of and meditated upon (10.17)?

As there is no end to Kṛṣṇa's extent, He promises only to list His manifestations which are most prominent (10.19). He begins with the most general manifestation, and the most important to us: "I am the Ātman abiding in the heart of all beings; I am the beginning and the middle of beings, and the end as well" (10.21). Continuing in this vein, He enumerates His principal manifestations one by one. For the sake of clarity, they are presented here in list form.

— Of *Ādityas*, I am Viṣṇu (10.21).

The *Ādityas* were a group of supreme gods, originally numbered at seven, later twelve. Viṣṇu, now one of the most widely worshipped manifestations of the Divine (along with Śiva and Devī) was originally considered an *Āditya*. On His own, He is the subject of the *Viṣṇu Purāṇa* and *Bhāgavata Purāṇa* (*Śrīmad Bhāgavatam*). The most beautiful, benevolent, and radiant member of the Hindu "trinity", Viṣṇu is a gorgeous god of love and light. Like Kṛṣṇa, His complexion is dark blue, He is dressed in yellow garments, and a peacock feather adorns His helmet. Kṛṣṇa is one of Viṣṇu's *Avatāras*, and will exhibit His Viṣṇu form for Arjuna in the next chapter. This four-armed form carries a conch, lotus, discus and club, which symbolize, among other things, creation, transcendence, the destruction of ignorance, and enlightenment. Viṣṇu rides atop the great bird Garuḍa, who will be mentioned in verse thirty, and with the thousand-headed serpent Ananta, whom we will meet in verse twenty-nine. At the dawn of each cosmic cycle, when the universe is created anew, Ananta lays down on the universal causal ocean like a bed while Viṣṇu reclines on him. Viṣṇu falls into a sleep-like trance and a lotus grows from His navel. As the petals of the lotus unfurl, Brahmā is found seated on the whorl of the flower and, after deep meditation, begins to create the universe element by element.

Perhaps the most glamorous and attractive of all the divine forms (excepting His own Kṛṣṇa and Rāma incarnations), Viṣṇu is the most benevolent because He incarnates Himself again and again on earth for the benefit of all humankind. His principal *Avatāras* number ten, though the tenth is yet to make His appearance. They are Matsya (the fish), Kūrma (the tortoise), Varāha (the boar), Nṛsiṃhadeva (the half-man, half-lion), Vāmana (the dwarf), Paraśurāma (the avenger with an axe), Rāma (the hero of the Rāmāyaṇa), Kṛṣṇa, Buddha, and Kalki (the eschatological destroyer). Notice how these forms mimic the evolutionary journey of the soul through increasingly sophisticated bodies — fish, amphibian, mammal, man-animal, diminutive human, full-statured human, prince, hero, enlightened one, liberator. Though Viṣṇu is worshipped in His original form, He assumes His greatest significance in His *Avatāra* forms.

— Of lights, I am the radiant sun (10.21).

— O the *Maruts*, I am Marīci (10.21).

Marīci was the chief of the storm gods, the *maruts*, who are associated with the Vedic pantheon.

— Among the nightly ones, I am the moon (10.21).

— Of the *Vedas*, I am the *Sāma Veda* (10.22).

The *Sāma Veda* is comprised of sacred songs (*sāmans*), drawn from the *Ṛg Veda* and rearranged for liturgical purposes.

— Of the gods (*devas*), I am Vāsava (10.22).

Vāsava is another name for Indra, the foremost of the Vedic deities. Today, he is thought of as the king of the *devas*, in other words, the leader of the celestial citizenry. Often compared to Zeus, he wields a thunderbolt, is lord of storms, and appears often in mythology, though in post-Vedic legends usually in a supporting role. Many hymns of the *Ṛg Veda* are dedicated to him.

— Of the senses, I am the mind (10.22).

In Hindu psychology, the mind is considered a sense organ, like the nose, tongue, or skin. It is a stimulus-responsive, or knowledge-gathering organ, not the source of consciousness, as is believed in the west.

— I am the consciousness of all beings (10.22).

Ātman is consciousness (*cit*), and Kṛṣṇa is the Paramātman, or Supreme Consciousness.

— Of the *Rudras*, I am Śaṃkara (10.23).

Śaṃkara is another name for Śiva. His Vedic prototype is Rudra, an ambivalent figure, on the one hand a fierce deity of tempests and destruction, on the other a bringer of fertility and well-being (through rains, for instance, or through the destruction of undesirable elements, such as animals that prey on livestock). Rudra is red-complected, hence his name is cognate with the English words "red" and "ruddy". So too does his ferocious personality correspond to western symbolism associated with the color red. The *Rudras*, as a group, are the sons of Rudra and Pṛśni, the Earth Goddess. They are also roaring, atmospheric deities associated with storms. The contemporary Śiva, whose name means "auspicious" is the creator and destroyer of the cosmos. Unlike Viṣṇu, who is the quintessence of sweetness and goodness, Śiva, like His earlier incarnation Rudra, is a god of paradox. He is benevolent and gentle, a loving protector of His devotees. Yet He is also fearsome and horrible, the personification of fury and death, the terrible destroyer who, at the end of each cosmic cycle, performs the cataclysmic dance which obliterates the universe. In this role He is known as Natarāja, the "Lord of the Dance". His dance is not an evil thing; it merely represents the natural dissolution that comes to all things, the sweeping away of the old and tired to make way for regeneration and rebirth. Śiva, then, is also the Creator. He is an erotic God, symbolized by the phallic *liṅgam*, which signifies His role as progenitor of the universe in conjunction with the Goddess, *Śakti*, His eternal consort. While an erotic figure, He is also the ascetic, ever deep in meditative trance at the summit of Mount Meru.

Śiva's body is white, but in popular iconography He is represented as grey, because He has smeared his body with the ashes of sacrificial fires. His throat is blue because He once drank an ocean of poison to protect the world from its effect. He has the third eye of high perception, the eye that turns inward and sees the Self. His long, matted hair indicates that He is an ascetic, while in it He bears the crescent moon, symbolic of the inevitability of time, the destroyer of everything. His tiger skin garment relates Him to *Śakti*, for the tiger is Her mount, and His accoutrement include the hourglass-shaped damaru drum, symbolic of the rhythm of time, a *japa mālā* (rosary), begging bowl, and trident. Around His neck He wears a garland of cobras, which represent the *kuṇḍalinī* power, the dormant libidinal-spiritual energy coiled at the base of the spine which can be manipulated in order to induce heightened states of consciousness.

— Of the *yakṣas* and *rākṣasas* I am Vitteśa (10.23).

Yakṣas are mysterious godlings or sprites which inhabit forests and jungles. Sometimes benevolent, sometimes malignant, they show up often in folklore and mythology. *Rākṣasas* are similar to *yakṣas* but are uniformly evil, monstrous even. Rāvaṇa, the antagonist in the epic *Rāmāyaṇa*, was a *rākṣasa*.

Vitteśa is better known by the name Kubera, or Kuvera. He is the leader of these earth spirits and the guardian of precious stones hidden in the earth. Thus he is sometimes referred to as "the lord of wealth". The half-brother of Rāvaṇa, he became an ally of Rāma when Rāvaṇa usurped His throne by force and consequently abducted Rāma's queen, Sītā.

— Of the *Vasus* I am Pāvaka (10.23).

Vasu is an umbrella term encompassing a class of atmospheric Vedic deities, some of which we have already become acquainted with. These "bright" gods (the term *vasu* means "good", "bountiful" or "wealthy") include the *Ādityas*, *Maruts* and *Rudras*. Pāvaka is better known as Agni, the god of fire. It is he who is personally manifest in the sacred fire.

— Of mountains, I am Meru (10.23).

Mount Meru, also known as Sumeru, figures prominently in Hinduism as it represents the central point and summit of the universe. It is Lord Śiva's abode, His meditation seat. The sacred Ganges flows from its peak. It is associated with the Himālayas, and its significance can roughly be compared to sacred mountains found in other traditions, such as Mount Olympus, Mount Fujiyama, etc.

— Of the chief household priests, know Me to be Bṛhaspati (10.24).

Bṛhaspati, whose name means "Lord of Prayer", is the celestial priest of the gods. He sanctifies the ritualistic worship of his human counterpart.

— Of commanders of armies, I am Skanda (10.24).

Skanda, better known as Kārttikeya, is one of Śiva's sons (the other being the elephant-headed deity Gaṇeśa), and is the principal deity of war.

— Of bodies of water, I am the ocean (10.24).

— Of great seers (*maharṣis*), I am Bhṛgu (10.25).

Bhṛgu was so illustrious he mediated quarrels among the gods.

— Of utterances, I am the single syllable Oṃ (10.25).

Oṃ is Brahman in sound form. It is the sacred syllable which is the basis of all mantras, the seed-sound of origination and dissolution. The whole of creation sprang forth from, and will eventually return to, what is known as "the Oṃ point". Sound is the subtlest of all elements that serve as building blocks of the universe, and Oṃ is the subtlest of all sounds. For a full treatment on the significance of Oṃ, the reader should consult the *Māṇḍūkya Upaniṣad.*

— Of sacrifices I am the muttered prayer (*japa*, or mantra meditation) (10.25).

Japa is the repetition of a *mantra*, often counted upon a *mālā*, or rosary of one hundred eight beads. Nowadays, when elaborate rituals and extended periods of meditation and austerity are impossible for nearly everyone, *japa* is considered the most efficacious "sacrifice", or method of worship.

— Of immovables, I am the Himālaya (10.25).

— Of trees, I am the sacred fig tree (10.26).

Kṛṣṇa, on the eve of His disappearance from this earth, is said to have meditated under a fig tree. Its shade is favored by meditators and yogīs.

— Of divine seers, I am Nārada (10.26).

Nārada figures prominently in the *Purāṇas* and is the traditional author of the *bhakti* classic, the *Nārada Bhakti Sūtras*, as well as some *Ṛg Veda* verses. A son of Brahmā, he is one of the first created beings, and is believed to still be alive. As a perfectly enlightened sage, he is not bound by the confines of time or space, and thus can travel all over the material and celestial universes without the aid of a vehicle. He pops up whenever the moment calls for it, and acts in various capacities, such as guru, devotee, oracle, and interceptor between *devas*, people, and God. Because of an early curse, he is fated to never stay in one place, but to travel constantly, and he uses this to his advantage by assuming the life of a traveling mendicant. Always carrying a *vīnā* (a stringed, musical instrument), he never stops singing devotional hymns and imparting spiritual instruction to everyone he meets.

— Of the *Gandharvas*, I am Citraratha (10.26).

Gandharvas are a race of heavenly musicians. They are supremely beautiful and winged, like angels. Citraratha is their leader.

— Of perfected beings, I am the sage Kapila (10.26).

Kapila is the founder of the *Sāṃkhya* school of philosophy, one of the oldest of the Hindu systems. An historical figure, he is guessed to have lived during the seventh century B.C.. Much of the third canto of the *Śrīmad Bhāgavatam* is devoted to his life and teachings, as he is considered therein to be an *Avatāra* of Viṣṇu.

— Of horses, know Me to be Uccaiḥśravas, born of nectar (10.27).

The reference is to the myth of the churning of the sea — ages ago the *devas* and *asuras* (gods and demons), engaged in a cosmic tug-of-war which churned up the elements of the primordial ocean and produced nectar and poison (which Śiva drank), as well as a number of celestial beings. Uccaiḥśravas, Indra's horse, was among the beings which sprang from the churning.

— Of princely elephants, I am Airāvata (10.27).

Also one of Indra's mounts, this celestial elephant was another product of the churning.

— Of men, I am the monarch (10.27).

— Of weapons, I am the thunderbolt (10.28).

The thunderbolt is the weapon of Indra, king of the *devas.*

— Of cows, I am Kāmadhuk, the wish-cow (10.28).

Also known as Surabhī, this mythical cow provides her master with anything desired. Legends describe her various captors and the battles that ensue for possession of her.

— Of procreators, I am Kandarpa (10.28).

Better known as Kāma (as in the *Kāma Sūtra*, the famous Indian treatise on erotic technique), Kandarpa is the Hindu Cupid, the god of love and passion.

— Of serpents, I am Vāsuki (10.28).

Among the species of snakes exists a unique race of celestial serpents, known as *Nāgas.* Vāsuki is their king.

— Of snakes, I am Ananta (10.29).

The word *ananta* means "endless", "eternal", and his spiraling coils represent eternity. As was mentioned earlier, Ananta is closely associated with Viṣṇu.

— Of water creatures, I am Varuṇa (10.29).

Varuṇa is another principal Vedic god, now reduced in stature to an elemental deity. He is the god of water.

— Of the ancestors, I am Aryaman (10.29).

Aryaman is one of the *Ādityas* mentioned earlier. He guides those who invoke him along safe and easy paths.

— Of subduers, I am Yama (10.29).

Yama is the god of death. Those who have undertaken the quest for spiritual perfection have nothing to fear from him. In fact, Yama is subdued by *them.*

— Of the *Daityas,* I am Prahlāda (10.30).

The *daityas* were a race of celestial adversaries, sometimes referred to as "demons", though this designation is misleading. Like *asuras*, they were godlings predisposed to wickedness. Their king was Hiraṇyakaśipu, a particularly dangerous tyrant, whose saintly son, Prahlāda, broke the mold and devoted his life to the worship of Viṣṇu. Prahlāda is a great hero to Hindus; as a mere child he risked everything, even his life, for God. The seventh canto of the *Śrīmad Bhāgavatam* contains the Prahlāda narrative. Viṣṇu's half-man, half-lion incarnation, Nṛsiṃhadeva, advented Himself in response to Prahlāda's devotion.

— Of calculators, I am time (10.30).

— Of the beasts, I am the lion (10.30).

The word for lion here is *mṛgendra*, "king of the beasts". The lion is considered the king of the beasts both in the West and the East.

— Of the birds, I am Vainateya (10.30).

He is better known as Garuḍa, the vehicle of Viṣṇu.

— Of purifiers, I am the wind (10.31).

— Of the wielders of weapons, I am Rāma (10.31).

Rāma, along with Kṛṣṇa, is the most important of Viṣṇu's *Avatāras*. His life is recounted in the epic poem, the *Rāmāyaṇa*.

— Of sea monsters, I am Makara (10.31).

This verse is also often translated: "Among fish, I am the shark." Makara is mythical creature resembling a crocodile, though he is also equated with the shark or dolphin. He is the vehicle of Varuṇa, god of the waters, and figures in many legends related to rivers, lakes or seas.

— Of rivers, I am the Ganges (10.31).

The most sacred of all bodies of water, the Ganges is personified as a Goddess who descends bodily from heaven and flows through the hair of Lord Śiva on Her way to earth. In another version, the river is said to flow from the toe of Viṣṇu. In either case, it is a spiritually purifying agent; bathing in it removes the taint of sin and accumulated *karma*.

— I am the beginning, middle and end of creation (10.32).

— Of varieties of knowledge, I am knowledge of the Supreme Self (*adhyātman*) (10.32).

— I am the discourse of those who speak (10.33).

— Of letters I am the letter A (10.33).

Like English, A is the first letter of the Sanskrit alphabet.

— Of compound words, I am the *dvandva* (10.33).

In Sanskrit grammar, there are several types of compound words. The *dvandva* is a simple compound where two or more words of the same case are joined into a single word to indicate a list. For example, the English phrase, "horses, elephants and men" would, as a *dvandva*, become "horseselephantsmen".

— I alone am infinite Time; I the Establisher, facing in all directions (10.33).

— I am all-destroying death, and the origin of what is yet to be (10.34).

Death is not something contrary to the divine purpose, the result of sin (as is believed in Christianity). Death, like life, is non-different from God. The seeming distinctions between death and life, God and not God, are the result of our deluded perception only. Associating death with beautiful Kṛṣṇa certainly removes its fearful connotations.

— Among the feminine, I am fame, prosperity, speech, memory, wisdom, courage, and patience (10.34).

Grammatically, all these are feminine nouns. They are also opulences embodied as Goddesses, one of the most prominent of whom is Vāc, speech. In Her form as Sarasvatī, She is the Goddess of learning, writing, and the arts.

— Of chants, I am the *Bṛhatsāman* (10.34).

Earlier, Kṛṣṇa identified Himself with the *Sāma Veda.* Within the *Veda* itself, He would be its most beautiful hymn, the *Bṛhatsāman*, which honors Indra.

— Of meters, I am *gāyatrī* (10.35).

The *gāyatrī* meter is found only in the *Vedas*; it consists of three lines of eight syllables each.

Of months, I am *mārgaśīrṣa* (10.35).

Roughly, November-December, the temperate season in India.

— Of seasons, I am the season abounding with flowers (spring) (10.35).

— I am the gambling of the dishonest, the splendor of the splendid; I am victory; I am effort; I am the goodness of the good (10.36).

— Of the Vṛṣṇis, I am Vāsudeva (10.37).

The Vṛṣṇis are the clan from which Kṛṣṇa is descended, and the name Vāsudeva refers to Kṛṣṇa Himself. It means "son of Vasudeva".

— Of the sons of Pāṇḍu, I am Arjuna (10.37).

Of the five Pāṇḍavas, Arjuna is the most illustrious.

— Of the sages, I am Vyāsa (10.37).

Vyāsa is the legendary compiler of the *Vedas, Purāṇas,* and *Mahābhārata.* He is also the grandfather of the Pāṇḍava and Kaurava princes.

— Of poets, I am the poet Uśanas (10.37).

A famous Vedic seer and poet, Uṣanas is frequently mentioned in the *Ṛg Veda*, some of the hymns of which he is the composer.

— I am the scepter of those who rule, the guidance of those seeking to conquer, the silence of things secret, the wisdom of the wise (10.38).

— I am the generating seed of all that lives (10.39).

So ends Kṛṣṇa's list of manifestations, but this represents only the minutest fraction, for His manifestations are infinite (10.40). Nothing whatsoever could exist without existing in and through and because of Him (10.39).

"Know," He says, "that whatever in this world is powerful, beautiful or glorious has sprung from but a spark of My splendor" (10.41).

Chapter Eleven: Arjuna's Vision of God's Universal Form

Chapter eleven marks the climax of the *Gītā*. Kṛṣṇa has gradually revealed His divinity to Arjuna, but in word only. Now He is actually going to demonstrate it. He is going to *prove* that He is God, the Original, All-Pervading, Infinite, Absolute, Fathomless, Supreme Truth, *Sat-Cit-Ānanda* by exhibiting to Arjuna His Universal Form. He will allow Arjuna to see — all at once and in one place — everything that ever was, is or will be. The past, present and future, the infinitude of worlds, the Divine in Its limitless multiplicity and blinding radiance will explode into Arjuna's perception. Arjuna is the only individual, celestial or terrestial, ever to be granted such a vision.

"O Supreme Lord," Arjuna prays, "You are as You describe Yourself to be; I do not doubt that. Nevertheless, I long to behold Your divine form. If You find me worthy of that vision, then reveal to me, O Lord of *yoga*, Your unlimited, universal Self" (11.3-4).

Kṛṣṇa is more than happy to. "But you are not able to see Me with your own eyes," He says. "Therefore I give you divine sight. Behold My mystic opulence!" (11.8).

What Arjuna witnesses is beyond the scope of the human mind to comprehend. The *Gītā* can only give us a hint, an inkling. If we can imagine the entire span of the cosmos, every event that has ever taken place, is taking place, and will ever take place, every form, every being, every thing, manifested endlessly in the infinite body of the divine Person, we can begin to understand.

"If a thousand suns should rise in the sky all at once, it might resemble the splendor of that Great Being" (11.12).

Arjuna sees all the gods at once, blazing with radiance (11.15-17). He sees the Divine, multicolored, roaring, without beginning, middle or end, with infinite faces, eyes, arms, bellies and fiery mouths (11.16-24). "You are the Unchanging," he says, "the supreme object of knowledge, the ultimate resting place of everything . . . Seeing this, Your marvelous and terrible form, the worlds tremble, O Great One" (11.20).

And so does Arjuna. Shaken to the core, overwhelmed with awe and fear, he witnesses terrifying cataclysms, the grotesque and monstrous drama of worlds being born and destroyed. "As moths dash into the blazing flame to their deaths, so to their destruction do the worlds rush into Your mouths" (11.29). Vanishing into His flaming gullet, all things are consumed by God.

"I am Time," the Lord thunders, "the destroyer of worlds, hastening to that hour that ripens to their ruin" (11.32).

Arjuna sees the warriors against which he is about to do battle hurled into the fiery mouth of annihilation. The outcome of the war is a foregone conclusion; as the force of their collective *karma* has brought all the soldiers to the field of battle, so has it already determined their fate. "Even without any action of yours, all these warriors on both sides shall cease to exist," Kṛṣṇa declares. "Therefore stand up and attain glory! . . . By Me they have already been struck down. Be merely the instrument, O Ambidextrous Archer" (11.32,33).

Trembling with fear and bowing down with reverence, Arjuna offers faltering prayers (11.36-40). He praises Kṛṣṇa, and begs forgiveness for having treated Him as an ordinary friend all these years. Ignorant of His true identity, Arjuna had always confided in and joked with Kṛṣṇa, treated Him casually, with ordinary human affection. He is grievously sorry for what he assumes to have been an offense, but we will later see that it is just this intimacy, this innocent warmth and affection, which constitutes *bhakti yoga*, the spiritual path most favored by Kṛṣṇa.

Though he knows Kṛṣṇa to be the "thousand-armed one . . . who has all forms" (11.46), Arjuna is curious for a glimpse of His four-armed Viṣṇu form. Kṛṣṇa assumes it, but Arjuna is still terrified. Only Kṛṣṇa's gentle, human form can calm his shaken sensibilities.

Of particular relevance are the chapter's concluding remarks that this universal form of God cannot be seen as the result Vedic study, nor austerity, nor alms-giving, nor ritual (11.53). "Only by single-minded devotion," Kṛṣṇa says, "can I be known in such a way" (11.54). This closely echoes the "secret teaching" of chapter nine, and will be elaborated upon fully in the next chapter.

Chapter Twelve: *Bhakti*, the *Yoga* of Devotion

Having regained his composure, Arjuna resumes the conversation by posing one of the most pressing of soteriological questions: which is better, to approach God as a personal Being, or as the formless, attributeless Brahman? (12.1). In Hinduism, these two aspects are known as *Saguṇa Brahman* (Brahman with qualities) and *Nirguṇa Brahman*

(Brahman without qualities) respectively. *Yogīs* attracted to the personal conception are given to *bhakti yoga*, the path of devotion, while those who are more drawn to the impersonal are the *jñāna yogīs*. Which path is superior?

The West tends to be biased toward the impersonal, considering it more sophisticated or more lofty. Perhaps this is due to the legacy of the Greek philosophers and their emphasis on reason, and to the Judeo-Christo-Islamic tradition and its horror of so-called "idolatry". In Islam, the most heinous of spiritual crimes is *shirk*, to associate anything earthly with God. This would include something as common as a form, or a distinct "personality". Asian religions, though generally more tolerant and universal, also tend toward the impersonal. Mahāyāna Buddhism, with its multitude of celestial Buddhas and *Bodhisattvas*, nevertheless conceptualizes the highest Truth as *Ādi Buddha*, the featureless, infinite Oneness. Many Hindus believe impersonal Brahman to be the higher, more "original" aspect, to which the personal aspects are but paths, but the *Bhagavad-Gītā* absolutely rejects this conclusion.

Kṛṣṇa says that those who worship Him with steadfast love come to Him. However, those who worship "the Undefinable, the Unmanifest, the All-Pervading" *also* attain Him (12.2-4). The means are different, but the destination is exactly the same.

Though both conceptions, both paths, are equally valid, Kṛṣṇa recommends the path of *bhakti* because it is easier. Concentrating on a limitless, featureless abstraction, though efficacious, is extremely difficult (12.5). Not only is fixing the mind and heart on an *Iṣṭa-devatā* (chosen Ideal) easier, but those who defer all their actions to Kṛṣṇa (or whomever their *Iṣṭa* may be), meditating on Him constantly, will find that He will help them in their efforts, that He will personally deliver them from the cycle of *saṃsāra* (12.7).

The basis of *bhakti yoga* is constant concentration on the divine Beloved: "Keep your mind on Me alone. Cause your intelligence to enter into Me. Thus you shall dwell in Me always. Of this there is no doubt" (12.8). If one is incapable of this, he or she may seek Kṛṣṇa through the practice of meditation (12.9). If meditation is impossible, one may consecrate ones actions to Kṛṣṇa, performing them for His sake (12.10). If even that is untenable, one may simply renounce the fruits of action and practice self-restraint (12.11).

How *bhakti yoga* is to be properly practiced, what qualities, attitudes, austerities the *bhakti yogī* cultivates, is discussed in verses thirteen through twenty. The *bhakti yogī* is free from attachment and egotism, is dispassionate yet friendly (12.13), has a mind fixed on God (12.14), yet does not shrink from the world (12.15), is alike to friend and enemy, honor and disgrace, heat or cold, pleasure or pain (12.18). Most of all, the *bhakti yogī* is full of devotion (12.14,16,17,19,20).

Some consider this simple teaching the most sublime aspect of the *Gītā*, for *bhakti yoga* offers a kind of "short-cut" to enlightenment. It is the easiest of all yogas, yet is as effective as rigorous meditation and austerity. It is not for everyone, though. The *Gītā* never insists that all people follow one particular practice or another. *Bhakti yoga* is for those of an emotional and imaginative temperament, or who find themselves drawn to a particular *Iṣṭa*. Often this attraction is irresistible, as though the *Iṣṭa* chose the aspirant, and not vice versa.

Chapter Thirteen: The Field and Its Knower

"I wish to know about *puruṣa* and *prakṛti*," Arjuna says. "I wish to understand the field of knowledge (the body) and the knower of the field (the Ātman)" (13.1). This chapter will deal with material nature (*prakṛti*) and how spirit (*puruṣa*) interacts with it. With the exception of chapter fifteen, the remaining chapters shift the focus away from the nature of the Divine, which has been fully explained, toward the world, how it is constructed, and how one may disentangle him or herself from it.

Kṛṣṇa begins by establishing the distinction between the knower, which is the Ātman, and the objective field which the knower experiences, namely the body and the world, of which the body is both a perceiver and a part (13.2). Kṛṣṇa, who is Brahman, consciousness itself, is also the knower (13.3).

The field is comprised of the principal elements (earth, air, fire, water and ether), the ego or consciousness of "I", the intelligence, the mind, the senses, and the five sense-fields, as it were, namely sound, touch, color, taste and smell (13.6).[9]

The body is also comprised of desire and aversion, pleasure and pain (13.6). All the aforementioned building blocks of the physical entity may at first strike the westerner as peculiar, but they are useful to know in that they help the aspirant to better understand his or her experience as a sensate being in contact with objects and matter, and to gradually disassociate from these. The *yogī* can carefully examine each element and systematically detach him or herself from it until complete renunciation is attained. This is possible because the senses are merely transmitters of information; it is the Ātman which actually senses, which actually experiences objects. (For a more detailed treatment of this idea, see the *Kena Upaniṣad.*)

But knowledge acquired through the senses is not true knowledge. Ironically, it is actually ignorance. Real knowledge is knowledge of the

Supreme Brahman, who is everywhere (13.12-13). One who knows the true object of knowledge, "the beginningless, supreme Brahman", attains immortality (13.13).

Verses fifteen through eighteen describe how Brahman interacts with material nature, a recap of Kṛṣṇa's teachings from chapter seven. Brahman maintains everything, but is unattached (13.15), It is outside and inside all beings, remote yet near (13.16). It is undivided yet appears as if divided into all things (13.17). While seated in the hearts of all, ". . . It is knowledge, the object of knowledge, and that which is to be attained by knowledge" (13.17).

Prakṛti and *puruṣa* are both beginningless and endless. The modifications in the field (the body), as well as the *guṇas*, arise from *prakṛti* (13.20). *Puruṣa* (in this case the spirit of the individual) experiences *prakṛti* and the *guṇas* which are born from it and becomes attached, thus subjecting itself to bodily rebirth (13.21). But there is a higher aspect to *puruṣa*, identified with Brahman: "The highest Spirit in this body is called the witness, the consenter, the supporter, the experiencer, the Great Lord, and also Paramātma, the Supreme Self (13.23).

These two aspects of *puruṣa* are sometimes compared to two beautiful birds seated on the same tree (we find this metaphor in both the *Muṇḍaka Upaniṣad* and *Śvetāśvatara Upaniṣad*). The tree is the body, and one bird represents the *jīva* which is attached to *prakṛti*. It flits about, constantly in search of new experiences, enduring pain and pleasure as it samples the sweet and bitter fruits of life. It is always hungry, always distracted, and almost incognizant of the other bird. The second bird is the Paramātma, the Supreme Self. Seated on the topmost branch of the tree, it is tranquil, self-satisfied, detached yet compassionate as it watches the restless bird. Some *yogīs* practice a meditation where they imagine the restless bird being absorbed into and becoming one with the supreme bird. They were never really separate in the first place.

In verse twenty-five Kṛṣṇa speaks of the "Self in the self", like the higher bird in the illustration. Some perceive this self through meditation, He says, some through *Sāṃkhya* (rationalistic, non-theistic philosophy), some through *karma yoga* (13.25). Again we see the tolerance and universalism so characteristic of the *Gītā*. Whatever the method of escape from *saṃsāra*, though, the means by which one has become entangled is the same for all: it is through the union of the field and the knower of the field, in other words the body and the soul, *puruṣa* and *prakṛti* (13.27).

The Supreme Self is the same in all people. "He who sees the immortal Supreme Lord existing alike in all beings truly sees," Kṛṣṇa says (13.28). The ethical implications of such an understanding are profound.

Sometimes Christians argue that their tradition embraces a higher ethical standard than any other, but the following *Gītā* verses prove this to be false. "Seeing the same Lord established everywhere, he (the aspirant) does not injure the self by the self" (13.29). In other words, seeing his own self as the self in others, and that self as God, he cannot do harm to anyone. Jesus taught that we should treat others as we would want to be treated ourselves, but the *Gītā* takes this a step further by establishing that there is no factual difference between ourselves and others, between all creation and God. Such a viewpoint naturally results in a commitment to social responsibility, which can be a yogic discipline in itself. It is known as *sevā*, selfless service to others.

Actions are performed by material nature on material nature. The individual who perceives that he is not himself the doer actually sees (13.30). Even though situated in the body, the Paramātma does not act and is never affected by actions (13.32). Still, it "illuminates" (animates by investing with consciousness) the body, just as the sun illuminates the entire world (13.34). Kṛṣṇa closes the topic by promising that knowledge of the distinction between the field and the knower (we can assume he means *experiential* knowledge, not just intellectual understanding) will result in one's attaining the Supreme (13.35).

Chapter Fourteen: The *Guṇas*, or Three Modes of Material Nature

The *guṇas* have been referred to several times already, but here in chapter fourteen, and again in chapter seventeen, they are examined in depth. It is important to learn how to recognize the *guṇas* at work if we are to achieve the state of super-perception described in the previous chapter. What does the *Gītā* mean when it says that we do not act, but that material nature is merely acting upon material nature, *guṇas* upon *guṇas*? When we learn to discern and categorize the *guṇas*, we can easily observe for ourselves what the *Gītā* means, and at the same time become increasingly detached from worldliness and ego, knowing that our actions and experiences are not, in any real way, attached to us.

The word *guṇa* means both "strand" and "quality". Like so many Sanskrit words, the pun is wonderfully appropriate because the three *guṇas* are like three strands which, when mingled, give rise to the various phenomena and qualities of material nature. They are categories in the *Sāṃkhya* philosophy, and according to this school, *prakṛti* at one time existed in an unmanifested, entirely potential state. The three *guṇas*, lying latent in *prakṛti*, were of equal quantity and perfectly still. When the primordial *puruṣa* united with *prakṛti*, the balance of the *guṇas* was disturbed and they began to fluctuate and blend. The result was a sudden, instantaneous cosmic upheaval which erupted into the birth of the material creation. Remember that Kṛṣṇa claimed *prakṛti* was part of Himself, only a "lower" part which does not affect Him.

The *guṇas* are *rajas*, *tamas*, and *sattva*. *Rajas* is impulse, movement, action, or passion. It is associated with the color red, with fast cars, with spicy food. *Tamas* is resistance, inertia, heaviness, ignorance, sleep. It is associated with the color black, with getting drunk in a dingy bar, with junk food and depression. *Sattva* is continuity, balance, harmony, purity, and goodness. It is associated with the color white, with spirituality and calmness.

"*Sattva*, *rajas*, and *tamas*," Kṛṣṇa declares, "the *guṇas* born of material nature, bind the Imperishable, Embodied One (the Ātman) down in the body" (14.5).

Even *sattva*, goodness, binds one to material nature. Though it is characterized by purity and illumination, it ". . . binds by attachment to virtue, and by attachment to knowledge" (14.6). When one is pleased with their own virtue, or a stickler in issues of purity and pollution, or preoccupied with the pursuit of knowledge for its own sake rather than as a means to a higher end, they are certainly in a state of bondage.

Rajas, characterized by passion and thirst, binds one by attachment to action (14.7). *Tamas*, born of ignorance, binds one with confusion, negligence, indolence, and sleepiness (14.8).

A predominance of one *guṇa* over the others may be discerned in different types of personality or behavior. For instance, those who seem illuminated by knowledge have *sattva* as their predominating *guṇa*. Avarice, activeness, and desire are present when *rajas* predominates. *Tamas* is dominant when the individual is foolish, lazy, heedless and confused (14.13)

The predominating *guṇa* determines the quality of birth one will take next (14.13-14), as well as the quality of the fruits of one's actions. *Sattvic* actions lead to purity, *rajasic* actions to pain, and *tamasic* to ignorance and darkness (14.16). The quality of *sattva* leads one upward, *rajas* leaves one in the middle, and *tamas* sends one down, into the lowest conditions of life (14.18).

Ideally, one should transcend all three *guṇas*, even *sattva* (14.20). How, Arjuna asks, can someone who has gone beyond the *guṇas* be recognized (14.21)?

By their dispassion and poise, Kṛṣṇa replies. Pain and pleasure are equal to them, a dirt clod, stone and gold are one in the same, the attractive and the repellent are perfectly equal in their eyes, blame and praise, honor and dishonor are exactly alike (14.24-25). "He who serves Me with the *yoga* of unswerving devotion," Kṛṣṇa says, "transcends these *guṇas*, is ready for absorption into Brahman. For I am the foundation of Brahman" (14.26-27).

Until one is ready to move beyond the *guṇas*, one should cultivate and gravitate towards *sattva*. As will be discussed in chapter seventeen, everything can be recognized as belonging to a particular *guṇa* or a mixture of *guṇas*. People, places, professions, foods, even religions are dominated by one *guṇa* or another. We should be able to intuit the *guṇa* at work and act appropriately. For instance, in walking into a room full of people, what *guṇa* predominates the scene? If *tamas* prevails, you can sense it immediately. The atmosphere feels low and dirty, "dark" somehow. Drugs always infect a situation with *tamas*. The standard adult cocktail party is usually characterized by *rajas*. A religious festival or spiritual gathering radiates *sattva*. Movies and television shows tend towards *rajas* and *tamas*; with increasing violence and mayhem being depicted, though, they are slipping toward complete *tamas*. Music strongly conveys different *guṇas*; certain forms of particularly angry, misogynistic and ugly rock and rap are seeped in *tamas*. The spiritual aspirant is advised to avoid them. Rock in general, jazz, country, salsa, and most other forms of popular music are primarily characterized by *rajas*. These should be taken in moderation, if at all. Many aspirants, as well as those of an aesthetically sensitive disposition, find themselves naturally growing disinterested in these forms of music. Classical moves back and forth between *rajas* and *sattva*. Religious music, or any music which is calming, uplifting and sublime is *sattvic*. This kind of music actually helps the aspirant in their spiritual development.

How the *guṇas* are reflected in different religious practices will be examined in chapter seventeen.

Chapter Fifteen: The Embodied Divine

The chapter begins by drawing upon the metaphor of the sacred *aśvattha* tree, an Indian fig tree, to describe the dilemma of the embodied soul. The roots of the enormous *aśvattha* grow down from its branches and become new trunks; this is like Spirit branching down into the material realm and taking embodiment. Kṛṣṇa exhorts us to cut down this tree with the "strong axe of non-attachment", and thus end the cycle of rebirth, returning instead to the "Primal Spirit" (15.3-4). The universal tree motif is found in many religious traditions, including the Tree of Life in the Kabalah, and the sacred ash of Germanic mythology, the death of which will be the end of the world.

The rest of the chapter is devoted to showing that the *jīva* which becomes embodied is a part of Brahman. "Merely a fraction of Myself in the world becomes an eternal (individual) self" (15.7). *Yogīs* always strive to see God situated within themselves (15.11). God has entered the heart of all beings and invested them with memory, knowledge, and reasoning (15.15). He is that part of us which is imperishable and unchanging, Paramātma, the Supreme Self, yet He is also higher than the Self within us (15.16-18). He is the worshipable Supreme Spirit (15.19).

Chapter Sixteen: Divine and Demoniac Tendencies

Human nature is malleable. The age-old philosophical question, "Is man basically good or basically bad?" is irrelevant in the Hindu scheme of things, which holds that we have the power to make ourselves into anyone we want to be. We are perpetually creating ourselves, and molding our future births by the actions we perform today. Stories abound of the most wretched people becoming great saints by the force of their own will (and a little divine grace). One of the best examples is the poet Vālmīki, who began his career as a robber, but after his awakening became a spiritual giant, and the author of the epic *Rāmāyaṇa*. We each have the infinite capacity for achieving sainthood, in fact it is the only reason we exist, the only true task before us. We must know, however, what a saint is like, which qualities, attitudes and behaviors we must strive to cultivate, which we must work to exorcise. It is to this end that Kṛṣṇa now turns to a discussion of divine and demoniac qualities.

Those of divine character have a divine destiny in store (16.3). They are fearless, pure, generous, self-restrained, austere, non-violent, without anger, serene, compassionate to all beings, desireless, gentle, modest, patient, prideless and steady in the yoga of knowledge (16.1-3).

The demonic, on the other hand, are destined for bondage (16.5). They are characterized by hypocrisy, arrogance, anger, harshness of language, ignorance, impurity, bad conduct and untruth (16.4-7). Clearly, there are varying degrees of the demonic in nearly every one of us. Some failings which we might dismiss as merely "human" Kṛṣṇa considers not human at all, but reminiscent of demons. Our characters ought to be perfect, and can be.

The demonic believe the universe is without a God (16.8), a view that leads to cruelty and actions which contribute to the destruction of the world (16.9). Their desire is insatiable, as is their lust; they are deluded and entertain false notions (16.10). Always fraught with anxiety, convinced that sense gratification is all there is to life, their only destiny is death (16.11). Hoarding wealth, accumulating enemies, they consider themselves great and erroneously believe that they are successful, powerful and happy (16.12-14). Whatever religious actions they perform are done in name only, for these acts are empty and hypocritical (16.17).

"Them, the hating, the cruel, the vile and vicious men, I constantly hurl into the circle of rebirth," Kṛṣṇa says (16.19). Because of bad karma, they enter the wombs of other deluded, demoniac people, grow up in barbaric circumstances, and the cycle is perpetuated. Birth after birth they descend lower and lower (16.19-20).

All demoniac qualities and behaviors spring from the triad of desire, anger and greed (16.21). The good news is that one can decide to break the vicious cycle at any time. Though raised badly by ignorant, cruel people, one always possesses the freedom to change. By abandoning desire, anger and greed, one begins gradually to rise out of their degraded position (16.22). Soon divine qualities will begin to develop instead.

Chapter Seventeen: The Three Kinds of Faith

The discussion of the *guṇas* begun in chapter fifteen now resumes, but here the concept is applied specifically to spiritual faith and practices. Not all activities and beliefs embraced in the name of religion are legitimate. As with anything in life, we must discriminate.

Arjuna inquires as to the standing of those who ignore the scriptural injunctions but are filled with faith. Are they *sattvic*, *rajasic*, or *tamasic* (17.1)?

Faith can reflect any of the three *guṇas*, Kṛṣṇa replies, depending on the person in question (17.2-3).

Verse four has been widely interpreted and with good reason; it seems that in any epoch or culture, examples of it are easy to find. It reads, "The *sattvic* worship the gods, the *rajasic* worship the spirits and demons, the *tamasic* men worship the departed and the ghosts" (17.4). Prabhavananda and Isherwood translate it, "Men whose temperament is dominated by *sattva*, worship God in His various aspects. Men of *rajas* worship power and wealth. As for the rest — the men of *tamas* — they worship the spirits of the dead, and make gods of the ghosts of their ancestors."[10] In India, as in some other countries where traditional, or tribal, practices can still be found, we can see how this verse might be taken literally. In the contemporary West, we can apply a broader interpretation, but it doesn't have to be too broad. We don't need to stretch very far. People preoccupied with hauntings, mediumship and such should be considered *tamasic*, as should individuals who partake in demon and/or Satan worship. By "worship" we can also mean revering excessively or following slavishly. Some popular New Age practices fall into the category of *rajas*, such as channelling or contacting "spirit guides", in other words, following disembodies entities, or the people who allegedly channel them, as teachers and guides. I would add to this category the worship of film and music stars, individuals not deserving of anyone's reverence, to be sure, and often even of a particularly low moral and spiritual fibre.

Dietary practices, sacrifices, austerities and gifts are analyzed in turn according to their predominant *guṇa*. *Sattvic* foods promote life, health and strength; they are smooth, firm, pleasant to the stomach, and bring happiness and satisfaction (17.18). Foods in the *rajasic* mode are excessively hot, pungent, sour or salty. Harsh and scorching, they cause pain and sickness (17.9). Hot peppers, for instance, might fall into this category, particularly if they lead to digestive problems. *Tamasic* food is stale, tasteless, left-over and foul (17.10). Fast food and/or junk food too often fits this description; some modern convenience foods are so overprocessed and denatured they render no nutritive value and thus become *tamasic*.

Sacrifice, or worship, if is to be *sattvic*, must be performed according to scriptural specifications and without desire for fruitive benefit (12.11). In other words, worship should be performed for its own sake, as an act of devotion, not because a reward is expected. Those who do perform sacrifice with a view to a reward are *rajasic* (17.12). Their motive is greed, not love. Worship performed without faith, without scripture and without an offering is *tamasic* (17.13).

Sattvic austerity of the body includes reverencing the gods and spiritual teachers, maintaining purity, virtue, and continence, and observing non-violence (17.14). *Sattvic* austerity of speech means speaking words which do not cause distress, are truthful, agreeable and salutary, as well as the reciting of sacred texts (17.15). *Sattvic* austerity of mind involves peace of mind, gentleness, self-restraint and purity of being (17.16).

Austerity performed in order to draw honor, praise and worldly reverence is *rajasic* and hypocritical (17.18). *Tamasic* austerities are to be avoided under all circumstances. They involve extremes in self-mortification and painful self-tortures. Such practices are motivated by egotism, passion and delusion; not only are they hurtful to the flesh, they desecrate the Brahman within (17.5-6,19).

Gifts given to a worthy recipient who has done no prior favor, given at the appropriate place and time, are *sattvic*. Those given grudgingly with the aim of recompense are *rajasic*. Those given to unworthy persons under inauspicious circumstances and in a mood of contempt are *tamasic*. Examples of such gifts could be donations to a legitimate religious or charitable institution, obligatory birthday or Christmas gifts, and a hand-out to a wino, respectively.

The final six verses of the chapter impart instructions on the execution of *sattvic* sacrifice, giving and austerity, based on the utterance *Oṃ Tat Sat*. This *mantra* means "Oṃ, That (i.e. God) Exists." In the *Upaniṣads*, Brahman is often referred to by the pronoun *Tat*, "That", as in the famous adage *Tat tvam asi*, "You are That."

"*Oṃ Tat Sat* ," Kṛṣṇa declares; "this is recorded as the threefold designation of Brahman" (17.23). Acts of sacrifice, giving, and austerity, therefore, always begin with the utterance of the syllable *Oṃ* (17.24). Those who desire release, and look not to the fruits of their work, take shelter in the Absolute by also uttering *Tat* (17.25). In praise of the reality and goodness of God (*Tat*), they lastly utter *Sat* (17.26).

One often sees the *mantra Oṃ Tat Sat* used as an invocation at the beginning of scriptures or as a concluding prayer at the end.

Chapter Eighteen: Action, Duty and Renunciation

We have come to the final chapter, which will bring us full circle thematically. Kṛṣṇa will reiterate His position that action is a necessary good, but that tranquility can only be achieved when one is detached from the fruits of his or her actions. As was stressed before, nowhere in the *Gītā* is inaction or complacency recommended. Beware anyone who suggests otherwise because this position indicates that the person has either not examined the text carefully or is the unwitting victim of a bad translation.

Chapter eighteen is the longest of the book, a full seventy-eight stanzas. It will not introduce any significant new teaching, but will forcefully drive home those which are the most important.

Arjuna asks Kṛṣṇa to clarify the difference between renunciation (*sannyāsa*, the fourth, or renounced, order of life) and non-attachment (*tyāga*, "leaving behind") (18.1.). Kṛṣṇa replies that renunciation is the relinquishing of those actions which are prompted by desire. Non-attachment, on the other hand, is the relinquishing of the *fruits* of action (18.2).

One must not renounce action itself. Indeed, certain actions, such as sacrifice, charity and austerity should always be performed, as they are uplifting and purifying (18.5). What ought to be renounced is attachment to the fruits of action (18.6). Kṛṣṇa has repeated this again and again throughout the poem.

"Renunciation of obligatory action is not proper . . . He who abandons action merely because it is difficult, or because of fear of bodily suffering, performs *rajasic* non-attachment" (18.8).

In other words, being a slob and calling it renunciation doesn't work. One who is truly renounced does not hate disagreeable action, nor is he attached to agreeable action. He performs action because it is his duty, and then renounces attachment to the result (18.9-10). All actions are accomplished through the cooperation of five factors: the seat of action (the body), the agent (the doer), the instrument (the sense organ), the activity itself, and divine providence (18.13-14). Therefore, anyone who sees himself has the sole doer is quite mistaken (18.16).

Knowledge, that which is to be known, and the knower are the threefold propulsions to action, while the instrument, act and agent are the threefold constituents of action (18.18). This analysis is highly technical, true, but understanding it is important because these elements, like everything else, are influenced by the *guṇas.* One is well-advised to scrutinize the workings of these elements of action in him or herself. Are they engaged in the mode of passion, ignorance, or goodness? The proceeding verses show us how we can tell.

Knowledge by which one sees the Imperishable Being in all beings, the Undivided in the divided, is *sattvic* knowledge (18.20). Knowledge which sees the various embodied beings as separate is *rajasic* knowledge (18.21). And knowledge which attaches itself to some object as if it were the all in all, even though it is insignificant, is *tamasic* (18.22).

Action which is controlled, free from attachment, performed with neither desire nor hate, is *sattvic* (18.23). Action performed with the obtainment of desires in mind, which is selfish and requires strenuous effort, is *rajasic* (18.24). *Tamasic* action is undertaken because of delusion and performed without regard to its consequences or the injury it inflicts on others (18.25).

The agent is said to be *sattvic* when he or she is free from attachment, free from talk of self, steadfast, resolute, and unperturbed in success or failure (18.26). The agent is *rajasic* when passionate, greedy, violent, impure, and filled with joy or sorrow (18.27), and *tamasic* when undisciplined, vulgar, obstinate, wicked, deceitful, lazy and despondent (18.28).

Kṛṣṇa continues in the same vein, applying the threefold *guṇa* categories to understanding, determination, and happiness (18.29-38).

Nothing in the material universe is free from the *guṇas.* Only by understanding them can we eventually transcend them.

Even the *varṇas,* the four social orders or castes, are determined by the *guṇas.* Though the *varṇa* system is not institutionalized outside of India, many commentators argue that it exists naturally in all societies. Ideally, *varṇa* is not determined by birth, but by character, by predisposition. One gravitates toward a particular profession according to their innate temperament and talent, and these are influenced by the *guṇas.* For *brāhmaṇas,* the priests, scholars and intellectuals, *sattva* predominates. For *kṣatriyas,* soldiers and government administrators, *rajas.* In *vaiśyas,* the mercantile class, we see a mixture of *rajas* and *tamas,* while the principal *guṇa* of the *śūdras,* or laborers, is *tamas.* This is not to say that individual members of the lower *varṇas* are bound to the lower *guṇas* and cannot attain spiritual liberation. Kṛṣṇa makes it abundantly clear that all *varṇas* have responsibilities and that members of each must adhere to high standards of morality and self-control. It ultimately doesn't matter which *varṇa* one belongs to, because the performance of one's own, unique *dharma* in a spirit of devotion and non-attachment is the basis of *yoga.* This is the most wonderful message of the *Gītā.* Whoever we are, whatever our situation, we can strive for spiritual fulfillment and achieve it. We do not need to be geniuses, or hermits, or adepts at extraordinary feats of self-denial. Simple people with unremarkable lives may scale the heights of spiritual illumination. "Content in his own work, every man can become perfect," Kṛṣṇa says (18.45). "Performing action prescribed by one's own nature, one does not incur evil. One should not abandon one's inborn action . . ." (18.47-48). "By renunciation (of attachment to fruits), one attains the supreme perfection of actionlessness" (18.49).

By attaining this perfection, one also attains Brahman (18.50). This requires determined self-control and detachment, however, as is indicated by Kṛṣṇa's long list of necessary conditions: controlling of speech, body and mind, meditation, dispassion, light eating, relinquishing of egotism, force, desire, anger and property, unselfishness, tranquility, etc. (18.51-53).

Such a person attains devotion to God (18.54), and one who comes to know God in truth immediately enters into Him (18.54). One can come to know God by offering actions to Him, taking refuge in Him and, most of all, constantly thinking of Him (18.57). One must not let egotism get in the way.

"If taking refuge in egotism you think, 'I shall not fight'," Kṛṣṇa tells Arjuna, "vain will be your resolve. Your own nature will command you" (18.59).

One cannot avoid acting, even for a second, because it is the Lord abiding in the heart which animates one in the first place (18.61). One must take refuge in this indwelling God and thereby attain release (18.62).

Once more Kṛṣṇa reiterates His most sublime teaching of all: "Fix your mind on Me, worshipping Me, sacrificing to Me, make reverence to Me. In this way you shall truly go to Me, I promise, for you are dear to Me" (18.65).

That this should be His final word on the subject is highly significant. The complexity of subjects covered in the *Gītā* is staggering, yet they all converge in this simple formula: "Take refuge in Me alone. I shall cause you to be released" (18.66).

The teachings of the *Gītā* have now formally come to a close. As is often the case in Hindu scripture, a few remarks concerning the preceding dialogue or narrative are spoken by a character contained in it. This device lends an intriguing layer of meaning; it is as though the characters know they are characters in a book, and comment upon their own story as if they are also outside it, reading about themselves. This would be fitting for Kṛṣṇa who, as divine, must be omniscient. "He who studies this sacred dialogue of ours," He says, "has worshipped Me with his intelligence" (18.70).

Kṛṣṇa warns Arjuna not to speak of this exchange to those who are unworthy or speak evil of Him, but to certainly pass it on to Kṛṣṇa's worshippers, who will be liberated thereby (18.67-68). Teaching the *Gītā* to others, in fact, is the most pleasing service one can perform for the Lord; such a person is dearer to Kṛṣṇa than any other on earth (18.69).

"Have your ignorance and delusion been destroyed, O Conqueror of Wealth?" Kṛṣṇa asks (18.72).

"Delusion is lost and wisdom gained through Your grace, O Unchanging One. I stand with doubt dispelled. I shall do as You command!" (18.73).

As the *Gītā* closes, we return to the narrator, Sañjaya, who is still addressing King Dhṛtarāṣṭra. Recollecting this wondrous dialogue makes him rejoice again and again (18.77).

"Wherever there is Kṛṣṇa, Lord of *Yoga*," Sañjaya says, "wherever there is the Arjuna, the archer, there will surely be splendor, victory, wealth and righteousness. That is my opinion!" (18.78).

A Note on Continuity

Some commentators have argued that the *Gītā* contains troublesome internal contradictions, but a close examination of the text, keeping in mind the overall world-view and theology it promotes, will reveal that these contradictions do not, in fact, exist at all. The *Gītā* presents certain cosmic paradoxes: Personal God/Impersonal Brahman, Oneness of the indwelling Spirit in all beings/apparent fragmentation of the Spirit in different embodied beings, etc. However, the universal divine scheme described in the poem cleanly and logically resolves such superficial paradoxes. This systematic, and quite deliberate, dispelling of so-called contradictions is precisely where the *Gītā's* greatest genius happens to lie.

Like the New Testament, or any sacred scripture, *Gītā* verses, in order to be understood, must be taken within their overall context. Single stanzas, lifted from the middle and plopped down somewhere in isolation, can give a misleading impression, or even obscure the intended meaning. Beware of unscrupulous commentators who offer a verse sample, then next to it print another one, out of context and from a different part of the book, which superficially appears to contradict it. Such methods are the mainstay of extremely poor scholarship, but one still finds this sort of work in print.

The *Gītā* maintains throughout that the Truth has infinitely complex facets and that a myriad of appropriate methods exist to approach It. The God of the *Gītā* is, perhaps, the most sophisticated and most equitable conception one can find anywhere. Being absolutely unlimited, It gives rise to a universe of unlimited possibility.

NOTES

1. Margaret and James Stutley, *Harper's Dictionary of Hinduism* (San Francisco: Harper and Row Publishers, 1977), p. 150.
2. A.C. Bhaktivedanta Swami Prabhupāda, *Bhagavad-Gītā As It Is* (Vaduz, Lichtenstein: The Bhaktivedanta Book Trust, 1983), p. xviii.
3. Quotations are adapted from Winthrop Sargeant, *The Bhagavad-Gītā* (Albany: State University of New York Press, 1984),
   Swami Prabhavananda and Christopher Isherwood, *The Song of God: Bhagavad-Gita* (New York: New American Library, 1972), and
   A.C. Bhaktivedanta Swami Prabhupāda, *Bhagavad-Gītā As It Is* (Vaduz, Lichtenstein: The Bhaktivedanta Book Trust, 1983).
4. Stutley and Stutley, p. 238.
5. Stutley and Stutley, p. 230.
6. Sargeant, p. 334.
7. Bhaktivedanta Prabhupāda, pp. 433-434.

8. All definitions in this chapter are drawn either from Sargeant, pp. 416-447 or Stutley and Stutley, assorted dictionary entries.
9. Sargeant, p. 533.
10. Prabhavananda and Isherwood, p.117.

Part IV

The *Upaniṣads*

CHAPTER SIX

Introduction

After having studied the *Bhagavad-Gītā*, the student or aspirant is advised to next move on the *Upaniṣads.* Composed over a period between 700 and 300 B.C., they represent the highly refined philosophical and mystical conclusions of India's saints and seers. Tradition holds that there are one hundred eight *Upaniṣads* (one hundred eight being a number sacred to Hindus), but only about thirteen have gained lasting prominence and, of these, eleven are singled out as preeminent. It is these eleven which we will examine in these pages.

The word *Upaniṣad* is probably derived from the roots *upa*, "near", *ni*, "down", and *sad*, "sit", or "come sit down near me", a teacher's exhortation to a student to sit down for instruction. The *Upaniṣads* are the product of a time of great spiritual and philosophical ferment in the world. Buddha appeared during this time, as did Mahāvīra, the founder of Jainism. In China, Confucius was teaching the path of superior conduct and reverence for tradition, while Lao Tzu was composing the *Tao Te Ching*. In Greece, the age of philosophers was in full swing, and scholars suggest that trade between India and Greece at this time may have contributed to a mutual exchange of ideas. This would account for some similarities between the teachings of the Greek philosophers and those of the *Upaniṣads.*

The *Upaniṣads* are mystical treatises, most of them very short. They attempt to describe the indescribable: direct realization of Brahman. These are not speculation, not the result of intellectual analysis and systematization, but the literary expression of actual experience. They represent, too, a move away from Vedic ritual towards a private, interior form of religion.

Around the seventh century B.C. and after, the Vedic religion began to run out of steam and metamorphose into what we now think of as Hinduism. One of the reasons for this was the priestly caste's tendency to abuse their power. As the sole keepers of Vedic knowledge — the hymns, the methods of ritual and the right to perform them — the *brāhmaṇas* managed to subordinate the other castes, who were dependent upon them for success in this life and the next. *Brāhmaṇas* charged fees for their services, so the business of ritual degenerated into a bit of a racket. Furthermore, because the sacred formulae and rituals compelled the universe to respond, *brāhmaṇas* began to envision themselves of pivotal importance in maintaining order in the universe and determining cosmic events. Priests could manipulate the gods; this suggested they were superior to the gods. Such a degradation of the religious system led to reaction and reform which ushered in the age of the *Upaniṣads.*

Another reason why Vedic religion declined was because religion is a living thing which evolves according to people's needs. India was becoming more sophisticated spiritually, and religion began to take an inward turn, towards a search for the Self. Spiritual seekers withdrew from the world and retired, in communities or alone, to the forest, where they engaged in intense spiritual practice and searching. It is believed that these *ṛṣis*, seers, discovered the Truth through experience and that these direct perceptions are expressed in the *Upaniṣads.* They are our clearest windows onto the Ultimate Truth.

While the *Upaniṣads* depart greatly from the *Vedas* in both style and content, they are, categorically, considered part of the Vedic corpus. When people speak of "Vedic wisdom", they are referring to both the four *Vedas* and the *Upaniṣads.* However, the *Upaniṣads* are further designated as *vedānta,* which means both "the end portion of the *Vedas*" and "the final word on all possible knowledge." The different *Upaniṣads* vary somewhat in outlook, yet they all address the same question: "What is that which, when known, everything becomes known?" (*Muṇḍaka Upaniṣad* 1.1.3). In other words, what is the Ultimate Truth and how can it be realized? The *Upaniṣads* take the view that it is not enough to understand intellectually what Brahman is or even to believe in Brahman. One can and must experience It directly. The culmination of this experience, which happens to be the experience to knowing one's own true Self, is liberation.

The core message of the *Upaniṣads* is contained in the four *Mahāvākyas*, or "Great Utterances":

Tat Tvam Asi — "You are That (i.e. Brahman)" (*Chāndogya Upaniṣad*)

Ayam Ātmā Brahma — "This Ātman is Brahman" (*Māṇḍūkya Upaniṣad*)

Prajñānam Brahma — "Brahman is Pure Consciousness" (*Aitareya Upaniṣad*)

Aham Brahmāsmi — "I am Brahman" (*Bṛhadāraṇyaka Upaniṣad*)

It is also an *Upaniṣad*, the *Bṛhadāraṇyaka*, which introduces the classic phrase which is the basis of *jñāna yoga* practice: *neti neti*, "not this, not this" (2.3.6).

Of the texts examined in this volume, the *Upaniṣads* are the most challenging. Their style is incredibly condensed; in few words amazing intensity is achieved and virtually infinite layers of meaning suggested. The language is often highly symbolic and obscure, with references that are too culturally specific for Westerners to initially understand without a commentary (which the present volume hopes, on a rudimentary level, to provide). However, once the reader cultivates an ear for Upaniṣadic language and imagery, they are not difficult to understand at all. Quite to the contrary, the reader will be amazed at how illuminating they actually are, and how brilliant the authors were to work so many dimensions into so few words. One does not read an *Upaniṣad* once through, like a novel, and put it on the shelf, never to be opened again. One has to explore it, live with it, change with it. Every time an *Upaniṣad* is re-read it reveals new depths.

The following sections are by no means meant to be an exhaustive treatment of the *Upaniṣads*. Only the most general points are touched upon in order to provide a foundation for further study.

> May quietness descend upon my limbs,
> My speech, my breath, my eyes, my ears;
> May all my senses wax clear and strong.
> May Brahman show Himself unto me.
> May I never deny Brahman, nor Brahman me.
> I with Him and He with me — may we abide always together.
> May there be revealed to me,
> Who am devoted to Brahman,
> The holy truth of the *Upaniṣads*.
> Oṃ . . . Peace . . . Peace . . . Peace.
>
> — Peace Invocation from *Chāndogya Upaniṣad*[1]

NOTES

1. Swami Prabhavānanda and Frederick Manchester, trnsl., *The Upaniṣads, Breath of the Eternal* (Hollywood: Vedanta Press, 1975), p. 101.

CHAPTER SEVEN

Īśā Upaniṣad: *A Meditation on Knowledge and Action*

The eighteen-verse *Īśā Upaniṣad* addresses three topics: knowledge, action, and the Self. Its title is derived from the first word of the *Upaniṣad* itself: *īśā*, "by the Lord". According to Swāmī Śarvānanda, it was probably composed in an attempt to reconcile the seemingly contradictory paths of *karma* (ritualistic works and the attainment of heavenly merit as a result of them) and *jñāna* (knowledge, or Brahman-intuition). In post-Vedic times, these divergent approaches were systematized by the philosophers Jaimini and Vyāsa respectively, and came to be known as the schools of *Mīmāṃsā* (Vedic apologists, or the path of action) and *Vedānta* (the path on non-dualistic Brahman-realization).[1] *Jñāna* is considered the superior of the two, but spiritual progress can be made through *karma* by those who are not ready for *jñāna.* As we shall see, the *Upaniṣad* suggests that the very best path is a combination of both.

Upaniṣads always open with a peace invocation, a brief prayer beginning with the syllable *Oṃ* and concluding with the benediction *Oṃ śāntiḥ śāntiḥ śāntiḥ*: "Oṃ. Peace! Peace! Peace!" The central prayer sometimes requests that "He" (the Lord) protect both the teacher and student and make their study fruitful. Sometimes it concerns the Infinite's permeating everything, the visible and invisible. Sometimes various deities are saluted or Brahman is saluted. Often several such prayers are used together. The peace invocation is not part of the *Upaniṣad* proper, but is a brief meditation to ready the consciousness for sacred study.

The first verse of the *Īśā* addresses the *yogī* who has taken to the path of knowledge. All that is changeful in this ephemeral world is pervaded by the Lord, it says; seek renunciation (1). The second verse addresses the *karmī,* one who is fond of life and work. If you desire to live a hundred years (the full span of life, according to the *Vedas*), then perform works ordained by scripture and thus be free from evil (2). In other words, if you are not yet ready for full renunciation and absorption into Brahman (*jñāna)* as endorsed by verse one, at least attend to the religious duties enjoined by the scripture (worship, self-control, etc.)

and cultivate the purity and righteousness that will eventually lead to *jñāna.*

Those who "slay the Self", in other words are indifferent to realization of Ātman and thus commit a sort of spiritual suicide, are enshrouded in blinding darkness. Their births are of a demoniac nature (3). (See *Bhagavad-Gītā*, chapter 16.)

The next five verses describe the Self (Ātman/Brahman) and the one who has perceived it. It is One. It is unmoving, yet faster even than the mind, beyond the reach of the senses. Ever steady, Its presence sustains all living beings (4). It is far, yet It is near; It is within everything yet outside of everything (5). One who perceives It sees all beings as nondifferent from himself and thus has no hatred for anyone (6). "What delusion, what sorrow is there for the wise one who sees the unity of existence and all beings as his own self?" (7). Compare these two verses to *Gītā* verses 13.27-28: "He who sees the Supreme Lord existing alike in all beings, not perishing when they perish, truly sees. Seeing indeed the same Lord established everywhere, he does not injure the self by the self." This perception is the highest ideal of *vedānta.*

Īśā verse eight describes this Self as self-existent, (in other words not depending on anything else for Its existence, nor having Its origin in anything else), everywhere, non-material (literally, "without a body", "without muscles"), without the taint of ignorance, radiant, whole, all-seeing, all-knowing, and all-encompassing. Employing mythological imagery, it adds, "He (Brahman) duly assigned their respective duties to the eternal *Prajāpatis.*" *Prajāpatis* are the primordial progenitors of the human race; one can take this passage to mean that Brahman designed Nature to be self-perpetuating.

The next three verses compare those who are devoted to *vidyā* and *avidyā.* The meanings of these two terms are quite enigmatic in this context. Literally, they mean "knowledge" and "non-knowledge", or ignorance. Unfortunately, these straightforward definitions are confusing here, so we need to employ some analysis. Ordinarily, *vidyā* refers to intellectual knowledge — book learning, scientific or specialized knowledge — not illumination, which is indicated by the term *jñāna.* If taken in this context, verse nine, which reads: "Those who are devoted to *avidyā* (ignorance) enter into blinding darkness. Into darkness greater than this, as it were, enter those who delight in *vidyā* (knowledge)," can be interpreted to mean that the uneducated dwell in spiritual darkness, but those who delight in their own secular book learning are worse off still. They are immersed in materialism and egotism. Education and learning are wonderful things but, from the spiritual perspective, useless if considered the all in all, rather than a means to a higher end.

Vidyā may also be assigned a meaning closer to that of *jñāna*; some believe it refers to the realization of all beings as One, *avidyā* being the perception of separateness. If this is the case, the particle *iva* ("like", "as if", "as it were", or "seemingly") is very important. The Sanskrit reads: *tamaḥ*, "darkness", *iva*, "as if", *praviśanti* "fall into". Therefore the darkness is a seeming darkness only. The verse could now be loosely translated: "Those who are engrossed in the perception of the many enter into a blinding darkness. Those who are absorbed in the perception of universal oneness enter *what seems to be* (to the ignorant observer) an even greater darkness." Taken in this sense the verse is, of course, expressing a profound irony. What appears to the uninitiated as the greatest darkness is, in fact, the greatest illumination.

A third definition, developed and promoted by Śaṅkarācārya, holds that the terms refer to ritualistic observances. *Avidyā* refers to those who perform the rituals without understanding their underlying significance or philosophy, while *vidyā* refers to those who cultivate theoretical knowledge about gods and sacrifices, but never rouse themselves to perform them.[2] In this context, *iva* has little significance and is more of a rhythmic filler, but the overall meaning sustains the continuity of the *karma* theme. The *Upaniṣad* would appear to be saying that religious actions ignorantly performed are more beneficial than dry speculation with no action to support it. Speculation alone amounts to nothing.

In any event, verse ten states that different results are obtained by *vidyā* and *avidyā*, while verse eleven says that one who understands *both* attains immortality. If we subscribe to the third interpretation, verse eleven appears to be saying that religious actions (*avidyā*, *karma*) coupled with theoretical knowledge (*vidyā*, *jñāna*) lead to immortality. One enhances the other.

If we hold to the second definition, that of perceiving the many (*avidyā*) or the One (*vidyā*), verse eleven simply means that the One can be seen in the many and the many seen in the One; *vidyā* and *avidyā* are thus "understood" in an absolute sense. There is no difference between the many and the One.

Finally, the first definition, that of secular learning and ignorance, can be applied to verse eleven and the *Upaniṣad* appears to be telling us to "understand", i.e. understand the illusory nature of both and to transcend them. Ignorance and knowledge in this realm are both irrelevant to the attainment of Self.

In a literary twist common to Upaniṣadic texts, the form of the last three verses is repeated with a change in the topical terms. Verse twelve reads: "Those who worship *asambhūti* enter into blinding darkness. Into darkness greater than this, as it were, do they enter who delight in *sambhūti*."

Sambhūti is a noun derived from the verb *sambhū*, "to arise", "to be born". It means, therefore, "the born", "the arising", or "the becoming". *Asambhūti* means "the unborn", "the not-becoming". Again, the exact meaning of these terms is ambiguous enough to suggest several possibilities. Some consider *asambhūti* to mean *prakṛti* (material nature) or *māyā* (the illusion that the material nature, the multiplicity, is real). "Unborn" refers to *prakṛti's* original state as the reservoir of all matter in potential before creation. As the *Gītā* clearly states (13.19), *prakṛti* had no beginning; its eternality is due to its being an aspect of Brahman. Therefore it is "unborn".

Sambhūti, "the becoming", "the arising" most likely refers to the manifest form of Brahman, Brahman with attributes. Swāmī Śarvānanda identifies this as Hiraṇyagarbha, the divine creator: "*Māyā* playing upon Brahman causes the first manifestation of Hiraṇyagarbha in the beginning of the cycle. He, in turn, creates the whole universe."[3] If this is true, then *sambhūti* refers to the personal deity ("born" in the sense that It has assumed form) and *asambhūti* to the Brahman without qualities.

We are still addressing the *karma/jñāna* question, but on an increasingly subtle level. The argument has been taken a step beyond the actual behavior pattern of the individual to encompass the largest, and most subtle, universal concepts. Action/ritual/*karma* is identified with *prakṛti* and the personal, anthropomorphic God, while knowledge/speculation/*jñāna* is identified with the impersonal Brahman. Though the phrasing of verses twelve through fourteen may at first seem baffling, remember that this thematic thread — the reconciliation of *karma* and *jñāna* — gives us insight into the *Upaniṣad's* intent. These paths are not mutually exclusive. Action and knowledge go hand-in-hand, as do *puruṣa* and *prakṛti*, and the personal and impersonal aspects of Brahman.

Verse thirteen, like verse ten, states that different results are obtained from the worship of *sambhūti* and *asambhūti*. Verse fourteen adds another dimension by introducing the *vināśa*, which means "destructible". It refers to the fact that anything which is born is destined for destruction; therefore it is a synonym for *sambhūti*, "the born". "He who understands *asambhūti* (the unborn) and *vināśa* (the destructible) both together attains immortality . . ." (14).

The last four verses are prayers to Brahman in the guise of two elemental deities. In the context of this *Upaniṣad* at least, they appear to be purely metaphorical, poetic representations of certain aspects of That which is indescribable.

In verse fifteen It is compared to the Sun, a fitting metaphor. The author asks the deity to remove Its effulgence so that he, the devotee, may have access to the Truth which lies beyond the light. The reader should take note of the fact that the light itself is not the final goal, not the highest realization. Verse sixteen has the devotee repeat the supplication, then add, "I am indeed He, that Being who dwells there (behind the effulgence)." Devotee and Deity are one.

The aspirant appears to be on the verge of death in verse seventeen, ready to be absorbed back into Brahman. He prays to have his breath merged into the all-pervading, immortal *prāṇa* (life force) and his body reduced to ashes. He sharply tells his own mind not to forget the lessons learned from past deeds. This passage is illustrates the art of conscious death.

A prayer to Agni closes the *Upaniṣad*, Agni being the god of fire. The radiance of fire suggests the infinite luminescence of Brahman. Agni also represents the power of Brahman manifest in the sacred fire. It was believed that oblations poured into the sacred fire rose, with Agni's help, to the gods. This beautiful image is here utilized as a metaphor for the soul's merging into the Absolute. The devotee asks for divine help, just as Agni helps the sacrifices along their route: "O Agni, lead us by the fair path that we may reap all the good we have sown. You know all our deeds. Lord, destroy all crooked-going sins against us. We salute you with our words again and again" (18).

NOTES

1. Swāmī Śarvānanda, *Īśāvasyopaniṣad* (Mylapore: Sri Ramakrishna Math, 1981), pp. 27-28.
2. Śarvānanda, p. 12.
3. Śarvānanda, p. 16.

CHAPTER EIGHT

Kena Upaniṣad: A Meditation on Brahman the Perceiver, Not the Perceived

Like the *Īśā*, the *Kena Upaniṣad* derives its name from the first word of the text. It means "by whom":

"Who impels the mind to alight on its object? Enjoined by whom does the vital force proceed to function? At whose behest do men utter speech? What intelligence, indeed, directs the eyes and ears?" (1.1).[1]

The body of the *Upaniṣad* is devoted to answering this question, first by direct discourse, then with an illustrative story. The text, divided into four sections, takes the form of a dialogue between a teacher and disciple. What, the student asks in the opening verse, is the animating principle behind the mind, senses and so on?

It is Ātman, the master replies, by whose power the ear hears, the mind understands, the life signs function, etc. The wise person separates the Ātman from these faculties, detaches him or herself from sense-life and is liberated (1.2). The premise here is simple but profound. The senses and mind are inert; if one were to pluck their eyeballs out and lay them on the ground, the eyeballs wouldn't see a thing. The Ātman within is what sees; the eyes are merely an instrument. Ātman is the sole intelligent principle. Those who are ignorant mistake the mind, senses and so on to be animate and intelligent and, therefore, identify Ātman with them, thinking "My thoughts are me, my fingers are me, etc." One must discern the distinction and, as a result, transcend identification with the senses.[2]

"The eye does not go there, nor the speech . . . we do not, therefore, know any process of instructing about It" (1.3). In other words, Ātman cannot be known by the senses or by other material means, such as words. Verse 1.4 says It is different from the "known", that is, ordinary objective reality, and the "unknown", whatever remains beyond our perception, or perhaps the fundamental ignorance which gives rise to the material manifestation, or, again, perhaps the non-objectiveness of Ātman.[3]

"That (the Ātman) which speech cannot reveal, but which reveals speech — know that alone as Brahman and not this that people worship here." (1.5). "This" refers to deities and their symbols, which people worship. The verse is not condemning deity worship, but clarifying that Brahman is behind everything, even the deities themselves. Speech cannot reveal the truth of Brahman because Brahman is the source of speech. In the preceding verses it was stated that Ātman is the source of the eyes' ability to see, the mind's ability to cognize, etc., and in the following verses these functions will be attributed to Brahman. Ātman is in Brahman.

"That which cannot be comprehended by the mind, but by which the mind cognizes, know that alone to be Brahman . . ." (1.6). This formulaic sentence is repeated (1.7, 1.8, 1.9) with reference to sight, hearing and *prāṇa*, the vital breath or life force. One cannot literally "see" Brahman because Brahman is what enables the eye to see. The *Upaniṣad* is impeccably logical.

Having established, in part one, that the senses and mind are useless for perceiving Brahman, part two will address how Brahman might be understood. The preceptor states that if you think you already know Brahman, you are mistaken. The form of Brahman seen in conditioned living beings and deities is but a trifle (2.1). Brahman cannot be known objectively; It must be intuited. This is because Brahman is not a thing outside of oneself. Knowledge of Brahman is a condition of pure Self-awareness, an experiencing of one's own being.

The disciple, after reflecting upon and realizing Brahman, states, "I think I have known Brahman" (2.1). But he feels compelled to explain such a statement. To say, "I know Brahman" suggests that It, the eternal and ultimate Subject, is an object among the many objects. On the other hand, to say "I don't know Brahman" sounds like a confession of ignorance. The disciple says, "Who amongst us comprehends It both as the Not-unknown and as the Known — he comprehends It" (2.2). In other words, from an objective point of view, the only viable description of one's understanding of Brahman is the statement, "It is not unknown." From the subjective point of view, however, one can safely claim, "It is known".[4]

As the ultimate Subject, the source of the seeing, the source of cognition, Brahman cannot be the object of mental conceptualization. In this regard, the teacher remarks that he who "conceives" It does not understand It. Similarly, one who "knows" It (as an object of knowledge) is actually ignorant, while one who understands that It can never be "known" in such a way possesses true knowledge (2.3).

It can be known through intuition, and such a realization leads to immortality. Knowledge of the Ātman equips one with "real strength" (2.4), that is, being so firmly situated in Self that one is never affected by ever-changing material conditions.

In the final verse of part two, the master proclaims that one who realizes the Ātman while in this world has attained "true life", while one who has not faces "destruction", or the inevitability of death and rebirth that is the result of living under the thrall of illusion. "Discerning the Ātman in every single being, the wise one rises from sense-life and attains immortality" (2.5). Compare this to the second half of verse 1.2: "Separating the Ātman from the faculties (senses, etc.), the wise one rises from sense-life and attains immortality." After discerning the Ātman in oneself, the aspirant discerns the same Ātman everywhere and in everyone.

Now the master relates the same teachings through an allegory. This myth is also found in the *Bṛhadāraṇyaka Upaniṣad* (3.14-25, 4.26-28). Briefly, the *devas* (gods) had won a victory over the *asuras* (demons) but only due to the force of Brahman behind them. Though not responsible for the victory, they became elated by it and thought, "We are victorious and the glory belongs to us!"

Brahman, aware of their vanity, appeared before them, but they could not fathom who this worshippable Spirit was. Agni, the deity of fire (here referred to as *jātavedas*, "all-knowing") was sent to find out. "Who are you?" Brahman asked the demigod. "I am Agni, the omniscient," Agni replied.

"What power do you possess?" Brahman asked.

"I can burn everything!"

Brahman lay a small straw before the god and said, "Burn it."

Agni dashed at the straw, but was unable to set it afire. He returned to the *devas*, saying, "I could not find out who that adorable Spirit is."

They next sent Vāyu, deity of wind. Brahman lay the straw before him and said, "Blow this away." Try as he might, the *deva* could not, and he returned, not having discovered who the Spirit was.

At last they sent Indra, their leader. As he approached, the Spirit disappeared and in that spot Indra beheld a wondrously beautiful Goddess, identified as Umā, "daughter of the snowy mountain Himavat". He asked Her who the Spirit had been (3.1-12).

"It was Brahman!" She exclaimed. "Through Brahman's victory you have attained greatness" (4.1).

These three gods — Indra, Vāyu and Agni — are to be considered the most excellent of the *devas* because they were the first to draw near to Brahman, and Indra is preeminent among them because he was the first to discover that the Spirit was Brahman (4.2-3).

Here the *devas* represent the senses. They cannot know Brahman through their own powers because Brahman empowers them in the first place. Trying to perceive Brahman as one would an object is useless.

The meaning of the Goddess' appearance is somewhat mysterious. If She is to be identifies with Brahman, a provocative layer of meaning is introduced. Perhaps She is merely acting as a mouthpiece; the name Umā means "possessor (of knowledge)", so She may have popped up simply to relay a fact. In any event, She is a manifestation of Mahādevī, the Great Goddess or Divine Mother, the feminine aspect of Absolute Truth. In Her various guises She is also Durgā, Kālī, Gaurī, etc.[5]

Verse 4.4 describes Brahman "as that which illuminates lightning and that which makes one wink." A lovely bit of imagery, the verse can be construed as saying that Brahman is behind every form of power and movement in the universe, whether as huge and dramatic as a bolt of lightning or as tiny as a wink. One might also interpret the verse to mean that through the contemplation of the material manifestation one can only gain a glimpse of Brahman, just as lightning, or a wink, comes in a flash and is suddenly gone.[6]

Verses 4.5 and 4.6 examine Brahman "from the point of view of His manifestation within the Self" (4.5). Because of the Brahman within, the mind is capable of knowing, remembering, and imagining (4.5). This Brahman within is known as *tadvana*, literally "adorable as being the Ātman of all".[7] It is to be meditated on as *tadvana* and as *tadvana* do beings love It (4.6).

The disciple asks whether the whole of "the secret knowledge" (*upaniṣad*) has been imparted (4.7). The preceptor replies that it has, but adds that austerity, restraint, and dedicated work are needed in order to fully comprehend it, that the *Vedas* are its "limbs", or a necessary course of complimentary study, and that Truth is its abode (4.8).

One who the knows the *Upaniṣad*, the master concludes, destroys evil and is established in boundless, blissful Brahman (4.9).

NOTES

1. Swāmī Śarvānanda, *Kenopaniṣad* (Madras: Sri Ramakrishna Math, 1981), p. 5.
2. Śarvānanda, p. 6.
3. Śarvānanda, p. 8.
4. Śarvānanda, pp. 18-19.
5. Stutley and Stutley, p. 311.
6. Śarvānanda, p. 39.
7. Śarvānanda, p. 36.

CHAPTER NINE

Māṇḍūkya Upaniṣad: *A Meditation on the Mantra Oṃ*

The twelve succinct verses of the *Māṇḍūkya Upaniṣad* embody the most sophisticated level of Upaniṣadic thought. Named for its author, Maṇḍūka[1], it is remarkable in its unequivocal non-dualistic (*advaita*) stance, and in its examination of the progressive states of consciousness one passes through in approaching Absolute Truth. The *Upaniṣad* dispenses with Vedic symbolism and references to deities, preferring to state the philosophical concepts outright. The only symbol employed here is the *mantra Oṃ*. In this context, it represents the spiritual and material totality, Brahman.

The first two verses express the substance of the entire *Upaniṣad*. In fact, they express the substance of *vedāntic* philosophy as a whole: "All this world is the syllable *Oṃ*. Its further explanation is this: the past, the present, the future — everything is just *Oṃ*. And whatever transcends the three divisions of time — that, too, is *Oṃ*" (1).

Everything is *Oṃ*. The material universe is *Oṃ*, as is that which transcends the material universe, namely Brahman. According to Swāmī Śarvānanda, Sanskrit philology dictates that the relation between *śabda*, sound, and *artha*, object, is inseparable. As the supreme, universal and all-inclusive sound form, *Oṃ* is an appropriate representation of the universe. The material universe is an emanation of the Divine and, therefore, is the Divine Itself. This naturally lends it to embodiment in the sacred sound *Oṃ*. *Oṃ* is also that which transcends material nature; it is Brahman.[2]

". . . everything is just *Oṃ*." The multitude of forms apparent in *māyā* dissolve as a result. There is nothing but *Oṃ*, nothing but Brahman. Meditation on the *mantra Oṃ*, therefore, will lead to realization of Brahman.

Verse two reads: "For truly, everything is Brahman. And this Self within (Ātman) is Brahman. The Self has four quarters" (2).

The text could not be more explicit. Everything is Brahman. The Self is Brahman. Therefore the Self pervades everything, is one with everything. The reference to "four quarters" will be explained in the following five verses. They are four states of consciousness culminating in knowledge of the Absolute. Each level corresponds to a sound inherent in the *oṃkara*: A, U, M, and, together, *Oṃ* (*Aum*).

Verse three identifies the first quarter as *vaiśvānara*, which literally means "common to all men". It is the waking state, outwardly cognitive, "seven-limbed, nineteen-mouthed and enjoying gross objects" (3). In other words, it is our ordinary, hum-drum consciousness. According to the *Chāndogya Upaniṣad* (5.18.2), the seven limbs of *vaiśvānara* are heaven, sun, air, sky, water, earth and sacrificial altar.[3] The *vaiśvānara* level, then, refers not only to the individual's perception, but also to that which is perceived, the universe. The nineteen mouths are the five sensory organs, five motor organs, five *prāṇas*, or division of vital energy, and four aspects of the mind. Together, these categorizations comprise the *jñānendriyas*, or knowledge-gathering senses.[4]

The second quarter, verse four states, is *taijasa*, "the brilliant". The dream state is its field, it is inwardly cognitive, and though it, too, is "seven-limbed" and "nineteen-mouthed", it enjoys subtle objects. *Taijasa* is a purely mental condition; the senses are withdrawn from gross objects, but now alight upon "subtle objects" — that is, impressions of waking life stored in memory.[5]

When one falls into a sleep state which is entirely dreamless, entirely desireless, it is a "deep sleep" (5). This state is called *prājña*, or "of one who knows properly". It is a purely intellectual state (notice how mind and intellect are considered distinct). Experiences are all unified in this state, "with cognition reduced to a mere indefinite mass, full of bliss, enjoying bliss, and forming the gateway to all definite cognitions" (5).

Prājña, in verse six, is compared to *Īśvara*, the Lord, because from this deep consciousness springs the whole phenomena of waking and dream states and back into it they dissolve (6). This is much like creation emanating from, and returning to, *Īśvara*, God.

Verse seven describes the fourth level, *turiya*, (literally, "the fourth") as qualitatively and categorically different from the other states, yet at the same time present in all the states. It is, in reality, not a fourth part of anything, but the whole of reality. It is the Self. The verse describes it beautifully as ". . . unseen, unrelated, inconceivable, uninferable, unimaginable, indescribable . . . All phenomena cease in it. It is peace, it is bliss, it is non-duality. This is the Self, and it is to be realized" (7).

Here the text returns to the topic of *Oṃ*. The Ātman, verse eight begins, is to be identified with *Oṃ* when *Oṃ* is to be considered a single syllable. When *Oṃ* is broken down into parts — A, U, M — the parts are to be identified with the "quarters" discussed earlier (8). In this way, *Oṃ* is identified with all states of consciousness, and with the macrocosmic-microcosmic designations which they represent. We see a progression, but at the same time a totality (A, U, M = *Oṃ*; no real difference exists at all).

Vaiśvānara, the waking state, is the A of *Oṃ* because both are all pervasive and have a beginning (9). A is considered "all-pervasive" because in Sanskrit the *a* sound is included in all the letters. It is the first letter of the Sanskrit alphabet and thus has no preceding letter or sound; it "has a beginning".

Taijasa, the dream state, is the U part of *Oṃ* because both are superior and in between (10). *Taijasa* is superior to *vaiśvānara* because it is more subtle, while U is superior to A, apparently, because it comes afterward. *Taijasa* is in between *vaiśvānara* and *prājña* as U is between A and M.

Prājña, deep, dreamless sleep, is the M of *Oṃ* because they are both at the end and both are like "the measure" (11). This analogy of a measure is quite subtle; it refers to a measure into which grain is put and from which it is then drawn out.[6] As far as *prājña* goes, this idea relates to verse six, where *prājña* was identified with *Īśvara*, the Lord. The waking and dream states appear to submerge in deep sleep and to emerge from it as well. Similarly, in chanting *Oṃ*, the repetitions run together in such a way that the A and U seem to sink into the M and then come out of it again.[7]

The twelfth and final verse of the *Upaniṣad* nicely ties together the various thematic threads. The syllable *Oṃ* in its unified aspect is *turīya*, "the fourth", as described in verse seven. It is devoid of phenomenal existence and is transcendental, full of bliss, and non-dual. "Thus the syllable *Oṃ* is verily the Self (Ātman)." One who knows this merges his own self into the universal Self (12).

The *Māṇḍūkya Upaniṣad* opens with the lesson that everything — both material and spiritual — is *Oṃ*. It closes by elaborating upon that same lesson — *Oṃ* is indivisible and identified with the Ātman. This simple, but extraordinary, concept is the essence of mysticism, the basis of *Vedānta*. Its full implication can only be grasped through further contemplation, and only perceived personally through meditation on the sound form of Brahman Itself: *Oṃ*.

NOTES

1. Swāmī Śarvānanda, *Māṇḍūkyopaniṣad* (Mylapore: Sri Ramakrishna Math, 1976), p. 3.
2. Śarvānanda, p. 8.
3. Śarvānanda, p. 10.
4. Śarvānanda, p. 10.
5. Śarvānanda, p. 11.
6. Śarvānanda, p. 21.
7. Śarvānanda, p. 21.

CHAPTER TEN

Aitareya Upaniṣad: A Meditation on Creation

In the opening chapter of the *Aitareya Upaniṣad* (named for its author, Aitareya),[1] we are introduced to a genre which we will encounter again and again as we work through the Hindu religious texts, namely the creation myth. It can be understood as symbolic, as a concrete point of reference to illustrate an abstract concept, in this case how the appearance of the many is created from the original, undifferentiated One. The first chapter seeks to show that the senses and their corresponding desires are separate from the Ātman and accomplishes this by personifying them. As the *Upaniṣad* progresses, the transmigratory cycle will be described, as will the means of escaping from it. Therefore, we have in one, small *Upaniṣad* a description of the entire cosmic cycle of creation, evolution, and involution, or return to the divine Source.

In the Beginning . . .

The text begins with a familiar idea: "In the beginning verily, all this was Ātman alone. There was nothing else existing as a rival."

In reality, all this still *is* Ātman alone, but for the sake of clarity, the *Upaniṣad* employs language which suggests potential differentiation. By "Ātman" he means Paramātman, the Supreme Ātman, or Brahman. Because there is nothing else, we can assume that Ātman alone is the source of material manifestation; in other words, matter is simply a transmutation of Ātman Itself, which is defined as absolute Existence, Consciousness, and Bliss (*Sat-Cit-Ānanda*).

"He (that Ātman) thought, 'Let Me create the worlds'. Thus He created these worlds, Ambhas, Marīcī, Maram, and Āpaḥ." Ātman is portrayed here as a conscious entity. It thinks.

The text proceeds to describe the four regions; Ambhas is above heaven, "superheaven"; Marīcī is heaven, earth is Mara, and the nether region, "The Region of Waters" is called Āpaḥ.

The reader can interpret this passage in several ways. It can be taken to mean that the first step in the cosmic manifestation would have to have been the creation of space, for without a place in which to occur, nothing *can* occur. The number of planes is a flexible detail in the Hindu scriptures. In the *Purāṇas,* for instance, the regions are numbered at fourteen.

Another, more subtle, interpretation depends on the opening statement that Ātman alone existed; it says that the regions have no absolute reality. In a sense, creation never took place because the indivisible, infinite Brahman is the only reality and therefore gross physicality cannot emerge from it. These are only apparent regions; space is an illusion. Brahman alone is real.

A third interpretation suggests that these regions symbolize states of consciousness, ranging from the lowest and most deluded (as if submerged in water), to the highest and most subtle (higher, even, than heaven). Brahman is the center, and these regions are to be thought of not as a series of vertical steps upward, but rather as concentric circles leading deeper toward the core, Paramātman.[2] "He (the Ātman) thought, 'These indeed are the worlds (I have created). Let me now create guardians of the worlds'. He then raised *Puruṣa* from the waters and fashioned him."

The word *puruṣa* literally means "man". In Hindu terminology, however, it takes on several important additional meanings, recognizable by context. Here it refers to *Virāṭ-Puruṣa*[3], the cosmic man, a sort of primordial, original body, or person, from which all individuals are derived. He represents the source of matter and multiplicity, originally undifferentiated from the One. He is also called *Hiraṇyagarbha,* which means "golden womb" and suggest his being the origin, the parent, of matter.

One can imagine him as a formless lump, an egg shape, or perhaps a featureless, though vaguely anthropomorphic body. The Ātman brooded over this *Puruṣa,* the *Upaniṣad* continues, and a mouth burst forth. From the mouth proceeded speech, and from speech, fire. In all Hindu creation accounts we see an evolution from the most subtle to the most gross as well as the idea that the gross elements have their origin in the subtle elements. They are not created separately; material manifestation is the result of a continuum. This is important because it means that all the universe, even its grossest aspects, is directly evolved from the subtlest element of all, Brahman. Therefore, all this world is non-different from Brahman, and divine.

The *Upaniṣad* states that two nostrils burst forth, and from them proceeded the power of smell, and from the power of smell, the air.

Next come eyes, sight, and the sun. Ears, hearing, the quarters. Skin, hairs, herbs and trees. The heart, mind, the moon. The navel, the down-breathing, death. The generative organ, seed, water. In the *Upaniṣads*, the senses are commonly associated with particular deities which govern them, and are often personified as such. This is the case here.

The First Person

In the second section of Chapter One the story continues: the senses, now personified as deities, fell into the "mighty ocean of existence". The mighty ocean can be taken to mean ordinary, worldly life and its requisite round of birth and death. Personifying the senses suggests separateness from Ātman. Swāmī Śarvānanda suggests another explanation of the sense-deities:

> The presiding deities, *Abhimānidevatās*, should not be taken in the sense that they are so many spirits or angels controlling the different organs of man; but they should be understood in the Vedāntic sense of the different expressions of the same *Ātma-caitanya* or Intelligence, working differently through the different sensations.[4]

In either case, they are submerged in *māyā.* The rest of section two deals with the emergence of desire, the natural result of entanglement in *māyā.* The Ātman, we're told, subjected the *Puruṣa* to hunger and thirst (that is, desire). In response, the sense-gods requested Him to provide them with a place in which to dwell and eat food (enjoy, fulfill desires). The human body is the best vehicle for sense enjoyment, as is suggested by the fact that the Ātman offered them first a cow body, then a horse body, both of which they rejected as insufficient. He finally offered them a human body, to which they exclaimed, "Well done!" Each deity then entered the corresponding organ to dwell there permanently. Fire, manifesting itself as speech, entered the mouth; air, having become scent, entered the nostrils, and so forth. This proto-human represents the first *jīva*, or individual person. Notice how his organs and their functions are exact replicas of those of the *Virāṭ-Puruṣa*, how the story establishes macrocosmic-microcosmic parallels.

Hunger and thirst, too, requested a dwelling place. They were told to dwell in the deities, to share with them. This makes sense, because without tangible sense organs to experience them, hunger and thirst are only abstract concepts.

The Evolution of the Consciousness

"He, the Creator, thought: There are these worlds and guardian deities; let Me create food for them." So begins the third section of Chapter One. Food is complex metaphor here. It refers both to gross objects which satisfy sense cravings, and to that force in matter by which it perpetuates itself — Nature, if you will. There is actually no difference between the two. This element nurtures matter and at the same time gives sensual satisfaction and pleasure, as does ordinary food. As we shall see, this nutritive force, this life support, is assimilated by means of the individual's *apāna*, or downward breath. Again, a two-tiered metaphor is brought into play, for *apāna* refers both to the "breath", or energy which courses down the body and thus makes swallowing and digestion possible, and to that aspect of *prāṇa*, or the general life-force, which is centered in the physical body and is invigorated by the life-force present in Nature. The human being and Nature are inextricably connected. Both contain the same vital force, here symbolized by food and *apāna*.

"He (the Ātman) brooded over the waters; and from the waters thus brooded over sprang up the form, or organic matter. And now the form thus born was verily the created food."

Form solidified into organic matter, organic matter is animated with life-supporting energy. The food, we learn, got up and ran away. The embodied being sought to seize the food by speech and, of course, could not. "Were he able to seize it with speech," the *Upaniṣad* asserts, "later man created by him would have been satisfied by merely uttering the name of food." He attempted to seize it with breath, and naturally failed. Had he been able to seize it with breath, people would have been satisfied merely with the scent of food. He similarly tries to seize it with each sense organ in turn — eyes, ears, skin, mind, and sexual organ. Finally he seizes it with the *apāna*.

The sense organs, though facilitating delight in fleeting objects, clearly cannot offer any lasting support or benefit. They do not sustain the individual, even bodily.

"He, the Creator, thought: How can this (aggregate of body, senses, etc.) remain without me?" Indeed, the one thing missing in this scheme was the Ātman Itself, the Soul, the presence of God which invests dull matter with life. Although the various characters in our story — the senses, the body, the food — behave as though they were animate and cognizant, in fact they are dead, inert matter before the Ātman entered them. What distinguishes living beings from inanimate objects is the Ātman within them. Plants, animals, people, even microorganisms, are alive because of the presence of Brahman/Ātman. The *Upaniṣad* says that the Ātman entered through the suture in the skull. That "door" is henceforth called *Nāndana*, the place of joy.

"For him there are three seats and three dreams." According to Swāmī Śarvānanda, the three seats might mean the three centers of consciousness — brain, neck and heart, or they might be the mother's body, father's body and one's own body (as will be mentioned in the next section), or they might refer to the residence of the *jīvātman* (individual soul) while one is in a waking, dreaming, or deep sleep state. The three dreams certainly refer to these three states.[5] The significance of these three states is that they are mundane modes and do not represent the highest state of consciousness one can attain. They are part of the gross material manifestation.

"Thus born, He named all things and thought if He could name anything beside Himself." Ātman, now embodied as an individual *jīva*, experienced the multiplicity of objects ("named all things"). By allowing Himself to come under the dreamlike spell of *māyā* He forgot His own real nature as the indivisible supreme One. This same cosmic drama is repeated in the life of every person. After perceiving and examining all objects, however, the *jīva* begins to look a step beyond them, which takes him to Brahman. He is identical to Brahman, thus he wonders if there is really anything besides himself at all. The world, we have seen, was created out of Brahman Himself; the building blocks of material manifestation evolve directly from Brahman and are, therefore, ultimately nondifferent from Brahman.

"He (the individual) perceived the very Being, Brahman, overspreading all, and with wonder He cried, 'Oh surely I have seen It!'" The *jīva* has achieved Self-realization. The goal of his life — to return to his source — has been achieved. The Creation drama is a giant circle, Brahman expressing Itself and returning to Itself. The purpose of creation is beautifully expressed here, so simple in theory but so profound in actuality.

Chapter One closes with a bit of punning: "Therefore Idandra is his name. For surely Idandra is his name and they call him who is known as Idandra by his mysterious name Indra. Indeed, the gods love mystery. Indeed, the gods love mystery."

Swāmī Śarvānanda explains Idandra as a term denoting the *jīva* who has realized his or her own Ātman as the universal Brahman. It is comprised of *idam* plus *dra*, "this-seeing". When the syllable "*dam*" is syncopated, the word becomes Indra, the chief of the gods and a designation of the Absolute.[6] Certainly, when one becomes Idandra, "this(Brahman)-seeing," one truly becomes Indra (Brahman Itself).

On Reincarnation

The first paragraph of chapter two describes the cycle of transmigration. It is quite explicit, stating that the preexistent *jīva* enters the body of a potential father and, through him, is placed in the womb of the mother. Settling into the mother is the first birth. The second birth is the physical birth. After attaining old age, the body dies and the *jīva* departs, only to be born anew in another body. This is the third birth. Though theoretically simple, the concept of reincarnation is one of the cornerstones of Hindu philosophy and religion. Very little else makes sense apart from it. It is Kṛṣṇa's first teaching in the *Bhagavad-Gītā*: "Truly there was never a time when I did not exist, nor you, nor all these princes, nor in the future shall any of us cease to be. Just as the embodied soul passes from childhood to youth to old age, so at the time of death does he pass into another body . . ." (2.12-13).

The second paragraph quotes a verse from the *Ṛg Veda* (4.27.1) uttered by Vāmadeva: "Ah! Dwelling inside the womb I understood all the births of all the gods. A hundred bodies strong as steel restrained me, but like a hawk I broke them by force and came out swiftly." Vāmadeva freed himself from the cycle of birth and death. He had had one hundred previous births and, while still in the womb of his one hundred-first, attained Self-realization and ended his bondage. The *Upaniṣad* states: "Emerging thus from the body (of his mother), enlightened with this supreme knowledge, and having enjoyed all delights in the abode of bliss (superconsciousness, knowledge of Brahman), he became immortal." Vāmadeva is also mentioned in *Bṛhadāraṇyaka Upaniṣad* 1.4.10.

One will notice that chapter one, after describing the material creation, ended with the event of Self-realization. So, too, does Chapter Two, after describing a microcosmic creation story — the creation of an individual body — end with Self-realization. Chapter Three will end in the same way.

Parabrahman

Chapter Three seeks to show that the Ātman is ever still and unchanging, neither attached to nor affected by modifications of mind and senses. Therefore, a firm distinction is drawn between that aspect of Brahman which experiences the world by acting as the perceiver behind the sense organs, and that which is the invariable, absolute, universal Spirit.

"Who is He whom we meditate upon as Ātman?" the chapter opens. "Which of the two (Parabrahman or Aparabrahman) is He?"

Parabrahman is translated as "Supreme Brahman". Aparabrahman means "*not* the Supreme Brahman". Is the Ātman Brahman or not? The text replies that Ātman is that by which the living being sees forms, hears sounds, and so forth. That the senses and the Ātman are separate was determined in Chapter One.

"That which is the heart and mind is the same as that," the *Upaniṣad* says. It goes on to list the properties associated with *prajñāna*, which means intelligence, consciousness, understanding. These include perception, firmness, power of reflection, memory, determination, desire, love, and so on. "All these are but names of *prajñāna*," the text states. The same intelligence which is characterized by so many variables is associated also with the unchanging Ātman. The point is that all this multiplicity is Brahman too. The many characteristics of *prajñāna* are an aspect of Brahman. But are they Parabrahman (Supreme Brahman) or Aparabrahman (Brahman, but not the *Supreme* Brahman)? The answer should be obvious: Aparabrahman.

The *Upaniṣad* continues in this vein, stating that light, water, and ether, as well as all the animals, plants, organisms and inanimate objects have their basis in *prajñāna*. Therefore *prajñāna* is Brahman. The message here is, again, twofold. On the one hand, we know that apparent multiplicity is an illusion due to the imposition of *māyā*; variegatedness, therefore, is unreal except for our perception of it. In other words, it is the condition of being perceived which gives an object its earthly reality. This perceiving is due to *prajñāna*, intelligence, which is a fraction of the Absolute Intelligence, Brahman. Objects, then, are invested with reality by *prajñāna* and therefore have their foundation in it.

On the other hand, *prajñāna*, natural elements, living beings, etc. are all created out of the material of Brahman Itself and, in that sense, are *never* separated from Brahman. "The whole world is founded on *prajñāna* and therefore *prajñāna* is Brahman." Limited knowledge is but a spark of Absolute Knowledge, which is Brahman. This Knowledge is referred to as *cit.*

The *Upaniṣad* closes with the veiled suggestion that the Ātman which lies behind and detached from the previously mentioned multiplicity is that which is to be meditated upon as Parabrahman. In the words "having transcended this world" lies the intent of the *Upaniṣad.* All this, verily, is Brahman, but there exists a supreme aspect of Brahman, a Parabrahman, which dwells within as the Ātman. It is immutable, limitless, absolute. It is entirely separate from the body, senses, and objects. The *Upaniṣad* reads: "He who has realized the Ātman, thus having transcended this world and having obtained all delights in the world of Bliss (superconsciousness, spiritual joy) gains immortality, verily, he attains immortality."

NOTES

1. Swāmī Śarvānanda, *Aitareyopaniṣad* (Mylapore: Sri Ramakrishna Math, 1978), p. 3.
2. Śarvānanda, p. 35.
3. Śarvānanda, p. 35.
4. Śarvānanda, p. 37.
5. Śarvānanda, p. 57.
6. Śarvānanda, p. 58.

CHAPTER ELEVEN

Praśna Upaniṣad: A Meditation on Prāṇa, the Life Force Within Us

Praśna means "question", and this *Upaniṣad* is so named because it is comprised of six questions put to a spiritual preceptor named Pippalāda.[1] Like the *Aitareya Upaniṣad*, the *Praśna* ushers the reader step by step from the gross to the subtle, from the material to the spiritual. This mode of exposition is known as *upāsanā*, or drawing the mind in steps from the mundane to the divine. Each question represents a thematic step toward a more abstract reality, so the first one begins at the beginning: how did we all come into being? The final question inquires into the nature of Brahman Itself, the conscious Being at our center. The consistent image upon which the entire discussion hangs is *prāṇa*, the life force. This *prāṇa* is the power which activates and animates everything but, as we shall see, it is the Ātman which activates the *prāṇa* and ultimately is identified with it.

Question One: Origins

As the piece opens, six students who are intent on realizing Brahman approach Pippalāda for instruction. The *Upaniṣad* immediately makes a distinction between the conception of Brahman to which the boys are presently devoted — *Brahmaparāḥ*, and that which they desire to know — *Parambrahma*. According to Swami Nikhilānanda, the first is a "lower" Brahman identified with *Saguṇa* Brahman or Brahman with attributes (*sa* - with, *guṇa* - qualities). The second is *Nirguṇa* Brahman, the "higher" or attributeless Brahman.[2] Also of note is that the seekers carry fuel with them to present to the guru as an offering. This is traditional Hindu etiquette; the fuel represents the students' willingness to serve the spiritual master. This fuel will be used in the sacred fire, and formerly it was not unusual for a disciple to earn his keep while under the tutelage of a *guru* by going out and collecting fuel daily.

Pippalāda does not immediately impart instruction, however. Verse 1.2 has him tell the boys to live with him for a year and practice *tapas* or sense restraint, *brahmacarya* or strict celibacy, and *śraddhā*, faith. After this period of purification, they may inquire as it pleases them. The indication here is that not everyone is eligible for discipleship; some preparation is necessary before the aspirant is ready to absorb spiritual teachings. He or she must be receptive.

A year later, the student named Kabandhī approaches the master (2.3). "Bhagavan (Venerable Sir)," he asks, "from whence are all creatures born?"

The logic of beginning with an examination of the ordinary world is that until one has understood it, one cannot rightly look beyond it. Several schools of Indian philosophy are grounded on the premise that a close analysis of the material world will lead the inquirer to discover its ultimate unreality, thus ushering him or her into an entirely different realm of reality which requires a wholly different form of inquiry. The *Praśna Upaniṣad* will, in a way, employ this method.

Verse 1.4, when translated rather literally, reads:

> To him he said: The Lord of all creatures became desirous of progeny. He deliberated on (past Vedic) knowledge. Having brooded on that knowledge, He created a couple — food and *prāṇa* — with the idea "These two will produce creatures for Me in multifarious ways."

The remainder of section one will explore the ramifications of this creation scheme. The Creator figure here is identified as *Prajāpati*, which literally means Lord (*pati*, a cognate with *pater*) of Procreation (*prajā*). He is the same primordial Person we met in the *Aitareya Upaniṣad* as *Puruṣa* or *Hiraṇyagarbha*. "He practiced *tapas*," the text continues. *Tapas* can denote many forms of austerity or discipline. It can also refer to meditation. The word actually means "heat", which is suggestive both of the power a *yogī* can acquire through the practice of hard austerities, and the actual generation of heat which is said to radiate from the *yogī's* body during such practice (see, for instance, the case of Hiraṇyakaśipu in *Śrīmad Bhāgavatam* 7.3.1-5, where the universe is set ablaze by the heat of his austerities). In any event, the *Prajāpati* performed some sort of meditation, deliberation, or austerity and the result was the creation of a cosmic duality from which the flow of generations of living creatures could continue uninterruptedly.

The duality is comprised of *prāṇa* and *rayi*, energy and matter. In the verse quoted earlier, *rayi* is translated as food. In Upaniṣadic imagery, food represents Nature, gross matter, tangible substance, whatever possesses form (1.5). It is referred to as "food" because it is drawn into the body through the senses and sustains us; thus objects are "food" for the eyes, "food" for the ears, etc. *Rayi* is also associated with the moon (1.5) which is believed to cause vegetables and grains to grow by the soothing power of its rays. In this way the moon is, indirectly, the source of food.

Prāṇa, on the other hand, is associated with the sun (1.5). It is the vital energy, the life force. Like the sun, *prāṇa* infuses all living things with vitality and strength. If *rayi* is their form, *prāṇa* is their animating principle. Verse six beautifully describes the all-pervading nature of *prāṇa* by comparing it to the way the sun, while moving through its course, showers its life-giving rays in all directions and upon all things and thus "illumines all". For *prāṇa* is not confined to living bodies; it is an all-pervading energy which binds the whole material universe together. It is everywhere.

The sun metaphor is carried over to verse seven, where the *prāṇa* is described as rising, like the sun, and as the *viśvarūpaḥ*, "the form of the world" (*viśva* - the whole world, the universe, *rūpaḥ* - form), in other words, the formless one which assumes all forms. This term has been translated variously as "the soul of the universe"[3], "the soul of all forms"[4], and "(the one) who is possessed of all forms"[5].

If this description of *prāṇa* is beginning to sound suspiciously like a description of Brahman, it's because the author is constructing descriptive parallels in layers. The discussion will eventually take us to Brahman, but for the time being Pippalāda is drawing our attention to things that are *like* Brahman. The sun is like Brahman, as was noted in the *Īśā Upaniṣad* (verse 15); the *prāṇa* is like Brahman, all-pervading yet centralized in the body, life-giving, radiant.

The first effect of this cosmic duality is time. "The year is *Prajāpati*," verse nine asserts. The sun and moon in their cyclical courses through days and nights constitute the passage of time. There are two paths which one can take through time — the Southern and Northern. These are metaphors for materialistic life and spiritual life. The Southern course is for those engaged in sacrificial rites, action, and performance of duty. These people conquer "the world of the moon", in other words the world of *rayi*, gross matter. They are reincarnated back here on earth. This course is appropriate for those desiring progeny. In other words, it is for those who wish to enjoy worldly life.

The Northern course is for the spiritual aspirant. The sun, as a metaphor for the Ātman, the Self, is "conquered" by the one who searches for It by means of sense-control, continence, faith and meditation (1.10). This sun-Brahman "is the resort of all that lives . . . indestructible . . . fearless; this is the highest goal, for from this they do not come back" (1.10). He who realizes the Self is liberated.

The sun is praised in verse eleven as the father (of the universe) and as possessing five feet which, according to Swāmī Nikhilānanda, refer to the six seasons of the Indian year, fall and winter being counted as a single season. He has twelve limbs (twelve months), is full of water (rain from the sky), is omniscient, has seven wheels (seven rays or colors), and has six spokes (six seasons).[6]

Verses twelve and thirteen further contrast sun and moon, day and night, light and dark and connect the interplay of these forces to the passage of time. In verse fourteen we arrive at the biological origin of creatures. *Prajāpati* is food; food is eaten and (by maintaining the existing body) becomes seed, or semen. From semen comes creatures. We have, then, a systematic progression: the Creator, through intense concentration, projects from Himself a cosmic duality from which evolves time and self-generating matter. Matter is enlivened by the presence of energy, or *prāṇa*, and the resulting individual creature is free to traverse either path it desires.

Those who undertake the vow of *Prajāpati*, in other words take up His creationary work here on earth, will produce sons and daughters, thus binding themselves to the world (1.15). Those who observe chastity and truthfulness, on the other hand, attain Brahmaloka ("Brahma's abode"), a state of liberation. "That taintless world of Brahman is for those in whom there is no crookedness, no falsehood, no deception" (1.16).

Question Two: The Supremacy of *Prāṇa*

The second student, Vaidarbhi, asks, "How many are the deities that sustain a creature? Which among them exhibit this glory? Which is chief among them?"

The "deities" are the sense organs. The word *deva* means "shining one", in other words, something which illumines or reveals. As the organs themselves are mere matter and, therefore, inert, they must be animated by some anterior force, and this force is symbolized by the deities, or powers.[7] Vaidarbhi wants to know how many of these powers there are, which ones manifest most through the body, and which one is supreme.

Pippalāda replies with a little story. He lists the powers which make sense perception possible, such as space, air, fire, water, earth (the five elements), speech, mind, eye and ear (the senses). After having exhibited their glory, each power boasted that it was he who supports and upholds the whole body (2.2). *Prāṇa*, who is superior to these powers said, "Do not be deluded. I alone, dividing myself into five parts, support this body" (2.3). The five parts of *prāṇa* are *prāṇa*, the main life force, *apāna*, the downward-moving force which is responsible for excretion and reproduction, *samāna*, the fire of digestion, *vyāna*, which empowers the circulatory system, and *udāna*, the upward-rising current which conducts the soul out of the body and to its destination at the time of death. These divisions of *prāṇa* will be examined further in the next section.

As the story continues, the senses were incredulous. To prove he was supreme among them, the *prāṇa* rose, as if in indignation. As he ascended, the others ascended with him, and as he settled down, the others followed. "As bees go out when their queen goes out and return when she returns, so similarly did speech, mind, eye and ear" (2.4). It is *prāṇa*, then, which empowers the senses; they are nothing without it.

Delighted, the senses began to praise the *prāṇa* and their exclamations comprise the remaining nine verses of part two. The content of their eulogizing sounds remarkably as though they were addressing Brahman. As has been noted earlier, the *prāṇa* here stands as a gross reflection of Brahman. In the next section, it will even be referred to as the "shadow" of Ātman. The reader should be alert to the suggestion here of a wonderful unity in all creation. Each subsequent level of manifestation is merely the expression of a single force, a single truth. The senses, the *prāṇa*, the sun, the Creator (*Hiraṇyagarbha*) are all identified with one another, are all multifarious aspects of a single, unified reality.

Prāṇa, the senses say, is the sun, the rain, the wind, the earth. It is Indra (chief of the *devas*); it is food; it is being and non-being; it is the nectar of immortality (2.5). We can glean from this verse that it is all-pervading (thus associated with the elements), supreme (associated with the highest of the *devas*), sustains the body (like food), and determines the difference between life and death (being and non-being in the bodily sense). As long as it is present, the body is alive, and as soon as it departs the body perishes. *Prāṇa* itself is always present everywhere in the world, though; it cannot die or be diminished. Thus it is associated with immortality.

Everything is fixed on *prāṇa*, including religion itself. The holy *Vedas* are dependent on *prāṇa*, as are the ritualistic sacrifices, the *brāhmaṇas*, and the *kṣatriyas* (2.6). This would make sense, because the *Vedas* and the sacrificial fire are considered vibrant, living things. Furthermore, without people to chant the Vedic verses or tend the sacred fire, these things would lose their vibrancy, their efficacy. The *brāhmaṇa* caste traditionally performed the sacrifices and recited the Vedic hymns while the *kṣatriya* caste sponsored these religious functions. Everything is interconnected here; everything is dependent on everything else and everything as a whole is dependent on *prāṇa*. Notice how the Vedic hymns are necessary in order to perform the sacrifice, the *brāhmaṇas* are necessary in order the chant the hymns, the *kṣatriyas* are necessary in order to support the *brāhmaṇas*, and the sacrifice is necessary in order to supply the *kṣatriyas* with wealth and blessings. *Prāṇa* is necessary to sustain all. The whole world functions in this way.

Prāṇa moves about in the womb, like *Prajāpati* (for the Creator expands Himself to form the various individual beings), and is born again (the first birth being entrance into the womb, the second being physical birth), and dwells thereafter in the body and organs (2.7). *Prāṇa*, then, is the basis of the human body. So, too, is it the basis of ritual sacrifice, a procedure traditionally thought to ensure happiness, health, and good fortune. Once the body is born, it needs sacrifice to support it, and *prāṇa* is that which bears the oblations to the gods and is the first offering made to the departed ancestors (2.8), a rite which would begin a fire sacrifice.[8] The *prāṇa* constitutes the activities of the senses and is the very essence of the material body (2.8).

Prāṇa is also the basis of the gods. Verse nine reads, "You are Indra. Through your valor you are Rudra. You are the Protector. You move through the sky; you are the sun, the lord of lights." This, and the two preceding verses, constitute a beautiful construction. *Prāṇa* is the sacrificer, the sacrifice, and the recipient of the sacrifice. It is present in the totality of all existence. It is indivisible. Notice how the three verses, taken together, are an expansion of verse six.

Verse ten eulogizes *prāṇa's* nourishing form of rain. Verse eleven elaborates on the nourishment theme while resuming the theme of sacrifice and begins, "O *Prāṇa*, you are unpurified." The term here is *vrātya*, which, according to Swāmī Nikhilānanda, is used to designate any individual of the three higher castes for whom the obligatory sacramental initiatory rites have not been performed[9] (*śūdras*, the lowest caste, are denied such a ceremony). These people are considered impure. *Prāṇa*, being the first born thing, had no one to perform the rites for it. Śaṅkarācārya offers another interpretation; the *prāṇa*, he asserts, was naturally pure and thus required no purificatory ceremony.[10] This interpretation is expressed most precisely in Swami Prabhavānanda's translation, which simply reads, "Thou art purity itself."[11]

The verse continues, identifying *prāṇa* as the *ekarṣi* fire, (one of the sacrificial fires associated with the *Atharva Veda*[12]), and as the Lord of all that exists. The senses identify themselves as worshippers of *prāṇa* with the statement, "We are the givers of your food." In other words, they symbolically "feed" the *prāṇa* by pouring out the butter oblation into the sacred fire. This ritual of feeding the chosen deity is still practiced today, though instead of pouring edibles into the fire, the supplicant usually places a tray of food before the image on the altar.

"Make calm," the senses request in verse twelve, "that aspect of yours which abides in the speech, the ear, the eye, and which pervades the mind. Do not rise up" (that is, do not leave). This sentiment may be embraced by everyone. Quieting the restless sense organs is a preliminary step in meditation and a necessary condition for spiritual life.

Section two concludes with the statement that everything in this world and in heaven is under the control of *prāṇa.* Heaven in the Hindu cosmology is not the state of liberation, nor an eternal divine abode. It is a level of the material sphere characterized by an abundance of *sattva* (goodness) and peopled with god-like, though mortal, beings. "Protect us," the humbled senses pray, "as a mother protects her son; bestow upon us prosperity and wisdom."

Question Three: How *Prāṇa* Works in the Body

Having eulogized the glorious nature of *prāṇa,* the *Upaniṣad* will now explore how it actually operates in the human body. This is significant because certain schools of yoga assert that through breath control and other disciplines, the *prāṇa* can be manipulated and higher states of consciousness achieved. Also, a study of the bodily *prāṇa* drives home the idea that the body is, in and of itself, an inert, dull, temporary object. The presence of *prāṇa* makes it work; it has no life of its own. That this force originates *outside* the body should certainly lead the aspirant to think of the body in a new way. It might help the aspirant develop a detachment from the body, knowing that these bones, organs, limbs, etc. are not the source of their own life, not the reason this body is animated.

A third student, named Kauśalya, asks: Where does the *prāṇa* come from? How does it come into the body? How does it dwell in the body after dividing itself? How does it depart from the body? How does it support that which is internal as well as that which is external? (3.1).

Pippalāda addresses each question in turn. *Prāṇa,* he begins, is born from the Ātman, the Self. Just as a shadow is cast by a person, the *prāṇa* is cast by the Ātman (3.3). Notice how section one of this *Upaniṣad* described, in the form of a myth, the creation of the universal, external, all-pervading *prāṇa* while this section describes, quite directly, the source of internal, or physical *prāṇa.* There is, in fact, no difference between the two *prāṇas,* nor between the two sources. The universal Self and the individual self are one in the same. Each section examines the same reality only from different perspectives, macrocosmic and microcosmic.

In answer to Kauśalya's question, "How does the *prāṇa* come into the body?" the *guru* replies, "Through the activity of the mind it comes into this body" (3.3). He means that through the desires, thoughts and volition arising from the mind in the previous lifetime, one chooses rebirth and hence the *prāṇa* enters a new body.[13] The kind of body one assumes is a direct result of the thoughts entertained during one's lifetime and especially at the moment of death. (The *Śrīmad Bhāgavatam* (5.8) offers a vivid warning about this in the narrative of Bharata Mahārāja who, because of his preoccupation with a pet deer, was reincarnated into a deer himself.) The next three verses address how the *prāṇa*, after dividing itself into secondary *prāṇas*, works through the body.

Just as a king commands officials to administer to various villages, so the *prāṇa* engages the individual bodily organs by means of secondary *prāṇas* (3.4). One of these is *apāna* ("breathing out") which dwells in "the two lower apertures" or the two orifices of excretion. It is a downward-moving force which is responsible for ejecting waste and for the reproductive functions (3.5). *Samāna* ("equal, uniform") is the force which distributes the nutrients of food equally throughout the body. It is the power of digestion and assimilation and is located in the mid-region of the body. "Seven flames" issue forth from it, namely the two eyes, two ears, two nostrils and mouth (3.5).[14] In other words, it is *prāṇa* alone which enables the sense organs to function. Food is necessary to sustain the body, but it is *prāṇa* which causes the food to be assimilated and utilized. This *Upaniṣad* does not contradict contemporary science; it merely suggests that biological functioning is impelled by an anterior force, a force too subtle to be detected by any instrument we as yet possess. The original *prāṇa* itself "issues out of the mouth and nostrils, resides in the eyes and ears" (3.5). In other words, it is manifest in the breath and is the animating principle behind the sense organs. The *prāṇa* is not to be confused with the breath itself, though this seems to be a common misunderstanding. *Prāṇa* is associated with breath for two reasons: because the life in the body is sustained, first and foremost, by breathing (we can go longer without food or water than we can without air!) and because the bodily *prāṇa* can be manipulated through *prāṇāyāma*, breath control.

The next verse describes *vyāna*, or that aspect of *prāṇa* which impels the circulatory and nervous systems. The Ātman dwells in the heart, and from the physical heart radiates one hundred one *nāḍīs*, which is translated variously as arteries, vessels, or nerves. For each of these one hundred one nerve branches there are one hundred sub-branches and for each of these an additional seventy-two thousand branches. Thus the *vyāna* permeates and invigorates the entire organism.

The fifth, and final *prāṇa* is the *udāna* ("breathing upwards). This important *prāṇa* propels the *jīva* (soul) out of the physical body at the

Divisions of *Prāṇa* According to *Praśna Upaniṣad*

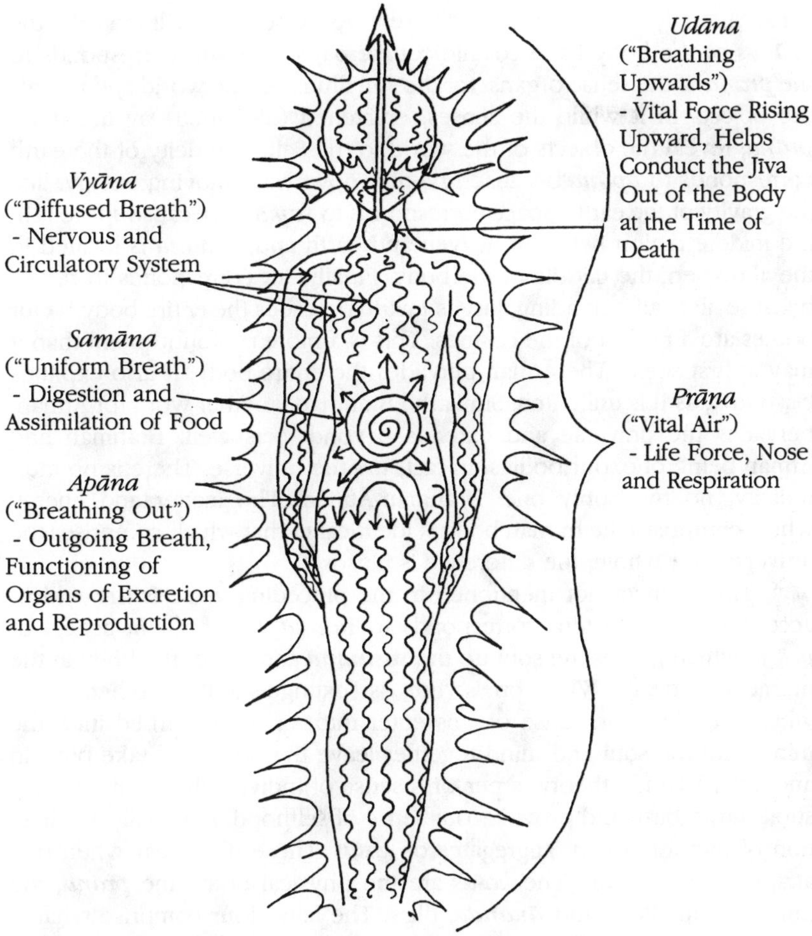

time of death and conducts it to its next destination (3.7). Described here as "ascending upward", the *udāna* is located in the *suśumnā*, the major *nāḍī* which is located in the spine.[15] The *kuṇḍalinī*, when awakened, is known to ascend the *suśumnā*; in the same way, the soul ascends by the power of the *udāna* and exits the body through the crown of the head.

Pippalāda will now address Kauśalya's last two questions, namely, how does the *prāṇa* support the external universe, how the internal universe? Actually, the two are nondifferent. As verse eight will indicate, the *prāṇas* of the body have cosmic counterparts. The sun corresponds to the *prāṇa* of the sense organs, for the sun illumines the world and reveals the objects in it while the senses, enlivened (illumined) by the inner *prāṇa*, reveal the objects of the world to the Self. The deity of the earth corresponds to *apāna* because *apāna* is downward-moving energy, like the gravity of the earth. Space corresponds to *samāna* because space is in the middle region between heaven and earth and *samāna* is located in the abdomen, the middle of the body. Finally, air corresponds to *vyāna* because air is all-pervading, just as *vyāna* pervades the entire body.[16] Our bodies are a replica of the cosmos. This is a more profound point than it may at first seem. The Ātman pervades the entire body; It also expands beyond it, as It is unlimited. Similarly, Brahman, another word for Ātman, pervades the universe and extends beyond it as well. Brahman and Ātman being one, our bodies, in fact, *are* the universe. There is no multiplicity, no two, only one: Brahman-Ātman. The matter and energy which comprises the human body is identical to that which comprises the universe as a whole; the difference is illusory.

The element not mentioned in the preceding verse is fire which, according to verse ten, corresponds to *udāna*, that brilliant aspect of *prāṇa* which guides the soul up the *suśumnā* and out of the body at the moment of death. When one's "fire" is "extinguished", in other words when one dies, the sense organs enter into, or are absorbed into, the mind, and the soul and mind together leave the body and take birth in another. In Hindu theory, a person's sense of individuality, that which is subject to rebirth and provides our sense of selfhood, is actually a collection of five temporary aggregates or *kośas*. These disappear when one attains emancipation. The *kośas* are the physical body, the *prāṇa*, the mind, the intellect, and *ānanda*, bliss. The latter four comprise what is known as the subtle body. According to this verse, the outgoing senses (not the physical organs, such as eye or ear, but the internal faculty which perceives impressions drawn in through the organs) recede, cease perceiving the outside world, and settle into the mind. The mind, as part of the subtle body, transmigrates into a new physical body, where the senses will turn outward again.

Verse ten takes up the idea suggested in verse three that the kind of body one assumes directly relates to the state of one's mind at the time of death. Generally, at the moment of death one thinks whatever one has thought about consistently through life. One gets what one desires. If one's mind is fixed on God, one attains God. If one fixates on a beloved spouse, one will assume a body resembling that person's. The *Upaniṣad* says that one's thought, combined with *prāṇa*, *udāna*, and Ātman propels one into a new existence.

The concluding verses of part three praise the preceding teaching, claiming that anyone who acquires this knowledge is fit for immortality.

Question Four: The Different States of Consciousness

Now Sauryāyaṇi ("the grandson of Sūrya"), also known as Gārgya ("of the Garga family") asks about the different states of consciousness people ordinarily experience, namely waking, dreaming sleep, and deep, dreamless sleep. This subject was also raised in the *Māṇḍūkya Upaniṣad*, though it is given more detailed attention here. The aim of the discussion is to establish that Brahman is beyond all normal states of consciousness, which are dependent on the mind, senses, or both. Consciousness of Brahman is known as *turīya*, "the fourth", meaning it is beyond waking, dream and dreamless sleep, though the bliss of dreamlessness is very close to it, and resembles it in some respects.

What is it, Gārgya asks, which goes to sleep in a person and what is it that is awake? What is it that experiences dreams? What is it that experiences the bliss of deep, dreamless sleep (here referred to only as "happiness")? In what do all these states culminate? Pippalāda will address each of these questions in turn.

Sleeping and waking are like the rising and setting of the sun, he says. When the sun is risen, the rays go outward. This is like an awake person whose senses go outward. When the sun sets, the rays seem to be drawn into the orb and all is dark. Similarly, in a sleeping person the senses cease to go out, and the outer world is unknown to the sleeper. In such a state one neither sees, hears, touches, tastes, grasps, or anything (4.2). The waking state is dependent on the senses.

The cessation of the senses in sleep, however, does not mean that the body is dead. The *prāṇa*, verses three and four say, is always awake, always keeping watch. The body is compared to a city, and the five *prāṇas* the three sacred fires which keep watch over the city, the priest which tends them, and the result of the fire sacrifices. At one time all householders of the three upper castes were required to perform ongoing *agnihotra* (fire) sacrifices as part of their *dharma*. The *Gārhapatya* fire was never allowed to go out, and the other two fires were kindled from it. These two verses construct an extremely elaborate metaphor, comparing the function of each *prāṇa* with its symbolic counterpart in the ritual. Suffice it to say, in the Vedic period rituals were believed to be necessary to maintain order in the universe. The functions of the cosmos depended on the performance of ritual. Similarly, the functioning of the body depends on the performance of *prāṇa*.

Now Pippalāda addresses the question, "What is that which sees dreams?" The answer is simple; it is the mind (here referred to as "the deity" or "the shining one"). As verse five explains, things that have been experienced while awake are experienced again in dreams, along with things that have not been experienced and things that are not even real. In dreams we see all because we *are* all; in other words, some dream material is drawn from our collective consciousness, the "universal mind", as it were, that we all share because of our shared humanness. The point is that in sleep the outgoing senses do not operate and yet we experience so much. It is the mind which is experiencing, an observation which suggests that since it does not require the physical senses to see, hear, taste, etc., there must be *internal* senses which do. The consciousness is not dependent on the senses.

The state beyond dreaming is a blissful dreamless deep sleep. In this state, verse six says, the mind is overcome by "light" and sees no dreams. "Light" refers to a state of undifferentiated consciousness, a complete absence of contrasted objects. Mind has ceased completely, and yet we are certainly not dead. In fact, this state is extremely sweet. It is akin to Brahman-realization, which is also a state beyond sensing, beyond thinking, beyond experiencing in any ordinary sense. In that state, verse eight suggests, everything is held still, settled quietly in the Ātman. The senses and their objects are stilled, mind and its content, the experience of egotism, the experience of understanding, everything is stilled.

This is not Brahman realization per se because it is temporary. However, Brahman is encountered in that state. It has to be so, for there is something that is the seer, feeler, hearer, thinker, knower, even when there is nothing to see, feel, hear, think or know. There is something behind all this, something still left. It is the supreme, changeless Self (4.9). One who realizes this — the "shadowless, bodiless, colorless, pure Immutable" — becomes It. That person becomes omniscient (4.11) because everything (senses, elements, *everything*) merges in That, everything is included in That; he or she who knows That "becomes all-knowing and enters into all" (4.12).

Question Five: *Oṃ* and the Gradual Stages Toward Brahman

In the *Māṇḍūkya Upaniṣad* the seed mantra *Oṃ* was analyzed as being of three parts, the sounds A, U and M, which correspond to the graduated levels of consciousness: waking, dreaming sleep and dreamless sleep. Together, they represent ultimate consciousness, Brahman. The *Praśna Upaniṣad* will analyze the threefold nature of *Oṃ* too, but from a different angle. *Oṃ* is All, but the All can be known by traversing it gradually, step by step. It will also be suggested here that *Oṃ* includes within it all the knowledge of the *Vedas.*

Satyakāma asks the teacher, "What world is attained by the one who meditates on *Oṃ* until death?" (5.1). *Oṃ* is Brahman, Pippalāda replies, both the lower Brahman (Aparabrahman, with qualities, as mentioned in the first chapter) and the higher Brahman (Parabrahman, beyond qualities). Through *Oṃ* one may attain either (5.3).

The sound *Oṃ* is broken down into three sounds — A, U and M. A, verse three says, represents the earth and humanity. The mantras of the *Ṛg Veda* lead one to an auspicious earthly birth; they are included in A. One who meditates on A attains such a birth.

U is identified with the mind, and meditating on U leads one to the "intermediate space, the world of the moon" (5.4). Mind is associated with dreams because dreams are a product of the mind. It is possible to take birth in a realm other than the earthly one and these states are rather like dreams because they are of the nature of ideas.[17] One enjoys them according to the deeds performed in the previous life, then returns to earth. U is associated with the *Yajur Veda.*

By meditating on M, one is led to the lower Brahman, the Brahman with qualities, known variously as *Puruṣa* (the Supreme Person), *Hiraṇyagarbha* (the Golden Womb, the Creator), and *Brahmā* (the First Born, the Highest). In verse five It is symbolized by the sun, and associated with the *Sāma Veda.*

Separately, each letter represents a relative reality, but together, they represent the total Reality, Brahman. One who knows them as joined attains an enlightened state beyond fear (5.6). This verse also makes a reference to their corresponding to "external, intermediate and internal courses of action," meaning the waking, dreaming, and deep sleep states.[18]

The three states mentioned above are, indeed, attainable, but the enlightened individual can, by meditating on *Oṃ*, achieve a state beyond all of them (5.7). This is Brahman — tranquil, quiet, not subject to decay, death, or fear.

Question Six: Brahman is the Origin and Destination of Everything

This last section explores how all things in the world have evolved from a single origin, Brahman, are nondifferent from Brahman and will eventually be absorbed back into Brahman. In Hindu theory, the cosmic creation and dissolution takes place in cycles, as though Brahman were breathing out, thereby creating the universe, then breathing in, thus drawing it back into Itself, into a state of non-being. Cosmic dissolution is known as *pralaya.* However, the cycle of creation and dissolution is constantly occurring on a microcosmic level, too. Everything that comes into existence — animals, plants, mountains, weather conditions, stars, works of art, civilizations, solar systems — disintegrates and disappears in time. It is merely the nature of things to vanish. Where do they go? They go into Brahman. So this cosmic drama of creation and dissolution is continuously happening, yet there is, in fact, never any increase or decrease because all of it is Brahman, both the manifested and the unmanifest.

Sukeśā, the final student, tells Pippalāda that he was once approached by a prince who asked a question that he could not answer. Now he puts the same question to Pippalāda: "Where is the Person with sixteen limbs?"

"Here inside the body," Pippalāda answers (6.2). In verse three the Person in question, who is of course *Puruṣa,* Brahman, ponders to Himself, "As a result of whose departure do I depart, and by whose continuance to I remain?" It is a rhetorical question; by His own volition He creates, maintains and destroys.

The "sixteen limbs" are primordial elements from which the material world evolves. In the Hindu view, creation is a gradual process of evolution from the most subtle elements to increasingly gross ones. Nothing pops up spontaneously; each element evolves naturally from a preceding one and is the natural cause of another element. Different scriptures give their own catalogue of number and order of the elements; in this *Upaniṣad* the basic ones are sixteen in number and are listed in verse four. The thing to remember is that the original cause is Brahman and that all elements share a oneness with Brahman. The sixteen "limbs" begin with *prāṇa.* Out of *prāṇa* faith evolved. From faith came space. From space, air. Then fire, water, earth, organs, mind, food (i.e. sense objects), vigor, self-control, sacred mantras, ritual, worlds, and names of things.

So it is that everything evolves out of Brahman. But Brahman is the destination of everything as well; all things evolve *back* into Brahman. The *Muṇḍaka Upaniṣad* uses the simile of a spider spinning a web from her body, then drawing it back in again (1.1.7). The *Praśna Upaniṣad* uses the metaphor of flowing rivers heading towards the sea, where "their names and forms are destroyed, and they are merely called the sea" (6.5). So, too, do the sixteen elements, which are representative of everything in the world, have *Puruṣa*, Brahman, as their goal. They, too, will disappear into Him, lose their names and forms, and simply be that *Puruṣa*. One who realizes this becomes "free from parts" and immortal (6.5).

All the parts, the multiplicity of the world, depend and rest firmly on Brahman, like spokes affixed to a wheel. "You should know that *Puruṣa* who is worthy to be known," Pippalāda exhorts his students and us, ". . . so that death may not afflict you anywhere" (6.6). One who knows Brahman is emancipated from the cycle of birth and death.

Pippalāda tells his students that he has taught them everything, for there is nothing beyond the supreme Brahman that remains to be known (6.7). This knowledge is *Vedānta*, the end-point of all possible knowing.

In the concluding verse, the students worship their teacher, for he is the gracious father who has ferried them across the ocean of ignorance to the "other shore". They also offer their salutations to all the great seers.

NOTES

1. Swāmī Gamhīrānanda, *Praśna Upaniṣad* (Calcutta: Advaita Ashrama, 1979), p. v.
2. Swāmī Nikhilānanda, *The Upanishads, Vol. II* (New York: Harper and Row, 1959), p. 153.
3. Swami Prabhavānanda and Frederick Manchester, *The Upanishads, Breath of the Eternal* (Hollywood: Vedanta Press, 1974), p. 44.
4. Nikhilānanda, p. 157.
5. Gamhīrānanda, p. 10.
6. Nikhilānanda, p. 160.
7. Nikhilānanda, p. 164.
8. Nikhilānanda, p. 167.
9. Nikhilānanda, p. 168.
10. Gamhīrānanda, p. 30.
11. Prabhavānanda, p. 47.
12. Nikhilānanda, p. 168.
13. Nikhilānanda, p. 171.
14. Nikhilānanda, p. 172.
15. Nikhilānanda, p. 173.
16. Nikhilānanda, p. 173.
17. Nikhilānanda, p. 189.
18. Nikhilānanda, p. 190.

CHAPTER TWELVE

Muṇḍaka Upaniṣad: A Meditation on the Realization of Brahman

According to Swāmī Śarvānanda, *muṇḍaka* means "razor", or a person who is shaven, such as the *sannyāsin* or monk with a shaved head. The ideal of renunciation as a requirement for Self-realization is enjoined in the text, yet the image may also refer to the shearing away of surface covering, such as ignorance, that obscures our perception of the Ātman.[1] The *Kaṭha Upaniṣad* also employs the image of a razor, there to suggest the difficulty of the spiritual path: "The sages say that the path to the realization of the spirit is as sharp as the razor's edge and very difficult to tread."[2] This *Muṇḍaka Upaniṣad* has a razor-like sharpness in style as well. Engaging and succinct, it describes the Ultimate Truth, Brahman, and how to attain realization of It.

Chapter One, Part One: Brahman is Explained

To begin with, the authority of the *Upaniṣad* is established by tracing its teachings back to the deity Brahmā who, it's said, imparted this knowledge to his eldest son, Atharvan. Atharvan taught it to Aṅgiras the elder, who taught it to Bhāradvāja, who taught it to Satyavāha, who taught it to the present Aṅgiras (1.1.1-2). Because of this unbroken line, the science of Brahman-realization is believed to be represented in this *Upaniṣad* in its pristine purity. Recall the disciplic succession described by Śrī Kṛṣṇa in the fourth chapter of the *Bhagavad Gītā.* Because the chain had been broken and the teachings lost, Kṛṣṇa had to incarnate Himself in order to restore them. In the case of this *Upaniṣad,* we can take the lineage back to Brahmā to mean that this wisdom originated with the Divine Itself; the Upaniṣadic *ṛṣis* are said to have arrived at their conclusions by *direct experience.* In other words, having achieved Brahman-realization through their own prolonged meditations, they can be said to have received this knowledge directly from Brahman.

Aṅgiras is approached by his disciple, Śaunaka, who asks the quintessential Upaniṣadic question, "What is that, knowing which, everything becomes known?" (1.1.3).

There are two kinds of knowledge, Aṅgiras begins, one higher and one lower (1.1.4). The Sanskrit term used here is not *jñāna* (spiritual knowledge), but *veda*, which refers both to the knowledge in the ordinary, worldly sense, and *the Vedas*. Both senses of the term are brought to bear here, it seems, because on the one hand the lower knowledge of which Aṅgiras speaks is the knowledge of Vedic scripture. Mere scriptural knowledge, as well as the disciplines associated with it, such as phonetics, grammar, etymology, metrics, etc., are mundane, the "lower" knowledge (1.1.5). Yet "lower knowledge" also refers to any knowledge which is not knowledge of the Supreme. It is knowledge of worldly subjects and things arrived at by our ordinary senses and mental processes. All knowledge as we ordinarily understand it, then, is lower knowledge. All experiences, all impressions, all thoughts, fall into this category.

Higher knowledge is direct perception of the Imperishable Being (Brahman). This Being is invisible, ungraspable, unoriginated and attributeless. The wise perceive that which is eternal, all-pervading and limitless as the source of all creation (1.1.6). We can infer that since Brahman is the source of everything, by knowing Brahman everything is known. Aṅgiras provides three similes for this, namely that of the spider emitting and withdrawing its web, herbs sprouting from the ground, and hair growing from a man's head (1.1.7). The first simile suggests that, like a spider emitting and withdrawing its web, Brahman projects the universe from Itself and at the time of cosmic dissolution draws it back into Itself. The universe and Brahman — its source as well as its destination — are non-different. Brahman expands and differentiates itself and becomes this world. The second simile illustrates how, like herbs growing from the ground, after creation the universe rests in Brahman as its sole support. Brahman is the substratum of all existence as well as that which exists upon the substratum. The third simile suggests that, like hair growing from one's head, creation is effortless and spontaneous.[3] Our hair doesn't grow by any act of volition on our own part; it is a natural process. Similarly, Brahman "grows", or differentiates itself to create the manifest world, without exertion or effort of any kind. Brahman is changeless; it is never affected by anything, nor does it in any real sense "act". This concept is reminiscent of the Taoist concept of *Wu Wei*, the "effortless effort" or "actionless action" of the Ultimate Truth, the Tao. The Tao doesn't work, it doesn't try or strive, yet as the active power which motivates the universe, it accomplishes all things.

Verse eight describes the step-by-step unfolding of the elements of creation from Brahman. This is a foreshadowing of what will be the main concern of Chapter Two. Brahman broods with Its own creativity and "food" is born. As we have seen in the *Upaniṣads* studied so far, "food" symbolizes the original Object — primal matter, Nature, that which is experienced (in a sense, "eaten" because it is drawn in through the senses). From food, *prāṇa* (life force, animating energy) comes into being, then mind (our individual minds are considered parts of a universal mind), the five elements, and then entanglement in works, *karma.*

Chapter One, Part Two: The Limited Role of Good Works

Vedic rituals, which were designed primarily for material safety and profit, bring their rewards, but they do not bestow immortality, which is the goal of our existence. Only the Seeker who knows the science of Brahman achieves this aim. Such is the message of Part Two.

The first seven verses of this section describe the sacred fire ceremony and the benefits which accrue from participation in it, for pouring oblations is considered a meritorious act which bears good fruit. Here the sacrificial act and the fruits thereof are a metaphor for all work performed with personal gain in mind. This entangles us in the snares of *karma,* the same *karma* mentioned in verse eight of the previous section. Even good *karma* is a bondage because it pulls us away from the perception of Brahman. Verse nine reads:

> Engrossed in the ways of the ignorant, these people childishly think that they have gained the end in life. But being subject to passions and attachment, they never attain knowledge, and therefore they sink down, wretched, when the fruits of their good deeds are exhausted.

Worldly works and their results are fine, but they will never lead us anywhere except into more worldly works. There is a profound futility about the whole thing. "Having scrutinized the worlds gained by deeds," verse twelve reads, "the man of spiritual inclination should become indifferent to them; for deeds which are originated cannot win the Supreme, who is unoriginated . . ." One should instead, with a tranquil mind and controlled senses, approach a teacher who is established in knowledge of Brahman and learn from him or her (1.2.11-13). The subject of spiritual practice will be taken up again in the second section of Chapter Two.

Chapter Two, Part One: All Creation Emanates from Brahman

Just as thousands of sparks spring from a blazing fire and fall back into it again, so too are manifold beings projected from the Imperishable

One (2.1.1). This section poetically describes how all of creation sprang from Brahman and is Brahman. He is the indwelling spirit of all, but He is also outside. The universe is Him. "Fire is His head, the sun and moon His eyes . . . the *Vedas* His voice, the wind His breath . . ." (2.1.4).

Verse five addresses a subject called *pañcāgnividyā*, or "science of the five fires". It is a poetic image suggestive of how Brahman is the starting point of nature's chains — food chains, the nitrogen cycle, etc.. The "five fires" are heaven, clouds, herbs, man and woman. Tradition has it that the moon in heaven puts forth rain clouds. The clouds shower rain onto the earth and cause the herbs to grow. The herbs are eaten by a man and endow him with vigor. The man then makes love to a woman and ignites her body with new life.[4] This elaborate metaphor makes a simple point, that everything has evolved from a single origin.

Everything is born from Brahman, the *Upaniṣad* continues, and everything rests in Him. Verse six describes how the *Vedas*, the rites associated with them, the time of the sacrifice, the sacrificer, and the fruits of the sacrifice all come from Brahman. This is a highly evolved idea, showing how religion itself, directed to the Absolute, has it source in the Absolute as well. In his lecture entitled *Ritualism*, Swami Ashokānanda points out how this concept is echoed in the Christian doctrine of the great sacrifice, where Christ is the priest (see Hebrews, seventh chapter), the God to whom the sacrifice is directed, and the object of sacrifice.[5]

That all living beings — *devas*, people, animals, birds and plants — come from Brahman is described in verse seven. Religious virtues, namely austerity, faith, truth, continence, and moral injunctions also come from Brahman, as do our ingoing and outgoing breaths, in other words our very life force and vital functions (*prāṇa*).

Our senses come from Brahman, as does their power to cognize (2.1.8). All of the objects which they perceive come from Him as well. In other words, our very perceptions, our experience of being ourselves and experience of the world beyond ourselves all have their source in Brahman. The verse refers to the "seven seats of sense-life traversed by the life forces." These are the active anterior principles, or nerve centers, associated with each bodily sense opening (two eyes, two ears, two nostrils, and the mouth).[6] The point of the verse is that it is Brahman which endows the living creature with the consciousness to perceive, the organs of perception, and the objects which are perceived. Our whole experience is derived from, and rooted in, Brahman.

The natural world is born of Brahman, including the oceans, mountains, rivers, and the food — here in verse nine referred to as "herbs and sap" — which supports the life of living beings. The Earth is our wonderful mother, a living, nurturing organism which feeds us and upon which we are dependent. Biologically and spiritually all living things are subtly and inextricably interdependent, and all things are dependent on Brahman, the source of everything.

The section ends by stating that the Omnipresent Being who is the source of all the aforementioned actually *is* all this — religion, knowledge, virtue, beings, nature, everything that exists. While everywhere and all, He is situated particularly in the heart, and He can be known.

Chapter Two, Part Two: How to Realize Brahman

Again, Brahman is described as "the great support" (2.2.1), as It was in the simile of the ground which sprouts herbs. Everything rests in It and is a part of It. Sometimes Brahman is known as *ādheya-ādhāra*, the ground of Being (*ādheya*) and that which stands upon that ground (*ādhāra*). It is fit to be adored (2.2.1). It is beyond understanding, yet the *Upaniṣad* exhorts us to know It. How can we know that which cannot be understood? Clearly, "understanding" is of the realm of lower knowledge spoken of in Chapter One. We "understand" with our ordinary intellectual and sensual faculties and these cannot bring us to knowledge of Brahman. We must avail ourselves to the higher knowledge, a radically different mode of knowing.

Verse two suggests how this higher knowledge can be approached. I say "approached" because at the outset we have nothing *but* our ordinary faculties to work with. Therefore, that is where we must start. We can use our senses and mind to transcend our senses and mind. Life, speech, and mind are all Brahman, the verse says. Just as we can't see our own eyeballs because the eyes are that by which we see (*Kena Upaniṣad*, 1.7), Brahman, being the mind, cannot be known as an object perceived by the mind. Yet, "That (Brahman) is the mark which should be penetrated by the mind. Penetrate it, O my friend" (2.2.2.).

The mind can be transcended when it is brought under control through meditation, and this is only done by the mind itself. The next two verses illustrate this point with the apt metaphor of the bow and arrow. The *Upaniṣads* furnish the mighty bow, which is *Oṃ*. The Ātman within is the arrow, made sharp by meditation. Brahman is the target. Drawing the arrow back is withdrawing the senses from external contacts. Aiming is fixing the mind steadily on Brahman. One should then hit the mark, and, like an arrow piercing its target, become one with It (2.2.3-4).

We are one with it anyway, but we just don't realize it. ". . . know Him alone as the one Self of all, and desist from all other talk" (2.2.5). While the Ātman pervades the entire body — nay, the entire cosmos —

yogīs like to meditate upon It as seated in the heart, and it is to this which verse six refers: "Within the heart, It moves, becoming manifold." "Becoming manifold" refers to the infinite modifications the embodied Ātman appears to undergo. In truth, the Ātman is unlimited and changeless, but due to our ignorance it appears, in the guise of ourselves, to change constantly (experiencing happiness, anger, pride, etc.) and to become many (the multitude of living beings).[7] Again, we are urged to "meditate on that Self as *Oṃ*" (2.2.6).

In both the Buddhist and Jain traditions, the image of crossing a river to an opposite shore is often employed as a metaphor for moving beyond the perceptual bondage of the world to a state of Enlightenment. So, too, does the *Upaniṣad*, which adds that this shore is characterized by darkness, which is a universal symbol for ignorance, and that the farther shore is beyond darkness, in other words, is a state of realization (2.2.6).

Verse seven further describes Brahman as dwelling within the body, in *Brahmapuram*, the "City of Brahman", or the heart.[8] The heart motif is carried over to the next verse, which employs a metaphor we see frequently in other *Upaniṣads*, the knots of the heart. "When a person realizes Him in both the high and the low, the knots of his heart are loosened, his doubts dispelled, and his *karmas* exhausted" (2.2.8). The knots of the heart are the desires, fixations and egoistic tendencies which keep us in bondage and ignorant of Brahman. When one realizes the Supreme, these "knots" are "loosened" and they vanish. By seeing Brahman everywhere, in the high and the low, the good and the bad, the beautiful and the ugly, the criminal and the saint, It is rightly known. One of the most persistent "knots" is prejudicial discrimination, thinking, "I'm attracted to this; I'm repulsed by that." Good and bad are transitory, relative, ultimately unreal. When the sage sees everything as Brahman, nothing can be viewed as high or low. The verse also refers to the *karmas* being exhausted. When one takes to spiritual practice, the accumulated past *karmas* are completely exhausted, and one is free.

"He is the light of all that shines," verse nine reads. A lovely and potent metaphor, "light" refers both to physical light, such as the sun, stars and fire, which make the world knowable to us, and to the light of knowledge, which makes the Supreme knowable to us. Both have Brahman behind them. Being full of Brahman, everything "shines"; the whole universe is the glorious manifestation of Brahman. Brahman is the beauty, the meaning , the power behind every object.

The section has examined Brahman from two angles: from the localized view, as the Ātman situated in the individual's heart, and from the universal view, as the all-pervading oneness. It is with this latter angle that the section ends, reminding us that Brahman is "everywhere —

above, below, in front, at the back, upon the right, upon the left! All this world is indeed the Supreme Brahman!" (2.2.11).

Chapter Three, Part One: On Brahman (or Self) Realization

The famous parable of the two birds perched on the same tree which opens the third chapter of the *Muṇḍaka* is also found in the *Śvetāśvatara Upaniṣad.* One bird is busy eating the fruits on the tree, sometimes enjoying, sometimes suffering, while the other calmly watches him (3.1.1-2). The busy bird is our limited self, compulsively and ignorantly gorging on sense objects and oblivious to our true Self, which is the changeless, peaceful One, symbolized by the observing bird. The two birds are, in fact, one, though they appear as two because of wrong perception, just as Brahman and the individual *jīva* appear as separate. When the first bird stops and sees the second bird as his own true Self, his suffering ceases. He sees his own true glory.

So it is when the seer realizes the effulgent One within and, attaining union with It, becomes perfect (3.1.3). Such a sage is always joyful; he sports with the Self, delights in the Self, speaks only sublime words of wisdom, never sliding into vain, useless chatter (3.1.4). How is this effulgent Self realized? Verse five explains: through vigilant truthfulness, austerity, concentration on the Supreme and continence. These practices cause impurities to dissolve and the Self to be realized. The supreme necessity of truthfulness is emphasized in verse six, which indicates that the "divine path", the path to Realization, is tread by those devoted to truthfulness.

But there is another sort of truth, a truth beyond the duality of lie or fact, and this higher truth is alluded to in verse seven. It is the truth of Brahman, the Ultimate Truth, which is both localized in the individual heart, and unimaginably vast, beyond the beyond.

Again the *Upaniṣad* suggests how It can be known. Verse eight says that It certainly cannot be described in words. Brahman is unlimited, and words define by imposing limitations on things. When we call a thing a chair, for instance, we mean it is not a book, not a mountain, not the sun. It is a chair only, a limited thing. Our reasoning, verbalizing mind creates a false perception of the world by placing limits upon everything. Brahman, however, cannot be reduced to the limitations of language and the divisions it naturally suggests.

The verse continues by stating that It cannot be known by means of the senses, an idea which should be well-known to the reader by now, so persistent is it a theme in the *Upaniṣads.* It cannot be known through rituals and penances, either. Only by purifying and refining the consciousness can It be known. When one draws the consciousness away from externals and fixes it, in meditation, on the Supreme, the Supreme is known.

"By means of thought one should know the subtle truth of the Ātman," verse nine reads, but "thought" here does not mean the ordinary, intellectual faculties, which have already been rejected as a means of knowing Brahman. "Thought" here means the rarified, purified consciousness, free from modifications, an intuitive sense. The Ātman is "permeated by life-force in a fivefold way." This is a reference to the five divisions of *prāṇa* as outlined in the *Praśna Upaniṣad*, in other words the energies which cause the body's vital functions to operate. As long as our mind and senses are fixed on such externals as the body, or sense objects, the Self will remain obscured. "Man's thought is interwoven with the senses" (3.1.9). However, if thought is turned inward, the Ātman is perceived: "When that (thought) is purified, the Self shines forth."

The section concludes by saying that whatever a Self-realized sage fixes his mind and desire upon, he obtains, therefore one should pay honor to such a sage (3.1.10). Of course, one should know that a Self-realized sage only fixes his mind on one thing — Brahman. This is, in fact, why the sage deserves honor. People of lesser realization might honor a sage because of his worldly reputation, his *siddhis* (supernatural abilities), or his retinue, but wise people honor him because of his knowledge of Brahman, as indicated in the first verse of the next section.

Chapter Three, Part Two: On the Sage Who Has Attained Brahman Realization

Wise people devoted to such a sage go beyond rebirth (3.2.1). Such is the nature of the *guru*-disciple relationship; following the master, the disciple achieves his or her own emancipation. Rebirth is the result of desire and longing for sense objects. The sage has found all longings fulfilled in the Ātman, and so his desires vanish completely (3.2.2). This is an important point to keep in mind. By giving up worldly desires we are only giving up our suffering. True joy, true fulfillment, can only be found in the Ātman, not in any material thing. Attachment to sense objects, ego, etc. only leads to perpetual frustration.

One sort of longing leads to emancipation, of course, and that is longing for the Self. Discourses, intellectualism and book learning alone do not liberate; when one longs for the Self wholeheartedly, the Self reveals Itself to the aspirant (3.2.4). The weak-willed, the careless, and those given to improper austerities (mortifications or ill-advised yogic experiments) will not gain the Self (3.2.4). Indeed, the path to Brahman-realization is full of failures, set-backs, dry spells and disappointments. Without strength of character and stubborn stick-to-itness, the aspirant will likely fall away. As verse four says, those "who strive with vigor, attention and propriety attain union with Brahman."

The next five verses discuss what a Brahman-realized soul is like and what he or she experiences. Such a person, verse five says, finds complete satisfaction, and longs for nothing more. He is perfect, not attached to anything, and wonderfully tranquil. Realizing that the all-pervading Spirit is everywhere and everything, he "enter(s) into the All." In other words, he recognizes himself as one with everything.

The illumined one becomes absorbed into the All, into Brahman. The second chapter discussed how all things evolved out of Brahman, though it did not offer meticulous details. Other scriptures, such as the *Praśna Upaniṣad*, *Aitareya Upaniṣad*, and *Śrīmad Bhāgavatam*, do give detailed accounts, and while they differ somewhat, they all agree that the universe gradually evolved from very subtle elements into increasingly gross ones, each element arising spontaneously as a result of the previous element. The sage's journey to oneness with Brahman is rather like the reversal of this process, moving backward from grosser elements to more and more subtle ones, each being absorbed into its predecessor. This is indicated in verse seven, which says that when Brahman is realized, the sage's "fifteen phases evolve into their sources." This is an involution toward oneness. According to the *Praśna Upaniṣad* (6.4), from *prāṇa*, the basic elemental building block, comes faith, from faith, space, from space, air, from air, fire, then water, earth, organs, mind, food (sense objects), vigor, self-control, mantras, rites, worlds, and names of things. Here, in the *Muṇḍaka Upaniṣad*, these "fifteen phases" are said to be absorbed back, one into the other, until fully absorbed into their original source, Brahman. This is the technical description of the phenomenon so aptly illustrated by the spider drawing her web back into herself.

In traditional Vedic imagery, each of the senses belongs to a presiding deity, and verse seven continues by saying that at the time of illumination, one's senses return to their corresponding deities. Thus, the material components of one's being are absorbed, as are one's senses. This is no loss, as oneness with Brahman means absolute and unlimited Consciousness, oneness with All, beyond limitations and the puniness of the material senses and their objects. At last, one's deeds (the need to perform actions as well as the *karma* that results from them) and one's personality are resolved into the Supreme.

> Just as rivers, flowing, disappear into the ocean, losing name and form, so the wise man, free from name and form, goes unto the highest of the high — the Supreme Divinity (3.2.8).

Whoever knows Brahman becomes Brahman (3.2.9). This is the ultimate conclusion to which the *Upaniṣad* has been alluding all along. There was never a time when any of us were *not* Brahman, but the task at hand is to realize this in truth. One's whole family is blessed when a member attains this supreme state; in fact, no one ignorant of Brahman is born into such an august family (3.2.9).

The *Upaniṣad* closes with two verses exhorting one who teaches the spiritual knowledge contained in this *Upaniṣad* to impart it only to the deserving pupil, one who is learned, devoted to God, full of faith, and attends to his ritualistic duties, in this case performing Vedic rites and making oblations into the sacred fire, the *ekarṣi*. The verse also mentions a rite called *śirovrata*, the exact nature of which is unknown. The word literally means "observance regarding the head", and Swāmī Śarvānanda writes that it may refer to shaving the head, as is alluded to in the title of the *Upaniṣad*. However, he also cites Śaṅkarācārya, who believed it referred to a rite mentioned in the *Atharva Veda* where a fire is carried on the head.[9] Westerners, of course, are not responsible for such culturally-specific ritualistic acts. The import is that the ideal pupil attends to the responsibilities of his or her station in life, whatever they may be.

"This is the very truth," the piece closes, as Aṅgiras Ṛṣi communicated it in ancient times. It is meant for the sincere spiritual aspirant only. "No one who has not observed any vow should study it" (3.2.11). This doesn't mean that it is privileged information and off-limits to secular readers, rather that only those of genuine spiritual inclination, those given to observing vows and performing regular spiritual practices, will fully understand and appreciate its message. This is true of any sacred literature.

NOTES

1. Swāmī Śarvānanda, *Muṇḍakopaniṣad*, (Mylapore: Sri Ramakrishna Math, 1974), p. 3.
2. Swāmī Ashokānanda, *Meditation, Ecstasy and Illumination* (Calcutta: Advaita Ashrama, 1990), p. 75.
3. Śarvānanda, p. 16.
4. Śarvānanda, p. 37.

5. Ashokānanda, pp. 144-145.
6. Śarvānanda, p. 40.
7. Śarvānanda, p. 48.
8. Śarvānanda, p. 49.
9. Śarvānanda, p. 76.

CHAPTER THIRTEEN

Kaṭha Upaniṣad: A Meditation on Death, Life, and Liberation

The *Kaṭha Upaniṣad* is so named because it belongs to the *Kaṭha Śākhā* section of the *Black Yajur Veda.*[1] It is perhaps the best-known *Upaniṣad* because it is framed in the charming story of Naciketā and his visit with Yama, the god of death. Several elements of this piece — the chariot metaphor, the razor's edge, and the upside-down peepul tree, for instance — are so well-known as to be Hindu standards, and certain verses are either identical or very similar to verses from the *Bhagavad-Gītā* and/or other *Upaniṣads.* The underlying theme is how to overcome death or, more precisely, how to become free from the cycle of birth-death-and-rebirth through knowledge of the Supreme Self. The teacher here is Death personified, the god Yama, whose name means "restrainer" or "cessation".[2] However, we learn that death is not an end, merely a means to acquiring a new body, because the true Self is eternal and changeless, beyond the jurisdiction of death. The secret is that there is no life or death, only ignorance and knowledge, and if a mere boy like Naciketā can attain such ultimate knowledge, so, too, can we.

Chapter One, Part One: The Story of Naciketā

The whole of section one is devoted to the story of Naciketā's descent into the abode of death. Though a mere boy, Naciketā is of a sterling character. He is selfless, reverent, polite, renounced, wise and of an advanced spiritual temperament. His self-sacrifice and disdain for material opulence are exemplary. Ultimately, he will achieve Brahman-realization, but even at the outset he possesses the qualifications of an ideal disciple, particularly an ability to discern what is important and what is not.

As the story opens, Naciketā's father is hoping to accrue merit by performing a special rite in which he gives away all of his possessions to the *brāhmaṇas.* The gesture is tempered, however, by the sorry state of his cows, which are skinny, old, and milkless. Seeing this, Naciketā hopes to rectify the situation by surrendering *himself* as an offering. "To whom do you offer me?" he asks his father, who is not paying attention. He asks a second time, then a third, only to annoy his father to such an extent that the man snaps, "To Death I offer you!", a sort of Vedic version of "drop dead!" or "go to hell!"

Naciketā considers the situation. Compared to some people he is the best, compared to others just okay. Is he a suitable offering to the god of death? What can his father achieve through him? Determined to find out, Naciketā journeys to the abode of death.

It just so happens that Yama is away when Naciketā arrives, so the boy sits down and waits. Three days pass. When Yama arrives, he is horrified, for having a *brāhmaṇa* in one's home without feeding him is a grievous transgression of etiquette, so terrible in fact, that it brings misfortune to the host. To compensate for his rudeness, Yama offers his guest three boons.

First, Naciketā asks that his father's anger be extinguished and that he be recognized and welcome when he returns. Yama is only too happy to grant such a wish. Next, Naciketā wants to be taught how to perform the sacred fire ceremony which leads to higher realms (though not Brahman-realization) after death. Yama goes him one better, and names the fire sacrifice after him. Finally, Naciketā asks his third boon. "Upon the death of a man," he asserts, "some say he exists; others says he does not exist. Explain the nature of death to me."

This is the one boon Yama does not want to grant. Even the gods, he explains, aren't privy to such knowledge. It is subtle, difficult to comprehend. Ask another boon, he insists.

Naciketā is persistent. What other boon is comparable to this? Yama tries to tempt him away by offering material opulence instead: riches, dancing girls, long life, children and grandchildren, chariots, elephants, vast expanses of land, all delectable things. But Naciketā is unmoved. These are ephemeral objects, he protests, which waste away the vigor of the senses and disappear in time. They are of the nature of Yama and his abode, subject to decay and death, no source of lasting happiness. Now that he has gone beyond the limits of the ordinary world and glimpsed death, how could he take delight in such vain pleasures? No, only that wisdom which can take him to the realization beyond birth and death will do.

Chapter One, Part Two: The Good and the Pleasurable

With Part Two the real substance of the *Upaniṣad* begins. As with other *Upaniṣads*, the speaker does not leap instantly into the highest philosophical teachings about Brahman, but develops the subject systematically and gradually, laying the foundation first, then building up to the most esoteric wisdom. Here, Yama begins by making a basic distinction. In this world, he says, there is *preyaḥ*, that which is pleasurable, and *śreyaḥ*, that which is preferable, i.e. good for you. The intelligent person can distinguish which is which, and chooses *śreyaḥ*, the preferable (1.2.1-2). In his commentary on the *Kaṭha Upaniṣad*, Eknath Easwaran draws a delightful picture to illustrate *preyaḥ* and *śreyaḥ*. If the world is a nightclub, *preyaḥ* is personified as "Mr. Popular", all decked out in the trendiest clothes and latest haircut. Surrounded by people drawn to his superficial charm, he is loud, vulgar, and shallow but flashy enough to attract the admiration of the greatest number of people. Across the room, alone and unnoticed by anyone, sits *śreyaḥ*, personified as a very subdued, quiet girl. Dressed plainly, wearing no makeup, she doesn't draw attention to herself, but perhaps one person in the room will notice that her sweet, serene face has a supernatural beauty. If that person takes the trouble to look her way, and possesses the character to recognize it, he or she will discover her to be of a vastly superior nature to anyone else present. In her subtlety and simplicity lies all wisdom, meaning, depth, love.[3]

Very few people are drawn to *śreyaḥ* because its superior nature is not immediately apparent. As Kṛṣṇa says is the *Bhagavad- Gītā*, "Out of many thousands, scarcely anyone strives for perfection, and of the striving, scarcely anyone knows Me in truth" (7.3). *Śreyaḥ* is renunciation, egolessness, selfless service, spiritual practice. *Preyaḥ* is the false glamour of worldly attainments and pleasures, just what Naciketā rejects. Those who choose *śreyaḥ* find their well-being assured, while those attracted to *preyaḥ* fall short of life's goal (2.1). Even in the material realm, *śreyaḥ* promotes well-being. Simple, wholesome food, for instance, is *śreyaḥ*, and promotes physical and emotional health, while rich, gourmet fare is *preyaḥ* and can contribute to illness. Similarly, simple, natural pleasures such as a walk, a conversation, or baking a loaf of bread are vastly more satisfying than the artificially arousing pleasures provided by technology.

The less evolved individual chooses *preyaḥ*, thinking that it promotes growth and security (1.2.2). This is, of course, a mistake. Verses five and six compare the courses in life taken by the wise and by the ignorant, and conclude that the ignorant, "thinking themselves intelligent and enlightened, go round and round following crooked courses, just like the blind led by the blind" (1.2.5). Lured by wealth, these people believe this world to be all there is, and thus fall under Yama's sway again and again (1.2.6).

The ignorant cannot understand the Self even if It is explained to them (1.2.7-8). On the other hand, wonderful indeed is the preceptor who imparts knowledge of the Self, and wonderful indeed the disciple capable of receiving It. It cannot be understood by the less intelligent because they will arrive at various opinions regarding It and It is not subject to interpretation or variation (1.2.8). It is what It is and one can know it only by direct perception. It is beyond argumentation; to speculate about It is to not know It in truth.

Yama praises Naciketā's wisdom and resolution (1.2.9) and explains that he, Yama, attained his present stature through austerity and sacrifice (1.2.10). By piling impermanent treasures into the fire as an act of sacrifice, the relative permanence of his abode was achieved. The *devas* such as Yama, Indra, Vāyu etc. are not immortal. So vast and powerful are they, they are considered gods and *seem* immortal, but they are not on the same level as Brahman or one of It's forms, such as Śiva, Kṛṣṇa or the Divine Mother. Some day, each *deva* is bound to die. Verse ten refers to the ritualistic system of the Vedic religion, a recurring metaphor in the *Upaniṣads* which symbolizes actions performed with gain in mind. The objects offered up in sacrifice are impermanent, and that which is impermanent can only produce something else impermanent. While Yama's state appears permanent from our point of view, it is not; some day his reign will end. We must never seek the permanent in the impermanent.

Naciketā, having examined worldly and heavenly things, rejects them all for something infinitely superior (1.2.11). This something is introduced formally in verse twelve. Giving up both happiness and sorrow (for they belong to the realm of the impermanent), the wise individual concentrates on the eternal Self. It is inscrutable and "lodged in the intellect", intellect here not referring to the ordinary, limited mechanism of thought, but to the pure, rarified consciousness that is anterior to thought. It is "seated in the midst of misery", in other words located within and thus covered by the modifications associated with being an individual, such as illness, old age, desire, frustration, and so on. The Self, however, is certainly separate from the body, and when one realizes It one experiences the ultimate delight, for It is the cause of all delight (1.2.13).

Naciketā now asks to be told of That which is beyond all dualities, beyond virtue and vice, cause and effect, past and future (1.2.14). Yama replies very simply, by imparting the mantra *Oṃ*. *Oṃ* is the sound representation of Brahman, and Brahman can be known by means of it. "I tell you briefly of that goal which the *Vedas* with one voice propound . . . it is *Oṃ*" (1.2.15). *Oṃ* is both the "inferior" Brahman, the aspect with qualities which unfolds itself as the universe, and the "superior" Brahman, the changeless, formless Supreme which transcends all. Anyone who meditates on *Oṃ* can achieve either aspect of Brahman he or she desires (1.2.16-17).

Verses eighteen through twenty-one describe Brahman. Verse eighteen is almost identical to the *Bhagavad-Gītā* verse 2.20 and verse nineteen to *Gītā* verse 2.19. The Self, verse eighteen says, is eternal; It is never born and never dies. It has no origin, but always was. It is not affected when the body dies. It is never killed, verse nineteen continues, nor does It kill. In *Gītā* terminology, killing refers to action or work in general (Arjuna being a *kṣatriya*, or warrior, killing is his *dharma* or duty, thus, in the broader sense, "killing" means any kind of action or work). The Self never acts. Only the *guṇas* act. The Self is changeless and serene. While It is the subtlest of all things, It is the greatest of all things, and It is located in the heart of every creature. When one becomes desireless and the bodily organs (the senses, mind, etc.) become serene, the Self can be perceived (1.2.20).

This Self is of a paradoxical nature. While It is eternally stationary (does nothing), It "travels far away" (does everything). While "sleeping" (devoid of all movement, all qualities, all volition) it "goes everywhere" (is all movement, qualities, volition) (1.2.21). What verse sixteen referred to as the "superior" and "inferior" sides of Brahman are examined here in greater detail. Brahman is both immanent, as the universe and everything in it, and transcendent, completely beyond the universe and unaffected by anything that occurs here. "Who but I," Yama asks, "can know that deity which is both joyful and joyless?" Yama is not suggesting that he and he alone knows Brahman, rather that only people of similar realization can. Brahman is "joyful" because It is supreme *ānanda*, bliss itself. It is "joyless" because It is beyond all attributes, all qualities, all experiences apart from pure Being.

Verse twenty-three is identical to *Muṇḍaka Upaniṣad* verse 3.23. It states that this Self (Brahman) cannot be known through intellectual speculation or theorizing. Reading books about It or thinking about It will not bring direct realization of It because It is that by which the mind is able to think, and not an outward object which the mind can contemplate. It is the Self itself, not a separate thing one can perceive. Verse twenty-four says that the Self is obscured by a dissipative mind and senses. The section closes with a curiously veiled metaphor: "How can anyone know where the Self is, for which both the *brāhmaṇas* and *kṣatriyas* become food, and for which death takes the place of a curry (condiment)?" The point is that *brāhmaṇas* and *kṣatriyas* are the highest castes; they are the protectors and rulers of the others, the upholders of *dharma*, very mighty in the worldly sense. Yet their earthly status, like all earthly things, means nothing. It is temporary, fleeting, and tiny. Before

Brahman they are mere food. Here now, gone in an instant, absorbed into the formlessness of Brahman, as all things eventually must. In the *Bhagavad-Gītā*, Kṛṣṇa says, "I am Time, the destroyer of worlds, come forth to annihilate all" (11.32). Nothing in this world is permanent; everything will eventually disappear. It is Brahman which causes this to happen, and all things flow into It, disappear into It. The *Gītā* illustrates this phenomenon with the image of all things rushing ceaselessly into the open mouth of God. Though couched in veiled language, the *Upaniṣad* is expressing the same idea. It takes it a step further, though, by suggesting that even death itself is a temporary, ephemeral thing, though an adjunct to the ever-destructive force of Brahman, the "condiment" on the "food".

Chapter One, Part Three: Self-Control as the Means to Realization

There are two dwellers in the body, or, in this case, "enjoyers of the inevitable results of work" (1.3.1). These are the limited self and the infinite Self, the "two birds on the same branch" spoken of in the *Muṇḍaka* and *Śvetāśvatara Upaniṣads.* The infinite Self is not an enjoyer in the same sense as the finite self because It is never affected by anything. It is an "enjoyer" in the sense that It is the perceiver. It is the consciousness behind all conscious experiences. These two enjoyers exist in the cavity of the heart, verse one says. Knowers of Brahman (the liberated), the worshippers of the five fires, and those who perform the *Naciketā* sacrifice compare the two indwellers to light and shade. The shade is the finite personality, a mere reflection of the infinite Self[4], which is the source of all light, an idea which will be taken up again in verse 2.2.15.

The *Naciketā* fire is a bridge to another world, verse two says, but there is also Brahman, the knowledge of which takes one beyond, to a wholly other shore, where fear does not exist. Hinduism believes that there are worlds other than this one, still material, still subject to decline and death, into which people may take birth in order to more intensely suffer or enjoy the karmic results of their actions here on earth. Their terms there are limited, and when their *karma* is exhausted they come back here to continue their spiritual struggle. Ritualistic performances, such as the *Naciketā* fire, are meritorious enough to warrant one's being born in a particular "heaven", but this is merely another realm of enjoyment, every bit as binding as our world. One is advised to renounce even this and concentrate on attaining freedom.

Verses three through nine introduce the famous metaphor of the driver and chariot. It illustrates our physical and psychological makeup and suggests the means of attaining self-control. Our body is like a chariot. The Self is the master of the chariot, in other words, the passenger. The intellect is the charioteer, the mind the reins. The senses are the horses and the objects of the senses are the roads. When the mind is undisciplined, the senses run rampant, just as horses grow unruly when the reins are slack. The intellect must control the wild mind, as the charioteer controls the reins. When the mind is controlled, the senses are quiet, like horses tamed. He who lacks a discriminating intellect lacks a controlled mind, and his chariot runs everywhere, returning ever to worldly existence. On the other hand, the one endowed with a discriminating intellect learns to control the reins of the mind, and can direct the chariot to the ultimate goal from which there is no rebirth, the abode of Viṣṇu (Brahman).

Similar to *Bhagavad-Gītā* verse 3.42 is verse ten, which begins, "Sense objects are higher than the senses." This does not refer to material objects observed by the senses, but to the inner organs of sense anterior to the senses themselves. The senses are merely conduits, holes through which waves of light, sound, etc. enter our bodies. They have no consciousness of their own, no powers of sensation or experience. There are inner organs which actually register the sensation; the outer objects are imprinted on these, actually *produced* by these if you consider that sight, for instance, is a phenomenon that occurs because an image is produced by and perceived by mechanisms confined entirely to the inside of our brains, as is taste, touch, and so on. Our perceptions of objects exist only in our own heads, so the objects can be conceived of a being created there. Thus the statement, "The sense-objects are higher than the senses." The verse continues, stating that mind is higher than the sense objects. Higher than the mind is the intellect. And higher than the intellect is the Great Soul (*mahān ātmā*), Brahman. In this verse we follow the layers of our experience of selfhood back, back and through more and more subtle stages until we reach That beyond which there is nothing more. The Self, we discover, is the supreme End, the Ultimate Truth.

Even within Brahman, though, there are levels of subtlety (1.3.11). The lowest level of Brahman is *mahat*. This is the cosmic principle of knowing, the ocean of awareness. It corresponds to *buddhi* in the individual.[5] The "Unmanifested" is higher than *mahat*. Śaṅkarācārya defines this as "that which is the seed of the whole universe, the essence of unmanifested name and form . . . like the power of a banyan tree in a tiny banyan seed."[6] Beyond even this is *Puruṣa*, the Supreme Self, the Ultimate Being. There is nothing higher than this, it is *the* culmination.

While He exists in all beings, He is hidden from them, and hence does not appear as the Self (1.3.12). He can, however, be known "through a pointed and fine intellect." By actually following the step-by-step progression of selfhood back, one can discover the Brahman within. Verse thirteen explains how to do this. First, one should "merge the organ of speech into the mind." This means all of the senses. Drawing the senses away from external objects, one should let them be absorbed and disappear into the mind. Mind, then, should be brought back and merged into the intellect. Intellect should be merged into the *mahat* (the universal ocean of awareness), and *mahat* merged into the "peaceful Self", Brahman. Thus each layer of our finite self is transcended until the Ultimate is revealed.

But no one ever said it was easy. "Arise! Awake!" verse fourteen exhorts, "and learn by approaching the excellent ones. The wise ones describe the path to be as impassable as a razor's edge which, when sharpened, is difficult to tread." One of the reasons it is so hard, the next verse explains, is because the Supreme is so subtle, without any tangible attributes upon which to grab hold. It is without sound, substance, color, taste, aroma, form or limit. There are no sides, no surfaces, nothing the rationalizing mind can use to construct a sense of understanding. Nevertheless, by knowing This, one becomes free.

A standard literary convention in many Hindu scriptures, the two concluding verses of chapter one express the power and efficacy of the text itself.

Chapter Two, Part One: Brahman in All

The Lord, Chapter Two begins, created the senses with a defect, an affliction: they are of an outgoing disposition.[7] We therefore perceive outer things and not the inner Self, which is the goal in life. A rare individual, however, turns the attention inward and sees the Self. External objects and the desire for them entangle one in the snares of rebirth; therefore those who are discriminating desire nothing of this impermanent world (2.1.2). The true Self is the only perceiver of external objects anyway, and It has no desires. The Self is that by which one cognizes color, taste, sound, smell, touch and sexual arousal; nothing is unknown to It (2.1.3), yet it is eternally unattached. The individual self is identical to the Absolute, and one who knows this does not cling to the individual self (2.1.5).

Verse six gets a bit technical, but its central point is that the primordial elements from which the universe evolved were born from Brahman, and this same Brahman exists in the individual's heart. Each person, then, is a microcosm, a universe. As the grand drama of the cosmos unfolds in the expanse, so does it unfold in the heart. Brahman, the verse reads, is identical to *Hiraṇyagarbha*. *Hiraṇyagarbha* is an ancient concept of

Vedic origin; the name literally means "golden womb", and it is the primordial creator-being or, alternately, creator-substance, the very substance from which the universe evolves. It represents an original, undifferentiated One from which the differentiated cosmos is derived. The actual terminology in this verse is *pūrvam jātam*, the "First Born". It is *Hiraṇyagarbha*, the original Thing or Person, one step away from Brahman, but non-different from It. This First Born precedes the elements (here referred to merely as "water", or "water" could be taken to mean the "cosmic waters", a universal symbol in creation myths for the formless primordial chaos before it is ordered and given form). In the midst of the mundane body and senses, this awesome original Divine Being dwells. When one deeply contemplates the enormity of it, it is mind-boggling.

Verse seven also draws upon Vedic imagery; it expresses the same idea as verse six, but through the image of Aditi. *A* means "not", *diti*, "limited"[8]; She is a Vedic goddess of the cosmic expanse, the unlimited sky, and the mother of the *devas* (*devamātṛ*). Swami Ranganathananda identifies Her as the "self of the cosmic powers"[9], while Swami Prabhavānanda calls Her "the power of all powers."[10] Here the primordial causal Being is understood as feminine, the infinite, original Mother, *Śakti*, the divine Power. She is Brahman, and dwells in the heart.

The multi-facted symbol of fire is introduced in verse eight. Like a fetus hidden within the mother, fire is hidden in two pieces of wood, and that fire is Brahman. Fire is energy and is the symbol for the all-pervading cosmic energy, the biological and divine energies in each of us. Fire is illumination, it is the sun, it is what lights up the world, endows it with life, causes all things to grow and thrive. Were the sun to go out, everything would die; it is the source and support of life, like Brahman. Just as fire lies unmanifest in wood, so does Brahman lie unseen in all things, living and inanimate. Brahman is the brilliance of all light, and physical light is a reflection of the divine light of Brahman, which is pure consciousness.

Brahman is the source and support of all the deities, verse nine asserts. *Devas*, remember, are the personifications of the powers of nature or, in some contexts, the senses. So nature and its forces are also Brahman. It is not in any way separate from the natural world.

Verse ten is one of my favorites both for its profound metaphysical dimensions and for its practical applications. "Whatever is here," it says, "is there; whatever is there is here. He who sees a difference goes from death to death." Everything is Brahman; Brahman exists in Its totality in the heart (in Its totality because It is not subject to the relativity of space; the totality of Brahman is as fully manifested in the atomic particle as in the limitless expanse). Strictly speaking, then, there is nothing of any true meaning or substance beyond the Self. Everything is within you. In practical terms, this means one need never long for anything. Whatever is of any value, whatever can provide lasting satisfaction is right here within you already. If you have to go somewhere to find it, it does not exist. This is the lesson Dorothy learned in *The Wizard of Oz*; you cannot fulfill your heart's desire by searching for it without. It is already at home, wherever you are. Those on the spiritual path who hanker for travel or experiences or meeting certain people are wise to remember this verse often. No matter how much we travel or how many celebrities or beautiful people we meet, the frustration, the longing, never abates. There is nothing outside you which can satisfy you. Only the Self can. "There is no diversity whatsoever," verse eleven says. Everything is an homogenous whole, Brahman. What is there to long for?

Again, Brahman's dwelling right within you is emphasized in verse twelve. Brahman is referred to as *Puruṣa* and is described as being "the size of a thumb", in other words, manifesting Itself within the space of the heart, about the size of one's thumb. Of course, we know that the localized Ātman is without dimension, both infinitesimal and, at the same time, limitless. According to Swami Ranganathananda, imagining It the size of a thumb is to facilitate meditation on It. In verse thirteen It is likened to a light without smoke, another image to use in meditation.[11] Light, of course, symbolizes consciousness, realization, purity, divinity, etc.

The section concludes with another potent metaphor — that of water. Water is always water, no mater what shape it takes or how it is divided. When water is poured into more water it is the same water it always was, though larger now. Perceiving the selves of people as being separate is like seeing water being poured on to a high mound. It gets dispersed as it runs down, separating into different streams (2.1.14). However, as pure water poured into pure water merges and is one with it, so does the knower of Brahman become identified as none other than that Brahman (2.1.15).

Chapter Two, Part Two: Brahman is the Controller of All

The unborn One (Brahman, unborn because It is eternal) lives in a city with eleven gates (2.2.1). The city with eleven gates is the body; the gates are the body's openings: the two ears, two eyes, two nostrils, mouth, navel (through which we were fed while in utero), anus, sexual organ and crown of the head (the subtle opening through which the soul is believed to pass when it departs the body at the time of death; obviously this metaphor is applicable to all people, though a woman's body is a city of twelve gates). This city is a veritable prison, but only for the unemancipated. Brahman is both within the city and beyond it (2.2.2). It is the sun (here called "the mover") in the heavens, It is the atmosphere, It is the guest in the house (a reference here either to a holy visitor, a *brāhmaṇa* guest, to the Paramātman in the heart, or, in a different reading, to *soma*, the sacrificial drink used in Vedic rituals, in a jar).[12] It is people, gods, water, the elements, everything.

Brahman is that which empowers and impels the *prāṇa* (vital energy). Verse three says that Brahman is "sitting in the middle", in other words in the heart, and "pushes the *prāṇa* upward and impels the *apāna* inward." In *kuṇḍalinī yoga*, superconscious states are reached by consciously manipulating the *prāṇa* up the *suśumnā*, or subtle channel along the spinal column, until it reaches the *sahasrāra cakra*, or energy center at the crown of the head. While this is not the conscious goal of other *yogas*, the *prāṇa* rises spontaneously during experiences of realization or enlightenment arrived at through any spiritual method. *Apāna* is one of the five divisions of *prāṇa*; it is the downward moving energy responsible for elimination and reproduction. So Brahman is identified with the biological energies of the body. This makes sense, for Brahman is the very life within living things, the original animating principle. When Brahman leaves the body, verse four asks rhetorically, what becomes of it? *Prāṇa* and *apāna* are not independent; they are not what endows the body with life. Without Brahman animating *them*, they are dead as well (2.2.5). Only Brahman is life, and only Brahman imbues matter with life.

According to the *jīva's* level of consciousness and the state of its *karma*, it acquires an appropriate body, perhaps an animal, sometimes a plant (indicated here by the term "the motionless") (2.2.7). These bodies are all created by Brahman. Even while we "sleep", or are unconscious of our true nature, Brahman goes along creating worlds (2.2.8). We may not be aware of It, but It is aware of us! It has assumed the shape of each one of us, just as fire assumes different shapes but remains ever fire. Yet Brahman is outside of us as well (2.2.9). Again, the metaphor of the sun comes into play in verse eleven. The sun illuminates everything. If there is a defect in one's eye and he or she cannot see light clearly, it is not the sun which is in any way diminished or dimmed. The sun is always fully brilliant. Similarly, the Self is never "tainted by the sorrows of the world." It is always pure, free and unaffected. Eternal peace is in store for the one who realizes this Self of all; the Brahman which "makes a single form multifarious," is "the eternal among the ephemeral," and "the consciousness of the conscious" (2.2.13).

At this juncture, Naciketā interjects with two questions. First, he asks, "How shall I know It?" then, "Is It self- effulgent?" (2.2.14). The section ends with an answer to the second question. The sun, Yama replies, does not shine on Brahman, for Brahman is the light that shines through the sun. The moon, stars and lightning do not illuminate Brahman for Brahman is the very light that shines from them. All light is merely a fractional reflection of Brahman's infinite lustre. This verse is identical to *Śvetāśvatara Upaniṣad* verse 6.14 and *Muṇḍaka Upaniṣad* 2.2.10.

Chapter Two, Part Three: The Path to Immortality

Like the section that preceded it, this final part opens with a colorful metaphor and one which is extremely pervasive in Hinduism. We find mention of it, for instance, in the *Bhagavad-Gītā*, verses 15.1-2. The World Tree, here in the guise of the peepul tree, is limitless and has its roots above and its branches below. The root is Brahman and the tree is the universe. Together they comprise everything. In his commentary on the *Kaṭha Upaniṣad*, Śrī Śaṅkarācārya explains the symbolism of the World Tree in depth. Its essence lies in its root, Brahman. Its vigorous growth results from the water of desire. Its sprouts are the objects of the knowledge-gathering senses. Its leaves are the *Vedas*, the *Smṛtis*, logic, learning. Its beautiful flowers are deeds such as sacrifice, charity, austerity, etc. Its many different flavors are the experiences of happiness and sorrow. Its infinite fruits are the means of subsistence for beings. There is an uproar of noise arising from the many beings living in the tree — laughing, grieving, making music, exclaiming, screaming, talking, playing — all induced by the ever-changing conditions of pleasure and pain in the tree. The winds of desire blow this unsteady tree about; it is a dangerous abode indeed. The tree is felled by the axe of detachment, forged from the realization of oneness with Brahman.[13]

Brahman, verses two and three say, is a great terror "like an uplifted thunderbolt . . . From fear of Him Fire burns, from fear shines the sun, from fear run Indra (storms) and Air, and Death, the fifth." Here death is counted among the primary elements. We are not actually to believe that Brahman is frightening and that the elements tremble before It. Brahman is the highest delight, the ocean of bliss. The *Bṛhadāraṇyaka Upaniṣad* states that Brahman is "like honey to all beings," and all beings "like honey" to It. Brahman is sweetness. The point, according to Śrī Śaṅkarācārya, is that Brahman is the supreme ruler of all forces, the regulating principle, like a monarch holding aloft a thunderbolt and keeping order in the state.[14]

If one realizes Brahman before the "falling of the body", or death, then one is emancipated (2.3.4). Verse five is a bit convoluted and requires explanation. Just as one can see clearly in a mirror, so too can Brahman be seen in the pure, unmodified intellect. In a dream, one's vision is confused, unclear. Similarly, Brahman is not clearly seen by those taking birth in heavenly realms and other planes of existence. There are other worlds, but they are no closer to Brahman than this one. Gandharvaloka is one such heavenly realm, believed to be peopled by beautiful, winged, music-making beings. Here vision of Brahman is like a reflection in rippling water — still unclear. In the world of Brahmā (Brahmāloka, the most sublime reaches within the material universe) the vision is fairly clear, but to get there is so difficult it makes no sense to even try. One should strive for Brahman right here, right now.[15]

The senses are separate from Brahman, as are their "rising and setting", their many experiences (2.3.6). Let us not seek Brahman through them. Let us never sorrow over what they witness or experience. Verses seven and eight are a recapitulation of verses 1.3.10-11: the mind is superior to the senses, the intellect superior to the mind, and so on up to supreme *Puruṣa*. Knowing that, one attains immortality.

How can It be known? The remainder of the *Upaniṣad* is devoted to answering this question. Again, It is not perceptible to the senses. Only the pure intellect, unoccupied by objects, can discern Brahman (2.3.9). The state of realization comes when one turns off the senses, silences the mind, and stills the intellect (2.3.10). This *yoga* is exactly parallel to the teaching of Patañjali in the standard text of *yoga* practice, the *Yoga Sūtras.* According to Patañjali, there is no need to adhere to any particular philosophy, theology, or doctrine in order to attain the Supreme. It can be known by direct experience when the senses, mind, and intellect are silenced. This is similar, too, to the teachings of the Buddha. One needn't believe anything. One need only practice and, in doing so, discover the Truth for oneself. This steadying of the senses is *yoga*, verse eleven says, and vigilance is necessary as one's practice can waver and "is subject to growth and decay."

Once again, it is stressed that It cannot be known as an object of the senses. But how can it be known apart from hearing about It and thinking about It? (2.3.12). Apparently, there must exist an entirely different way of knowing. This is suggested in verse thirteen. We begin by merely knowing that It exists — perhaps not in our immediate experience, but existing nonetheless. Then there is direct knowledge of It "as It really is", actual perception of Brahman. The difference involves knowing *about* It and knowing *It.* Eventually the Self which was initially only known *about* reveals Itself and is *known* (2.3.13).

It is desire which obstructs our knowledge of Brahman, the "knots in the heart" (longings, fixations, egoistic tendencies). The one who lets go of these becomes immortal (2.3.14-15). "This much alone is the instruction (of all the *Upaniṣads*)" (2.3.15). This sentiment is echoed in the words of Sri Ramakrishna, who said that the *Gītā* could be understood in full merely by reversing the syllables of its title, which becomes *tāgī*, "renunciation". In nearly all the world's religions, renunciation is espoused as *the* key to spiritual realization.

References are again made to *kuṇḍalinī* theory. According to verse sixteen, the "nerves of the heart are one hundred one in number. One of them passes through the head." This is the *suśumnā* mentioned earlier, the canal running up the spinal column through which the *prāṇa* rises during superconscious states. The "nerves" mentioned in this verse refer to *nāḍīs* or nerve channels through which *prāṇa* moves, as well as pathways through which sensate data moves in order to be experienced by the conscious being within. Of course, the nerves are connected to the brain, but by associating them with the heart, the *Upaniṣad* is drawing attention to the Self, located in the heart, as the only Experiencer of sensate signals. Of the nerve that passes through the head, the verse says, "Going up through that nerve one gets immortality." It is believed that Self-realized *yogīs* can decide to leave their bodies and merge with Brahman at will. They can decide the moment of their own deaths and execute them by drawing the *prāṇa* up the *suśumnā* and completely out of the body. Self-realized people who die a natural death also undergo this process. The soul destined never to return rises up the *suśumnā* before departing. The rest of the nerves, the verse concludes, those that have different directions, "become the causes of death." In other words, when a person follows the other nerve channels — the outward going senses — they fall prey to desire, craving, and bondage, the causes of rebirth. One should carefully separate the indwelling One, the *Puruṣa*, from one's body. He is pure and immortal. He is our own Self (2.3.17).

Having had this knowledge imparted to him, Naciketā became Brahman-realized. Anyone who becomes a knower of the Self, like our young hero, also attains Brahman, says the penultimate verse. This is a promise the *Upaniṣad* makes to us. Anyone can attain this highest realization if they try, for it is the very purpose of our existence.

The final verse is a peace invocation, asking the Supreme to protect the teacher and pupil, to reveal to them the knowledge they seek, to vouchsafe this knowledge, and to make their spiritual study fruitful. *Oṃ*, the narrator prays, Peace, Peace, Peace!

NOTES

1. Swāmī Gambhīrānanda, *Kaṭha Upaniṣad* (Mayavati: Advaita Ashrama, 1980), p. v.
2. Stutley and Stutley, p. 346.
3. Eknath Easwaran, *Dialogue With Death: the Spiritual Psychology of the Kaṭha Upaniṣad* (Petaluma: Nilgiri Press, 1981), p. 32.
4. Swami Ranganathananda, *The Message of the Upaniṣads* (Bombay: Bharatiya Vidyā Bhavan, 1971), pp. 397-398.
5. Ranganathananda, p. 417.; Organ, pp. 221-222; Swāmī Nikhilānanda, trnsl., *The Gospel of Sri Ramakrishna* (New York: Ramakrishna-Vivekananda Center, 1942), p. 1039.
6. Gambhīrānanda, pp. 71-72.
7. Ranganathananda, p. 446.
8. Stutley and Stutley, p. 3.
9. Ranganathananda, p. 470
10. Prabhavānanda, p. 31.
11. Ranganathananda, p. 485.
12. Ranganathananda, p. 492; Gambhīrānanda, p. 98.
13. Gambhīrānanda, pp. 112-114.
14. Gambhīrānanda, p. 116.
15. Gambhīrānanda, p. 118.

CHAPTER FOURTEEN

Śvetāśvatara Upaniṣad: A Meditation on the Presence of Brahman in All Creation

The beauty of the *Śvetāśvatara Upaniṣad* is twofold. First, its style is clear and vivid. Instead of shrouding its wisdom in mystifying symbolism and esoteric references, it states its philosophical premises outright in powerful, crystalline phrasing. Second, it brilliantly harmonizes what were, at the time of its composisiton, the viewpoints held by rival philosophical schools. It is a work of synthesis and, in this sense, resembles the *Bhagavad-Gītā*. The Divine is presented here in various aspects — personal, impersonal, immanent, transcendent, dualistic, monistic — yet there is no sense of conflict. The diverse methods of attaining realization of the Divine are also presented with equal emphasis. The text advocates *jñāna yoga* and *bhakti yoga*, seeing no sense of exclusivity between them.[1]

The name of this *Upaniṣad* is derived from the sage who is said to have expounded it to his students. The word *Śvetāśvatara* is not a name, but rather an appellation honoring the spiritual attainment of the guru to whom it refers. *Śveta* means "pure", and *aśva* "senses", together meaning "one who possesses purified senses".[2] It might also be interpreted as "white calf" or "white mule", and would indicate simply that the bearer of this epithet owned one.[3]

This *Upaniṣad* deals exclusively with the subject of Brahman, Its nature, and Its attainment. However, unlike its sister *Upaniṣads*, it identifies Brahman not just as an abstract, absolute Oneness, but as *God* (*Īśvara*, *Deva*), personal, sovereign, glorious. Being of a relatively late date, the *Upaniṣad* was no doubt influenced by the devotional tradition. It is sometimes referred to as the "Śaivite *Bhagavad-Gītā*"[4] because of its references to Rudra and Śiva, and its similar slant toward philosophical synthesis. Each of its six chapters addresses a specific topic, yet its themes and ideas overlap and intertwine with such complexity and smoothness, one scarcely notices thematic divisions at all.

Chapter One: An Overview of the Nature of Reality

The *Upaniṣad* opens with questions posed by a group of students to their teacher. What is the cause of everything? Is it Brahman? What is our final destination? Is there something controlling this world, controlling us?

Different possible answers are considered and rejected (1.2). Time, nature, universal law, chance, energy and intelligence are all posed as possible causes, but none provide a suitable explanation because these are all created things, things that have their origins in some previous cause. What preceded even them? The answer can be discovered by the practice of meditation (1.3). Through meditation one can realize firsthand that God is the cause of all causes, the "self-luminous power in everyone", the "God of religion, the Self of philosophy and the Energy of science" (1.3). This truth cannot be comprehended through the intellect, because the intellect is limited and Brahman is not.

We can, however, attempt to conceptualize Him through the vehicle of metaphor, and at this juncture the *Śvetāśvatara Upaniṣad* utilizes two: Brahman as a wheel and Brahman as a river (1.4, 1.5). The symbol of the wheel is the most complex we will encounter in this *Upaniṣad*, and it exemplifies Hinduism's great love of categorizing, dissecting and listing. He, verse four says, is the universe, which resembles a wheel which has one rim, a triple tire, sixteen extremities, fifty spokes, twenty counterspokes and six sets of eight, and is driven along three roads by means of a belt. In simple terms, this image symbolizes the elements comprising the material universe, moving from the most basic elements to the most differentiated and complex. Swāmī Tyāgīśānanda identifies the imagery thus:

— One Rim: the circumference of Nature (i.e. *māyā*, *prakṛti*).

— Triple Tire: the three *guṇas*: *sattva*, *rajas*, and *tamas*.

— Sixteen Extremities: the sixteen products enumerated in the *Sāṃkhya* philosophy, namely the eleven organs and five gross elements.

— Fifty Spokes: the five misconceptions, twenty-eight disabilities, nine satisfactions, and eight *siddhis* (supernatural powers).

— Twenty Counterspokes: the ten senses and ten objects.

— Six Sets of Eight: 1.) Eightfold Nature: the five elements, mind, intellect, and ego. 2.) Eight Ingredients of the Body: bone, blood, fat, etc. 3.) Eight Psychic Powers 4.) Eight Mental States (*dharma*, *adharma*, renunciation, attachment, etc. 5.) Eight Superhuman Beings (*Devas*, *Gandharvas*, *Rākṣasas*, etc.) 6.) Eight Virtues.[5]

The three roads are virtue (*dharma*), vice (*adharma*) and knowledge (*jñāna*). The belt is desire, which keeps the wheel turning.[6]

The wheel as a whole suggests the dynamic nature of the universe, its perpetual motion, and the cyclical character of all natural phenomena. The traveler in this world is whirled round and round, living and dying, experiencing pleasure and pain, success and failure.[7]

The metaphor of the river suggests flowing, spontaneity, perpetual change within a constant unity. Just as the river flows into the sea, so does all living creation flow back to its source in the Divine. The river of creation and the ocean of God are of a single substance.[8]

Five streams flow into this river; these are the five senses. The river has five great curves, which are the five elements (earth, air, fire, water, ether).[9] There are five waves; these are the *prāṇas,* or five vital airs. The mind is the source of this river, earthly misery its rapids.

So long as the pilgrim considers him or herself to be separate from the Divine, he or she will rotate on the wheel endlessly, futilely, and be hurled hither and thither in the powerful, frightening rapids. However, when one realizes him or herself to *be* the very moving force which makes the wheel spin, makes the water flow, immortality is his or hers.

This whole cosmic manifestation is the Supreme Brahman, while at the same time Brahman is the divine support underlying it. The world is comprised of that which is perishable (matter) and that which is imperishable (spirit). Those who grow attached to the perishable become enmeshed in it, imprisoned in it, while those who know Brahman are freed from it (1.7, 1.8, 1.10).

The concept of *tripuṭi,* the three elements of thought, is introduced in verse nine. The *tripuṭi* are the conscious subject, the object of perception, and *māyā,* that inscrutable magic force which brings the two into relation to each other and creates the illusion of separateness, of observer and observed. When all three are recognized as Brahman, however, "the Self becomes infinite, universal and free . . ." Meditation is the key to this realization, and nothing beyond this remains to be known. It is the Ultimate Truth (1.12).

This Ultimate Truth is within us, but normally It is hidden from our perception, just as fire is hidden in a piece of wood. The wood must be struck in order for the fire to be released, and similarly we must perform spiritual practices if we want to "release" our hidden Ātman. Building upon the wood metaphor, if we imagine our own body as the lower piece of wood, the upper piece of wood is the *praṇava,* the syllable *Oṃ.* By meditating on *Oṃ,* the Ātman is gradually revealed, just as rubbing two sticks together gradually reveals the fire latent within them (1.13-14). Through concentration, truthfulness, self-control, meditation and inner searching, one finds the divine Self and becomes the Supreme Brahman (1.15).

Chapter Two: The Practice of *Yoga*

Chapter Two concerns itself with the actual means of achieving Brahman realization, offering both theory and practical instruction. Simply put, when the mind and senses are controlled, stilled, focused on realizing the Truth, the Self is revealed and supreme bliss attained (2.1-2). This is the practice of meditation, a technique lauded throughout the text.

Verse six uses the imagery of Vedic sacrifice to suggest that any of several different yogic paths may be followed to attain the Supreme. "Where fire is churned out," it reads, "where air is controlled, where *soma* juice overflows — there the mind attains perfection." According to Swāmī Tyāgīśānanda, fire represents the intellect, the fire of intelligence, hence, the path of *jñāna yoga*. Air represents *prāṇāyāma*, breath control, and thus refers to *rāja yoga*. *Soma*, an intoxicating beverage, represents worldly enjoyments, so offering it up in sacrifice is symbolic of *karma yoga*.[10]

Spiritual practice destroys old *karma*, thus freeing us from having to suffer or enjoy the results. Both suffering and pleasure are unwelcome states of arousal and distraction.

Now the *Upaniṣad* gives nuts-and-bolts directions for meditation. Posture, breath, location, and holding the mind still are all discussed, as are signposts along the way which indicate the aspirant is making progress. Visions appearing, old age and disease being staved off, a lightness in the body, clear complexion, beautiful voice and so on are indications that one is entering *yoga* (2.8-13).

The *yogī* realizes that the Divine exists in all persons as their own Selves. He alone is born, He alone enters the wombs of living creatures, He is present in the fire, the water, the plants, the trees, the whole universe (2.16-17).

Chapter Three: *Saguṇa* Brahman and *Nirguṇa* Brahman

Chapter Three explores the aspects of Divinity which are *Saguṇa* Brahman, Brahman with qualities, forms, activities, attributes, and *Nirguṇa* Brahman, Brahman without qualities and attributes. In doing so, it reconciles the rival philosophies of *Advaita Vedānta* (non-dualism) and *Dvaita Vedānta* (dualism, or conceiving the Ultimate Truth to be a Reality or Supreme person separate from the individual). For the Ultimate Truth to be truly unlimited and all-encompassing, It must necessarily include both conceptions. One of the central teachings of Sri Ramakrishna was that God is both with form and without form. This position is upheld in the *Śvetāśvatara Upaniṣad*.

The chapter opens by describing Brahman very much in terms of a personal God. He is the Creator, the Divine Lord, the Protector of all the worlds, and the controller of forces working within them. He is identified with Rudra, a form of Śiva. He projects all worlds from Himself and is the very beings inhabiting these worlds. "He is the real owner of all the eyes, faces, hands and feet in the universe" (3.3, compare to *Bhagavad-Gītā* verse 11.16). He is the force of their *karma*, and the inspiration to work and live. He created the gods and bestows bliss, wisdom and freedom from sins on the devoted, while unleashing justice on the evildoers. He blessed the world by imparting the sacred scriptures. He holds an arrow, which he aims at whomever He chooses; it is the weapon which destroys ignorance — divine grace. The author prays, "O protector of devotees, do not destroy that benign personal form of Thine which has manifested as the universe" (3.1-6). These verses could have comfortably fit into any scriptures from the *bhakti* tradition.

Now the text turns to that aspect of Brahman which is without form. "Higher than this is the infinite Supreme Brahman . . . who, though remaining single, envelops the whole universe" (3.7). Nothing is greater than This, or smaller than This; nothing is different from This. It fills the whole universe, yet is beyond this universe. It is formless (3.7-10). These verses speak from a more *jñāna* perspective, that of an impersonal, all-pervading, attributeless Divine.

A third aspect of Brahman must be addressed, that of the indwelling soul, the Brahman which is the Self of all beings. It is the consciousness which causes the senses to perceive, the intellect to know; It is the life force which causes all things to move, live and be. Though It expands Itself into manifestation, It remains in Its original state at the same time. Though It ultimately has no eyes, It is that which sees when we see. Though It has no ears, It is what hears. Though It has no hands, It is what grasps and feels. All that occurs is It; all that is experienced is It; all that does the experiencing is It (3.12-19).

Chapter Four: *Puruṣa* and *Prakṛti*

The *Upaniṣad* now examines in greater depth the interaction of matter (*prakṛti*) and Divine Consciousness (*Puruṣa*), and their ultimate oneness. *Prakṛti*, Nature, is the solid manifestation of Brahman, Its own Self-expression, yet Brahman is beyond it as well.

Brahman, though colorless, becomes all colors. It is the entire universe, the sun, moon, sky, stars. It is Prajāpati, the Creator Being. It is man and woman, the young and the old, the dark blue butterfly and the green parrot, the seasons, the oceans. All this is It, yet It is beyond time and space (4.1-4).

Verse five is notable because it introduces the image of the Divine Mother. As an archetypal Creatrix, or Mother Goddess, She represents Nature, matter, substance, *prakṛti.* "There is a single Female, of red white and black colors who is unoriginated and produces various offspring resembling Herself" (4.5) The three colors refer to the three *guṇas* — *rajas, sattva,* and *tamas* — which are the subtle building blocks of material nature. "By Her side," the verse continues, "lies one unborn Male out of attachment for Her, while another unborn Male, also unoriginated, forsakes Her, after having enjoyed Her."

These two males represent *Puruṣa,* the pure, spiritual, divine Consciousness. One is attached to Her, and this is the soul in bondage, attached to the world and sunk in ignorance. The other walks away from Her; this is the liberated soul, who has cast off attachment to the world and has attained spiritual freedom.[11] They are of an identical nature; ultimately they are the same being, only their consciousness is different.

The famous "birds of beautiful plumage" analogy follows. It is one of the most oft-referred to metaphors in Hinduism and is also found in the *Muṇḍaka Upaniṣad.* "Two birds of beautiful plumage, who are inseparable friends, reside on the self-same tree. Of these, one eats the fruit of the tree with relish while the other looks on without eating" (4.6). The eating bird is the conditioned consciousness, the consciousness in bondage, attached to the pleasures and pains of the world, like the clinging lover of the previous verse. The watching bird, detached and serene, is the Ātman, the true, divine Self which remains ever changeless, ever unaffected. When the eating bird stops and notices the watching bird, the Ultimate Truth, it will be liberated (4.7).

Book learning alone cannot grant one realization of Brahman, nor can religious observances, for these are material things, limited things, part of the gross world of *māyā* (4.9). However, one can look beyond the multiplicity inherent in *māyā* and see that *māyā* is actually an aspect of Brahman. "The whole world is filled with beings who form His parts" (4.10). While Brahman is the Creator, the Sovereign, the Lord, the Bestower of Blessings, in other words, God, the separate and transcendent (4.11-13), He is ultimately immanent, for it is He who has assumed all forms and become all things (4.14).

For those whose ignorance is dispelled and who perceive Brahman, all the dualities of *Māyā* disappear: "There is neither day nor night, neither being nor non-being. There is only that Auspicious One" (4.18). The actual word here is *śiva,* "Auspicious One". This may be interpreted to mean Brahman in general, or Lord Śiva, the divine form which most closely represents the infinite, still, unmanifest state. Interestingly, the verse states that this One is "worthy of being adored by the creator"

(4.18). In other words, the creator aspect is a step below the supreme Brahman or Parabrahman. "Creator" may also refer to Lord Brahmā, who, though the agent of creation, is considered to be of a lower status and mortal. The actual word used here, *savitṛ*, can also refer to the sun.[12]

Both the formless, unmanifest Brahman and the Brahman with personality are the Ultimate Truth. Two verses (4.19-20) state that It is so unfathomable It cannot be perceived, understood or conceived of through the senses or the mind, only through intuition. The two verses which conclude the section, however, address a personal deity. Calling upon Rudra by name, the author says that those who are frightened by the thought of rebirth approach God for help. He prays for Rudra to protect the devotees from harm with His "benevolent face" (4.21). This verse is a standard in liturgical and personal prayer; it reads: *Rudra yat te dakṣiṇam mukham tena mām pāhi nityam*, "O Rudra (God), evermore protect me by Your sweet and compassionate face." Notice how the dual aspects of the Divine as terrible and awesome (Rudra, compare to the *Bhagavad-Gītā*, eleventh chapter) and as gentle and benevolent are juxtaposed and harmonized in this verse.

Chapter Five: God as Controller of and Indweller in Nature

Continuing and building upon a theme introduced in the previous chapter, this section examines the specifics of Brahman's presence in all things. It begins by stating unequivocally that Brahman is, when viewed from Its ultimate sense, beyond all dualities, including such crucial ones as death and immortality, wisdom and ignorance. Brahman is, in fact, manifested in all dualities, yet, paradoxically, transcends all dualities (5.1). This is the profound Vedāntic paradox, the paradox that allows the *jñāna yogī* to approach Brahman either through the mental discipline of *neti neti*, "not this, not this", or *iti iti*, "this, this". In other words, one can view the world with the constant thought in mind, "This is not Brahman. None of this is the Reality. The multiplicity is an illusion and Brahman is beyond it." Or, one can see the world with the thought, "Everything is Brahman. There is nothing which is not Him. The multiplicity is an illusion because everything is but the Oneness of Brahman." In either case, the result is the same, entering into a realization of Brahman.

The next four verses describe the aspect of Brahman which presides over Nature, which is its master, its controller. The *Upaniṣad's* author is expressing the idea that Brahman is both the prime mover of Nature and Nature itself. He is attempting to synthesize philosophical viewpoints which see Brahman as either beyond material nature or inherent in it. Verse two mentions the ancient Vedic creator figure *Hiraṇyagarbha*, the primordial first differentiation. *Hiraṇyagarbha* means "golden womb" and is the original cause of the universal manifestation. It is, of course, non-different from Brahman, but it represents one of the most primal states of Brahman's self-differentiation. This verse says that Brahman "witnessed the birth" of *Hiraṇyagarbha*. In other words, It has always been aloof and detached from creation.

Yet it is He who is evolving in creation, both as gross matter and as living beings. The text now turns to the subject of the soul, the Brahman within. One who is attached to worldly pleasures acts in the world only with an eye to attaining them. Thus he is bound by the three *guṇas* and is forced to be reborn again and again ("assuming various forms"). His deeds create karmic reactions which he is compelled to receive, and depending on the quality of this *karma*, he may live a life of *dharma* (righteousness), *adharma* (evil) or *jñāna* (knowledge) (5.7). This, in a nutshell, is the human condition, and empty cycle of futility.

But within each of us there exists the divine spark, "effulgent and infinite like the sun." It has assumed physical forms and dwells in the heart. We do not ordinarily experience It, however, because of egotism and *saṅkalpa*, the aspect of the mind which finds attraction for something which does not deserve it (5.8).[13]

What is that divine spark like? It is so subtle, It cannot be perceived by means of the senses. It is "as subtle as a hair-point divided and subdivided hundreds of times." Yet It is also infinite (5.9). The *jīva*, or embodied soul, has no gender, but becomes identified with whatever body it assumes (5.10). The kind of body it assumes depends upon the quality of its *karma* (6.11) as well as the quality of its mind (5.12). In other words, a low-minded individual will necessarily take a low birth.

This process can be escaped from, however, by one who realizes the Supreme Divinity, "the blissful, the incorporeal, and the nameless" (5.14).

Chapter Six: The Power and Greatness of Brahman

The ultimacy and magnificence of Brahman is extolled in this last chapter, which is a meditation on Brahman's qualities and powers. Here he is very much presented as *Saguṇa* Brahman, the Divine with attributes.

The first verse constructs a clever thematic bridge which brings us full circle: "Some deluded thinkers speak of Nature and others of time as the force that revolves this wheel of Brahman" (6.1). This is an echo of verses 1.2 and 1.4, a device which gives the text a sense of completion and closure.

Brahman is praised as the creator and destroyer (6.4), the source of all virtue, destroyer of sins, the abode of the universe (6.5). He transcends *saṃsāra* (reincarnation), time, and form (6.6). He is the Supreme God over all gods (6.7). He has nothing to achieve for Himself, yet He causes all things to happen (and in this sense very much resembles the Chinese concept of Tao) (6.8). He is the witness, the Pure Consciousness (6.10).

Only those who attain realization of Brahman know lasting happiness, and no one else (6.11). Identical to *Kaṭha Upaniṣad* 2.2.15 and *Muṇḍaka Upaniṣad* 2.2.10, verse thirteen indicates that no light — neither the sun, the moon, nor the stars — can illuminate Brahman because Brahman is the light that causes *them* to shine. The deeper implication is that Brahman cannot be known through our sensory faculties — eyes, ears, mind — because Brahman is that consciousness which sees through the eyes, hears through the ears, thinks through the mind. This theme is also central to the *Kena Upaniṣad*.

Hinting at the personal aspect of Brahman and the phenomenon of divine grace, verse fourteen calls Him "the one destroyer of ignorance in the midst of this universe." It is He, then, that grants liberation. Yet He is not remote, "up there" somewhere, but rather the Supreme Self within us. That the Divine would dwell so absolutely in the world and within ourselves appears to the uninitiated as an irreconcilable incongruity: "He alone is the fire stationed in water" (6.14). Nevertheless, realizing this fact is the only means of emancipation (6.14). Because He is all, liberation cannot take place without His causing it to happen; He is the only Doer (6.15).

Yet He is free from actions, without parts (6.17). Understanding the ultimate rationality behind the seeming contradictions is the basis of *jñāna* realization.

God realization is the only source of real joy, the only end of misery: "Only when men shall roll up the sky like a skin, will there be an end of misery for them without realizing God" (6.18). In other words, any effort to be free of pain and misery apart from spiritual realization is as futile as trying to roll up the sky.[14]

Praising the sage Śvetāśvatara, who has expounded this highest of mystical teachings, the author suggests that not everyone is fit to receive it. It should not be taught to those whose passions are not subdued, who are loath to attend to their duties and responsibilities or who are otherwise unworthy (6.20). Trying to teach so sublime a philosophy to these kinds of individuals constitutes, to borrow a phrase from another religious tradition, casting pearls before swine.

Only in the high-souled ones (*mahātmas*), those who have cultivated devotion to God and devotion to the spiritual teacher, can such truths take hold, grow, and eventually shine forth like a radiant light (6.21).

NOTES

1. Swami Tyāgīśānanda, *Śvetāśvatara Upaniṣad* (Mylapore: Sri Ramakrishna Math, 1979), p. 4
2. Tyāgīśānanda, p. 3.
3. Organ, p. 165.
4. Organ, p. 164.
5. Tyāgīśānanda, p. 22.
6. Tyāgīśānanda, p. 23.
7. Tyāgīśānanda, p. 21.
8. Tyāgīśānanda, p. 24.
9. Tyāgīśānanda, p. 24.
10. Tyāgīśānanda, p. 45.
11. Tyāgīśānanda, p. 81.
12. Stutley and Stutley, p. 275.
13. Tyāgīśānanda, p. 108.
14. Tyāgīśānanda, p. 131.

CHAPTER FIFTEEN

Taittirīya Upaniṣad: *A Meditation on the Journey Within*

The *Taittirīya Upaniṣad* is one of the more difficult *Upaniṣads.* Of early composition, it avails itself heavily to obscure symbolism and mystifying references. The meanings inherent in the very archaic and culturally specific language and imagery may have been perfectly clear to aspirants living at the time of the text's composition, but Western aspirants of today might, on a first reading, find it impenetrable. It is not. With a little patience, imagination, and a helpful commentary (such as that provided by Swāmī Śarvānanda with his translation, which I consulted in the preparation of this chapter[1], or the book you are now holding) the *Taittirīya Upaniṣad* can be deciphered, and it is well worth the effort.

At once informative, practical, technical, philosophical and ecstatically mystical, the *Taittirīya* takes the reader on a multidimensional journey, a ride as dizzying, colorful and radiant as light through a kaleidoscope. Within the limited scope of its length, it touches upon a remarkable array of subjects, then grows progressively more focused until its climactic final verse, which explodes, like a starburst, in the rapture of Brahman realization.

The origin of the *Upaniṣad's* name is highly unusual, and narrated in a story found both in the *Mahābhārata* (12.319) and the *Viṣṇu Purāṇa* (3.5). In brief, Yājñavalkya, the nephew and disciple of the Vedic sage Vaiśampāyana, in order to prove his preeminence among his fellow disciples, disgorged the *Yajur Veda*, which he had committed to memory, in tangible form. The other disciples turned themselves into partridges and pecked up the pieces of the *Veda. Taittirīya* is derived from the word *tittiri*, which means "partridges".[2] The serious student of this *Upaniṣad* is like one of these partridges, devouring and internalizing spiritual knowledge.

The reader is advised to progress through the text slowly, pondering the underlying significance of each verse until it is clear before moving on. The *Taittirīya Upaniṣad* contains the highest and most subtle mystical truth, and deserves to be studied thoroughly and carefully. It is divided into three major sections, or *vallis*, each of which contains several *anuvākas*, or lessons. These are longer than the verses usually found in Upaniṣadic literature, and sometimes shift abruptly from one topic to the next in mid-lesson. Be prepared for this.

Chapter One: *Śikṣā* (Phonetics) *Valli*, Concerning the Readying of Oneself for the Search for Brahman

Like all *Upaniṣads*, the *Taittirīya* opens with a peace invocation, but this one is particularly beautiful. The different Vedic atmospheric deities are revered as perceptible manifestations of Brahman. This is a foreshadowing of a theme that will be developed much later, that of Brahman's presence in all phenomena.

The *Mahāsaṃhitas* — The Great Conjunctions

The *Upaniṣad* proper opens, "We proceed to explain the science of phonetics. It deals with vocalic sounds, accent or pitch, quantity . . . etc." (1.2). To the untrained reader, this seems curiously incongruous with the whole purpose of an *Upaniṣad*. The reference is, in fact, extremely Vedic, and draws upon the Vedic preoccupation with grammar and phonetics. In the ancient Vedic ceremonies, it was crucial that the priests chant the Vedic hymns flawlessly, for any mistake could counteract the efficacy of the ritual. In addition, the *Vedas* themselves were revered as the tangible manifestation of Divinity in this world as well as the means by which the *brāhmaṇas*, through vocalizing the Vedic *mantras*, ceremonially ordered, perpetuated and recreated the universe. Sounds, words, sentences, euphonic combinations and poetic meters were literally of ultimate significance and thus scrupulously studied and lovingly poured over.

An ancient reader of the *Taittirīya Upaniṣad* would have recognized and felt comfortable with the imagery invoked in this verse and would easily have interpreted the symbolism. The following verses will employ the imagery of conjunction — the combination of words — as a prototype for how things in the world fit together in general, the basic interconnectedness of things.[3] In Sanskrit, there is a concept called *sandhi*, or principles concerning euphonic combinations. If certain letters appear as the last letter in a word, and certain others appear as the first letter in the next, these letters may change slightly in order to make the sound combination more beautiful. Technically speaking, there are three sounds: the concluding letter of the first word, the initial letter of the second word, and a third cementing element between them.[4] All three are united into a single unit. Here is an example: *yoga* + *īśvara* (Lord) becomes *yog-e-śvara* (*Yogeśvara*, "Lord of Yoga").

Very cleverly drawing upon this principle, the author compares the unified nature of all reality with the unified nature of grammatical conjunction. "The teaching concerning the universe is this: the earth is the prior form, the firmament is the posterior form, the atmosphere is the conjunction, and the air is the means of joining" (1.3). Everything is connected to everything else. One should meditate on this, the lesson says. By contemplating concrete counterparts of abstract concepts, the mind is gradually drawn into increasingly subtle levels until the analogy falls away and the pure concept is left. Many *Upaniṣads* employ this same technique of leading the reader in steps from the gross to the subtle (a device known as *upāsanā*). The *Taittirīya Upaniṣad* brings the imagery of grammatic conjunction to bear on the phenomena of light, learning, progeny and vocal expression respectively, directing the aspirant to meditate upon these *Mahāsaṃhitas*, or "Great Conjunctions", and their deeper meaning.[5]

The Prayers of the Teacher

The backdrop of universal unity having been set, we now embark upon the task of striving to know Brahman. Before initiating any momentous undertaking, one should seek the grace of the Divine for strength and help. Lesson four provides a series of prayers uttered by the spiritual teacher to Brahman, both praising Its form as the mantra *Oṃ*, and requesting It to bestow upon him or her the qualifications necessary to assume the role of teacher, including intellectual vigor, knowledge of the *Vedas*, sweet speech, an able body, an openness to lifelong learning, and the material means to perform the proper religious rites and support sincere students. "May celibate students of hallowed wisdom come to me . . . may they come from far off and different directions! May they come in large numbers! May they be self-controlled and calm!" (1.4).

The teacher is not praying for his own benefit, but strictly for the benefit of his disciples. Traditionally, disciples of a *guru* lived in his house with him and were supported, both spiritually and materially, by him. This is why the *guru* supplicates for material favor, so that he may provide his students with all necessities, thus freeing them to concentrate entirely on their study and *sādhanā*. It is not egotism, nor a desire for name and fame that motivates a teacher to pray for the arrival of first-rate students, but rather a desire to serve others. The legitimate spiritual teacher is entirely beyond ego. "O gracious Lord, may I enter into Thee . . . ," he prays, ". . . O Gracious Lord, enter into me . . . take possession of me."

Readers using a very literal translation will find each exhortation of lesson four followed by the exclamation "*Svāhā*!" This is a mantra uttered by both Hindus and Buddhists following the offering of an oblation to the gods and is roughly translated, "let it be so," or "may good come out of it." It is rather like the Biblical "Amen".[6] Brahman is referred to here as "that Self of Thine with a thousand branches." This may refer to the myriad of gods and goddesses, all of which are aspects of the divine One, or may refer to the many sacred scriptures, which are the literary incarnation of Brahman. Swāmī Śarvānanda notes that just as the many gods and goddesses are expressed in the one Brahman, so, too, do all of the scriptures find their unity and expression in the syllable *Oṃ*.[7]

The *Vyāhṛtis* — The Mystical Names of the Worlds

Oṃ, *Bhūḥ*, *Bhuvaḥ*, *Svaḥ* (or *Suvaḥ*) — these are the opening syllables of the *Gāyatrī mantra*, the most sacred polysyllabic *mantra* in Hinduism. In four words a universe of meaning is suggested, and lesson five examines them in some detail. These four words comprise what are known as the "Four *Vyāhṛtis*", or "four utterances", and represent the four realms of reality — the earthly, the atmospheric, the celestial and the spiritual. *Oṃ*, *Bhūḥ*, *Bhuvaḥ*, *Svaḥ* are the basis of a sophisticated meditation on the graduated levels of consciousness leading to the most subtle, that of Ātman consciousness.

The fourth *Vyāhṛti* (*Oṃ*), lesson five says, was discovered by the sage Mahācamasya through divine intervention.[8] It is Brahman/Ātman, and everything else comprises Its "limbs", i.e. Its parts. A breakdown of the *Vyāhṛtis* and their associations is as follows:

	Bhūḥ	*Bhuvaḥ*	*Svaḥ*	*Oṃ/Mahaḥ*
Realm	This World	Intermediate Realm Between Heaven and Earth	Heaven	Brahman
Element	Fire	Air	Sun	Food
Veda	*Ṛg*	*Sāma*	*Yajur*	*Oṃ*/All *Vedas*
Vital Air	*Prāṇa*	*Apāna*	*Vyāna*	*Udāna*

"Food", here categorized under the *Oṃ Vyāhṛti*, symbolizes that which is the fundamental support of all life. It also symbolizes knowledge. This will be taken up in depth in chapter three. In essence, lesson five expresses that all the worlds are but aspects and outgrowths ("limbs") of the *Virāṭ*-Brahman, or the all-pervading Spirit which has assumed the form of the universe.[9]

Yogic Death

What happens to us when we die? Lesson six addresses this question from the point of view of the *yogī* who dies in a state of divine consciousness. It is said that what we meditate upon we become, so if we fix our minds on Brahman in the heart, that is what we will attain after death. "There is within the heart a bright space known to all," lesson six begins. This is Ātman, the true Self. There also exists within us a subtle energy system consisting of the *suśumnā*, a hollow canal running up the spine and through the crown at the seam of the skull, two major *nāḍis*, or nerve channels, situated on either side of the *suśumnā*, a hundred or so auxiliary *nāḍīs*, which permeate the body, and seven wheel-like energy centers along the spinal column, known as the *cakras*. Lesson six refers only to the *suśumnā* and its opening at the crown. "The worshipper, at the time of his final departure, gains his exit from the body through this passage." In other words, the life force ascends the *suśumnā* and exits the body through the top of the head. From here, the illumined soul passes through various states of consciousness, each increasingly subtle, until pure Brahman is reached.

Here is where knowledge of the *Vyāhṛtis* becomes relevant, for it is said that these are each experienced in turn as the *jīva* journeys to its final goal, the ultimate abode of peace, Brahman.

Meditation on the Elements of the Macrocosm and Microcosm

In Western esoteric literature, there is what is known as the Law of Correspondences, an idea expressed most simply: as above, so below. That which occurs on the macrocosmic level, out in the universe, is reflected on the microcosmic level, within ourselves. This is because the macrocosm and microcosm are intimately and inextricably connected and comprised of basically the same thing. From the view of modern physics, this is demonstrated by the fundamentally identical nature of everything at the subatomic level. From the Hindu point of view, this is demonstrated by the observation that all things, when broken down to their elemental properties, are revealed to be comprised of the same

The Subtle Energy System

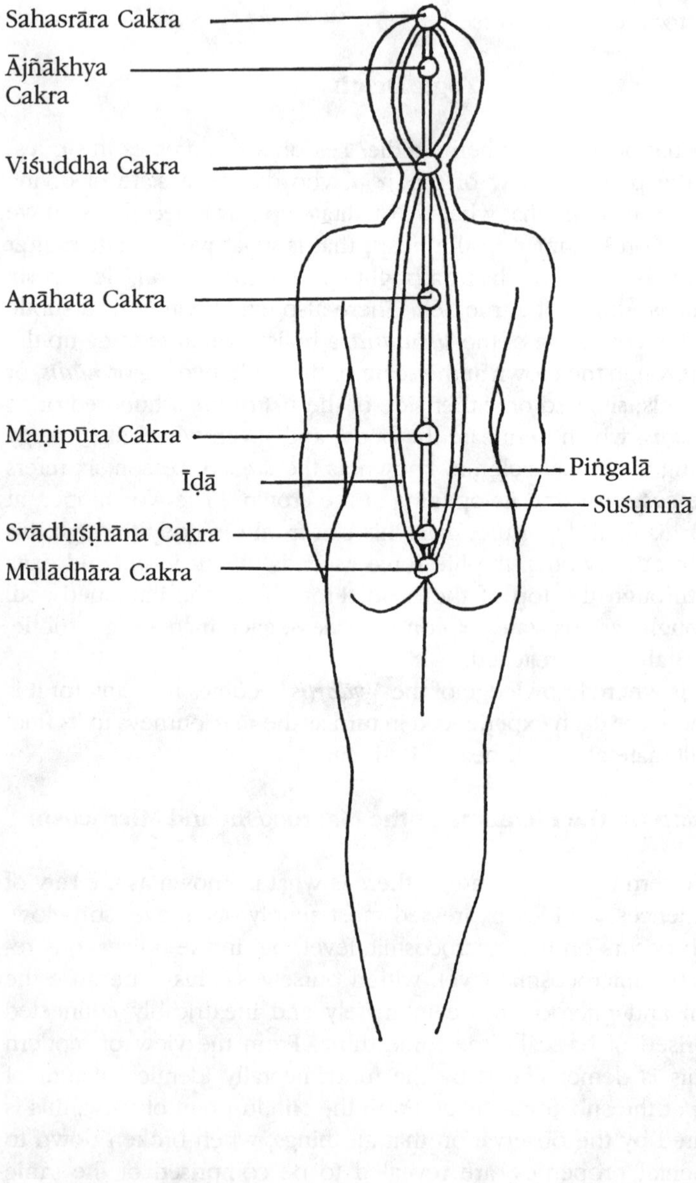

elements as all other things. Seen from this standpoint, the multiplicity, the individuality of things, fades away and a common, underlying oneness is seen.

Lesson seven guides the reader through a meditation based on such a dissection, encouraging the aspirant to examine, in turn, the elements which comprise the universe, the world, the body, the vital air, and the senses, a progression from the enormity of the macrocosm to the enormity of the microcosm.

The Power of *Oṃ*

The supremacy of *Oṃ* over all other *mantras* is colorfully illustrated in lesson eight, which describes a Vedic fire sacrifice replete with many levels of personnel being directed in their various duties. In the traditional ceremony, several different priests would preside, each with their own functions and *mantras.* The *Taittirīya Upaniṣad* here makes it clear that *Oṃ* is so direct, so ultimate, it is included in, and precedes, all *mantras.* Each priest in turn — the *Agnidhra*, *Udgātṛ*, *Hotṛ*, and *Adhvaryu* — begins his chanting with *Oṃ*. *Oṃ* is the basis of all sounds, of all ideas, of all reality.

Principles of Right Conduct for a Virtuous Life

Having touched upon the duties of the priests in the worship sacrifice, now the *Upaniṣad* turns to the duties compelling all of us. For the spiritual aspirant, one's entire life is worship, every thought, deed and act is surrendered to God in a perpetual mode of sacrifice. The Upaniṣadic mystics transformed the Vedic sacrifice into an internal worship of symbolic dimensions. The sacred fire was now the divine Self within, the offerings into the flames were now the mind, *prāṇa*, ego, desires, etc. Each one of us is a priest attending the sacred ceremony of our everyday lives. How, then, is this ceremony performed? Lesson nine is very explicit.

The codes of proper conduct are "fixed by the scriptural rules and *one's own reflection*" (italics mine). Blindly following rules for their own sake, like a robot, is no virtue. Consciously, deliberately, intelligently, and with a capacity for flexibility, we must live our lives so as to pursue the ideals of virtue, duty and growth. Often we must decide for ourselves what is right, and that requires maturity and conviction. Most of all, it requires selflessness.

Our duties, then, are studying and teaching the scriptures, truthfulness, self-denial, self-restraint, tranquility, attending to religious obligations, hospitality, helping others, and raising a good family. The lesson goes on to quote, however, certain sages who reduced the duties to just one or two. Rāthītara, for instance, held that truthfulness was the only necessary discipline. Pauruśiṣṭi believed devout austerity to be enough, while Mudgala insisted on the study and imparting of the *Vedas.* It would seem that any spiritual discipline, if carried out to perfection, would include in it all others, and would lead one to the ultimate Goal.

Identification with the Absolute

Short but powerful, lesson ten is a meditation on one's own divinity. "I am the stimulator of the tree of the universe," it says. In other words, I (the speaker of this verse is the sage Triśaṅku, but could just as well be you, or I, or anyone) am God, I am Brahman, the Supreme. We encountered the symbol of the tree in the *Kaṭha Upaniṣad* (2.3.1) and the *Bhagavad-Gītā* (15.1-2). In brief, it is the expression of the Divine as the universe, a single organism branching out into an infinite spectrum of phenomena.

"I am the excellent immortal Being, as He is in the sun." The sun, because of its radiance and its role as the sustainer of all life on this planet, is often used as a symbol for Brahman. But more than that, Brahman *is* in the sun, just as Brahman is within us. The *Bṛhadāraṇyaka Upaniṣad* expresses this concept exquisitely:

> This sun is like honey to all beings and all beings are like honey to this sun. The same with the shining, immortal being who is in this sun, and the shining, immortal being identified with the eye in this body. These four are but the Self. This Self-knowledge is the means of immortality; this underlying unity is Brahman; this knowledge of Brahman is the means of becoming all (2.5.5).

The one who realizes his or her own divinity becomes imperishable, immutable, resplendent.

Instructions for Disciples

Assuming that the disciple has mastered the instructions imparted in lesson nine, and has studied the *Veda* sufficiently, the preceptor now expands and elaborates upon those instructions, adding new duties and disciplines for the serious aspirant.

Again, truthfulness is admonished, as is faithfully attending to one's *dharma.* The scriptures should be recited mindfully, with heartfelt concentration, not mechanically. One should be attentive to the gods and forefathers, see to their own health, and always look upon their mother, father, *guru* and houseguests as gods. Carefully following the *guru's* instructions, one's conduct must be irreproachable and virtuous. When in the august company of those who are more distinguished, particularly in regard to spiritual attainments, one must be quiet and deferent.

Gifts, particularly those intended for a holy person or a needy or sick individual must be given gladly and willingly, not grudgingly. However, too extravagant of gifts, or gifts which stir pride in the giver, are not recommended (the text admonishes "modesty"), nor are forcing gifts upon those who disagree with the nature of the transaction (a range of possible scenarios present themselves here, such as bribery or gifts intended to instill guilt or obligation in the receiver).

If in doubt, compare your conduct to that of the *brāhmaṇas* and model yourself after them. The ideal *brāhmaṇa* is "experienced, independent, gentle, and intent on the *dharma*." The *Bhagavad-Gītā* says, "Peacefulness, self-control, austerity, purity, tolerance, honesty, knowledge, wisdom and religiousness — these are the natural qualities of a *brāhmaṇa*" (18.42). This is a standard against which to assess our own behavior. When unsure of what to do, one can ask oneself, "What would St. Francis do in this situation?" or "What would Swami Vivekananda do?" or "What would the Dalai Lama do?" and the answer should be obvious. In the West today there are few literal *brāhmaṇas* and even too few figurative ones to observe and pattern our behavior after, but we do have descriptions of great spiritual heroes of the past, the lives and teachings of the great saints and sages from around the world. Or perhaps we might know a great man or woman, not necessarily a spiritual aspirant, whose courtesy, compassion, strength, sweetness and poise are so great, they typify the *brāhmaṇa* ideal, and deserve to be emulated.

Chapter One ends with a closing peace invocation which reflects the one which opened the *Upaniṣad*, though with some variation. The preceding course of study having been successful, the speaker now offers thanks to the gods for their gracious help and protection.

Chapter Two: *Brahmānanda* (the Bliss of Brahman) *Valli*, Concerning The Five *Kośas*

Now that the preliminaries of discipleship have been addressed, we come to the core of the *Upaniṣad*, which deals directly with the aspirant's journey inward, the search for the divine Self in the center of one's being. One doesn't leap instantly from ordinary consciousness to realization of Ātman. There are layers which have to be dug through, barriers obstructing our understanding which must be recognized and overcome.

Westerners familiar with the fundamentals of psychotherapy will immediately recognize a similarity between its approach to the human condition and this aspect of Hindu philosophy. According to the psychoanalytic theory, a central component of our being, the unconscious, is normally unknown to us, hidden as it is behind a formidable barrier of amnesia and denial. We usually experience the conscious mind as all there is, identifying ourselves wholly with it, though all the while the unconscious is directing us and motivating us without our knowledge. Therapy is the means for removing the barrier and discovering the content of the unconscious.

Similarly, the Ātman is one's true Self, the fundamental basis of being, yet we are normally unaware of it, fixated as we are on the superficial. Just as the unconscious is buried under the consciousness, so is the Ātman buried under the five *kośas. Kośa* means "sheath", and the *kośas* are the five layers which cover the Ātman. They are the physical layer, the *prāṇic*, or vital energy layer, the mental layer, the intellectual layer, and the bliss layer. Chapter Two will elaborately examine the *kośas*, but a general outline of their form and function may be useful at this point.

The value of identifying and analyzing the *kośas* is that they help us to understand who we are. They comprise what we ordinarily experience as our personalities. We are not integrated beings, but fragmented ones, and we encounter this fact constantly. One part of the mind is telling us to do one thing while another part seems to be telling us to do another. The body has a craving which the intellect tries to suppress. We have feelings and longings we may disapprove of, or lack feelings for things we think we should have. This fragmentation of self is a source of constant torment for us, but there is consolation in the fact that the *kośas* do not comprise the true Self. The sense of selfhood derived from identifying with the *kośas* is an illusion, the play of *māyā*.

In meditation, the aspirant can discover and peel away each *kośa* like peeling away layers of an onion, until he or she severs identification with them and is left with the pure, divine consciousness of Ātman.

Anna. The *annamaya-kośa* is the gross, physical sheath, the body. The word *anna* means "food" and is so named because the physical body is sustained by food and, in the animal kingdom, is food for another. In Upaniṣadic symbolism, food represents material nature, for anything which is drawn in through the senses is a kind of food (so we have food for our ears, food for our fingers, a "feast for the eyes", "food for thought", etc.). Food also symbolizes knowledge, and the body is the organ through which we gather all manner of information. This food metaphor will figure prominently in the third chapter.

Prāṇa. Prāṇa is the life force, the vital energy, and it permeates all existence. Motion, gravitation, magnetism, and the vital principle which sustains physical life are all expression of *prāṇa.*[10] When the *prāṇa* leaves, a body dies. The *prāṇamaya-kośa* is the vital energy sheath, more subtle than the physical sheath, but more gross than the sheaths which follow.

Manas. The *manomaya-kośa* is the mental sheath. This is the rumbling cauldron where images, ideas, information, all the stuff which thoughts are made of dwell — snippets of songs, sudden memories, the mad, irrational constant babble in our heads. Indian psychologists many centuries ago noticed that our minds seem to be divided. One part rumbles merrily along while the other coolly watches it and imposes reason upon the chaos. They named the rumbling part *manas* and the reasoning part *vijñāna.* We have no corresponding terms in English, but the accepted, if misleading, English equivalents are "mind" and "intellect".

Vijñāna. The intellectual, or discrimination sheath, *vijñānamaya-kośa*, is rational thought, individual will. It is this which most people mistake for the true "self". But this, like all the *kośas*, is in a state of constant change, endless flux, and therefore is not the Self. This faculty is also known as *buddhi.*

Ānanda. The *ānandamaya-kośa*, the most subtle of the sheaths, is the closest to the Ātman. *Ānanda* means "bliss", and at the center of our beings is sweetness and joy, if we can reach down that far. The rapture we feel on the earthly plane has its source in the *ānandamaya-kośa.* Though the bliss of this sheath is akin to the bliss of the Ātman, it is not the same, and the two should not be confused.

At the center of the *kośas*, but always separate and unaffected by them, is the Ātman. One might think of it as a light bulb burning brightly, and the *kośas* as scarves of increasingly dark color and thickness wrapped, each in turn, around the light. By removing the scarves, the light is gradually revealed.

Though we can diagram the *kośas* as concentric layers to facilitate understanding, the fact is they are not actually layered one atop the other. They all occupy the same space, but as each is more subtle than the last, they do not interfere with each other.

Now, it appears that the combination of *kośas* are what comprise an individual. This is only partly true. They contribute to the illusion of individuality, but the reality is that each person does not possess his or her own private *kośas.* There are not five billion *annamaya-kośas*, there is only one, which we all share. The physical plane, as contemporary physics has revealed, is not a collection of individual objects, but an organic

The Five *Kośas*

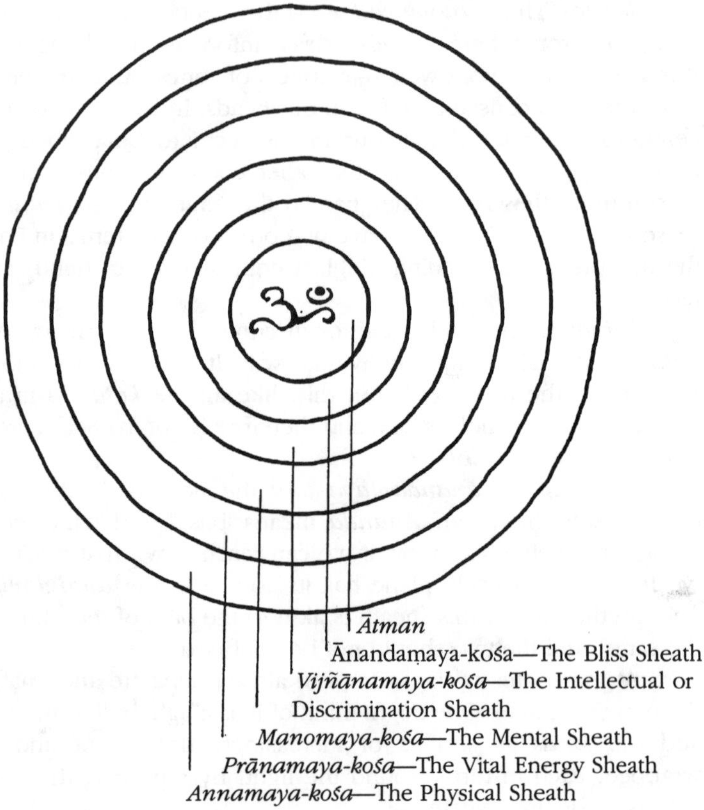
Ātman
Ānandamaya-kośa—The Bliss Sheath
Vijñānamaya-kośa—The Intellectual or Discrimination Sheath
Manomaya-kośa—The Mental Sheath
Prāṇamaya-kośa—The Vital Energy Sheath
Annamaya-kośa—The Physical Sheath

oneness, a single substance. The physical matter of which your body is comprised is literally connected to, bonded with, at one with, that of someone on the other side of the planet. The crazy soup of your mind is drawn from a communal soup, a common mind which we all share. Why do cultures that have never had contact with each other have the same myths? Perhaps because all people draw their images from the collective mind. So it is with all the *kośas.*

One of the most profound, and most comforting, meditations is on the universality of the *kośas*, and the second chapter of the *Taittirīya Upaniṣad* will walk the reader through it. To imagine one's body not one's own, but part of an indivisible oneness, helps one to detach from it. Similarly, seeing one's life force not as an individual event but as part of an energy field that connects all life, one can disown the particular life and become merged in the general life. The mind, too, is merely a fragment of the universal mind, the intellect a reflection of the universal intellect. The sense of "I-ness" which you feel right now (your ego or, in Hindu terms, *ahaṃkāra*, "I-maker") is the identical "I-ness" your neighbor, cat and bitterest enemy are experiencing as well. There are no two egos, just one ego, one *ahaṃkāra.* Why, then, do you feel that you are you while your cat feels she's your cat? It is the inscrutable magic of *māyā.*

Of course, the truth underlying all of this is that *anna* is Brahman, *prāṇa* is Brahman, *manas* is Brahman, *vijñāna* is Brahman, *ānanda* is Brahman and the Ātman is Brahman. That everything you can imagine is Brahman is the truth to which the *Upaniṣads* return again and again. The aspirant can meditate upon each *kośa* in turn and merge it into the oneness of Brahman until the Ātman is revealed and the aspirant is merged into It. This is one of the most efficacious meditations.

Now let us turn to the text.

After the invocation, lesson one gets right to the point: "He who realizes Brahman attains the Supreme." This is the whole of Upaniṣadic wisdom in a nutshell. There is no higher philosophy than this, and it is the conclusion to which all *Upaniṣads* point. What is Brahman? According to the text, Brahman is Existence (*Sat*), Intelligence (*Jñāna*), and Bliss, or Infinitude (*Ānanda*). This formula diverges slightly from the standard *Sat-Cit-Ānanda* (Existence-Consciousness-Bliss), though basically conveys the same idea. Brahman can be found "in the cave", in other words in the heart, "in the highest ether", in other words in the space in the heart, the inner Self, which is identical to the space outside, the universal Self.

Lesson one continues by tracing the unfolding of the elements of creation from the most subtle (beginning with the Ātman) to the most gross (the human body) to establish the continuum and oneness underlying all things. Food is identified as being the essence of the body; remember that the physical sheath is termed *anna*, "food", and that food is the Upaniṣadic terminology signifying matter, Nature, sense objects, knowledge.

The body is now poetically conceived of in the shape of a bird: "This indeed is his head; this his right wing; this his left wing; this his trunk; this his hind part forming the support and foundation." Why imagine our bodies as the bodies of birds? This is a literary device to better draw out the philosophical implications of the topic at hand, which will be the interconnectedness of the individual with various aspects of the *kośas*. The shape of a bird's body is better suited to this analogy. Like a cross, it has a front part, and left part, a right part and a back part (here considered the "support and foundation"). There is a sense of connecting, intersecting, uniting. The human form is cumbersome in this particular case. Swāmī Śarvānanda explains:

> Only when the body is conceived in the shape of a bird can we speak of a tail and support; and only when each *kośa* is pictured as endowed with this support, the last *kośa* can be spoken of as having its ground in Brahman. This is the significance of the bird analogy.[11]

So let us imagine ourselves to be birds.

Annamaya-kośa, the Physical Sheath, and *Prāṇamaya-kośa*, the Vital Force Sheath

Food, that is, matter, is the ground of all things in the physical world, lesson two begins. Everything is born from it, has its being in it, is sustained by it, and returns to it. Matter, we know, is nothing more than energy, and energy is never created or destroyed; it merely changes its form. This discovery of modern science was prefigured by approximately twenty-five centuries in this *Upaniṣad*. Matter is Brahman; it is sacred and divine. Hinduism is not a pessimistic or world-denying religion; to the contrary, it reveres the divine in all things, including Nature, inanimate objects, and even the human body, which it does not look upon with disgust, but respects as an expression of God and a tool for attaining spiritual perfection. There is no antagonism between matter and spirit because there is no real dichotomy between them. They are both aspects of a unified Reality.[12]

Contained within this physical form, or sheath, is another form, the *prāṇamaya-kośa*. It fills the same space as the physical sheath and has the same shape: "That one (the *annamaya-kośa*) being in the form of a person, this one (the *prāṇamaya-kośa*) also, accordingly, is in the form of a person." It gives form and support to the preceding *kośa*, which would disperse without it. *Prāṇa* is the life force, the vital energy; when it departs, the physical sheath disintegrates. In our bodies, this *prāṇa* is further broken down into five distinct subcategories, each energy being responsible for different bodily functions. These five vital energies are termed *prāṇa*, *vyāna*, *apāna*, *samāna*, and *udāna*; together they comprise, nourish and uphold the *prāṇic* sheath. Here the bird analogy is used. *Prāṇa* is his head, *vyāna* his right wing, *apāna* his left wing, *samāna* his trunk, and *udāna* his tail, or "support and foundation".

Lesson three continues on the subject of *prāṇa*, indicating that all life is dependent on it, and that an individual life is but an eddy in the ocean of the universal Life, the one *prāṇic* field we all share.[13] *Prāṇa* is Brahman.

Manomaya-kośa, the Mental Sheath

The lesson now proceeds to the *manomaya-kośa*, the mental sheath. Just as the *prāṇic* sheath was the same form and gave support and structure to the physical sheath, so, too, is the mental sheath of the same shape as the *prāṇic* and supports its existence. Each *kośa* is wholly dependent on the more subtle one preceding it. The *prāṇamaya-kośa* is "filled" by *manas*. Clearly, a profound mind-body continuum is suggested here; it is no wonder that stress, depression and negativity foster physical illness, while joy and positivity promote health.

Our mental life is supported by learning. *Manas* is the repository of all sense impressions, experiences, knowledge, facts. It is crucial that we fill this repository with ennobling and intelligent things, rather than with trash. One of the best-loved peace invocations reads, "O gods, may we hear with our ears what is auspicious. O Ye adorable ones, may we see with our eyes what is auspicious."[14] Every sound and image our senses encounter enter our consciousness and fix themselves there permanently. On a conscious level we may not remember them or may choose not to think about them, but they are there, subtly influencing us, informing our character and actions. If we subject ourselves to images of violence, misogyny, sexual degradation and general ghastliness so prevalent in films, music and books today, our poor *manas* will be filled with such horrors. They will haunt us and motivate us in ways we are not even aware of. On the other hand, if we expose our *manas* to that which promotes wisdom, beauty, *dharma*, art, those things will become part of us. We are what we eat.

In this regard, the *Upaniṣad* states that wisdom, learning, literature, particularly sacred literature comprises *manas*. The *Vedas* are *manas'* mainstay and support: "*Yajus* is his head, *Ṛk* is his right wing, *Sāma* his left wing, the injunctive part of the *Vedas* (the *Brāhmaṇas*) is his trunk and the hymns of the *Atharva Veda* are his support." Further, the *Vedas* can be viewed as the concrete manifestation of the universal *Manas*, which has its origin and grounding in Brahman.

Vijñānamaya-kośa, the Intellectual or Discrimination Sheath, and *Ānandamaya-kośa*, the Bliss Sheath

In a verse very similar to many in the *Kena Upaniṣad* ("That which cannot be comprehended by the mind but by which the mind comprehends, know that alone to be Brahman" (1.6)), lesson four opens by reminding us that neither by speech nor by mind can Brahman be known, though one that does know Brahman sheds fear completely and permanently.

Resuming the thematic thread, the *Upaniṣad* introduces the *vijñānamaya-kośa*, the sheath of intellect or discrimination, the reasoning faculty, the will. It fills and supports the *manomaya-kośa*. The higher virtues are its manifestation, the expression of the universal *vijñāna*. Thus, *śraddhā*, faith, is his head, right is his right wing, truth his left, *yoga* his trunk, and *mahat* (the cosmic intellect or *Hiraṇyagarbha*, the universal ego which is the ground of all egos[15]) is his tail, or foundation. Lesson five picks up the topic; *vijñāna* is Brahman, it says, and one who meditates on this is freed from all sins.

Within the *vijñānamaya-kośa* is the bliss sheath, the *ānandamaya-kośa*. Love is his head, joy his right wing, delight his left wing, bliss his trunk. Brahman Itself is his foundation. It is very close to the Divine, and the source of all our experiences of joy. It is extremely subtle and pure.

How Do We Know Brahman Is Real?

The *kośas* having been explained, the aspirant now knows how to proceed, through the vehicle of meditation, through the various layers of the personality until the kernel of Selfhood, Ātman, is discovered. But the *Upaniṣad* now raises an objection. How do we know that when the five sheaths are, figuratively speaking, stripped away, there will be anything there? How do we know they aren't all there is of us? This question is actually posed in the middle of lesson six, while the answer frames it in two parts, one before it, one after.

"If a person takes Brahman for an unreality, truly be becomes a nonentity." In other words, the skeptic's life is tragic and useless. Such a person has no ultimate ideal, no ultimate goal, only an endless stream of unfulfilled desires and fragmentary flashes of sense-enjoyment. Their pursuits are vain because no matter how conspicuous the trappings of their worldly "success", without an underlying foundation of meaning, life remains empty and absurd. Brahman is that meaning. Conversely, "If he understands that Brahman is an existent entity, in consequence of that, the wise will consider him right and good." Even if one fails to achieve the measure of material "success" set so arbitrarily by society, if one commits one's life to seeking Brahman, it has been an infinitely superior life to that of the majority of people.

Yeah, yeah, we think, but how do we *know* that? Lesson six says that the existence of Brahman can be proved because Brahman *is* existence. That anything exists, instead of there being nothing, is proof that Brahman is real. Creation is Brahman Itself; the Divine has entered into and permeates all creation.[16] To question the existence of Brahman is absurd, because that is questioning the existence of anything, including oneself. The *Upaniṣad* says,

> He, the Ātman, desired: May I become many; let me procreate Myself. He brooded over Himself. Having brooded, He projected all this — whatever there is here. Having brought it forth, verily He entered into it; having entered into it, He became the Being and the Beyond. He became the defined and the undefined, the founded and the foundationless, the conscious and the unconscious, the real and the unreal.

The Sweetness of Brahman

It is the presence of Brahman, lesson seven says, that lends creation its loveliness. "He, truly, is the flavor (*rasa*) which is the essence of existence." It is because Brahman underlies creation that we derive pleasure from this world. *Rasa* is sweetness, nectar, delectability. "Who, indeed, would breathe, who would remain alive if this Bliss were not in the ether!" We derive pleasure from breathing because Brahman is in the air, deeply enjoy eating because Brahman is in the food, become intoxicated by beautiful music because Brahman is in the music, long for love because Brahman is in the beloved. This sting of bliss is *rasa*, and it is a microscopic reflection of the unlimited, ecstatic bliss which can be had from the direct experience of Brahman.

The antithesis of bliss is fear. Brahman is absolute fearlessness. The *Upaniṣad* states that fear comes into being only when there is a sense of "two", rather than of "One": "Whenever it (the individual) assumes the smallest interval in that state of identity (with Brahman), then it has fear." In Oneness there is no possibility of fear, no other thing to be afraid of, no subject to be threatened.

Continuing the topic through lesson eight, a verse identical to that of *Kaṭha Upaniṣad* 2.3.3 appears to contradict the preceding lesson: "Out of fear of Him, the wind blows, through fear of Him the sun rises . . . etc." This is picturesque speech only, because Brahman, being bliss and fearlessness itself, cannot be feared. The verse is indicating that all earthly phenomena occur because of the power of Brahman and are subordinate to It. On the other hand, phenomena occur because of the illusion of differentiation, because of, to quote the preceding lesson, the "interval in that state of identity." Brahman, in Its undifferentiated state, is actionless. So, the differentiation makes possible all action and phenomena. It also creates fear. Hence, fear and phenomena are linked.

The rest of the lesson concentrates on the sweetness and bliss of Brahman. It tries to give the reader some semblance of how intense the bliss of Brahman realization is by following a sort of joy hierarchy through higher and higher levels. If we have a youth in the prime of life, perfect health, with great learning and the entire earth laden with all riches, this is one unit of joy. A *Gandharva's* joy (*Gandharvas* are winged, celestial beings, heavenly musicians) is one hundred times greater than this. The joy of the *Pitṛs* (celestial progenitors) are one hundred times greater than the joy of the *Gandharvas*. The joy of the gods in the *Ājāna* heaven is one hundred times greater than this.

So up the ladder does it go, until we reckon the joy experienced by Lord Brahmā as a million billion times more intense than the joy of the happiest human on earth.[17] The bliss of the knower of Brahman, however, is greater even than that of Brahmā because it is the bliss of Brahman Itself, a bliss which cannot be calculated. The *Upaniṣad* says it is the same as the bliss "in the yonder sun". The sun, which is radiant and is the sustainer of all life, here symbolizes Brahman.

This liberated one, after departing from this life, transcends all five of the *kośas*, casts them off, and is unlimited and free. The liberated one who is still in the body, the lesson concludes, is free from all fear. Furthermore, he has reached such a state of perfection, he never has to discern and decide between the right thing to do and the wrong thing to do. He need not expend any special effort to be virtuous. Such a person cannot do wrong, cannot err, and so is free from society's conventions.

Chapter Three: *Bhṛgu Valli*, Concerning *Anna*, the Sustaining and Transforming Energy of Brahman

The young Bhṛgu approaches his father, the sage Varuṇa, and requests that he be instructed about Brahman. So begins the third chapter. As is generally the case in the *Upaniṣads*, the teacher does not reveal the full implications of Brahman right away, but leads the student through various levels of understanding, from the gross, through the subtle, and to the Divine, allowing the student to draw inferences and make conclusions for himself. The *kośas* will figure prominently in Bhṛgu's search, as will the symbol of *anna*, food, which will assume another level of meaning here.

As a preliminary, Varuṇa instructs his son about "Food, vital airs, sight, hearing, mind and speech." Food, vital airs and mind correspond to the physical, *prāṇic* and mental *kośas*, while hearing and speech can refer either to the knowledge-gathering senses or, collectively, to *vijñāna*, the intellectual sheath.[18] In either case, all of these functions are gateways to knowledge, and as such must be understood, developed, and disciplined as a preparation for spiritual practice. We read that Bhṛgu then plunged himself into performing austerity. The phrase, "He (Bhṛgu) performed austerity," will be repeated five times, a powerful reminder that austerities (*tapas*, literally "that which burns")[19] are necessary in the pursuit of spiritual perfection.

After performing *tapas*, Bhṛgu realizes that food, or matter, is Brahman. All beings have their origin in matter (their parents' bodies), are kept alive by matter (food, water, fire, etc.), and upon departing, will return to matter (as the body decomposes and returns to the elements). This discovery corresponds to the *annamaya-kośa*. Approaching his father again, Bhṛgu is told to practice further austerity.

His next discovery is that *prāṇa* is Brahman. Like *anna*, all beings are born from, sustained by, and reabsorbed into it. "More austerity," Dad says, and Bhṛgu discovers that *manas*, mind, is Brahman. On he goes, step by step, through *vijñāna* and *ānanda* in the same way, until he passes beyond the *kośas* and arrives at the abode of "Supreme Bliss hidden in the cave." The cave, of course, means the heart, the seat of the Self.

From here through lesson nine, the *Upaniṣad* will analyze and extol the powers of food, *anna*. As was explained earlier, food is a subtle and complex metaphor suggesting a number of meanings. It can represent matter, or Nature, vital substance which is constantly transforming and causing transformation. All food — meat, vegetables, milk, eggs, etc. — must possess life force, must have its origin in living things (though some of the junk we eat is so processed, so de-vitalized, its connection to a living source is difficult to trace). In order for a substance to nourish life, it must possess life. Thus Nature is a massive food chain.

On another level, food symbolizes anything taken in by our senses. As was mentioned before, all stimuli that reaches our senses penetrate us and become a part of us. Our eyes "eat" images and those images imbed themselves our consciousness and inform who we are and how we react. Our ears "eat" sounds, our minds "eat" books, our fingers "eat" surfaces. All these experiences are absorbed, processed, and relegated to some level of consciousness or forgetfulness, but they never entirely go away. They are always a part of us, influencing us in subtle ways (that is, until one takes up spiritual practice, for *sādhanā* helps incinerate, as it were, these old sense impressions — remember the etymology of *tapas* is "that which burns").

When we eat literal food, we may react to different foods in different ways.[20] One delights us, one disgusts us, one keeps us up all night, another calms us, one gives us vitality, another saps our energies. And each person reacts differently to each food. What is perfectly fine for one person may be dangerous to another, depending on their constitution. This is true, too, of the myriad of sense impressions bombarding us all the time. What may be life-alteringly significant to one person may be impossibly incoherent or banal to another because the two are at different phases in their lives. What frightens one man may invigorate his brother. Music which soothes a teenaged girl may irritate her mother. Does this "food", then, have an objective reality of its own? Is it significant or incoherent? Frightening or invigorating? Soothing or irritating? Does it have any qualities we can unequivocally label as true, or are those labels dependent on our reactions and definitions, which may vary from person to person? What nourishes one child, another cannot swallow.

On yet a third level, food symbolizes knowledge, and by now it should be easy to see the connection. Everything that is taken in through the senses is a kind of knowledge. Some of it is very mundane knowledge ("it is daytime," "that is a flower", etc.), some very sophisticated ("light is both a wave and a particle"), some divine ("He who realizes Brahman attains the Supreme"). Some knowledge we are ready to understand and accept, some we are not. Still, everything we encounter, in one way or another, contributes to our store of knowledge.

With all this in mind, the next three and a half lessons are not difficult to interpret. One can replace the word "food" with "matter," "Nature", or "knowledge" to reveal slightly different, yet complimentary readings. Lesson six states that the knower of Brahman "commands food and gets the power to assimilate and enjoy it." In other words, such a one has insight into the true nature of things; one sees the Reality underlying everything and enjoys the bliss of realization; one commands knowledge, assimilates knowledge, enjoys knowledge.

The Interconnectedness of All Things

"One should not blame food," lesson seven says. In other words, one should not disdain the world. The Western horror of "the flesh" (a pathology which has led not only to people's disrespect of their own bodies, but of Nature as well and, as a result, the destruction of the earth's natural environment) is unequivocally rejected here. Matter, the physical world, is knowledge; it is good. It is Brahman.

"Life, indeed, is food. Body is the eater of food. Body is set in life; life is set in the body. Therefore food is established on food." *Anna* and *prāṇa* are mutually dependent.[21] In the lessons that follow, this same formula will be repeated, with slight variation of the element under scrutiny, to show how everything is interdependent. We begin with the body, then move on to water, of which the body is primarily comprised, then to fire ("Water , indeed, is food. Fire is the eater of food . . . etc."), then to earth, and finally to ether ("the earth, indeed, is food. Ether is the eater of food . . . etc.").

There is a unity connecting everything. The *Upaniṣad* repeatedly exhorts the aspirant to contemplate this unity: "He who contemplates food which is based on food is firmly established." If everything is food — life, the Earth, the eater (subject) and eaten (object) — then food takes on yet another, deeper level of meaning. Food is Spirit, food is Brahman, food is God. We are established in That. God is eater and eaten, both subject and object. It is the nourisher and that which is nourished. It is both knowledge and the knower. One who realizes this sublime reality, this unity beyond all dualities, is blessed with all happiness: "He becomes the enjoyer of food (knowledge, reality, Brahman), commanding plenty of food." All abundance, both physical and spiritual, are his: "In the effulgence born of sacred wisdom, he becomes great."

Sharing Food / Remembering Brahman

Lesson ten extends the food theme by advocating, in very direct and worldly terms, the sharing of food as a religious duty. In India, food does have a central role in religious observance. Merit is accrued by offering food to *brāhmaṇas*, holy people, and the poor. Food is offered to household and temple deities and, thus consecrated, distributed. Feasts accompany all major festivals, and it is considered a matter of *dharma* to offer the utmost hospitality, in other words food, to any and all visitors to one's home, even enemies. But there is a deeper, symbolic significance to the sharing of food. Sharing food symbolizes the partaking of the universal Oneness, the Oneness of our collective *anna*, *prāṇa*, *manas*, *vijñāna*, *ānanda*, and Ātman. By supporting each other's physical wellness, we are supporting and honoring the divine Whole.

Suddenly shifting without warning, lesson ten now turns to the subject of the many different ways one can meditate on and remember Brahman. It rather resembles, in theme at least, the tenth chapter of the *Bhagavad-Gītā.* Brahman being all-pervading, anything can be associated with Brahman. We can remember Brahman constantly by observing It in all worldly phenomena: one's body, the rain, the stars, space, even sexual pleasure. However, it goes on the say that the meditator comes to possess whichever attributes he or she meditates upon. If she meditates upon Brahman as the *Veda*, she will possess Vedic wisdom. If she meditates upon Brahman as the universal mind, she will possess mindfulness. If she meditates upon Brahman as destructive power, her enemies will die around her! Thus, it is necessary to discriminate in choosing which attribute to concentrate on.

The Boundless Joy of Mystical Realization

At last we reach the climax of this extraordinary scripture, and an ecstatic one it is. In an explosion of Bliss, the realization of one's Brahmanhood is achieved. The Aspirant casts off the five *kośas* and "traverses the worlds, enjoying food and assuming forms at will." Going beyond the limitations of individuality, the aspirant has now become everything. She "traverses these worlds" because she is everywhere at once. She assumes "forms at will" because she is now all forms, all things, living and inanimate, everything that ever was, is, or will be.

And the liberated one is singing in joy: "I am food! I am food! I am food! I am the food-eater! I am the food eater! I am the food-eater!" She realizes herself to be both the universe and the Spirit that pervades and transcends the universe. She is the consciousness in all beings. "I exist even prior to the gods, I am the center and source of immortality! . . . I am a splendor like the sun!"

No higher realization exists than this, no greater state of rapture.

NOTES

1. Swāmī Śarvānanda, *Taittirīyopaniṣad*, (Mylapore: Sri Ramakrishna Math, 1977).
2. Śarvānanda, p. 3.
3. Śarvānanda, p. 26.
4. Śarvānanda, p. 26.
5. Śarvānanda, p. 25.
6. *Ramakrishna-Vedanta Wordbook* (Hollywood: Vedānta Press, 1962), p. 76.; Stutley and Stutley, p. 293.
7. Śarvānanda, p. 39.
8. Śarvānanda, p. 43.
9. Śarvānanda, p. 43; *Ramakrishna-Vedanta Wordbook*, p. 84.
10. *Ramakrishna-Vedanta Wordbook*, p. 56.
11. Śarvānanda, p. 89.
12. Śarvānanda, p. 93.
13. Śarvānanda, p. 98.
14. Swami Parasharānanda, ed., *Garland of Prayers* (Singapore: Ramakrishna Mission Singapore, 1990), p. 7.
15. Śarvānanda, p. 104.
16. Śarvānanda, p. 114.
17. Śarvānanda, p. 130.
18. Śarvānanda, pp. 139-140.
19. Swami Harshānanda, *A Dictionary of Advaita Vedānta* (Bangalore: Sri Ramakrishna Ashrama, 1990), p. 78.
20. The ideas in the following paragraph are drawn, in part, from a lecture by Dr. Margaret Bedrosian at the Vedanta Society of Sacramento, June 28, 1992.
21. Śarvānanda, p. 156.

A Note on the Longer *Upaniṣads*: *Chāndogya* and *Bṛhadāraṇyaka*

If you study the nine short *Upaniṣads* with care, you can consider yourself well-educated in the genre. You will have developed a grasp of Upaniṣadic language, simile, metaphor, and modes of argument as well as more technical matters, such as the *prāṇas* and the *kośas*. The basic Upaniṣadic philosophy of *Vedānta* will be clear. I strongly suggest reading the shorter ones before attempting the longer ones. If you do, much of what you encounter now will be familiar to you and you can glide through it without a struggle. Plunging into the lengthier texts first will probably frustrate the average reader to the point of exasperation.

Both the *Chāndogya* and *Bṛhadāraṇyaka Upaniṣads* are seeped in archaisms. Both draw heavily upon the imagery and language of Vedic ritual and cosmology, which are very removed from the experience of contemporary Westerners and obscure their understanding of the philosophical concepts rather than illuminate them. There is much here which is wonderful and useful, but it is sandwiched between long passages which are of virtually no relevance to the Westerner, save the devoted Indologist, linguist or religious studies scholar.

As the present text is designed to be a guidebook for the general reader, the two remaining *Upaniṣads* will not be examined in their entirety nor in as great of depth as the preceding ones. The reason is threefold. First, analyzing each verse would result in too much repetition of what has been covered in the preceding chapters. No doubt the reader has noticed that the contents of the *Upaniṣads* overlap each other greatly, even word-for-word at times. Having studied most of the *Upaniṣads*, the reader will find much in the *Chāndogya* and *Bṛhadāraṇyaka* which is already familiar to them.

Second, certain parts of the longer texts are so obscure and difficult, the general reader is probably better off skimming through them and noting the general ideas but not lingering over them. A painstaking analysis we leave to the scholars. Instead, we will focus on the sections that are the most relevant and interesting to us, the "good parts". My job is to help you locate them, to guide you through this dense forest to the treasures that lie hidden within it. And the treasures *are* there — some of the most celebrated of all Upaniṣadic verses, in fact. That some sections are relevant to us while others are not is testified by the fact that Swāmī Prabhavānanda and Frederick Manchester, in their translation of the principal *Upaniṣads* simply omit large sections of the *Chāndogya* and

Bṛhadāraṇyaka Upaniṣads. We can confidently do the same without worrying that we are cheating ourselves.

Thirdly, were we to examine each verse, the size of the present volume may be close to doubled. The *Chāndogya* and *Bṛhadāraṇyaka* (in fact, all of the *Upaniṣads*) deserve an entire book to themselves. I imagine my readers would tire before completing the chapter anyway and would skip on to the *Śrīmad Bhāgavatam*, which is more fun.

And spiritual life should be fun. Study of the scripture should be enlivening and delicious, not an ordeal. To that effect, let us bite straight into the juicy parts.

CHAPTER SIXTEEN

Chāndogya Upaniṣad: A Meditation on the Practice of Upāsanā, or Drawing the Mind, in Steps, from the Mundane to the Divine

An *upāsanā* is an Upaniṣadic meditation. The goal is realization of Brahman, but the method favored by the *Upaniṣads* is not to try to fix the mind straightaway on Brahman (for one's mind would be flailing helplessly if one did, it being unaccustomed to thinking of something without form, quality, limit or context), but to draw it gradually, step by step, from the mundane to the Divine. *Upāsanā* employs sets of correspondences, relationships, connections, causes. We have encountered them in preceding chapters, but no *Upaniṣad* utilizes them as heavily as the *Chāndogya.*

The *Chāndogya Upaniṣad* also relies heavily upon storytelling as a means of conveying its wisdom. It contains both allegorical tales and lofty dialogues between illumined teachers and their students. We will meet the patient Satyakāma, who learns the wisdom of Nature, and humble Upakosala, who is instructed by the sacred fires. We will see the caste system turned topsy-turvy when the *brāhmaṇa* Gautama approaches the *kṣatriya* king Pravāhaṇa for instruction. Even celestials enter into the *guru-śiṣya* relationship when Indra, king of the *devas,* and Virocana, king of the *asuras,* surrender to the primordial progenitor, Prajāpati, as disciples. Swans talk, the senses have a contest, and bulls teach the wisdom of Brahman.

Interspersed with these stories are passages devoted to the performance of ritual, to chanting, to cosmological correspondences with ceremonial objects, and the like. The *Chāndogya Upaniṣad* is associated with the *Sāma Veda. Sāma* means "song" and it is a *Veda* geared to liturgical uses, specifically the performance of elaborate fire sacrifices. As such, the *Chāndogya Upaniṣad* is preoccupied with the subject of singing, its efficacy and symbolism, the meanings of various *mantras* and syllables. The reader needn't get discouraged climbing through this jungle of symbolic semantics if he or she keeps in mind that the *Upaniṣad* is always headed in the same direction: Brahman. The basis of all sounds, we will learn, is *Oṃ*, and *Oṃ* is Brahman. The *sāmas* are designed to lead us to the realization of Brahman if we are wise enough to see into their true nature.

Before commencing study of the *Chāndogya Upaniṣad*, it will be helpful to understand a few particulars regarding the *Soma* sacrifice, for it provides the underlying context for much of the *Upaniṣad's* terminology and imagery.[1] At one time, every *brāhmaṇa* family was expected to stage a *Soma* sacrifice at least once every three generations. A ceremony in honor of the Vedic god Soma, it was an elaborate and expensive undertaking, requiring costly paraphernalia and the services of no less than sixteen priests. The four major priests were known as the *Hotā*, *Adhvaryu*, *Brahmā*, and *Udgātā*, each presiding over a specific function of the ceremony and each assisted by three additional priests. Central to the *Soma* rite were the hymns of the *Sāma Veda*, which are divided into five sections, each sung by a different priest. The five divisions are the *Prastāva*, *Udgītha*, *Pratihāra*, *Upadrava*, and *Nidhana*. The *Prastāva* was sung by a priest known as the *Prastotā*, the *Udgītha* by the *Udgātā*, the *Pratihāra* by the *Pratihartā*, the *Upadrava* again by the *Udgātā*, and the *Nidhana* by the priests collectively. At the commencement of the ritual, the *Oṃkāra* (the *mantra Oṃ*) and the *Hiṃkāra* (the *mantra Hiṃ*) were chanted by the priests together. Other elements of the sacrifice included preparing the altar, kindling the fire, pouring the *Soma* juice into the ceremonial receptacles, offering oblations into the fire, and animal sacrifice. Each phase of the ritual had its own corresponding *mantras* and hymns, which had to be sung perfectly and by a priest especially trained for the function.

The *Chāndogya Upaniṣad* raises the significance of this ritual to a subtle, symbolic level. The implements, the *mantras*, etc., are seen as earthly counterparts to spiritual realities. The performance of the sacrifice draws the mind beyond the earthly phenomena to the cosmic phenomena it manipulates and represents, then to the divine Reality beyond the cosmic phenomena. This imposition of a symbolic dimension upon the ancient Vedic rituals was a major contribution of the Upaniṣadic *ṛṣis*, who saw the ceremonies as so much empty formalism otherwise. Keeping the *Soma* sacrifice in mind will be helpful in understanding the *Chāndogya Upaniṣad*, particularly the first two chapters.

Chapter One: On *Oṃ*

Oṃ is the first syllable which is chanted in the sacrifice. Thus we begin at the very beginning. Yet *Oṃ* is Brahman, the Ultimate, the Supreme, the very End. The beginning is the end, the end the beginning.

"One should meditate on this letter *Oṃ*, which is *Udgītha*," the *Upaniṣad* opens. The term *Udgītha* refers to the second part of the *Sāma Veda* or to the *Sāma Veda* as a whole. The word literally means "to chant aloud."[2] *Oṃ* is the seed-sound from which all other sounds are derived, the *mantra* which is basis of all *mantras*. It is the sound which corresponds to Brahman, and just as *Oṃ* is the source, substance and underlying support of all sounds, so is Brahman the source, substance and underlying support of everything. Both *Oṃ* and Brahman are all Reality. The various verses of section one demonstrate that whatever thing one chooses to examine, its essence can be traced back to *Oṃ*.

The Story of the Gods, Demons and Senses

Of all the functions of the body, *Oṃ* (*Udgītha*) is the most closely associated with the *prāṇa*, for the *prāṇa* is so subtle it cannot be polluted or tainted by any outside influence. This fact is illustrated by a story narrated in section two wherein the *devas* (gods) and *asuras* (demons) were fighting, as usual. The perpetual battle between the *devas* and *asuras* is generally believed to represent the maintenance of universal balance through the harmonious tension of the cosmic duality, rather like the Chinese Yin-Yang.

Believing they could defeat the *asuras* with the *Udgītha*, the *devas* took it up. First "they meditated on the vital force in the nose as *Udgītha*." But the *asuras* afflicted the nose with vice. Hence our sense of smell can lead us to sensual attachment. The *devas* meditated upon the eye as *Udgītha*, but the *asuras* afflicted that as well. Hence our eyes lead us to worldly bondage. So it went with the ear and the mind. Then they meditated upon it in the mouth, in other words in the breath, the voice, speech, *prāṇa*. Approaching it, the demons were destroyed, like a dirt clod dashed against a rock.

Section three draws connections between the power of speech, the *Vedas*, which are chanted, the universe, which corresponds to the *Vedas*, and *Oṃ*.

The Deities Escape Death Through *Oṃ*

Oṃ is immortality. This is illustrated in a brief story (1.4.2-3) in which the deities, seeking to flee death, hid in the *Vedas*. But death saw them there, as though they were fish visible through water. They then fled into *Oṃ*, and there were safe from death's clutches. Thus the gods became immortal and fearless, as can anyone who takes refuge in *Oṃ* (1.4.5).

The *Upaniṣad* introduces several *upāsanās* at this point, each demonstrating that any cause is dependent on a previous cause, which is dependent on yet another previous cause, until we are drawn back to the ultimate and original Cause. In sections eight and nine, the *rājarṣi*, or king-sage Pravāhaṇa, whom we will meet again later, explains to his companions that the singing of *sāmans* (sacred hymns) is dependent on vitality. Vitality is sustained by food, which is produced through the nourishing properties of water. Water comes from the atmosphere, which sits upon and is supported by the earth. The earth is dependent on Brahman. Thus we trace the sacred hymns, which are the cause of all abundance and well-being, back through their successive causes to the Cause of all causes, Brahman.[3] The point of this meditation is to draw the consciousness from the familiar to the unfamiliar, from the concrete to the abstract.[4]

Chapter Two: On *Sāma* and Sacrifice

Chapter Two elaborately describes the symbolic meanings underlying the different sections of the *Sāma Veda* and the sacrifices performed in accordance with it. A unity underlying all reality is suggested; the *Sāma*, in its wholeness and perfection, is a reflection of the wholeness and perfection of the Divine. Both the *Sāma* and the Divine encompass all things. This idea culminates in the exclamation, "He who knows that (*sāma*), knows everything . . . His vow should be, 'I am everything'" (2.21.4). The first mention of Brahman in this *Upaniṣad* comes five verses later: "The man established in Brahman attains immortality" (2.23.1).

The rest of Chapter Two discusses the significance of the *mantras* *Bhūḥ, Bhuvaḥ*, and *Svaḥ*, which signify the physical plane, psychic plane and causal plane respectively or, according to more traditional Vedic cosmology, the terrestrial, atmospheric and celestial realms. They are part of the celebrated *Gāyatrī mantra.* They correspond also to the three elements of *Oṃ*: A = *Bhūḥ*, U = *Bhuvaḥ*, M = *Svaḥ*[5], to the three classes of Vedic celestial beings, the *Vasus* (benevolent, atmospheric gods), *Rudras* (storm deities), and *Ādityas* (gods of light, time and manifestation), and to the three phases of the day. The *Upaniṣad* offers directions for performing ritual worship of the three deities associated with *Bhūḥ*, *Bhuvaḥ*, and *Svaḥ*.

Chapter Three: Honey, the Sun, and Other Luminous Things

The *Vedas* are compared to a honeycomb. They are sweet, beautiful, golden like the sun, life-sustaining. The gods "eat", in other words enjoy and are nourished by, the Vedic *mantras*, as if they were a honeyed elixir, the *amṛta*, or nectar of the gods (3.1- 3.10).

Sections six through ten make reference to the rising and setting of the sun; section eleven picks up the thread of this image, using the sun as a metaphor for worldly life. Just as the sun performs actions in its rising and setting, so are we bound to action. Just as the sun exists within the realm of duality — day and night — so do we perceive duality. But what of the one who goes beyond action, beyond duality, who is God-realized?

> Having transcended (all these phases) and risen, he (the sun) will not rise, he will not set down. He will remain established only in himself above . . . It (the sun) certainly does not rise up nor does it set down for him who knows this mystic teaching of Brahman. For him it is daylight forever (3.11.1,3).

An *upāsanā* on the sacred *Gāyatrī mantra* is outlined in section twelve. *Gāyatrī* is the foundation for the earth, earth is the foundation for the human body, the body is the foundation for the *prāṇa*, the *prāṇa* is the foundation for the space in the heart, which is the dwelling place of Brahman. That Brahman is within us and also outside of us is expressed in verses seven through nine. "That, indeed, which is Brahman is surely this which is the space outside a person. That space indeed which is outside a person is surely this which is the space within a person" (3.12.7-8).

The Light Within

After a discussion of the five *prāṇas* (sections 12-13.7), chapter three attends to the serious business of Brahman. "Now, that Light which shines beyond this heaven, beyond the whole creation . . . is certainly this which is the light within a person" (3.13.7). Brahman is the consciousness by which the body lives and senses (3.13.8).

Sarvaṃ khalvidaṃ Brahma, "All this is Brahman," section fourteen begins. Verse 3.14.1 is very dense. It includes this quintessential Upaniṣadic dictum, endorses meditation and inner calm, explains that one's conviction during his life will determine his or her fate after death. This topic will be elaborated upon further in chapters Five and Eight. The section now concentrates on describing Brahman, the Self within. It is consciousness, formless like space, the only Doer (3.13.2), smaller than the smallest, larger than the largest (3.14.3), all-pervading, desireless (3.14.4). Anyone who vows to become identified with Brahman will surely become Brahman (3.14.4).

The universe is a treasure, section fifteen says; it is a positive, nurturing place because of the presence of Brahman in the *prāṇa*, earth, intermediate space and heaven.

Life as a Sacrifice

We can no longer perform Vedic sacrifices as in days past, but sections sixteen and seventeen indicate that if seen in the correct light, we ourselves are a sacrifice; the living of life is one big sacrifice. This idea is in keeping with the disciplines of *karma yoga* as echoed throughout the *Bhagavad-Gītā*, which enjoins the surrender of the fruits of one's actions, as well as one's entire being, to God. Hunger and thirst, the *Upaniṣad* says, are the initiation of the sacrifice. Eating and drinking are the oblations poured into the fire (here symbolized by the fire of digestion). Laughter and lovemaking are the chanting of the scriptures. Austerity, charity, truthfulness and non-violence are the offerings to the priests (3.17.1-4). Just as at the close of the ceremony special *mantras* are chanted, so, too, at the time of death should one chant *mantras* which will elevate the consciousness to Brahman: "You are undecaying. You are unchanging. You are the vital force made completely fine " (3.6).

The Light of Supreme Brahman

Knowers of Brahman "visualize everywhere that supreme Light which shines like the all-pervading daylight" (3.17.7). Everything is Brahman, and anything can be utilized for the realization of Brahman. One can meditate on the mind as Brahman, or space as Brahman (3.18.1), or the consciousness behind the sense organs as Brahman (3.18.2-6), or the sun as Brahman (3.19.1).

Chapter Three closes with a characteristically Upaniṣadic creation account (3.19.1-4). In other words, it is brief, pithy and highly symbolic, its aim not so much to describe the process of creation as to trace all things to their ultimate cause, Brahman, their ultimate destination, Brahman, and the substratum of their existence, Brahman.

Chapter Four: Satyakāma, Upakosala and their Non-Human Teachers

Chapter Four is comprised of stories and dialogues. Characters and voices weave in and out in a complex web of multi-generational anecdotes. We will concern ourselves only with a few of them, one of the most celebrated of which is the tale of Satyakāma, who proved that brāhmaṇahood is a state of mind, not a matter of birth. (This story begins at section 4.4.)

The Story of Casteless Satyakāma

Single-parent homes are not as recent a phenomenon as many people seem to think. Young Satyakāma, the son of a maidservant, approached his mother one day to ask about his lineage. He wanted to live in a spiritual teacher's house as a celibate student (*brahmacārī*), but knew that he would be asked his parents' lineage and caste.

His mother, without shame or regret, told him truthfully that she didn't know who his father was. She had been young at the time, very busy, and her attention had been focused on her duties. "But my name is Jabālā," she said proudly. "And your name is Satyakāma. So you speak of yourself as Satyakāma Jābāla."

The youth humbly submitted to the teacher, Haridrumat Gautama, who did, indeed, inquire into his lineage. "Sir, I do not know to which lineage I belong," he answered guilelessly, and explained his mother's situation. "Such as I am, I am Satyakāma Jābāla."

"A non-*brāhmaṇa* will not be able to say this," the *guru* replied. "I shall initiate you since you did not depart from the truth" (4.4.1-5).

Truthfulness is the mark of a high-souled individual. Clearly, a *brāhmaṇa* — a man or woman of impeccable character — is not a *brāhmaṇa* on the basis of family connection, but on the basis of character, personal cultivation and merit. By a traditional society's standards, a child born out of wedlock is considered of the lowest birth, but wise Gautama saw beyond the superficial trappings of society's labels to the true personality beneath.

Satyakāma Learns from Nature

Section five continues the Satyakāma story. As an education in loyalty, patience and self-surrender, Satyakāma was sent off to tend his *guru's* herd of cattle, four hundred in number, and he vowed not to return until they had multiplied to a thousand. Many years passed in exile until his vow had been fulfilled. One day, a bull turned to him and spoke. "I wish to tell you of one foot (i.e. aspect) of Brahman," the bull said, and explained to him that Brahman can be conceived of as the Unmanifested, and that anyone who meditates upon Brahman this way will achieve the unmanifested State (in other words, one becomes what one meditates on) (4.5.2-3).

Later, fire spoke to him, showing him that Brahman can be thought of as the Limitless, and that one who meditates on Brahman in this way becomes limitless. The next evening a swan flew down and settled next to Satyakāma. He said that Brahman is the Effulgent, and one who meditates on Brahman as such will attain the Effulgence. Finally, a diver-bird came to him and told him that Brahman could be conceived of as *Āyatanavān*, "Possessing an Abode", and that abode is one's very own self.

When he returned to his *guru*, the teacher remarked that Satyakāma's face shone like a knower of Brahman (4.9.2). This story demonstrates that we do not cultivate all of our spiritual wisdom at the feet of our master. Life is a teacher, our friends are teachers, Nature is our teacher, animals are our teachers, fire, air, water are our teachers. A similar story appears in the *Uddhava Gītā* (chapters two through four, the "twenty-four teachers of the *Avadhūta*").

Upakosala Learns from the Sacred Fires

In section ten we meet the disciple Upakosala, whose teacher allowed all his students to graduate except him. Humble and sorrowful, the student stayed in his teacher's house, fasting and tending the sacred fires. Then the fires spoke to him.

"The person who is seen in the sun," one of the fires said, "that am I. I am that very one."

"This Person that is seen in the moon," the second fire said, "that am I. I am that very one."

The light in a fire, the light of the sun, the light in the stars, the light of our own awareness, this is but one light, the light of Brahman, which is the source of all effulgence, of all phenomena. In the *Bhagavad-Gītā* God says, "I am the Ātman abiding in the heart of all beings, and I am the beginning and middle and the end of all beings as well . . . Of lights, I am the radiant sun . . . among the mighty ones, I am the moon" (10.20.21).

The fires represent ourselves, their radiance the Ātman within us, which is the same consciousness which pervades the universe and, hence, is "in the sun . . . in the moon."

Upakosala's teacher returned, and picked up where the fires left off, relaying in explicit terms what the fires hinted at implicitly. Section 4.15 describes the Self. It is deathless, fearless; It is Brahman (5.15.1). It is all-attractive, the goal of all good things (4.15.2). It is the bestower of all merit (4.15.3), that which shines in all the worlds (4.15.4).

The remainder of Chapter Four gives instructions for rectifying a sacrifice in case of a defect.

Chapter Five: Life and Death in the Body of the Cosmic Person

Chapter Five explores matters of life, death, reincarnation, *karma* and the *Virāṭ-Puruṣa*, the all-pervading Self envisioned as the cosmic Person whose body is the universe.

The Organs Have a Contest

On what does our life depend? On our sensing? On our speaking? On our thinking? One day the bodily organs decided to have a contest to see which of them was the most important. First the speech left the body and lived in exile for a year, sure that the body could not manage in his absence. When he returned, he found that everyone got along quite nicely without him. What they lacked with the speech missing, they made up for in sight, touch, thought, *prāṇa* and so on.

Now the eye departed for a year. When he returned, he found the same thing — the body was blind, but managed just fine without him. The ear left and returned to the same story. Even the mind could go and the body survived! But when the *prāṇa* pulled out, it was like "a spirited horse pull(ing) out the pegs to which its legs have been tied" (5.1.12). The body could not survive even a moment without it. The organs pleaded with him, "O venerable sir, please be the ruler. You are the greatest among us. Please do not depart!" (5.6-13). This story is also narrated in the *Praśna Upaniṣad*, 2.1-4, and in the *Bṛhadāraṇyaka Upaniṣad*, 6.1.7-13.

The *prāṇa* is the vital force which causes the organs to function. Without it, they are dead matter, mere orifices in a corpse. We must not, therefore, identify with what our eye sees, what our ear hears, even with what our mind thinks. They are not at all connected with our true Self, but are implements of perception only.

Section two continues on the subject of *prāṇa* and offers instructions for a ceremony known as the *Mantha* rite, which promotes meditation on the *prāṇa*.

The Sage-King is Questioned

A *brāhmaṇa* youth, Śvetaketu (who will figure prominently in the next chapter), went to an assembly of *kṣatriya* wise men. A king among them, Pravāhaṇa (who also shows up in the *Bṛhadāraṇyaka Upaniṣad*, 6.2.8), asked the boy if his father had properly instructed him. "Surely he did," Śvetaketu replied. The king then asked him if he knew where beings go after they die, how they are reborn, and of the two paths the soul can take after death. Poor Śvetaketu admitted he did not and, shaken, went home to his father to find out why he had not been instructed in such matters. "If I knew myself," his father replied, "don't you think I would have told you?" At that, Śvetaketu's father, Gautama (also called Uddālaka), visited the king, determined to learn the answers for himself.

Just like the story of Satyakāma, the institution of *varṇa*, or caste, is challenged. *Brāhmaṇas* are supposed to be the wise ones, the scholars, mystics and sages, but here a *brāhmaṇa* approaches a *kṣatriya* for instruction. Pravāhaṇa indicated that in the past, *kṣatriyas* were the keepers of mystical knowledge, but now he gladly imparts it to a *brāhmaṇa*. Clearly, the Upaniṣadic *ṛṣis* who composed these texts did not think much of the rigidity of the caste system, and saw no connection between the social stratum of one's birth and spiritual attainment. It is significant that so many of India's greatest spiritual reformers, including Kṛṣṇa, Siddhārtha Gautama (the Buddha), and Guru Nanak (the founder of Sikhism), were of *kṣatriya* background.

The Wheel of Birth and Death

In sections four through six, the king identifies the Vedic fire sacrifice as a microcosmic recreation of the universe. This leads into a discussion of the cycle of birth and death. Human beings are themselves a fire sacrifice. The woman is the fire, the man's semen the oblation, the child the outcome. We are born, then, of fire, the fire of a woman's womb. After living the number of years to which we are destined, we die, and our bodies are committed once again to the fire, this time the funeral pyre. So we come full circle, from fire to fire. Our whole lives are framed in the ritual of the fire sacrifice (5.7-9).

So much for the body, but what of the soul? During the interim period between births, there are two possible paths the soul may traverse, the "solar path", which leads to Brahman, and the "lunar path" which leads to the realm of the gods. Which path one will take depends on the kind of life they've led, the consciousness at the moment of death, and the time of death. One who takes the solar path does not return. One who traverses the lunar path, after enjoying the karmic results of their good works in a heavenly realm, returns to earth to be reborn (5.10.1-6).

The type of birth one takes depends on the quality of one's actions in the previous life. Though the *Upaniṣad* does not use the word *karma*, such is the metaphysical law which is described in verse 5.10.7: "Those who were performers of meritorious deeds here will attain good births. . . . On the other hand, those who were performers of bad deeds here will indeed attain bad births in a quick manner — birth as a dog, or birth as a pig, or birth as a *Caṇḍāla* (outcaste)" (5.10.7).

***Virāṭ-Puruṣa*, the Universe as God**

In section two, the scene suddenly shifts and we are now listening in on a group of illustrious householders who are conducting a discussion about Brahman and the Self. They need to consult someone wiser than themselves, so they pay a visit to the sage-king Aśvapati. After duly initiating them, he asks each one individually which aspect of the Self they meditate upon. As each answers, he identifies that aspect with the Universal Self, which is here referred to as *Vaiśvānara* (a name of the fire god Agni, in other words "Light").

One disciple meditates on heaven. That, Aśvapati explains, is the head of the Universal Self. Another meditates on the sun. That is the eye of the Universal Self, the king says. Yet another meditates on air. That is the *prāṇa*. Space is the abdomen. Water, the bladder. Earth, the two feet (5.11-18).

Thus the divine Self encompasses the entire universe. Everything in the world is part of this Oneness, part of Its universal body.

Chapter five continues with a description of the ritualistic sacrifice to the five *prāṇas* and their correspondences on the cosmic level, then concludes with the assurance that the *agnihotra*, the fire sacrifice, burns up the worshippers' sins, just as fire consumes fuel.

Chapter Six: *Tat Tvam Asi*, That Thou Art, O Śvetaketu

We meet up with Śvetaketu again, now a young man, fresh back from his twelve year stay with a *guru.* He has become conceited and immodest, proud of what he believes to be his superior learning. His arrogance is quickly deflated, however, when it turns out that he cannot answer the very first question his father puts to him: "Through what does the unheard of become heard, the unthought of become thought, the unknown become known?" (6.1.3).

Śvetaketu's father, here referred to as Uddālaka, begins by establishing and validating his analytical method, which relies on the use of inference.

"By knowing a lump of earth, all things made of earth become known . . . by knowing a lump of gold, all things made of gold become known," he says (6.1.4,5). By understanding a part, we understand the whole, and the knowledge which Uddālaka is about to impart is a knowledge so all-inclusive, knowing it, one knows the All. It is knowledge higher than the knowledge of ordinary objects on the relative plane: "All transformation has speech as its basis, and it is name only"

(6.1.4). In other words, things that are not eternal are not wholly real; they are words only, names, subjective designations dependent on our limited and preconceived definitions of them. We create the reality of the material world by assigning things definitions and names.

In the Beginning . . .

That is not to say that the world does not actually exist; in fact, there is nothing *but* Existence. The world is real, but its multiplicity is not.

"In the beginning," Uddālaka explains, "this was Existence alone, One only, without a second" (6.2.1). Some say that in the beginning there was non-existence, and that existence issued from non-existence, but Uddālaka holds this view to be absurd. Something cannot come from nothing; it must come from something else, so existence requires an antecedent Existence.

That original, divine One Existence decided to become many, and out of Itself projected the universe, into which It entered. It became every being and every thing. Nothing has an existence independent or apart from That.

After an examination of how ordinary things can be broken down into constituent parts, but that those parts are still one with the original things, Uddālaka leads us back to the subject of Brahman by means of an *upāsanā.* We depend on food for our existence. Food depends on the vegetation. Vegetation depends on its roots. Roots depend on water. Water depends on fire; in other words, the rain falls in response to the priests' oblations into the sacred fire. The fire depends on the divine Existence (6.8.4). Existence, then, is the "root" which sustains everything: "All these beings have Existence as their root. Existence is their abode. Existence is their place of merger" (6.8.4).

Tat Tvam Asi

Now we reach the climax of the *Upaniṣad,* in some people's opinion the climax of *all* the *Upaniṣads.* The quintessential Upaniṣadic dictum, or *mahāvākya,* is *tat tvam asi*: "That thou art." In other words, "You are a part of Brahman, the Supreme, the Ultimate Truth, the Infinite, the Fathomless, the Divine, the All."

"That which is the subtle essence, all this has got That as the Self. That is Truth. That is the Self. That thou art, O Śvetaketu" (6.8.7).

This refrain repeats eight times, as Uddālaka substantiates this extraordinary claim with example after example.

Just as bees make honey by collecting the essences of different flowers, when they are reduced to a homogenous whole, the different essences do not think, "I am from this flower," "I am from that flower." They have merged into a single Existence. So is our existence one with the divine Existence (6.9.1-2).

Similarly, when rivers flow into and merge with the sea, they do not continue to think, "I am the eastward-flowing river," "I am the westward-flowing river." Their very existence is one with the ocean's essence (6.10.1-2). So, too, is our essence the Self, the ocean of consciousness which is God.

If we hack off the branch of a tree, the branch will die. If we hack off the trunk, the trunk will die. But so long as the roots are healthy, the tree will live. In the same way, our bodies may die, but our root — the soul, the divine Self — cannot die. It is immortal, eternal, the Ultimate Truth, Brahman. *Tat tvam asi*: you are That.

Just because you cannot see this all-pervading Truth doesn't mean it isn't there. Uddālaka has Śvetaketu dissolve salt in a cup of water. Śvetaketu cannot see the salt, but wherever he tastes, be it at the top, the bottom, or the middle of the cup, he finds salt. So it is with Brahman. The spiritual aspirant is like a blindfolded man trying to find his way. Lost and disoriented, he cries out for help. Someone comes to his rescue, removes the bandage from his eyes, and points him in the direction he needs to go. This kind soul is the *guru* (6.14.1-2).

The states of bondage and spiritual liberation are akin to the man accused of theft who pleads innocence. A legendary test of guilt was to tie the accused's hands and have him hold a heated axe. The guilty, it was said, having defiled himself by his act, would be burned, while the innocent, pure as he was, would not. Likewise, the one who lives a life of falsehood (egotism, materialism, etc.) will remain in bondage and endure the suffering of worldly existence. The pure soul, the spiritually realized, is beyond suffering and is released from the bondage of birth, death, and individuality (6.16.1-2).

Chapter Seven: Nārada and Sanatkumāra

Nārada is an ubiquitous figure in Hindu literature. He is prominent in the *Purāṇas*, where he is depicted as a son of Lord Brahmā and as a minstrel-sage, forever roaming the universe, singing devotional hymns and occasionally stopping long enough to impart spiritual wisdom to those who seek it. He shows up also in the *Mahābhārata*, is mentioned in the *Bhagavad-Gītā* (10.13, 10.23), and is, according to tradition, the author of the *Nārada Bhakti Sūtras.* Sanatkumāra is one of the celebrated *kumāras* (literally, "boys"), quadruplets, also sons of Brahmā, who, in order to safeguard their purity, vowed never to grow up. They also figure prominently in the *Purāṇas.*

Chapter Seven is devoted entirely to the dialogue between Sanatkumāra, here assuming the role of *guru,* and Nārada, here the disciple.

"Teach me, O venerable sir," Nārada requests.

Sanatkumāra replies, "Tell me that which you know. I shall tell you things that are beyond them" (7.1.1).

Worldly Knowledge and Self-Knowledge

Nārada proceeds to list a prodigious array of subjects of which he is conversant, from the *Vedas* to mathematics, from grammar to mineralogy, from logic, ethics and etymology to science, archery and the fine arts. However, all this worldly knowledge does not satisfy him. They are just so many words, so many facts; they cannot dispel sorrow. Only knowledge of the Self can dispel sorrow. "And I am full of sorrow," Nārada sighs. "O venerable sir, please take me beyond sorrow" (7.1.1-3).

Yes, the *guru* agrees, all worldly knowledge is mere name only, mere words, nothing substantial. But even name is Brahman (7.1.4). So begins yet another progressive *upāsanā* which takes us through a good part of the chapter. Greater than name, Sanatkumāra says, is speech, for without speech, names cannot be uttered. Speech is Brahman. Greater than speech is mind, for without thought, there is no speech. Mind is Brahman. Greater than mind is will, for will impels thought. Will is Brahman. Greater than will is intelligence; greater than intelligence is meditation; greater than meditation is understanding; greater than understanding is strength; greater than strength is food (without which there is no strength); greater than food is water; greater than water is fire; greater than fire is space; greater than space is memory; greater than memory is hope; greater than hope is *prāṇa*; and the only thing greater than *prāṇa* is Brahman (7.1.4-15.4).

Nārada wants to know this Truth firsthand; so begins the second *upāsanā* of Chapter Seven, outlining the qualities and disciplines an aspirant must cultivate in order to realize divine Truth. Truth requires understanding; understanding requires reflection; reflection requires faith; faith requires devoted service; devoted service requires action; action requires joy; and joy requires the Infinite! (7.17-23).

The Infinite and the Finite

"There is no joy in the finite. The Infinite alone is joy" (7.23.1).

There cannot be any division in the Infinite; division would create limitation, finiteness. Infinity must necessarily be a Oneness. "The Infinite is that where one does not see anything else, does not hear anything else, and does not understand anything else" (7.24.1). Subject and object are merged; there is only One, and this One is boundless joy and immortality. "That which indeed is Infinite is immortal. On the other hand, that which is finite is mortal" (7.24.1).

This Infinite One is everywhere — below, above, behind, in front — and therefore *you* are everywhere — below, above, behind, in front. "I indeed am all this," one should think (7.25.1). The Self is everywhere, the Self is all; anyone who realizes this "revels in the Self, disports in the Self, has union with the Self, has pleasure in the Self. He becomes a sovereign" (7.25.2).

Those who do not realize this, "come under a different ruler." They are subject to suffering and death, to bondage and ignorance; they belong "to the worlds that are subject to decay" (7.25.2).

Everything you can imagine "spring(s) from the Self" (7.26.1). The realized soul transcends the clutches of death, disease and sorrow. He "sees everything, attains everything in every way" (7.26.2). By all means, discover the Self.

Chapter Eight: A Demon and a God Become Disciples

The City of Brahman

The body is known as *Brahmapura*, the City of Brahman, because it is the abode of the Divine. Within the body, the heart, which is "lotus-like", is the seat of the soul (8.1.1). So opens the final chapter, which begins with the lofty philosophical ponderings which represent the *Upaniṣads* at their best. "The space within the heart is as vast as this space outside," verse three reads, an assertion substantiated by our knowledge of the sub-atomic world. Infinity is within you. All that is outside is within you; there is, in fact, no inside, no outside. "Within it (the heart) indeed are included both heaven and earth, both fire and air, both sun and moon, lightning and stars. Whatever this one has here and whatever he has not, all that is included" (8.1.3).

There is never cause to feel envy, loss, deprivation or separation, knowing that everything and everyone is yours, and is a part of you.

What, verse 8.1.4 inquires, survives when the body dies? Brahman, verse five replies, which is ever unaffected by the changes in the body. Brahman is the Self, and It is joyful, changeless and immortal. Those who pass away without realizing the Self find no happiness in any world they enter, and eventually must come back. They are bound to this world, bereft of freedom. However, knowers of the Self are liberated (8.1.6). Their perception is without restriction, so they can be anywhere and see everyone they wish instantly, because they already are everywhere (8.2.1-10).

During deep, dreamless sleep we lose consciousness of ego and merge back into Brahman. However, because we are blinded by ignorance, we are not cognizant of this experience (8.3.2). One can overcome ignorance through serenity, detachment, and severing identification with the body. In this way one becomes "established in his true nature," which is the Self — immortal, fearless, Supreme (8.3.4). The Self is beyond all dualities, beyond change, beyond even virtue and vice. It is ever pristine, ever untouched (8.4.1). Having attained It, all of one's imperfections fall away, "even night surely turns into day" (8.4.2).

The Virtue of Celibacy

Celibacy is extolled as one of the paths to God-realization. Its power is well-known to Hindu, Buddhist and Catholic monastics alike. The egolessness, self-denial, sense-control and surrender needed to embrace a life of celibacy propel one toward the divine Goal. Here the *Upaniṣad* asserts that celibacy is so potent a *sādhanā*, it includes all other *sādhanās* in it. Celibacy is a form of sacrifice, a form of worship (8.5.1). It is contemplation (8.5.2). It is the same as going to the forest, in other words, renouncing the world (8.5.3). Verse three indulges in some punning, saying that there are two oceans in the heaven of Brahman, named Ara and Ṇya. *Araṇya* means "forest", so retiring to the forest is practically the achieving of Brahman (8.5.3). One need not literally live in the forest; forest-dwelling is a metaphor for inner renunciation, for detachment from the world. The forest can be within yourself.

Enlightened Death: The Psychic-Spiritual Nervous System

Because the advanced *yogī* can die and be liberated into Brahman-realization at any moment he or she chooses, section six briefly outlines the mechanics of how this occurs. Such a death is willed, conscious — an enlightened death, where the *prāṇa* is deliberately lifted upward, through the central nerve in the spine (the *suśumnā*), and expelled through the crown *cakra*, thus freeing the soul from its mortal prison (8.6.1). The *nāḍīs* (nerves) branching out from the *suśumnā* and extending throughout the body are the channels through which our *prāṇa* circulates and nourishes the physical and psychic organism. Verse 8.6.6 (which is repeated verbatim in the *Kaṭha Upaniṣad* 2.3.17) states that raising the *prāṇa* through the *suśumnā* leads to immortality, while following the other nerves, in other words following the fancies of the senses, leads to desire and bondage. According to Śrī Śaṅkarācārya, this information is given for those aspirants whose consciousness has not yet gotten beyond the qualitative mindset which still holds on the ideas like "traveller", "travel", and "destination". To those who realize the complete unity of Self, such ideas are absent.[6]

Indra and Virocana Seek Spiritual Instruction

The last story of the *Chāndogya Upaniṣad*, and definitely one of the best, concerns the king of the gods and the king of the demons both surrendering to the same *guru*, yet both interpreting his instructions very differently. The tale illustrates beautifully how at any given time we hear and understand only what we are ready to hear and understand, not a speck more, and how our mental predispositions shape what we hear into exactly what we want it to be. Just as Jesus spoke of casting pearls before swine, the *guru* here, Prajāpati, cast his pearls of wisdom before an undeserving disciple, who failed to understand a word of it.

One day, Prajāpati said aloud,

> The Self which has no sin, no death, no sorrow, no hunger, no thirst . . . That has to be known, That has to be enquired into for realization. He who, after knowing the Self, realizes It, attains all the worlds and all desires (8.7.1).

Both the *asuras* and the *devas* overheard him, and excitedly discussed it amongst themselves. From among the *devas* Indra, their sovereign, emerged carrying fuel for the *guru's* fire, a sign of discipleship. From among the *asuras* emerged their king, Virocana, also carrying fuel. Together they approached Prajāpati for initiation (8.7.2).

After practicing celibacy for thirty-two years in preparation, they asked Prajāpati to teach them what the Self was. "You are the Self", he told them, and had them look at their own reflections in a plate of water. Well-adorned, groomed, handsome, they gazed upon their physical forms and liked what they saw. "This is the Self," Prajāpati told them. "This is immortal, fearless. This is Brahman" (8.8.1-3).

Satisfied, the students departed.

Watching them leave, Prajāpati thought, "They are going away without attaining the Self, and without realizing It" (8.8.4). Virocana returned to his people and told them, "This worldly self is to be worshipped and adored. Attend to it and pamper it!" (8.8.4). He had completely misunderstood his teacher's point. Yes, the worldly persona is the Self in the sense that everything is the Self, but it's not the *entirety* of the Self. Most people labor under the same misunderstanding.

Indra was heading back home, but right before he got there he suddenly stopped and pondered, "This body can go blind, get a runny nose, become lame, die. It can't be the entire Self of which Prajāpati is speaking." So he went back and inquired further (8.9.10).

"The Self is the consciousness of the dream state," Prajapati said. "Dreams are beyond the realm of physical illness, decrepitude and death." Satisfied, Indra departed, but partway home he stopped again and thought. "Even in dreams we see scary things, cry, suffer. That can't be the Self." So again he returned (8.10.1-4).

"The dreamless state of deep sleep is the Self", Prajāpati said, "for in that state there is perfect tranquility." Good enough, Indra thought, but on his way home he stopped again to think it through. "True, there is tranquility, but there is also no consciousness!" Back he went (8.11.1). Having considered and rejected ordinary states of being as the Self, Indra was now ready to be taught the highest spiritual truth.

The body is mortal. The Self is immortal. Anything which is embodied is conditioned by the duality of "desirable" and "undesirable." The Self cannot be touched by such polarities; it is entirely independent of them (8.12.1).

The Self is formless, yet all forms have come from It and are one with It. Observe, for instance, how clouds, lightning, and thunder, all things with form and quality, emerge from the air, which has no form or quality. They are also absorbed back into the formless air, as all forms are absorbed back into the formless Self (8.12.2).

We are joined with this body, our bondage, just as a horse is harnessed to a vehicle. But by detaching ourselves from this transitory body and cultivating tranquility, we can achieve union with the "Supreme Light", the "Supreme Person" (8.12.3).

By analyzing ourselves a little we can see how the true Self is not this body. The Self is the consciousness behind the eye, that by which the eye sees; It is the consciousness behind the nose; that by which the nose smells. The senses are mere organs. To be attached to them or identify with them is sheer folly (8.12.4).

The purified mind, verse five says, is the "divine eye". While the restless, impure mind is just another organ, the purified mind is a means of discerning spiritual Reality, the "world of Brahman" (8.12.5).

All desires are fulfilled in realization of the Self, Prajāpati concludes. Even the gods adore this Self within each one of us as the Self within them. One who attains It has attained All (8.12.6).

Prayers for Liberation

This *Upaniṣad*, infinitely rich, extraordinarily deep (according to some scholars, as many as one hundred thirty topics are touched upon)[7], concludes with two prayers for God-realization and a synopsis of the perfectly-lived life.

The first prayer is a solemn oath to attain that unmanifested state which is our point of origin. "From the dark I wish to attain the variegated. From the variegated I have attained the dark." Dark here means the attributeless, the fathomless, the formless Brahman. Like a horse shaking its hair, the speaker vows to shake off sin. Like the moon being freed from the mouth of Rāhu, he will be liberated from all bondage. Rahu is a demon responsible for eclipses of the sun and moon. One day he snuck a gulp of *amṛta*, the *deva's* nectar of immortality. It got as far as his throat when Viṣṇu lopped off the demon's head with His fiery discus. The body toppled over dead, but Rāhu's head was endowed with immortality. It rose into the sky, and in its anger has eternally been swallowing the sun and moon, only to have them escape right out of him again. This story is related in the eighth *skandha* of the *Śrīmad Bhāgavatam*.

The second prayer is a supplication for Brahman-realization, the attainment of which endows one with all glory. Using striking imagery, the speaker prays not to be forced to take rebirth: "May I not enter into that white slippery place which is a toothless swallower" (8.14.1). This rather unnerving turn of phrase refers to the birth canal.

This divine wisdom originated first with Lord Brahmā, the final verse says. He imparted it to Prajāpati, who passed it on to Manu, who taught it to the earth's creatures. Thus its sacred origin and authority is established. Before closing, the *Upaniṣad* gives one last teaching, one last bit of advice. We have learned so much theory, so many *upāsanās*. We have been given a clear picture as to the Goal of life. Where do we go from here? How do we put this information to practice? In four sentences, the entire span of a life beautifully lived is expressed. One can study the sacred scriptures under the tutelage of a *guru* and serve him or her devotedly. After finishing this course of study one can assume the responsibilities of a householder, all the while keeping up with study, practicing *sādhanā* and passing spiritual values on to the children. Then the time comes to leave the world and practice intense meditation ("withdrawing all his organs into the Self") while following the austerities and etiquette prescribed by the scriptures for a member of the renounced order of life. This is a life lived well, a life lived with purpose and meaning. What's more, "He does not return again, he does not return again" (8.15.1).

NOTES

1. For this exposition of the *Soma* sacrifice, I am wholly indebted to Swāmī Gambhīrānanda, *Chāndogya Upaniṣad* (Calcutta: Advaita Ashrama, 1983), pp. 675-678.
2. Gambhīrānanda, p. 676.
3. Gambhīrānanda, p. xxxiii.
4. Gambhīrānanda, p. xxxiv.
5. Swāmī Mukhyānanda, *Oṃ, Gāyatrī and Sandhyā* (Mylapore: Sri Ramakrishna Math, 1989), pp. 18, 36.
6. Gambhīrānanda, pp. 571-572.
7. Gambhīrānanda, p. v.

CHAPTER SEVENTEEN

Bṛhadāraṇyaka Upaniṣad: A Meditation on the Infinite Which Emanates From the Infinite

Bṛhadāraṇyaka means "great forest"[1], and the title lends itself to many interpretations. The ancient *ṛṣis* whose realizations are expressed in the *Upaniṣads* were forest dwellers. They left mainstream society and mainstream religion, which at the time was largely ritualistic, to seek ultimate Truth through meditation in the solitude of the forest. Yet the "forest" can also be understood as a metaphorical forest, the dense and mysterious terrain of the consciousness, where all spiritual treasures lie hidden. Sri Ramakrishna used to tell the story of a woodsman who met a *brāhmaṇa* holy man at the edge of a forest. "Keep going farther," the *brāhmaṇa* said. The woodsman entered the forest and discovered a grove of sandalwood trees, very valuable. He was delighted, until he remembered the *brāhmaṇa's* instructions, "Keep going farther." He went deeper into the forest, and discovered a silver mine. He was rich! But again he recalled the *brāhmaṇa's* instructions, and went farther. He found a gold mine. Farther still he went, and discovered a diamond mine. So it is with the spiritual journey. We must forge ever farther and deeper, never satisfied until that most precious of all treasures, God, is fully ours.

In a very real way, the *Bṛhadāraṇyaka Upaniṣad* is itself the diamondiferous forest. It yields up philosophical gems of exquisite brilliance, fire and clarity, but not easily. It is the longest *Upaniṣad*, traditionally considered the most illustrious, but it is also the most challenging. In the introduction to his volume of lectures on this *Upaniṣad*, Swāmī Krishnānanda admits that it is "very rarely studied by people and very rarely still discussed . . . because of its complicated structure, difficult to grasp."[2] Indeed, the imagery and phraseology relies so heavily on ancient Vedic ritual, the contemporary reader may find much of it bewildering. But this is a case where the reader, to draw upon an English adage, "can't see the forest for the trees." The difficult surface language merely veils, and thinly at that, a very simple theme which forms the foundation of the entire text and runs as a connecting thread through each verse and chapter. It is stated clearly in the *Upaniṣad's* opening peace invocation:

> Brahman is Infinite. This universe too is Infinite. The Infinite emanates from the Infinite. Assimilating the infinitude of the Infinite, the Infinite alone is left.[3]

This is the basic premise of the text, explored through various dialogues, analogies, poetic exclamations and clear, literal exposition. We find the idea dramatically illustrated in the Creation accounts which open the book. Later, the sage Yājñavalkya explains it to his disciple-wife Maitreyī by means of analogy. The celebrated *Madhu-Vidyā* (literally, "honey wisdom") section of Chapter Two describes it as a loving delectation the Infinite derives from experiencing Its own Self. With this clue in mind, patient readers can find their way through this forest of an *Upaniṣad*, the most august piece of literature of its kind. I am deeply indebted to Swāmī Krishnānanda's commentary on the *Upaniṣad* for many of the insights offered in the following pages.

Chapter One: Creation, or How Brahman Itself Has Become Everything

The opening chapter is appropriately devoted to accounts of the creation of the universe. Just as the Old Testament book of Genesis gives, in fact, two versions of the Creation and three of the births of Adam and Eve, so too does the *Bṛhadāraṇyaka Upaniṣad* offer several Creation accounts. All, however, illustrate the same point: that Brahman Itself became all this, dwells in all this, is non-different from all this. Like all the *Upaniṣads*, the *Bṛhadāraṇyaka* promotes a philosophy of non-dualism.

Section One: An Initial Creation Account — the Cosmic Horse Sacrifice

With what may be the most awesome piece of imagery in all *Upaniṣadic* literature, the scripture dramatically begins with an allusion to the *aśvamedha*, the Vedic horse sacrifice. This was a rite only performed by kings, where the creation of the cosmos was reenacted through the literal dismemberment of a sacrificial horse. The universe was ceremonially created afresh, and thus the balance of the cosmos kept intact. Even back then, the fundamental connectedness of the microcosm and macrocosm was understood.

In this *Upaniṣad*, the sacrificial horse represents God. In the opening verse, its different body parts are identified as various phenomena in the universe:

> The head of the sacrificial horse is the dawn, its eye is the sun, its vital force the air, its open mouth the fire called *Vaiśvānara* (a.k.a. Agni, the deity of fire)[4], its trunk the year, its back is heaven, its belly the sky . . . (1.1.1).

Fire is associated with the mouth because because digestion is considered a kind of "fire".[5] As an archetype, the horse is strongly connotative of beauty, vigor, power and eroticism, the creative impulse, life itself. In Britain it is considered lucky to see a white horse because the horse is a symbol of life; similarly, the Celtic goddess of creativity, Epona, was shown riding a horse, or was personified as a white mare.[6] The image of dismemberment echoes the myth of the dismemberment of the Cosmic Person, Prajāpati (from *prajā*, "procreation", *pati*, "Lord"), which resulted in the creation of the universe. This story is recounted in many Hindu texts, including this one, in the next section. This original, divine Person is known by many names, including Hiraṇyagarbha ("golden womb")[7], Virāj ("universal ruler")[8], Brahmā (a masculinized form of the noun Brahman[9], which suggests a supreme father, or supreme progenitor) and, interestingly, Hayagrīva ("horse-necked"). Underlying this complex imagery is the simple premise that the material manifestation is merely the "body" of God. There is only Brahman, the one, non-differentiated Reality. Yet, if we concentrate on one part of Brahman or another (the dawn, let's say, or the sun), there appears to be a multiplicity. This is an illusion. It is like looking at the head of a horse, or the eye, and saying, "Look, here is an individual entity, a head; here is another individual entity, an eye," whereas these things are not separate from the horse at all. The horse is not a collection of parts, but rather a unity, a totality. So it is with Reality in general.

The second verse of part one expands the imagery to include the utensils used in the sacrifice, particularly a gold cup and silver cup which were placed before and behind the animal. They represent day and night respectively. The source of the horse itself is identified as the "sea", which is a universal symbol for a primordial chaos, a formlessness, hence limitlessness, which exists prior to the delineations of form and duality imposed on the One at the time of creation. Compare this to the Biblical Genesis account:

> Now the earth was a formless void, there was darkness over the deep, and God's spirit hovered over the water . . . God said, "Let there be a vault in the waters to divide the waters in two . . ." (Gen. 1.2, 1.6).

Section Two: A Second Creation Account — The Unfoldment of the Universe from the Cosmic Person, Prajāpati

"In the beginning there was nothing whatever in the universe," section two begins, and a step-by-step narrative of Prajāpati's creation of the universe by imposing differentiations on Himself ensues. The first stirrings are very subtle: "This universe was enveloped by Death alone, or Hunger, for hunger is death." Notice that death exists before life. Death is non-being. The first thing that came about was non-being, absence, but in order for non-being to exist, there must be its opposite, being. In the primordial, static Brahman there actually is neither, for Brahman is beyond all duality. So the first manifest thing was nothing, and inherent in this nothing was "hunger", which here means desire — desire for an object, for differentiation. Desire necessitates awareness: "May I be possessed of a mind." And what is this primordial One aware of? There is nothing *to* be aware of except Its own infinite divinity, hence, "He moved about worshipping Himself." This worshipper gives rise to water. Water can refer to the formlessness of the One. Fire will soon develop, and is referred to as *arka*, which means "light-bringer" or "shining", an epithet of the sun,[10] though on a subtler level it can mean knowledge, consciousness of a subject. The verse is operating on exoteric and esoteric levels simultaneously, on the one hand recounting the creation of the material elements such as water, fire, earth, air, etc., and on the other suggesting that creation is a matter of the unfolding of the divine Consciousness with its awareness of the concepts of being, of space, of subject and object, etc. The term *arka*, our text is delighted to point out, is a pun, for the root *arc* means worship, which was the first act ever performed, and *ka* means water or happiness.[11] Water is a primary element in Hindu worship, as is fire, the creation of which is mentioned in the next verse. It seems the Cosmic Being became the elements with which it worships Itself. This idea will climax in the end of section two, when Prajāpati will become the sacrificial horse which is sacrificed to Himself, bringing us full circle and establishing the fundamental Oneness of everything.

In verses three and four Prajāpati continues to divide Himself and becomes air, *prāṇa* (vital energy), the directions, mind and speech. These are all subtle elements, without substance. However, the Creator desired, "May a second body be born to Me," in other words a true *other*, substance, a tangible, subjective reality. The cosmic "baby", matter, is born. As soon as the baby is born, however, Prajāpati devours It! He goes on to create everything — the *Vedas*, people, animals — and everything He creates He devours. Verse four reads, "Whatever He created He resolved to devour. Verily He devours everything; that is why He is called *Aditi*." *Aditi*, which is also the name of the Vedic goddess of space, means "not limited",[12] a quality of Brahman. Everything which comes into being disappears in time and returns to its formless source, Brahman. For everything that is born, death is certain, for everything that comes into being eventual non-being is certain. Such is the nature of the world. This idea is dramatically illustrated in the eleventh chapter of the *Bhagavad-Gītā*, where Kṛṣṇa reveals to Arjuna His universal form. There all creation, past, present and future goes racing into the fiery gullet of God, Who, in time, devours and reabsorbs everything. The *Bṛhadāraṇyaka* verse 1.2.5 ends, "He who knows the import of this name of *Aditi* becomes the eater of the universe and the universe becomes his food." In other words, he becomes one with Brahman.

Now Prajāpati's body begins to swell (1.2.6). He becomes a horse, the very horse that is sacrificed to him, the very horse that opened the *Upaniṣad*. Another pun is brought into play here, for the Sanskrit word for swell is *aśvat*, and the word for horse is *aśva*.

Section Three: *Prāṇa* (the Vital Force) and the Analogous Workings of the Universe Within Us and Outside of Us

Throughout the Upaniṣadic literature, *prāṇa*, the life force or vital energy, is subtly associated with Brahman, for where life exists, consciousness exists, and consciousness, *cit*, *is* Brahman. The *Praśna Upaniṣad* is primarily concerned with the science of *prāṇa*, and the *Chāndogya Upaniṣad* (1.2.1-9) contains, with slight variations, the same story which is here narrated from verses 1.3.1 to 1.3.11.

In their ongoing rivalry with the *devas* (gods), the *asura* (demon) forces charge violently at each of the bodily sense organs which attempt to chant the sacred hymns (our senses are traditionally believed to be governed by particular deities). Each organ is easily pierced with evil, hence our senses are proved unreliable and may lead us to vice. However, when the demons rush upon the *prāṇa*, they are crushed and scattered in all directions. *Prāṇa* is the basis of all physical functions; the organs do not, by themselves, possess perceptual powers. It is the presence of *prāṇa* and, by inference, Ātman, the Brahman within, which animates them. We are not, therefore, to identify with our senses, but rather with the conscious Self which is behind them.

The text now takes us through a meditation where we ourselves assume the role of Prajāpati, mentally dismembering ourselves and becoming all. Verses 1.3.12-17 ask us to associate each of our sense organs with elements in the universe and thus arrive at a realization of our own all-pervading nature. Each of us is a perfect replica of the universe, because each of us has Infinity within.

The remainder of section three continues to examine the role of *prāṇa*, identifying it as "food", i.e. that which gives life, to all organs of the body (1.3.18), as the very essence of bodily existence (1.3.19), as expression (1.3.20), and so forth. The real point behind this examination of *prāṇa* is that it sets the foundation for a system of analogies which will appear later in the *Upaniṣad*. The various senses are dependent upon, fixed in, indeed merged with, *prāṇa*. So is all worldly phenomena dependent on, fixed in, merged with Brahman. We can understand the workings of the entire cosmos by understanding the workings of our own beings, the inner cosmos.

Section Four: A Third Creation Account — Creation from the Universal Self

The *Upaniṣad* resumes the subject of creation, or the infinite which proceeds from the Infinite. In this version, "In the beginning, this universe was verily the Self . . . He pondered and beheld nothing but Himself. He first said 'I am He.' Therefore He got the name 'I'" (1.4.1). This idea is echoed in the Old Testament where, in the book of Exodus, God reveals His name to Moses as Yahweh, literally "I am". Another name for Brahman is *Sat-Cit-Ānanda*, "Existence-Consciousness-Bliss". Brahman is not something that possesses consciousness, Brahman *is* consciousness, It is the awareness of "I am" which all living things share. Verse 1.4.1 says that He has another name too: *Puruṣa*. A cognate with the word "person," *puruṣa* literally means "man" or "male". In the Hindu sense it refers to that aspect of Brahman which is pure consciousness, pure Spirit. Symbolically, it is associated with the masculine aspect of the cosmic polarity, the Yang, Śiva. Its counterpart is *prakṛti*, which is a cognate with "procreate" and signifies the cosmic feminine, Yin, matter, energy, substance, *Śakti*. Brahman must necessarily include both these polarities. The *Sāṃkhya* philosophy holds that creation came about as a result of a sort of big bang when the principles of *Puruṣa* and *prakṛti* combined.

In verse 1.4.3 the divine Self does, indeed, divide into these two, the universal Male and Female joined in the sexual embrace. From their union all manner of living beings sprang forth (1.4.3-4). But nothing in creation is to be understood as separate from the Creator: "He knew, 'I am indeed the creation, because I created all this.' Hence He became known as creation" (1.4.5). Then He manifested Himself as the many different deities but, again, they are to be understood as dimensions of a single divine Reality, not separate entities (1.4.6).

The multiplicity is nothing more than name and form (1.4.7). Brahman exists *as* the names and forms as well as the conscious Self within them. "This supreme Self has penetrated into all these bodies up to the nail-ends — just as a razor lies in its case" (1.4.7).

This Self is dearer to us that anything. If we hold anything else as dearer — children, wealth, etc. — we will find that what we hold so dear will perish. The Self never perishes (1.4.8).

Further exploring this concept of the Self, verse 1.4.10 states that those who know Brahman become Brahman and thus become All. Those who think of the Divine as something separate from them do not know the truth. The gods, apparently, would prefer people not know the truth and lose their individualities in the totality of Brahman because then there would be fewer people around to worship them!

The next four verses describe how Brahman created the four castes (and thus lend justification for India's highly stratified social system, though in its ideal form, the four *varṇas* are not determined by birth) and the deities which govern them. Brahman is also attributed with the creation of *dharma*, every individual's divinely designed duty in life. While divisions do exist, Brahman is personally present in all castes (1.4.15). It is not the mere performance of one's caste duty which secures liberation, but meditation on the Self. The implied import is that birth in a high caste is no assurance of liberation or even of closeness to it. Brahman is present in all people as the indwelling Self and it is realization of this which confers liberation. Social standing is completely irrelevant. (Compare this to *Bhagavad-Gītā* 9.32: "Even those of low birth — women, *vaiśyas*, and *śūdras* too — can reach the highest spiritual realization if they take refuge in Me.")[13]

Section Four closes with a description of the fivefold sacrifice obligatory to householders, a ritual which, like the earlier horse sacrifice, holds the cosmos in order (1.4.16), and a discussion of how the sacrifice can be performed mentally, through metaphor, and be equally efficacious (1.4.17).

Section Five: Prajāpati's Creation of the World as "Food" For Himself

In *Upaniṣadic* symbolism, "food" refers to anything that is taken in by the senses — all sights, sounds, sensations, objects of observation, in fact all of objective reality. "Food" refers to creation itself, and the "eater" of food, i.e. the subjective experiencer, is the spiritual Self, Brahman. In the words of Swāmī Krishnānanda, "*Prakṛti* is the 'food' of *Puruṣa*".[14] Section Five examines this concept and will emphasize two connecting philosophical points: that the conscious Self actually creates the food/ world which It eats/experiences and that this individual Self is one with the cosmic Self (God, here called Prajāpati) which pervades the universe.

Verse 1.5.2 is a restatement and explanation of verse 1.5.1, so we will approach them as a single unit. Prajāpati, here called the Father, created seven kinds of food. That He created them "through meditation and rites" suggests that during the event of creating, the Father was both in a state of Self-contained repose and in a state of willful activity, a paradox which is characteristic of Brahman, which is ever changeless yet ever becoming all that is. One kind of food was "the general food of all beings," in other words the material manifestation. We are warned not to become infatuated with this food nor to hoard it, "for this is the common food of all." Nothing actually belongs to us, but is the property of God. This injunction against greed and accumulativeness is echoed in the *Īśā Upaniṣad*, verse 1.

Two foods were assigned to the gods, and the text itself offers variant interpretations. The two foods could be taken to mean sacrificial libations and other offerings in general, or could mean the full moon and new moon sacrifices, known as *Darśa* and *Pūrṇamāsa*.[15] The objects of the gods' senses, then, are more subtle than ours, for they are sustained by worship, not by matter and physical sensations. The animals, on the other hand, being of a lower consciousness, require less to sustain them. In general, they do not require ideas, music, stories, meaning, philosophy, complex amusements, etc., and thus the food allotted to them is milk, the food of babies. Animals, though spiritually identical to humans, are as infants on the evolutionary scale of consciousness.

Before discussing the three foods Prajāpati created for Himself, the text asserts that rituals (in Upaniṣadic symbolism ritual refers to any physical action, for, like sacrificial ritual, all actions bring about tangible results through the force of *karma*) do not bring the worshipper immortality. Only by a knowledge of the nature of reality — what is the "eater", what is the "food" — is immortality achieved.

A question is raised, "Why are the foods not exhausted, though they are constantly being consumed?" The answer is given, because the eater creates the food. The implication is twofold. If we take the eater to be God, the eater is unlimited and so the scope of His expression, food/creation, is also inexhaustible. If we understand the eater to be the individual person, the meaning is even more intriguing. The *Upaniṣad* says, ". . . the eater is indeed the cause of their inexhaustiblility because he creates this food . . . If perchance he does not do this, it surely will be exhausted." In other words, we create the objects of our desire through our attachments to them. It is the desire of the individual to remain individual and enjoy separate sense objects that keeps the material manifestation going. According to Swāmī Krishnānanda,

> . . . if desire is to be absent, the world itself would become absent. The world in front of you exists because of your desires. If the desires of all created beings get absorbed into their own sources, the universe will vanish in a second.[16]

So it was Brahman's desire for separateness that gave rise to creation and our continued desire that sustains it. However, the one who can eat food, as verse 1.5.2 says, "prominently . . . attains identity with the gods". Prominently here means being superior to it. In other words, the embodied individual can have contact with material nature and still remain aloof from it, thus attaining immortality, symbolized in these two verses by the word nectar. In Hindu mythology the *devas* possess *amṛta*, the nectar which confers immortality.

Beginning with verse 1.5.3, the three foods of God are described. They are speech, mind and *prāṇa*. As is typical in Upaniṣadic exposition, a system of correspondences is developed linking the individual's inner being to the material and divine macrocosms. Speech, mind and *prāṇa* are, of course, a part of our personal makeup. Yet, the text asserts, they are also the three worlds: earth, atmosphere, and heaven, which comprise the Vedic *Triloka*, or three abodes (1.5.5). They are the three principal *Vedas* (1.5.5), the gods, manes and men (1.5.6), mother, father, child (1.5.7), the known, the yet to be known, and the unknown (1.5.8). The point is that each person is a microcosm containing the infinitude of the macrocosm and reaching beyond the limits of individuality to pervade the universe. "Heaven (the sky) is the body of the mind . . . as far as the mind extends, so far does heaven" (1.5.12). One who sees the world and the self as limited remains limited, while one who sees them as unlimited becomes unlimited (1.5.13).

This Prajāpati is associated with Time and with the moon, which is the marker of time with its waxing and waning (1.5.14). The fortunes of men also wax and wane, but wealth is merely a passing ephemera, and does not affect that aspect of a person which is changeless (1.5.15). According to Śaṅkarācārya, the word wealth here refers to one's family, particularly sons, which, because they were able to perform sacrifices on behalf of their father after his death, were a great asset to a man.[17] Verses 1.1.16-17 elaborate on this fact, describing how after death one can enter into any of the three worlds, and that it is through a son that one enters into the world of men, by means of the son's carrying out of the father's instructions and performing sacrifices. If spiritual liberation is attained, the father "penetrates" and "pervades" the son in the sense that he, the father, is now all-pervading and the son is his worldly representative.

Again, the preeminence of *prāṇa* over all other sense organs is extolled, for it is the foundation of all activities, of the functioning of the sense organs, and of the very elements, here personified as deities. *Prāṇa* is all-pervading, the substance of the cosmos, and is symbolically identified with Vāyu, the god of wind or air (1.5.21-22). Section five closes, then, with an exhortation to observe the "vow" of merging all the other senses into *prāṇa*. In his commentary of this verse, Śaṅkarācārya suggests that the *yogī* contemplate thusly: "The vocal and other organs in all beings as well as fire and the other gods are but a part and parcel of me, and I, the vital force, the Self, initiate all movement."[18]

Section Six: The General Category as the Basis of the Particular

In this short section, three analogies are drawn to explain how Brahman, the general reality or category, is the substratum from which particulars arise. Names, for instance, are particulars, but they all have their basis in sound. "It is their common feature, for it is common to all names. It is their self, for it supports all names" (1.6.1). Similarly color, or form, is the general category, while individual colors or forms are particulars within that category. They could not exist were there not "color" or "form" as a concept (1.6.2). Particular actions rise out of the common substratum of action as a concept; it is their "self" (1.6.3).

Name, form and action comprise our bodies, our outward personas, but just as these three phenomena are merely particulars of a general category, so do they hide "the deathless principle" within, that is the Divine, which is the general background of all phenomena.

Chapter Two: The Conditioned Self and the Divine Self

The second chapter is the most celebrated portion of the *Bṛhadāraṇyaka Upaniṣad* because it contains the *Maitreyī Brāhmaṇa*, a lofty dialogue between the sage Yājñavalkya and his wife, Maitreyī, as well as the *Madhu Vidyā* or "honey knowledge", a poetic reflection on the Oneness of everything. This chapter is lucid, lyrical and accessible, scaling the clear philosophical heights for which the *Upaniṣads* are revered.

Section One: King Ajātaśatru and Proud Bālāki (or Gārgya)

In former times, it was the custom for kings to endow *brāhmaṇas* with gifts of cattle in exchange for the *brāhmaṇa's* services as teachers, priests, and spiritual guides. So it is that king Ajātaśatru and the *brāhmaṇa* known as Proud Bālāki (henceforth refered to as Gārgya, or descendent of the Garga family) strike a deal — a thousand cows for a discourse on Brahman. Ajātaśatru remarks that everyone flocks to King Janaka's court to hear discourses on spiritual subjects and that he is glad that Gārgya has come to him instead (2.1.1).[19]

For the next twelve verses, Gārgya proposes facets of Brahman, each of which the king shoots down with the remark, "Please do not talk about Him. I adore Him . . ." and the addition of his own commentary. In other words, the king is saying, "I already know this, so there's no point in your talking about it. Tell me something I *don't* know."[20] Gārgya identifies Brahman as that Being who is in the sun. Yes, King Ajātaśatru replies, I know: "I adore Him alone as transcendent, as the head of all beings and as radiant. He who adores Him thus becomes transcendent, the head of all beings, and radiant" (2.1.2). It is a well-known adage in Hinduism that what we long for and worship we become. The subsequent verses follow this same pattern, identifying Brahman as the Being who is in the moon, in lightning, in the ether, the air, fire, water, the looking glass (i.e. all shining, pure things),[21] in sound, in the directions, in darkness, and in *Hiraṇyagarbha* (2.1.3-13).

"Is this all?" the king asks. When Gārgya replies in the affirmative, the king says, "No, that is not all," and in a striking, even politically subversive role-reversal, the *brāhmaṇa* submits to the *kṣatriya* as a disciple (2.1. 14). Clearly it is not caste identification but personal realization which qualifies one to be a *guru*.

Ajātaśatru begins by drawing Gārgya by the hand up to a sleeping man. He calls to him, nudges him, but the man is insensate. Finally he manages to wake him up and asks Gārgya, "When the self that is associated with the intellect was thus asleep, where was it?" (2.1.16). The king explains that when the intellect is drawn away from the external world through sleep, it becomes fixed in the Supreme Self in the heart. It becomes *svapiti*, "absorbed in itself"[22], and all of the sense organs become similarly withdrawn (2.1.17). This Self is the source of everything: the senses, the worlds, the gods, all living beings. It is the Ultimate Truth, the "Truth of truth".

Section Two: The Sacredness of the Human Body, the Abode of *Prāṇa*

As Brahman is the foundation of everything, all phenomena is sacred. However, the human body is especially sacred because the divine consciousness is more highly developed here than anywhere else. The *Upaniṣads* often use *prāṇa*, the vital force, to signify Brahman, and in this short section, the sacredness of the human body, the dwelling place of *prāṇa*, is defined by drawing correspondences between certain body parts and certain holy things and entities.

According to Śaṅkarācārya, the analogy of the calf in verse 2.2.1 refers to the subtle body.[23] The *Taittirīya Upaniṣad* describes five *kośas*, or sheaths, which envelop the Ātman and comprise the individual. They are the physical sheath (*annamaya-kośa*), the prāṇic sheath (*prāṇamaya-kośa*), the mental sheath (*manomaya-kośa*), the intellectual sheath (*vijñānamaya-kośa*), and the bliss sheath (*ānandamaya-kośa*).[24] The subtle body to which Śaṅkarācārya refers is comprised of the *prāṇic*, mental, and intellectual sheaths. These do not disintegrate at death, but form the basis of a new body.[25] The subtle body is fixed in the physical body, just as a calf is fixed to a certain spot by means of a post and tether. Whoever understands the science of the subtle body can overcome his "seven jealous relatives", namely the seven sense organs: the eyes, ears, nostrils and mouth.[26]

The *prāṇa* is revered and tended to by seven "decay preventing", in other words life-sustaining, gods, each of which is given a symbolic correspondence to a portion of the eye (2.2.2). All of these deities are extremely ancient, of the earliest Vedic pantheon. The red of the eye corresponds to Rudra, "the ruddy one", a red-complected proto-Śiva; the water belongs to Parjanya, the personification of rain[27]; the pupil is Āditya, the sun; the iris is Agni, fire; the white is Indra, the chief of the gods; the lower eyelid is the Earth goddess Pṛthivī[28], and the upper eyelid is the very ancient god Dyaus, the sky (a cognate and forerunner of the Greek Zeus).[29] So within the globe of the eye an entire universe is represented, with Father Sky above, Mother Earth below and all manner of elemental activity in between. Once again the *Upaniṣad* points to a macrocosm in the microcosm. This imagery is extremely powerful.

The Seven orifices of the head are our knowledge-gathering instruments. Hence, in verses 2.2.3-4 they are associated with the seven great

Vedic sages Bharadvāja and Gotama (ears), Viśvāmitra and Jamadagni (eyes), Vasiṣṭha and Kaśyapa (nostrils) and Atri (tongue). Each of these famous figures have legends associated with them and show up in the *Mahābhārata* and the *Purāṇas.*

Section Three: The Two Forms of Reality

The thesis of section three is stated clearly at the outset: "Brahman has only two forms — gross and subtle, mortal and immortal, limited and unlimited, perceptible and imperceptible" (2.3.1). The remaining five verses merely elaborate on this idea. The analogy of the sun is used; the gross form of the sun, the aspect we see, is the shine of the sun (2.3.2). However, behind the shine is that which *causes* the shine, the source of the shine, which we cannot see. The text refers to this as, depending on the translation, the solar orb[30], or the being that is in the sun[31] (2.3.3). It is the subtle, imperceptible aspect which causes the gross, perceptible aspect to be.

We, too, have a gross and subtle aspect. The body is the mortal, limited, perceptible dimension (2.3.4), but within it is the immortal, unlimited, imperceptible dimension (2.3.5). There are many analogies we can use to describe the subtle body within, and verse 2.3.6 refers to some. It is like a tongue of fire. Like a white lotus. Like a flash of lightning. However, there is an inner Reality even beyond the subtle body, a Reality so profound it cannot be described. The most accurate means of speaking of It is to say It is *neti neti*, "not this, not this" (2.3.6). In other words, any mental conception one can formulate, any quality or characteristic one can apply to Brahman is incorrect because Brahman is beyond all limitations, all conditions, and hence all attributes. It is safer to think, "Brahman is not this, nor is It this other thing, nor is It that, etc." *Neti neti* is one of the principle disciplines of *jñāna yoga.*

Section Four: Yājñavalkya Instructs His Wife Maitreyī That the Self Encompasses Everything

Perhaps the most famous portion of the *Upaniṣad*, the *Maitreyī Brāhmaṇa*, so named after the woman disciple to whom this teaching is imparted, is a straightforward treatment of the Ātman as the source, substratum and content of everything.

The section opens with the sage Yājñavalkya preparing to renounce the world and dividing his estate between two beloved wives, Kātyāyanī and Maitreyī. Maitreyī inquires, "Even if you endow me with the whole earth, will such wealth bring me immortality?" Yājñavalkya replies that it will not. "Then of what value is it?" Maitreyī asks. "Please, instead bestow upon me the knowledge that is the means of attaining immortality" (2.4.1-3). Expressing his love not only for her, but also for the sublime subject into which she is inquiring, Yājñavalkya invites her to sit with him and learn (2.4.4).

The two wives represent the two life paths one can follow, the path to liberation and the path of worldliness. We always have a choice, and while the latter is not necessarily bad, the former is infinitely superior. The *Kaṭha Upaniṣad* also speaks of the two paths, calling them *preyaḥ*, the pleasurable, and *śreyaḥ*, the preferable, stating, "The intelligent one selects the electable (*śreyaḥ*) in preference to the delectable (*preyaḥ*)" (*Kaṭha Up*, 1.2.1-2). Material comforts do not bring lasting happiness and freedom, only spiritual attainment can.

Yājñavalkya begins by asserting that when we love a thing, be it a spouse, a child, money, places, whatever, we do not love the object for the sake of the object, but for our own sakes (2.4.5). The emotions and attachments we feel have no actual connection to things outside of us. The inner world is psychological, the outer physical, our feelings completely subjective, inner operations that have no tangible relation to outside phenomena.[32] When we yearn for things outside of us, what we are really yearning for is a sense of inner wholeness, and the object holds out the promise of completing us. So long as we are bound by limited consciousness we will suffer this sense of deficiency, because our true natures are infinite.[33] "The Self, my dear Maitreyī, should verily be realized . . . By realization of the Self alone, my dear, through hearing, reflection and meditation, all this is known" (2.4.5). Only through realization of Ātman is wholeness attained, for the Ātman is infinite and includes everything. The lover will no longer need to love things outside him or herself because he or she is complete in the Self. There are no external objects, no internal subjectivity.

Unless you understand the oneness of everything with the Self, Yājñavalkya suggests, you will suffer loss after loss (2.4.6). "Worlds reject him who knows worlds to be different from the Self. The gods reject him who knows the gods to be different from the Self . . . All rejects him who knows all to be different from the Self." So long as there is a sense of separate*ness*, separa*tion* will occur. Swāmī Krishnānanda puts it well: "Everything shall leave you if you regard anything as other than you . . . Anything that is outside you cannot belong to you and cannot satisfy you and will leave you."[34] However, the verse concludes, everything — the worlds, the gods, all beings — are, in fact, "only the Self." Paradoxically, therefore, one is never separate from anything or anyone but in eternal union with all. It is a matter of perspective.

The separate notes of a drum, a conch or a lute are not different from the sound in general which comes from the instrument. They are simply variations on a single phenomenon (2.4.7-9). Similarly, all branches of knowledge are but the "breath of this limitless Reality" (2.4.10). The breath of a man is nondifferent from the man himself, yet emanates from him; so too do the *Vedas*, history, mythology, philosophy, art, etc. emanate from the Divine. As the sea is the merging place of all water, so too is the Self the merging place of all multiplicities (2.4.11). Just as a lump of salt dissolved in water cannot be located as a separate thing, and wherever you taste the water the salt is there, so too is "this great, endless, infinite Reality the only homogenous Intelligence" (2.4.12). Because of its contact with material elements, such as the body and senses, It appears to have separateness, subjects and objects. However, when these are eliminated, separateness is eliminated and no particular consciousness remains (2.4.12).

At this point, Maitreyī objects. "You have confused me, saying that after attaining oneness the Self has no consciousness" (2.4.13). This is an oft-misunderstood point; Maitreyī is in good company. Some people find the Hindu and Buddhist philosophies anathema because they mistakenly think that the extinction of the individual self means oblivion, total extinction of being. This is absurd. Liberation from the confines of individual consciousness brings realization of one's infinite existence, infinite consciousness and infinite bliss (*sat-cit-ānanda*). It is Being at its utmost.

Yājñavalkya puts it this way. When there is duality, one sees things outside oneself, hears things outside oneself, thinks things outside oneself, and so on. There is the other, a subject and an object. However, when everything is realized as the very Self, the distinction between Knower and known disappears. Without a subject and object, there is no longer a seer and a seen, experiencer and experienced. It is only in this limited sense that the consciousness of which Yājñavalkya speaks is no more. In its place is unlimited, Supreme Consciousness (2.4.14).

Yājñavalkya ends his discourse here, but will resume where he left off in the third chapter, when he addresses questions posed by a group of sages. In the meantime, the *Upaniṣad* turns to one of its loveliest and most contemplative segments.

Section Five: This Earth is Like Honey . . . or the Universal Exchange of Bliss

Perhaps the most beautiful and meditative set of passages in the Upaniṣadic corpus, the *Madhu-Vidyā*, or "honey wisdom", is a contemplation on the sublime joy which binds all reality together and is the Self. We don't say that the Ātman possesses joy, because the Ātman *is* joy. The Western adage, "God is Love" is echoed here; the *Upaniṣad* speaks of a sweetness, a bliss, a love that permeates everything. This love is Ātman, God, the Self. It derives ecstasy from experiencing Its own being.

In addition, the *Madhu-Vidyā* proposes an awesome and mysterious doctrine that in any one thing the totality is experienced because everything is equally representative of the whole. Again to quote Swāmī Krishnānanda, "When you touch anything, you are touching everything. If I touch a table, I am touching the sun at once . . . When I speak to anyone, I am speaking to everybody. . . . when I know one thing, I know everything."[35] Like much sacred literature which is meant to be memorized and meditated upon, the *Madhu-Vidyā* is repetitive. The same phrase is repeated a full fourteen times with only slight variations between them. So profound are these words, one can read or chant the verses one after the other, like the refrain of a piece of music, allowing the ideas to soak in, or one can select a single verse and contemplate it deeply. The pattern goes:

> This air is like honey to all beings and all beings are like honey to this air. The same with the shining immortal being who is in this air, and the shining immortal being who is the vital force in the body. These four are but the Self. This Self-knowledge is the means of immortality; this underlying unity is Brahman; this knowledge of Brahman is the means of becoming all (2.5.4).

So complete is this statement, it encompasses the wisdom of all the *Upaniṣads*. If God-realization were one's only goal in life, this paragraph is the only thing one would ever have to read.

Succeeding verses replace the word air with earth, fire, water, sun, directions, moon, lightning, cloud, ether, *dharma*, truth, human and other species, and cosmic body (the sum total of all bodies and things).[36] Anything at all could be fitted into this paragraph: sunset, music, constellation, wind, mouse, etc., because everything is equally pervaded by "the shining, immortal being," Brahman.

Tradition has it that the *Madhu-Vidyā* was first spoken by the sage Dadhyac to the celestial Twins, the Aśvins. He learned it from Indra (in other versions the roles are reversed and Indra is the disciple of Dadhyac), who was jealous of this knowledge and threatened to chop Dadhyac's head off should he speak of it to anyone. When the Twins approached him as disciples he regretfully turned them down, but they came up with a plan to trick Indra. With his permission, they cut off

Dadhyac's head themselves, kept it safe, and replaced it with a horse's head. When Dadhyac, through the horse's head, began to speak the *Madhu-Vidyā*, an enraged Indra swooped down and sliced off the horse's head. The Twin Aśvins restored Dadhyac's human head and he was saved.[37] The last four verses of section five make reference to the *Madhu-Vidyā* (here called "that meditation on things mutually helpful") being imparted to the Aśvins by Dadhyac.

Notice that the theme of the horse, which so dramatically opened the *Upaniṣad*, reemerges. The Aśvins, while embodying the universal archetype of the divine twins, are also strongly connected to horses. The name *aśvin* means "possessed of horses" and they were born of deities who assumed the forms of a mare and a stallion for the purpose of sexual union. Throughout the Aśvin's mythology, horses are a recurring motif.[38]

Section six closes the third chapter with a list of the line of spiritual teachers from the most current at the time, Pautimāṣya, spanning fifty-five generations back to Brahman Itself, the Supreme Teacher.

Chapter Three: The Sages Test Yājñavalkya

The next two chapters take place in the court of King Janaka. The term Janaka does not necessarily refer to a particular person, but is rather a title conferred upon the most august saint-kings. There were sixty-four Janakas in all.[39] This particular Janaka, the emperor of Videha, staged an enormous sacrifice and invited all of the most learned *brāhmaṇas* in his kingdom. He wanted to see which was the foremost and offered a thousand cows, each with ten gold coins tied to its horns, to the most knowledgeable among them (3.1.1). Yājñavalkya was present in the assembly, and he at once turned to his pupil and said, "Drive these cows back to my house, son." The sages were aghast! What nerve! A person doesn't just proclaim themselves the greatest scholar in the land without proving it, so the sages set about testing him with a series of progressively more subtle and difficult questions. This provides the substance of the third chapter.

The Warm-Up Questions

First, the king's own priest, Aśvala, drilled Yājñavalkya with questions about the performance and results of ritual sacrifice, all of which Yājñavalkya answered perfectly (3.1.3-10). Then Ārtabhāga took over and threw down questions about the bodily organs, their objects and their destinations after death. Again, Yājñavalkya responded correctly (3.2.1-13). Next, Bhujyu asked as to where the descendants of King

Parīkṣit, that is, performers of the horse sacrifice, go after their deaths. Yet again, Yājñavalkya knew (3.3.1-3). These were easy questions. Having passed the preliminaries, Yājñavalkya was now ready for the real test.

Brahman in Its Immanent Feature

Henceforth the dialogues will address a deeper level. The questions will turn to spiritual subjects, and will concern themselves largely with the idea that any phenomenon, element, or thing has its cause in, its foundation in, and is part of a more general thing which, in turn, has its foundation in a still more general thing, and so on. In his conversation with Maitreyī, Yājñavalkya used the example of notes emitted by a musical instrument. The individual notes are variations of, and have their basis in, the general sound coming from the instrument. The sound made by the instrument has its basis in sound in general, and so on. If we take anything far enough back eventually we reach a point beyond which there is no place to go. This supreme reality is Brahman.

Uṣasta is the first to ask about Brahman, particularly in Its immanent feature. Yājñavalkya tells him that It is the Self within everyone and is manifest in the vital energies or airs, such a *apāna*, *vyāna* and *udāna* (3.4.1). Inquiring further, Uṣasta asks for a description of Brahman, but Yājñavalkya replies that none can be given, for just as the eyes cannot see themselves because they are the things doing the seeing, so too can Brahman not be experienced as an objective reality because It is the one doing the experiencing. That which does the hearing can't be heard; that which does the thinking can't be thought about (3.4.2).

Kahola continues the questioning on the immanent aspect of Brahman, to which Yājñavalkya replies that Brahman is beyond conditioned, worldly life. Therefore, the true *brāhmaṇa* (or true spiritual aspirant) renounces the world to become a mendicant and master meditation (3.5.1).

A woman sage named Gārgī now introduces the overarching theme of the discussion, that everything has its foundation in a more subtle antecedent, but that when we get to Brahman we can't go any farther, for It is the ultimate Ground of all Being (3.6.1).

The Inner Controller

Uddālaka poses two questions. First, what is that *sūtra*, or thread, by which this world, the next world and all beings are strung together, like beads on a necklace? It is Vāyu, Yājñavalkya replies (2.7.1-2). In other words, it is *prāṇa*, the vital air, for Vāyu is the god of air.[40] Second, who is that Inner Controller (*Antaryāmin*, also translated to "Supreme

Immanent Principle")[41] who governs this life, the next life, and all beings? The answer resembles the *Madhu-Vidyā* both in form and theme. It is poetically and meditatively repetitive and speaks of an ultimate being or reality which is present in all individual things as well as the collectivity of all things. Though It is the very being of all things, those things are not cognizant of Its presence:

> He who dwells in water but is within it, whom water does not know, whose body is water, and who controls water from within, is the Inner Controller — your own immortal Self (3.7.4).

No clearer exposition of *advaita vedānta* could be given. The twenty-one verses of this section will repeat the refrain verbatim, but will substitute the word water with earth, sky, directions, moon and stars, ether, darkness, mind, all beings, and so on. It winds up with a restatement of what was the crux of section four: "He is never known, but is the Knower. There is no other seer than He, there is no other hearer than He, there is no other thinker than He . . ." (3.7.23).

Brahman in Its Transcendent Feature

Once again the illustrious Gārgī takes the floor. The most outspoken of the sages, she tells the others that if Yājñavalkya can answer the questions she is ready to pose, no one can defeat him (3.8.1). In sporting fashion she warns Yājñavalkya that like their royal host's stalking of an enemy with sharp arrows in hand, she is closing in on him with two killer questions. "Ask, Gārgī," he says.

First, what pervades the earth, sky, and heaven, what is in between, and is the past, present and future? The unmanifested ether, he answers (3.8.3-4). Ether is the subtlest of all elements, but even more subtle is the undifferentiated, non-physical ether which, in its unmanifest state, precedes ether.[42]

What, then, she asks, pervades the unmanifest ether? (3.8.7). It is, he replies, Brahman, the Absolute, which has no qualities, no perimeters, no senses or organs, no interior, no exterior (3.8.8). Under the rule of the Absolute, the whole universe is kept running in its proper course. The constellations hold their positions, time is kept regular, and the rivers flow in their proper directions (3.8.9). One who performs rituals and penances, but doesn't know this Absolute Truth, finds the results of his works transitory. And should he leave this world in such a consciousness, he is "pitiable". However, one who leaves the world knowing this Absolute knows Brahman (3.8.10).

Brahman, the Ground of All Being

"Certainly none of you can ever defeat him in expounding Brahman," Gārgī announces. But one opponent is still not convinced. Vidagdha, henceforth referred to as Śākalya ("son of Śakala") takes up the challenge by posing obscure technical questions that carry underlying philosophical significance. Yājñavalkya, of course, responds on both levels. Though the terminology of section nine is highly stylized and obscure, the point is fairly direct. If we analyze any object or phenomenon, we find that it has its basis in a more general thing, which has its basis in a still more general thing, and so on. The farther you go, the fewer particulars there are, until the multiplicity is eliminated entirely and there is only the One. For instance, I am a woman. The concept of woman has its basis in the category human. Humans are based in the general category mammals. To be a mammal, one must be an animal. Animals are living beings. Living beings are part of matter. Matter is a phenomenon. Phenomenon is based on existence (as opposed to non-existence). What, then, is the antecedent of existence?

Śākalya will test Yājñavalkya on three subjects — the gods, the elements, and the directions — to see if Yājñavalkya can name the subtle causes upon which each level of phenomena rests. The Hindu pantheon is a good example of particulars resting in generalities resting in even greater generalities because many different gods can be the aspects or emanations of a particular god (like Viṣṇu and His *Avatāras* or Śrī Devī and the many goddesses that are Her manifestations), and all the gods are merely dimensions of the one Brahman. Śākalya asks Yājñavalkya to name how many gods there are and receives the answer "three hundred and three and three thousand and three." Pushed further, he reduces the number to thirty-three, then to six, then three, then two, then one and a half, then just one (3.9.1).

The verses that follow (3.9.2-9) are particularly relevant to those interested in the ancient Vedic pantheon, for they give a good overview of the general categorization of deities. The thirty-three gods are comprised of eight *Vasus*, benevolent atmospheric gods[43], eleven *Rudras*, storm gods, and twelve *Ādityas*, gods of light, such as sun, moon and stars[44], Prajāpati ("Lord of Creatures") the creator, and Indra, the celestial monarch (3.9.2). All of the deities predominate over a particular realm of the universe. The *Vasus* govern the natural elements, the *Rudras* govern the body, the *Ādityas* time, Indra the thundercloud and Prajāpati the ritual sacrifice (3.9.3-6).

The thirty-three gods are really aspects of six primary gods, Agni (fire), Pṛthivī (Mother Earth), Vāyu (air), Antarikṣa (sky), Āditya (sun) and

Dyaus (heaven) (3.9.7). These can be reduced further to three gods, those of earth (in which fire and earth are combined), sky (air and sky combined) and heaven (sun and heaven combined)[45], then further to only two, energy and matter.[46] One and a half refers to God manifesting Itself as individuals who think themselves separate and unique (hence the "half") (3.9.8-9). Finally, there is the one God, Brahman, known simply as *Tyat*, "That" (3.9.9).

Now for the elements. Śākalya will deal with eight: earth, desire, general forms, particular forms, ether, water, darkness, and seed (reproductive potency). In each case, an unvarying pattern of inquiry will ensue which reveals, layer by layer, the subtle antecedents which provide a ground for what has preceded them. Beginning with verse 3.9.10 the pattern is as follows:

Phenomenon
(Body)
=
=
Chief Sense Organ
=
=
Mind
=
=
Special Manifestation
=
=
Supporting Deity

One of the eight elements is named as the body of Brahman (earth for instance). Bodies are knowledge-gathering organisms and are based in sensate experience, thus a chief sense organ is named, referred to poetically as the "eye", so the eye of the earth is fire, or vital force, the eye of desire is intellect, the eye of colors, which means form, is the eye, the eye of ether is the ear, and so one. Each of the organs have an underlying support, and it is common in all of them — the mind. Then a special manifestation of each element is named, for instance the earth element is manifested as the human body, desire is the libido, form is the sun (because the light of the sun allows us to see forms), etc. Finally each element is supported by a particular deity.

The five directions — north, south, west, east and skyward — are treated to a similar analysis, each resting upon a more subtle cause which rests upon an even more subtle cause, ending up with the heart, which is the seat of the Self (3.9.20-24). When Śākalya asks on what the heart rests, Yājñavalkya chastises him. The heart is the very basis of life in the body, it being the seat of the animating principle, the Self. Without it the body dies and becomes carrion for scavengers (3.9.25).

Undeterred, Śākalya presses on with his questions, now turning to the five *prāṇas*, or vital airs, of which one rests upon the other (3.9.26). Ultimately, everything rests upon Brahman, though. This is the whole point, the final conclusion of all knowledge (*vedānta*, the "end of knowledge") and nothing more remains to be said. Yājñavalkya tires of Śākalya's incessant interrogation and turns the tables on him, demanding that he prove *his* learning. "If you cannot clearly tell me of Him (Brahman) your head shall fall off," He says. Beware a *brāhmaṇa's* curse, for they always come to pass. Śākalya was not a knower of Brahman and couldn't speak of Him. So his head fell off! As his disciples were carrying his shrouded body away for cremation, they left it alone for a moment on the roadside and some robbers, thinking it might be a treasure, carried it away. Thus Śākalya was denied even decent funeral rites (3.9.26).

Ever the gentleman, Yājñavalkya offers to field more questions, *but* he reserves the right to ask questions of anyone. No one dares (3.9.27). Yājñavalkya has clearly proved himself the foremost scholar and knower of Brahman in the kingdom, so he offers the sages a short discourse.

The Tree Simile — Rebirth into Brahman Consciousness

A tree is like a man, Yājñavalkya says. A tree has leaves, a man has hair; a tree has bark, a man has skin; a tree has sap, a man has blood. While a tree stands, it can sprout again from seeds, and while a man is alive he can reproduce through his seed. If a tree should fall, it might still sprout again by sending new shoots through the roots. But what of man? If he should be felled by death, does he find life again? Yes, through rebirth into Brahman consciousness. Brahman is life itself and one who realizes Brahman becomes Brahman. "It is Brahman which is Absolute Intelligence and Bliss, the ultimate resort . . . of the knower of Brahman who lives in It" (3.9.28).

Chapter Four: The Three States of Cosciousness and the Journey of Reincarnation

Sometime after the sacrifice Yājñavalkya pays another visit to King Janaka, and their private conversation comprises the *Upaniṣad's* fourth chapter. In general, it will address two topics: the three states of consciousness experienced by an unliberated soul (waking, dreaming and dreamless deep sleep) and how we progress on the journey of reincarnation. The final two sections are reiterations of the *Maitreyī Brāhmaṇa* and the line of teachers, from the fourth and sixth sections of chapter two. Perhaps at one time, before the *Bṛhadāraṇyaka Upaniṣad* was compiled, the *Maitreyī Brāhmaṇa* existed as an independent text, maybe even its own *Upaniṣad*, and these two versions represent the inclusion of two different recensions. The list of teachers differs somewhat from the version in chapter two and may also represent an alternative recension. It is possible, in that case, that the *Maitreyī Brāhmaṇa* and line of teachers segments were included as parts of longer texts which have been joined together to create the *Bṛhadāraṇyaka Upaniṣad* in its present form.

Section One: Partial Definitions of Brahman

So as to avoid redundancy, Yājñavalkya asks the king what he has already been taught by other *gurus*. Each *guru's* definition of Brahman is true, in its way, and Yājñavalkya affirms this, but they are flawed in that they are only partial definitions. Indeed, Brahman is included in the parts; It is present in each proton and electron, but while present in all, It encompasses all and is also beyond all.

The various teachers with whom King Janaka has conferred, Jitvan, Udaṅka, Barku, etc., isolate Brahman as one or another of the bodily organs, which, as has been indicated earlier in this *Upaniṣad*, is associated with a particular deity, for instance the organ of speech which has its correspondence in Agni, fire, (because it is through the sacred fire that we communicate with the *devas*, and also by chanting Vedic mantras make the fire efficacious). The organs and deities have one "foot", that is support or foundation, and It is the Undifferentiated, Brahman. Every one of these "bodies", or abodes of Brahman, have a special form by which they should be meditated upon, as in the case of speech being meditated upon as intelligence (the discriminating voice inside our heads). Included in this system of correspondences is Brahman as speech, *prāṇa*, eye, ear, mind and heart, which is the seat of the Self. The reader should remember that eye, mind, *prāṇa*, heart, etc. are not simply isolated, limited phenomena that belong to this particular person or that. Each is unlimited, pervading and collective. Our individual minds are but whirlpools in a universal mind which is shared by all; *prāṇa* is everywhere, binding all life and matter together, and so it is with all the constituents of our being.

Sections Two and Three: The Three States of Consciousness

"Where do you think you go when you die?" the king is asked, and he replies that he does not know. Yājñavalkya's answer spans three sections, each serving as an introduction to the proceeding one. Section two is a short prologue to section three. It introduces by means of symbolism the concept of the three states of consciousness. Normally we are bound to three states of consciousness: waking, the dream state, and dreamless deep sleep, in which we temporarily return to our true natures, to Brahman. We need to merge ourselves back in our source, immerse ourselves in truth and bliss on a regular basis in order not to despair and/or go insane. Beyond these three states is the superconsciousness of Brahman realization, known as *turīya*, "the fourth" state.

In verse 4.2.2 the waking consciousness[47] is hinted at in a veiled way as the "being" who inhabits the right and left eyes, and is symbolized by Indra, who represents light, and his consort Virāj, who symbolizes matter (because one sees by a combination of light and matter). The obscure reference to Indra's direct name being Indha is connected to a text called the *Nirukta*, which is the oldest commentary on the *Vedas*. It says there that the gods dislike being addressed by their actual names (as do any people of high rank), therefore the lightning deity Indha whose name is derived from *indhana*, meaning "fuel" is addressed as Indra.[48]

The dream state is hinted at by mention of the heart in verse 4.2.3. When we sleep, our consciousness is withdrawn from outer objects and absorbed into the heart. Yet we have intense dream experiences in this state. "The subtle body has finer food than the gross body" means that dream images are objects of experience (food) for the subtle body. Dreams are experienced through a network of subtle nerves which are as fine as the circumference of a hair split into a thousand parts. As will be disclosed in section three (4.3.20), these nerves are called *hitā* and run with white, blue, brown, green and red serums. According to Swami Jagadīśwarānanda:

> These nerves are the seat of the subtle body, which is the repository of impressions. It is transparent, but on account of its contact with the serums, it manifests itself in dream, under the influence of man's past work, as images which take varied forms.[49]

As of this writing, scientists know what kind of chemical and electrical processes occur in the brain when we dream, but they still aren't sure what a dream actually is nor why we have them. Perhaps some day they will construct sufficiently sensitive instruments to confirm the existence of the *hitā*, just as they have documented the existence of bodily energy fields (auras) and the acupuncture meridians.

The third state, dreamless deep sleep, is suggested in verse four by the image of *prāṇa*, which is said to span all directions. It is associated with Brahman, which we experience in deep sleep but do not remember upon awaking. Swami Krishnānanda again puts it well:

> The *Prāṇas* are not only inside our bodies. They are powers which operate throughout the universe. And so, the vital *Prāṇa* that is sustaining the whole world, all creation, becomes part and parcel of one's being and sustenance comes from all sides when the ego subsides temporarily . . . Empty space does not exist . . . all space is filled with *Prāṇa*.[50]

The lovely "Light of Man" dialogue opens section three, culminating in the conclusion that when the sun and moon have set, the fire gone out, the sounds hushed, the Self serves as the guiding light (4.3.6). This Self is a traveller, and can pass between this life and the next, between waking and dream (4.3.7). In dreams, the Self creates a dream body through which It acts and experiences. Obviously, there is no sun or electricity to provide the light in our dreams; by what are they illuminated? The Self provides illumination (4.3.9). In dream, this Self creates worlds of its own (4.3.15-16). We pass easily between different states of consciousness and think nothing of it (4.3.18).

There is a third state too, beyond dreaming. In deep, dreamless sleep, our consciousness is reabsorbed into Brahman, and it is to this subject that verses 4.3.18 through 4.3.32 turn. We must hasten back to this state, "As a hawk or falcon, flying variously in the sky, is exhausted, and stretching its wings directs itself toward its nest" (4.3.19). There are no experiences to garner and bring back from this state, for by being fully merged in Brahman, there is no more subject or object, nothing external from the Self to observe. "That It does not apparently see in that state is because, although really seeing in that state . . . there is not that second entity differentiated from It which It can see" (4.3.23). Nevertheless, the bliss that is experienced in that state is one trillion times more intense than the greatest bliss possible on earth (4.3.33).

The last four verses introduce the subject of bodily death, and thus serve as a transition into section four, which will discuss the transmigratory journey.

Section Four: Death, Reincarnation and Liberation

We reincarnate because we still want or need certain experiences on this plane. The least amount of attachment will bring us back, and the situations we are destined to encounter here are the direct karmic result of our past actions. We create our own future bodies and lives by the choices we make now. But no matter how fortunate or luxurious our situations, so long as we are in this world we are fated to endure suffering and ignorance. Only Brahman realization can liberate us from the pains of life and death.

At death, the senses are withdrawn from external objects, separated from their corresponding physical organs, and settle back into the subtle body (4.4.1-2). The old body is abandoned and the Self creates a new body which, depending on one's *karma*, can take birth in any of several worlds (4.4.4). Our acts and choices form us into who we are and what will happen to us (4.4.5). As long as we have attachment for this or any world, we will transmigrate back for new experiences, but should we attain non-attachment, there is no motivation to come back and we will merge into Brahman, even while still in this body.

Those who are satisfied with mere outward forms of religion will not attain this liberation (4.4.10), nor will sectarian dogmatists or narrow thinkers who believe in a God so limited He must be conceived of in a certain way and not others: "Some speak of It as white, or blue, or grey, or green or red" (4.4.9) (though some interpreters believe these colors refer instead to celestial colors experienced in heightened spiritual states).[51] Worse still are the ignorant, who enter into realms of joylessness and darkness. These places exist both in this world and in others.

Those who know themselves to be Brahman, however, escape misery while in this body and become immortal (4.4.14). There is no diversity whatever in Brahman; one who thinks there is will be reincarnated perpetually (4.4.19). Yet this is an illusion, for the Self within is ever unborn and indestructible (4.4.20). It is infinite, birthless, unaffected by our deeds, the Lord (*Īśvara*) and protector of us all (4.4.22). Those who desire It give up all mundane desires and renounce the world, for It is beyond dualities and definitions (4.4.22).

The sublime qualities of a knower of Brahman are described in verse 4.4.23, and the section closes by reiterating that Brahman is "the eater of all foods," or the sole experiencer of all objects, while at the same time is the objects that are experienced (4.4.24). When we come to know ourselves as Brahman, we know ourselves to be unchanging, neverending, fearless and infinite (4.4.25).

For an outline of sections five and six, please refer back to Chapter Two, sections four and six, of which these are a reiteration.

Chapter Five: Various Meditations on Brahman as Energy and Light

Chapter Five is a collection of fifteen short meditations, each independent and complete in itself. Though all are unique, many share the same theme of light and energy as manifestations of Brahman, whether it be as the sun, or lightning, or *prāṇa*, or the metabolic fire, or the sacred *Gāyatrī* mantra, the Vedic hymn to the sun. Brief synopses of each are given below.

Section One: The Infinite from the Infinite

The universe emanates from Brahman — the infinite from the Infinite. *Oṃ* is Brahman and *Oṃ* is the means of becoming Brahman (refer, too, the *Māṇḍūkya Upaniṣad* for a more complete treatment of *Oṃ*).

Section Two: The Three Virtues

Prajāpati engendered three races — the *devas*, or gods, the *manuṣyas*, or humans, and the *asuras*, or demons. Each group, in turn, came to him for instruction. To the *devas* he gave the syllable "*da*". "Do you understand?" he asked them and they replied, "Indeed. You are instructing us to practice self-control." "Correct," he said. To the humans he also gave the syllable "*da*". "You have told us to be charitable," they said, and he affirmed it. Finally the *asuras* came to him, and he gave them the syllable "*da*". "You have taught us to be merciful," they said and they were correct.

"*Da*" refers to the first syllable of the words *dāmyata*, self-control, *datta*, charity, and *dayadhvam*, mercy.[52] The *devas* are known for their capacity for pleasure, hence self-restraint is the most important austerity for them. Humans are most given to greed, hoarding, accumulativeness, so charity is our principal discipline. *Asuras* are violent and cruel, hence it most efficacious for them to cultivate merciful compassion.[53] Of course, these three classes of beings can be taken to represent classes of ordinary people who are characterized by sensuality, covetousness and cruelty, and suggest the principal virtues they should strive to embody.[54]

Section Three: God in the Heart

The divine Self, here referred to as Prajāpati, resides in the heart. The word "heart", *hṛdaya,* itself is a subject for meditation, for its component elements each suggest something of the nature of the Self. The root *hṛ* means to draw, attract, or pull towards, and everyone gravitates to a knower of the Self. The root *da* means to give, and as the Self encompasses all, everything naturally comes to the knower of Self. *Ya* means to go, and the one who knows Brahman goes to Brahman.[55]

Section Four: Truth

Satya means truth, and Brahman is Truth Itself.

Section Five: the *Mahāvyāhṛtis*

In the beginning, the universe was only "water", that is, primordial chaos and formlessness. The water created *satya*, truth, out of which emerged *Hiraṇyagarbha*, the cosmic womb. *Hiraṇyagarbha* gave birth to *Virāj*, matter, from which the gods were formed. *Satya* is Brahman and even within the word *satya* one sees both the conditioned and unconditioned aspects of Brahman represented. The syllables *sa* and *ya* are truth, or unconditioned, infinite Brahman, while nestled within them is *ti*, untruth, or the conditioned Brahman. They are both a single Reality.

The section now turns to what is known as a *sūrya upāsanā*, or graduated meditation, from the most gross to the most subtle (*upāsanā*), on the sun (*sūrya*).[56] The sun is symbolic of Brahman as Brahman is the original energizer, sustainer, life-giver, light-giver, etc.[57] It is contemplated through the *Gāyatrī mantra*, the most sacred Vedic *mantra*, which goes,

Oṃ bhūr bhuvaḥ svaḥ
tat savitur vareṇyam
bhargo devasya dhīmahi
dhiyo yo naḥ pracodayāt

> *Oṃ*. Salutations to the terrestrial sphere (*bhūḥ*). Salutations to the sphere of space (*bhuvaḥ*). Salutations to the celestial sphere (*svaḥ*). Let us contemplate the deity of Light, the Divine Creator. May He guide our minds (so that we may realize the Supreme Truth).

Our *Upaniṣad* verse 5.6.3 draws from the three *mahāvyāhṛtis*, or great sacred formulae, *Bhūr, Bhuvaḥ, Svaḥ*,[58] which represent, respectively, earth, atmosphere, and heaven. The *vyāhṛtis* correspond to the body of the divine Person in the sun. "His secret name is *Ahar*" — a pun, for *ahar* means "to destroy or shun" (in this case evil),[59] but also means "daylight".[60] The next verse is similar, only His name is identified as *Aham*, "I am". He is Brahman, the one universal consciousness.

Section Six: The Light of the Mind and Intellect

Brahman is in the mind and the heart, and provides the light that illumines both.

Section Seven: The Lightning

Brahman is the light in lightning, that is, the light of knowledge that dispels the darkness of ignorance (Tibetan Buddhism is, by the way, known as *Vajrayāna*, the "Thunderbolt Vehicle").

Section Eight: the *Vedas* are Like a Cow

The *Vedas* are like a cow that distributes the milk of knowledge. Her four nipples are the concluding syllables chanted at the end of Vedic *mantras — Svāhā, Vaṣaṭ, Hanta,* and *Svadhā.* Because *Svāhā* and *Vaṣaṭ* are uttered when offerings are made to the gods, these are said to be the nipples that feed the gods, while *Hanta* and *Svadhā* mean "if you want" and "food", so these feed people and manes. *Prāṇa* is her bull because chants cannot be performed without breath, and bull is cow's constant companion. Mind is her calf because calf stimulates the production of mother's milk, and the hunger of the mind to know stimulates the acquiring of knowledge.[61]

Section Nine: Brahman as Metabolic Energy

The metabolic fire (*samāna*, one of the five *prāṇas*) is representative of Brahman as it is a life-giving energy, an "eater" and "creator". It is identified as *Vaiśvānara*, an epithet for Agni, the god of fire.[62]

Section Ten: The Levels of Ascent to Brahman

When an enlightened person dies, he or she usually doesn't break instantly into union with Brahman, but ascends gradually through higher and higher levels of consciousness until attaining the highest. This ascension process is known as *krama-mukti.*[63] In this verse, the stages are symbolized by the different guiding deities one meets at each stage of the journey, such as Vāyu, the god of air, Āditya, the god of the sun, and Candra, the moon god.

Section Eleven: Illness and Death as Spiritual Austerities

Consider illness and impending death, both of which are inescapable for everyone, as *tapas* — spiritual austerities. Meditate upon them as a means of transcending aversion and attraction.

Section Twelve: The Interdependence of Matter and Energy

Matter (*anna*, "food") and vital energy (*prāṇa*) are interdependent; neither exists without the activating force of the other. Thus, matter is called *vi*, from the word *viṣṭa*, to be rooted, because all things are rooted in matter, and *prāṇa* is called *ram*, from *ramaṇa*, to be happy, to take joy in life,[64] because the delight we experience in life is due to the presence of *prāṇa*.

Section Thirteen: The Vedic *Mantras* are Imbued With *Prāṇa*

The *prāṇa* is associated with four great Vedic chants: the *Uktha*, which is a laudatory hymn used mainly in the *Mahāvrata* sacrifice, a fertility festival marking both the end and beginning of two successive solar periods;[65] the *Yajus*, verse-*mantras* to accompany ritual sacrifice;[66] *Sāman*, sacred songs, and *Kṣattra*, power and protection.[67]

Section Fourteen: the *Gāyatrī* Encompasses All Phenomena

This section returns to the subject of the sacred *Gāyatrī mantra*, which it praises and analyzes. Being connected to the sun, the *Gāyatrī*, like the root *mantra Oṃ*, is associated with Brahman, hence by meditating upon it and its components, one is led to realization of the highest Truth.

As it is comprised of four verses, the *Gāyatrī* is compared to a four-footed creature. One of its feet encompasses the earth, sky, and heaven. In verse 5.14.1 these spheres are identified by their predominating deities, Bhūmi, Antarikṣa and Dyaus respectively. Each letter of the *Gāyatrī* has a deity who wipes away the sins of whomever utters it,[68] thus the *mantra* encompasses the universe and its powers.

The three *Vedas* — *Ṛg, Yajus* and *Sāma* — form another of the *Gāyatrī's* feet (5.14.2), and the three principal *prāṇas* — *prāṇa, apāna* and *vyāna* — yet another (5.14.3). The fourth foot is the sun, i.e. Brahman, and therefore is described as supramundane and resting on the truth (5.14.4). It is called *turīya*, "the fourth", as in the fourth state of consciousness beyond waking, dreaming and dreamless deep sleep in which we temporarily merge back into Brahman. The verse refers to *Sāvitrī*, which is another name for the *Gāyatrī* and is also another name for Sūrya, the sun god.

The benefits of knowing the *Gāyatrī* are elucidated in verse 5.14.6, and verse 5.14.7 offers both a salutation to the *Gāyatrī* and the means for sending a curse using the *Gāyatrī*. Verse 5.14.8 gives an overly concise rendering of a cautionary tale concerning the recitation of the *Gāyatrī* (perhaps the author of the *Upaniṣad* assumed his or her readers were already familiar with the story).

Buḍila Aśvatarāśvi, a reciter of the hymn, made an error in its execution and, as a result, became an elephant in his next birth. Janaka, riding the elephant one day, asked him how this strange thing could have happened, and the elephant replied, "Because I did not know its mouth, O Emperor. Fire is indeed its mouth."[69] The *Gāyatrī* is like fire. On the one hand, it burns away sins and purifies the consciousness of the reciter, but on the other hand, fire is dangerous and can cause harm if handled incorrectly. The *Gāyatrī* is powerful and must be treated with caution.

Section Fifteen: Prayer to Brahman as the Sun

The chapter closes with a gorgeous prayer to Brahman in Its form as the sun. Honoring Divinity through the beautiful and life-giving sun is a universal spiritual practice, still observed in Japan by worshippers of the Shinto Sun Goddess Amaterasu (who is certainly an embodiment of the Great Goddess archetype) who rise early every day, face the sun and offer prayers, and also by practitioners of certain Native American traditions, who greet the sun each morning with jubilant songs.

Very similar verses to this one can be found in the *Īśā Upaniṣad*, verses sixteen and eighteen.

Chapter Six: The Preeminence of *Prāṇa*; Meditation of the Five Fires

The concluding chapter seems not to address a particular theme, but rather scrambles together whatever loose bits were hanging about. Swāmī Krishnānanda does not even include it in his commentary, nor do Swami Prabhavānanda and Frederick Manchester include it in their translation. The latter three sections offer directions for ritual and another list of the line of spiritual teachers, this time identified matrilineally. The beginning two chapters discuss the senses' dependence on *prāṇa* and the famous Five Fires meditation, both of which can also be found in the *Chāndogya Upaniṣad*.

That the *Bṛhadāraṇyaka Upaniṣad* does not progress systematically to a philosophical climax but instead reads like a collection of independent, unrelated episodes suggests that it may be a compilation.

Section One: Which of the Sensory Organs is Most Essential?

The first six verses describe how each of our vital sensory functions, namely the *prāṇa*, the speech, the eye, the ear, the mind, and the sexual organ, is important in its own way and contributes to our well being (6.1.1-6). However, *prāṇa* is the most essential of them all, as is illustrated in a story (this episode is also recounted in the *Chāndogya Upaniṣad*, 5.1-5.22). One day the senses decided hold a contest to see which of them was the most important. The speech left the body and went on vacation for a year. When it returned, it asked how everyone held up. "We lived as a mute, but otherwise were just fine," the senses said. The eye then left for a year and on his return was told, "We were blind, but got along perfectly well otherwise." The ear left, and the body held up, the mind left, and though the senses were in the body of an idiot, they functioned normally. The sex organ left, and though no offspring were produced, everything was fine. But when the *prāṇa*, the life force, left it pulled the other senses out with it, for without the vital energy the body dies.

The senses have their very foundation in *prāṇa*. In order to hold the *prāṇa* in the body, it must be "fed and clothed", in other words given food and water (6.1.14), which we ingest to sustain our lives. As has been the case throughout the *Upaniṣad*, *prāṇa* is meant to be associated with Brahman, the original animating force, the presence of which is the life of all living things, "dogs, worms, insects and moths" (6.2.14).

Section Two: Śvetaketu's Father, Gautama, Learns the Meditation of the Five Fires

We met the student Śvetaketu before, in the *Chāndogya Upaniṣad*, where he was given the quintessential Upaniṣadic dictum, *tat tvam asi*, "That thou art, O Śvetaketu" (*Chānd. Up.* 6.8.7). That text also includes the following episode (*Chānd. Up.* 5.2-5.10), where Śvetaketu visits the court of King Pravāhaṇa during an assembly. The king asks Śvetaketu if his father has given him instruction. Receiving an affirmative answer, he tests the boy with five questions, not a single one of which the young *brāhmaṇa* could answer. Mortified, Śvetaketu hurries home and asks his father Gautama why he has withheld information from him. "I taught you everything I know," Gautama says. "Clearly this king has greater knowledge than I. I shall approach him myself as a student" (6.2.1-4).

Throughout the *Upaniṣads*, several incidents of radical caste reversal take place, where a *brāhmaṇa* becomes the disciple of a *kṣatriya*. The strong message inherent in these stories is that wisdom and spiritual realization are not the property of any particular class, race or group of people. They are certainly not conferred or denied because of birth into a particular caste. Passages such as the above are a direct challenge to India's caste system based on birth.

From King Pravāhaṇa, Gautama learns the *pañcāgni-vidyā*,[70] or doctrine of the five fires (6.2.9-13). In this meditation, heaven, rain, earth, man and woman are all seen as sacred fires. All creation is sacred, its cycles are sacred, and the human passages of birth, death and rebirth are sacred. During the Vedic period, the ritualistic *agnihotra*, fire sacrifice, was considered more than just worship. Chanting the Vedic *mantras* and making oblations into the fire helped to sustain and renew the cosmic order. The universe depended on the ceremony for its balance and perpetuation, just as the worshippers depended on the universe for their maintenance. Everything is delicately interconnected to everything else, and the *pañcāgni-vidyā* brings us into a deep contemplation of this fact.

Heaven-rain-earth-man-woman, each is nourished by what precedes it. Woman gives birth, but first must be impregnated by man. Man derives his vigor from eating vegetables, grains and herbs which grow from the earth. Earth is nourished by rain, which falls from heaven. Tradition has it, too, that when a *jīva*, an individual soul, is to be incarnated, it journeys to earth in a raindrop, is absorbed by a plant, which is eaten by a man, and then enters the semen. This may be a fanciful explanation, but its philosophical underpinnings lie in the complex connectedness of all organic phenomena.

Fire is a metaphor for vitality, life itself. The mother is a sacred fire, and the semen which impregnates her an oblation. The fruit of the sacrifice is a child (6.2.130). We are born of fire, and to fire we will return, for one day we will be consigned to the funeral pyre (6.2.14). Perhaps we will be born on earth again, the fire thus rekindled, the cycle perpetuated. When we die, there are two paths we can take. If we are ready for liberation, we will take the solar path, the path of emancipation, from which we need never return (6.2.15). If we must come back for another birth, however, we take the lunar path, a journey through the transmigratory process (6.2.16). The many levels described in these passages may refer to states of consciousness one passes through, and/or to deities which help guide the soul through the transition. The solar and lunar paths are also mentioned in the *Bhagavad-Gītā*, 8.23-27, and the *Chāndogya Upaniṣad*, 5.10.1-6.

Sections Three, Four and Five: Directions for Ritual; the Line of Spiritual Teachers

Section three offers directions for a universal fire sacrifice honoring virtually all of the deities, while section four describes rituals for conceiving and blessing a child. They are interesting reading because they offer a glimpse into a religious system and world-view very different from ours today, but compelling in its power and gradeur. These passages help us to imagine what the Vedic ceremonies were like and what worshippers valued and prayed for.

The *Upaniṣad* closes, in section four, with another listing of the line of spiritual teachers, the third such list in the *Upaniṣad*. This one is unique, however, because it identifies each *guru* after his mother, perhaps because mothers were the topic of the previous section, and it is mothers who give birth to illustrious men.[71]

If you are reading this, you've made it through the most formidable of all the *Upaniṣads* and, therefore, the most difficult text in this book. Congratulations! You deserve a round of applause. It has been an odyssey, hasn't it?

NOTES

1. Two translations were consulted for this chapter: Swāmī Mādhavānanda, *The Bṛhadāraṇyaka Upaniṣad* (Calcutta; Advaita Ashrama, 1965); Swāmī Jagadīśwarānanda, *The Bṛhadāraṇyaka Upaniṣad* (Mylapore: Sri Ramakrishna Math, 1985).
2. Swami Krishnānanda, *The Bṛhadāraṇyaka Upaniṣad* (Shivanandanagar: The Divine Life Society, 1984), p. 9.
3. Adapted from Swāmī Jagadīśwarānanda, p. xxxix.
4. Stutley and Stutley, p. 318.
5. Jagadīśwarānanda, p. 4.
6. Carl G. Jung, et. al., *Man and His Symbols* (Garden City: Doubleday and Company, 1964), p. 98.
7. Stutley and Stutley, p. 112.
8. Stutley and Stutley, p. 334.
9. Stutley and Stutley, p. 48.
10. Stutley and Stutley, p. 19.
11. Jagadīśwarānanda, p. 8.
12. Stutley and Stutley, p. 3.
13. Prabhavānanda and Isherwood, p. 85.

14. Krishnānanda, p. 239.
15. Krishnānanda, p. 245.
16. Krishnānanda, p. 247.
17. Mādhavānanda, p. 158.
18. Mādhavānanda, p. 171.
19. Prabhavānanda and Manchester, p. 134.
20. Mādhavānanda, (Śaṅkarācārya's commentary) p. 178.
21. Mādhavānanda, p. 183; Jagadīśwarānanda, p. 117.
22. Jagadīśwarānanda, p. 124.
23. Mādhavānanda, p. 222-223.
24. *Ramakrishna-Vedanta Wordbook*, p. 42.
25. Ibid, p. 75.
26. Jagadīśwarānanda, p. 129.
27. Stutley and Stutley, p. 221.
28. Stutley and Stutley, p. 224.
29. Stutley and Stutley, p. 84.
30. Jagadīśwarānanda, p. 147.
31. Mādhavānanda, p. 230.
32. Krishnānanda, p. 259.
33. Krishnānanda, p. 265.
34. Krishnānanda, pp. 268, 269.
35. Krishnānanda, p. 289.
36. Jagadīśwarānanda, p. 171.
37. Krishnānanda, pp. 287-288.
38. Stutley and Stutley, pp. 28-29.
39. Krishnānanda, p. 510.
40. Krishnānanda, p. 374.
41. Krishnānanda, p. 368.
42. Krishnānanda, p. 387.
43. Stutley and Stutley, p. 327.
44. Stutley and Stutley, p. 3.
45. Jagadīśwarānanda, p. 260.
46. Krishnānanda, p. 414.
47. Krishnānanda, p. 488.
48. Stutley and Stutley, p. 116.
49. Jagadīśwarānanda, p. 331.
50. Krishnānanda, pp. 494, 995.
51. Krishnānanda, p. 607.
52. Krishnānanda, pp. 671-672.
53. Krishnānanda, pp. 671-672.
54. Jagadīśwarānanda, p. 405.
55. Krishnānanda, pp. 682-684.

56. Krishnānanda, p. 705.
57. Krishnānanda, p. 705.
58. Jagadīśwarānanda, p. 412.
59. Jagadīśwarānanda, p. 412.
60. Krishnānanda, p. 707.
61. Jagadīśwarānanda, p. 416.
62. Stutley and Stutley, p. 318.
63. Krishnānanda, pp. 725-726.
64. Krishnānanda, p. 741.
65. Jagadīśwarānanda, p. 423; Stutley and Stutley, p. 173.
66. Stutley and Stutley, p. 344.
67. Stutley and Stutley, p. 153; Krishnānanda, p. 746.
68. Stutley and Stutley, p. 97.
69. Krishnānanda, p. 760.
70. Gambhīrānanda, *Chāndogya Upaniṣad*, p. xv.
71. Jagadīśwarānanda, p. 511.

Part V

The *Purāṇas*

CHAPTER EIGHTEEN

Introduction

The religion of *bhakti*, devotion to God, reaches its highest expression in the *Purāṇas*. These gorgeous literatures are unrivaled in their poetic beauty, in the scope of their themes, and in the breadth of their theology. While the *Upaniṣads* are given more to an exploration of *Nirguṇa* Brahman (Brahman devoid of attributes), the identification of Brahman and Ātman, and the realization of this oneness through direct perception, the *Purāṇas*, though not contradicting this teaching, take us even further. We find in them the glorification of Brahman in His/Her manifest aspects, particularly Kṛṣṇa, Viṣṇu, Śiva, and Śrī Devī. Devotees of the personal aspect of the Divine consider it a more complete, more sophisticated and ultimately "higher" conception than that espoused by the *Upaniṣads.*

As we approach the *Purāṇas*, we must always keep in mind that the sectarian nature of the different texts is of a surface nature only. Each *Purāṇa* lauds the deity to which it is devoted as the Ultimate and Original, superior to and the creator of everything, including other conceptions of the Divine. The reason for this is not to establish narrow, dogmatic beliefs in the supremacy of one divine ideal over another, for within the framework of Upaniṣadic and Bhagavad-Gītic Hinduism such a fanatic outlook is absurd. This is not to say that it doesn't happen, but this sort of bigotry is not scripturally sound. Each *Purāṇa* holds to the supremacy of its own Godhead because the chosen Ideal of any given devotee is supreme to him or her. All conceptions of the divine are true, therefore each one achieves ultimacy in the heart of the aspirant. It is important for the devotee to respect all the manifestations, but equally important to hold his or her own divine Beloved in a special place of exaltation. As Kṛṣṇa says in the *Bhagavad-Gītā*, "Whoever desires to honor with belief any worshipped form, on him I bestow immovable faith" (7.21).

The word *Purāṇa* means "ancient" or, more broadly, "narratives of ancient times".[1] They are difficult to describe because the scope of their subject matter is so diverse. One often hears them referred to as "books of mythology", but they, like the Old Testament, contain far more than mere narratives. Within the contexts of stories and dialogues, the most sophisticated philosophy, practical instruction, and lofty poetry are expressed. The beauty of the Purāṇic language makes these books a delight to read and the stories are both entertaining and spiritually uplifting. Some are fable-like, with clearly defined instructive messages, while others are of a more subtle nature because they describe the *līlā*, or divine activities, of God. The tenth *skandha* (canto) of the *Śrīmad Bhāgavatam*, for instance, is devoted entirely to the life and times of Lord Kṛṣṇa. His advent is minutely chronicled and analyzed, and the reader finds him or herself transported by it. One's frame of mind is altered by such narratives, drawn into a more rarified state, because the *līlā* of Kṛṣṇa, as well as of other divine manifestations, has the power to engender devotion, joy, deep tranquility, and spiritual illumination.

The *Purāṇas* as we now posses them represent a period of composition which spans from the sixth century B.C. to the twelfth century A.D. Though each one is traditionally attributed to the sage Vyāsa, they are most likely compilations. The result is a particularly rich and fascinating collection of texts which beautifully synthesize the teachings of numerous saintly teachers and devotional cults which rose from time to time to address the changing spiritual needs of their age. While Vedic revelation was considered static and unalterable, it was, nevertheless, incomplete, and the ever-renewing, wonderfully fluid nature of Brahman with Its all-encompassing Truth left much room for continuing revelation throughout the centuries.[2] These innovations are embodied in the *Purāṇas*, which are, by their own admission, not intended exclusively for mystics or priestly elites, but for everyone, regardless of social status, gender, or level of learning. That the intended audience was a broad spectrum accounts, no doubt, for the sweetness and approachability of the texts. Yet they never talk down to the audience nor pander to cruder sensibilities.

The validity of the Purāṇic literature is further substantiated by the fact that the nucleus from which its present form is derived is believed to have existed as early as the Vedic *Saṃhitās*. During intervals in Vedic sacrificial ceremonies, Purāṇic lore was regularly recited. This included creation stories, proverbial anecdotes, ancient histories and genealogies of kings and *ṛṣis*, all features of the *Purāṇas* in their present form.[3]

The class of literature categorized today as Purāṇic is fixed, but not without its share of controversy. Of the extant *Purāṇas*, eighteen are distinguished as *Mahā-Purāṇas*, or major *Purāṇas*, and an additional eighteen as *Upa-Purāṇas*, or supplementary *Purāṇas*, though which volumes belong to which group is the subject of some debate. Specifically, the *Devī Bhāgavata*, one of the principal scriptures of Śakti worshippers, is claimed by its admirers to be a *Mahā-Purāṇa*, but if this is so, one of the titles included in the traditional list of *Mahā-Purāṇas* must be demoted to *Upa-Purāṇa* status.[4] This is an academic problem only and shouldn't be of undue concern. Devotees of the Universal Mother will benefit from a study of the *Devī Bhāgavata* whatever its official status.

The eighteen *Mahā-Purāṇas* are listed as (the order is not indicative of importance): *Brahma, Padma, Viṣṇu, Śiva, Bhāgavata, Nārada, Mārkaṇḍeya, Varāha, Agni, Bhaviṣya, Brahma-vaivarta, Liṅga, Skanda, Vāmana, Kūrma, Matsya, Garuḍa,* and *Brahmāṇḍa*.[5] The most beloved of these is the *Bhāgavata Purāṇa*, better known as *Śrīmad Bhāgavatam*, which holds a unique status among the Purāṇic literature and will be afforded the most attention here.

The *Upa-Purāṇas* are: *Sanatkumāra, Narasiṃha, Vṛhannāradīya, Vāyu, Durvāsasa, Kāpila, Mānava, Auśanasa, Vāruṇa, Kālikā, Śāmba, Nandi, Saura, Pārāśara, Āditya, Māheśvara, Bhārgava,* and *Vāsiṣṭha*.[6] As was mentioned above, the *Devī Bhāgavata*, though not included in the preceding lists, must be recognized on account of its esteemed status among devotees of the Divine Mother.

Though each *Purāṇa* is unique in structure and content, all are required to touch upon five subjects, namely the first stage of the creation of the universe (*sarga*), the secondary stage of creation (*pratisarga*, or *visarga*), genealogies of kings, *ṛṣis*, and gods (*vaṃśa*), the cyclic epochs of history (*manvantaras*) and the histories of the Solar and Lunar dynasties (*vaṃśānucarita*).[7]

Why are these topics of interest to the spiritual aspirant? Because the Supreme Being is constantly present in these histories. The Deity is shown to personally direct the flow of history and to interact with individuals. The kings and sages are not ordinary people, but extraordinary spiritual giants whose austerities, devotions, prayers and teachings have great significance for men and women of today. What they accomplish on an epic scale we can imitate, if only in a small capacity, in our own lives. The Divinity is no less involved with our existence than with that of these legendary persons, and reading about the affectionate exchanges between God and His devotees helps us keep this in mind.

More important than the histories, though, are the detailed descriptions of the nature, appearance, attributes, powers and activities of God, whatever forms He/She happens to assume. By studying these narratives, our inherent devotion to the Absolute is aroused. In the words of the *Śrīmad Bhāgavatam* itself:

> The teachings it (*Śrīmad Bhāgavatam*) imparts is concerned with the supreme Truth that brings about the good of all . . . For this Text is itself sufficient to fortify faith and devotion to God in the minds of men who hear and study it with attention. O connoisseurs! O devotees! Quaff, quaff to inebriation this nectar that is the *Bhāgavata* . . . (1.2.2-3).[8]

And nectarean the *Purāṇas* are, but potential readers may be daunted by their sheer volume. Each one is long, and it is, of course, unlikely that the average person would attempt to plow through all thirty-seven. However, the *Śrīmad Bhāgavatam* stands above all the rest. So superb is this work, it has practically obscured the others from the attention of both aspirants and scholars. No other *Purāṇa* has been translated into so many languages nor rendered into English so many times. It is the one most widely commented upon and most often cited in religious discourse. All Hindus, despite their sectarian orientation, are expected to have some knowledge of the *Śrīmad Bhāgavatam* because the stories it contains weave in and out of the very fiber of Hindu consciousness and life. Once the Western reader has made contact with these stories, he or she will find that they are constantly referred to in writings on Hindu spirituality. A good knowledge of them is an essential tool for further study.

For all these reasons, the aspirant is advised to initially concentrate on the *Śrīmad Bhāgavatam*. It is a *Vaiṣṇava* text, in other words devoted to Viṣṇu and His *Avatāras*, with particular emphasis on Śrī Kṛṣṇa. If, after studying it, an aspirant devoted to a different divine Ideal still hungers for this type of literary sustenance, he or she should proceed to the corresponding *Purāṇa*.

As to the sheer bulk of the *Bhāgavatam*, or any *Purāṇa*, there is no way around it. Like the fearless pilgrims who work their way through the Old Testament one page at a time, so too should the spiritual aspirant tread the *Bhāgavatam* gradually. Be patient. Read a chapter or two daily and enjoy them. It is so worth the time spent. Try not to skip ahead or bounce around haphazardly, basing your choice on the chapter headings in the table of contents, for you will miss the wealth of material which is not strictly a part of the narrative thread. Soaring hymns, sublime meditations, as well as sound, practical advice on spiritual life are woven throughout the tapestry of the *Bhāgavatam*. Do not deprive yourself of the bliss they impart.

NOTES

1. Organ, p. 275; Swāmī Tapasyānanda, *Srimad Bhagavata* (Madras: Sri Ramakrishna Math, 1980), vol. 1, p. xix.
2. Tapasyānanda, vol. 1, pp. xix-xx.
3. Tapasyānanda, vol. 1, p. xix.
4. Tapasyānanda, vol. 1, p. xxiii.
5. Stutley and Stutley, p. 237.
6. Stutley and Stutley, p. 237.
7. Stutley and Stutley, p. 236; Tapasyānanda, vol 1, p. xxi.
8. Tapasyānanda translation.

CHAPTER NINETEEN

Śrīmad Bhāgavatam (or *Bhāgavata Purāṇa*)

The *Śrīmad Bhāgavatam* appears to have taken shape in a succession of phases beginning in the early half of the sixth century[1] and concluding approximately in the eighth century.[2] Some scholars place the date as late as the tenth century[3], or ascribe portions of the piece to as early as the fourth.[4] For the general reader, it is enough to know that the text is of a relatively late date, and thus reflects an extremely mature level of theological and philosophical development. Like the *Bhagavad-Gītā*, it attempts to synthesize various approaches into a workable system. The foundation of this system is *bhakti*, devotion, and the numerous philosophical and mythological strains of Hindu thought are viewed, as it were, through the lens of *bhakti*, resulting in a unified vision.

Like the *Bhagavad-Gītā*, the *Śrīmad Bhāgavatam* incorporates the traditions of *Sāṃkhya*, *yoga*, *Vedānta*, etc., but while the *Gītā's* central theme is the reconciliation of knowledge (*jñāna*) and action (*karma*), the *Śrīmad-Bhagavatam* is more concerned with the reconciliation of knowledge and devotion (*bhakti*). It enjoins a passionate love for God in one of His personal aspects while attending to sense restraint and the cultivation of *jñāna*, in other words, the perception that the material world is merely the empty play of *māyā*, and that it is to be rejected in favor of that which is eternal, God. This seemingly simple premise is explored in the most painstaking detail and from a kaleidoscopic range of angles. We see it illustrated in the life stories of saints, seers, and devotee-kings. We see it justified through extensive metaphysical and philosophical analyses, as well as through elaborate accounts of the process of creation and cosmic dissolution. We see it substantiated through practical instructions on how to do it ourselves, how to realize the Absolute through time-tested spiritual exercises. In a way, the *Śrīmad-Bhagavatam* is an encyclopedia of spirituality. So multifarious are its topics, a thorough exposition would require an entire volume unto itself. This treatment will therefore be limited to only the most general points.

The Structure of *Śrīmad Bhāgavatam*

In one sense, the *Bhāgavatam* has a chaotic feel to it. While it dwells upon historical narrative, it is not chronological. It skips merrily back and forth in time as theme dictates. Furthermore, it is couched in a web of conversations between teachers and students. A *guru* describes to his disciple what another *guru* told his disciple what yet a third *guru* taught his disciple. Once well into the discourse, we are likely to forget who, in fact, is saying what to whom.

Yet the reader will find that this seeming confusion does not, in fact, pose a problem. These are minor structural details. The substance of the words are far more important than who speaks them. However, the overall text does have a systematic structure, an understanding of which will enable the reader to safely concentrate on the message of the work.

The *Bhāgavatam* is comprised of 18,000 stanzas divided into twelve cantos, or *skandhas*. Though it adoringly describes all of the *Avatāras* of Viṣṇu and holds the worship of any one of them to be a key to liberation, Kṛṣṇa is uniquely exalted here as the most perfect and complete earthly and transcendental manifestation of the Divine. He is the supreme Incarnation, the fullest manifestation of *Sat-Cit-Ānanda Parabrahman*. The structure of this *Purāṇa* reflects this; it is as if the book is cradled in Kṛṣṇa. The first canto opens onto the later life of Kṛṣṇa, then we depart from Him, only to meet up with Him again in the tenth canto, which is the longest in the *Purāṇa* and is devoted solely to the narration of His life. The eleventh canto contains the *Uddhava-Gītā* (Kṛṣṇa's last discourse) and an account of His departure from this world. The second through ninth cantos contain the stories of Viṣṇu's other incarnations, major and minor, as well as important myths, fables, and genealogies. The twelfth, and final canto is of a concluding nature, and suggests that since the departure of Lord Kṛṣṇa and the subsequent commencement of *Kali-yuga*, the world is in a state of gradual entropy. It cites the beginning of the end.

The whole of the *Bhāgavatam* is narrated by the sage Sūta to an assembly of sages in the forest of Naimiṣāraṇya. They had collected in order to perform a *Brahma Satra*, or fire sacrifice of thousand year duration, and their spokesman, Śaunaka, approached Sūta with the request that he speak on spiritual topics, particularly the advents and activities of Lord Hari (Viṣṇu).

Sūta replied by recounting in full the recitation of the *Śrīmad Bhāgavatam* by the supremely elevated sage Śukadeva to Mahārāja Parīkṣit. Sūta had been in attendance when the king, cursed to die within a week, retired to the banks of the Ganges at Hastināpura (now Delhi) to perform religious austerities in preparation. An assembly of holy men and their disciples collected around the king and were privy to the dialogue between the dying man and his master. "What is the duty of one facing death?" the king asked Śrī Śukadeva. "What should he hear, do, remember and worship?" The answer to this, and further inquiries, comprises the *Bhagavatam* proper. In essence, then, the reader is hearing Sūta relate the conversation between Mahārāja Parīkṣit and Śukadeva. Sometimes, though, Sūta answers questions put directly to him by Śaunaka. There are, therefore, two simultaneous dialogues. When Śukadeva relates the conversations between yet another master and disciple, such as that of Brahmā and Nārada in the second canto, or Maitreya and Vidura in the third, we are hearing three dialogues at once.

Mahārāja Parīkṣit is the grandson of Arjuna, the hero of the *Mahābhārata* and disciple of Kṛṣṇa in the *Bhagavad-Gītā*. Thus, Parīkṣit is more than just a spiritual seeker; he is personally involved in the very narratives which he is hearing, both part of the story and a listener to the story. We see a similar double-layered identity in the *Rāmāyaṇa*, when Lord Rāmacandra listens to a recitation of his own life story (a *Rāmāyaṇa* within a *Rāmāyaṇa*) by his own twin sons, whom he does not at that point recognize. With Parīkṣit as the central prop of the overall structure here, the *Bhāgavatam*, like many good novels, begins at the end. Parīkṣit's death will mark the end of the dynasty and the end of the *Bhāgavatam*, while Kṛṣṇa's appearance in this royal line will serve as the climax, both religiously and narratively. We begin at the end and then, in the third canto, go back to the very beginning, to the creation of the cosmos. The *Bhāgavatam* then winds its way through time until we end up at the end again with the close of the Kurukṣetra war, the passing away of the Pāṇḍavas and of Lord Kṛṣṇa, and of the curse upon the last remaining monarch, Mahārāja Parīkṣit, who sits down to fast unto death and hear this *Śrīmad Bhāgavatam*. The circular structure reflects the cyclical nature of time and creation. The story is eternally repeating itself and, therefore, resembles that which is universal, transcendent, timeless and perpetually meaningful.

The *Avatāras* of Viṣṇu

If the dialogue between King Parīkṣit and Śrī Śuka provides the framework, the recounting of the *Avatāras*, or earthly incarnations, of Viṣṇu provides the thread that draws us through it. Each *Avatāra* story marks a high point in the text, and with every subsequent appearance the Divine is more fully manifest until He reaches His most complete and magnificent revelation in Śrī Kṛṣṇa.

There are ten principal *Avatāras* as well as a number of secondary ones. An examination of the primary ten reveals that the earthly form of God evolves gradually through the biological species, just as the individual *jīva* moves through increasingly sophisticated bodies until it reaches the human form. Viṣṇu appears first as a fish, then an amphibian, a mammal, a half-animal half-human, a dwarf, a full-statured man, etc. Of particular significance is that the historic Buddha is counted among Viṣṇu's *Avatāras*. According to Swāmī Vivekānanda, Buddhism as an individual sect has all but disappeared from India not because India rejected it, but because it was absorbed into Hinduism and is expressing itself there. Hinduism adapted itself to accommodate Buddha's teachings, and identified Buddha himself as a divine Incarnation, thus honoring him with the highest possible stature.

In brief, the ten principal *Avatāras* are as follows:

Matsya

Matsya means "fish", and the most interesting aspect of His story is its similarity to the Biblical legend of Noah. The seventh great lawgiver and patriarch of the human race, Manu Satyavrata, found a tiny fish in the water he used for ablutions. The fish told him that He would save Manu from the world-wide deluge, and instructed him to build a ship which could rescue all of the sages, the plants, the animals and the four holy *Vedas*. As soon as the deluge came, the fish grew to a monstrous size and protected the vessel until the waters subsided. (This narrative is found in the eighth canto.)

Kūrma

Viṣṇu next appeared as the giant tortoise, Kūrma, to recover some sacred items, such as *amṛta*, the elixir of immortality, the wish-cow Surabhī, the celestial jewel Kaustubha, and so on, which were lost in the deluge. As if churning milk to produce butter, the *devas* (celestials) and the *asuras* (demons) churned the cosmic ocean, and Kūrma laid Himself down as a pedestal upon which they placed Mount Mandana as a churning rod. One of the substances to emerge from the ocean was *hālāhala*, the primordial poison. So destructive was this substance, Śiva drank it Himself and thus He is known as Nīla-kaṇṭha, the Blue-Throated One. The few drops that escaped His lips and fell to the ground became all of the venomous animals and plants which exist in the world today. (Eighth canto.)

Varāha

With Varāha, the Boar, Viṣṇu evolves into a mammal. When the earth was submerged in the chaos of the primordial Cosmic Waters, Varāha delved down, like an ordinary boar delves into the soil for roots and truffles, and picked the earth up on His snout. After setting it back in place, He destroyed the demon Hiraṇyākṣa. Varāha has been a popular subject of iconographic sculpture; it's rare to visit an Asian art museum and not find Him represented there somewhere. (Third canto.)

Nṛsiṃhadeva

One of the most awesome of Viṣṇu's *Avatāras* is the half-man half-lion Nṛsiṃhadeva (also called Narasiṃha, from *nara*, "man", *siṃha*, "lion"), who incarnated in order to deliver His devotee, the young child Prahlāda, from his murderous father, the demon-king Hiraṇyakaśipu (the brother of the Hiraṇyākṣa mentioned above). As the demon had received a boon that he could not be slain by man nor beast, Viṣṇu took the form of Nṛsiṃhadeva and destroyed him. Nṛsiṃhadevas's ferocity is dramatically juxtaposed with His beauty and benevolence. He could not be pacified by the adorations of the *devas*, only by the loving prayers of a small boy, a compelling reminder that the perfect way to approach God is not with fear, but with the simple devotion, love and purity of a child. (Seventh canto.)

Vāmana

Now Viṣṇu takes the form of a human being, but a physically diminutive one. Bāli, the king of the *asuras*, gained dominion over the three worlds through the power of his asceticism and valor. To correct this situation, Viṣṇu took birth as a beautifully-featured dwarf in the *brāhmaṇa* caste. As it is the duty of *kṣatriyas*, the royal and military class, to ritualistically bestow gifts to visiting *brāhmaṇas*, Vāmanadeva approached King Bāli in his palace and asked for as much land as He could encompass in three steps. Bāli readily agreed, and Vāmana suddenly grew to such an enormous size that with one step He covered the entire material cosmos, with the second He covered heaven and, having nowhere else to go, with the third touched Bāli on the head with His beneficent foot. The Vāmana story has an Iranian parallel, the three steps of Ameśa-Spenta.[5]

Paraśurāma

Now Viṣṇu is a fully developed man, Paraśurāma, which means "Rāma with an axe". He was born a *brāhmaṇa*, and among His many activities the most important is His single-handed destruction of every male in the *kṣatriya* caste. The social order had been disrupted when the kings wrested spiritual leadership from the *brāhmaṇas* in a full-fledged revolt. After eliminating the royal males "twenty-one times", Paraśurāma reestablished the peaceful monarchical theocracy by allowing the widows of the slain *kṣatriyas* to be impregnated by *brāhmaṇas* or, in another version, by *kṣatriya* survivors hidden by the sages during the massacre. Though gory in the extreme, this story vividly illustrated the necessity of the separation of powers, and of the dangers of presuming religious authority without the qualifications for it. Paraśurāma is an important figure in the *Mahābhārata* and appears also in the *Rāmāyaṇa*. The advents of Paraśurāma and Rāmacandra overlap. Somewhat jealous of His own younger Incarnation, Paraśurāma challenges Rāma to a battle. Paraśurāma was a student of Lord Śiva, who taught Him the art of weaponry and gave Him the axe for which He is named. (Ninth canto.)

Rāma

Rāma is the glorious and widely popular hero of the epic *Rāmāyaṇa*. Apart from Kṛṣṇa, He is the most adored of all incarnations. The perfect sage, perfect king, perfect warrior and perfect family man, Rāma is considered the very embodiment of *dharma*. He is discussed in full in chapter twenty-six of this book. (Canto nine.)

Kṛṣṇa

The greatest of Viṣṇu's Incarnations (or, according to the Gauḍīya Vaiṣṇavas, the Supreme Deity who even precedes Viṣṇu), the darling of the *Bhāgavatam*, the enchanting cowherd boy and precious lover of the *gopīs*, the speaker of the *Bhagavad-Gītā*, the quintessential Godhead, Kṛṣṇa surpasses all other divine manifestations in popularity, sweetness, beauty and splendor. While mention of Him is sprinkled throughout the text, the tenth canto is devoted solely to Him.

Buddha

The *Śrīmad Bhāgavatam* does not include a narrative of the life of Siddhārtha Gautama, the Buddha, because he was born in the sixth century

B.C., long after the recitation of the *Bhāgavatam* is said to have taken place. Buddha's advent is mentioned as prophecy only. He taught a thorough rejection of brāhmiṇical ritualism and instead stressed a hands-on system of spiritual practice by which *Nirvāṇa,* extinction of the individual "I" and resulting liberation from the cycle of rebirth, is achieved.

Kalki

The Kalki *Avatāra* is yet to come. At the end of this *Kali-yuga,* the age of degeneration and anxiety in which we now live, yet before the final dissolution of the material universe, Kalki will appear atop a white steed. Sword in hand, He will destroy the creatures of the world, all of them wallowing in depravity, corruption and utter degradation. Once all people are released from their bodies, and the world purged, universal obliteration will take place, followed by the re-creation of the cosmos. We cannot expect Kalki to appear any time soon; many millennia are scheduled to pass before His arrival.

The secondary *Avatāras,* some of whom are as dazzling as the principal ten, include but are not limited to:

The Four Kumāras

Kumāra means "son" and these quadruplets are the sons of Lord Brahmā, born directly from his body during the primordial creation. They remain children eternally so that they may never slip from a state of perfect celibacy. They spend all of their time in spiritual austerities. (Third canto.)

Nārada

Another son of Brahmā, Nārada is the perfected sage who fills many roles. A cosmic minstrel, he travels through the universe constantly singing hymns in praise of God and enlivening the hearts of all who encounter him. Mercurial in nature, this gentle and appealing saint is not restricted by time or space and so tends to appear suddenly to impart spiritual instruction or participate in important religious functions. (First canto and throughout.)

Nara and Nārāyaṇa

These are divine twins, a religious archetype found in diverse traditions across the world. In this case, they are brilliantly beautiful forest ascetics who appear as a blessing to the humble sage Mārkaṇḍeya.

Lord Kapila

Much of the third canto is devoted to the teachings of this remarkable philosopher, who synthesizes the traditions of *bhakti* and *jñāna* against the backdrop of *Sāṃkhya.* (Third canto.)

Dattātreya

The son of one of the primordial *ṛṣis*, Atri, Dattātreya is the spiritual preceptor of non-Āryan beings, such as Prahlāda.[6]

Yajña

By this time, the deities of the *Vedas* — Indra, Vāyu, Agni, etc. — had not only lost their eminence as divine manifestations, they were now considered merely posts which are filled by various people for a period. Yajña temporarily occupied the post of Indra.

King Ṛṣabhadeva

King Ṛṣabha was a great teacher who demonstrated in his own life the ideal of renunciation and *bhakti* for householders. (Fifth canto.)

King Pṛthu

This Incarnation demonstrated the art of blending devotion and statecraft. He restored prosperity to a famine-stricken kingdom and organized the country into villages and towns for the first time. All the while he broadcasted the gospel of *bhakti.*[7] (Fourth canto.)

Dhanvantari

During the churning of the ocean, Dhanvantari emerged. He was the proto-physician who introduced the art of medicine to the world. (Eighth canto.)

Mohinī-mūrti

The only female *Avatāra* not identified as an Incarnation of Śrī Devī, Mohinī-mūrti appeared to retrieve the nectar of immortality from the *asuras.* However, Her identity as Mahā-Māyā is established in an incident wherein Lord Śiva, spotting her captivating beauty, is swept away by passionate ardor. Such loss of control is out of character for Him, and accounts such as this are meant to establish the supremacy of Viṣṇu over other conceptions of God. (Eighth canto.)

Vyāsa

The word *Vyāsa* means "editor", "arranger" or "compiler"[8] of literary compositions. Vyāsa is traditionally believed to be the arranger of the *Vedas* (their origin being purely divine), and the author of the *Purāṇas* and *Mahābhārata.* This marvelous, mythical wordsmith also happens to be the father of Śrī Śukadeva, the narrator of the *Bhāgavatam* (Śuka heard it from Vyāsa, then recited it to King Parīkṣit). Historically, there were probably many "Vyāsas", but poetically they are combined into a single figure. (First canto.)

Balarāma

Balarāma is the brother of Lord Kṛṣṇa. Their advent together, plus the advent of the Devī in the form of Rādhārāṇī, constitute the divine Trinity. We find the precedent for this triple Incarnation in the forms of Lord Rāmacandra, His brother Lakṣmaṇa, and His consort, Sītā. (Tenth canto.)

Canto One: Setting The Scene

After a salutary invocation to the Divine and a brief passage in praise of the text itself, the *Śrīmad Bhāgavatam* launches straight into an account of the assembly of sages at Naimiṣāraṇya forest and the questions they put to Sūta. The sages are particularly interested in hearing the story of Kṛṣṇa's incarnation, as well as of God's other manifestations and deeds.

Two chapters are devoted to Sūta's preamble, an involved exposition on the cultivation of *bhakti*, which is identified as the supreme duty of all, and on Vāsudeva, the *Bhāgavatam's* favored name for God. Other favorite appellations include Nārāyaṇa, Hari, and, of course, Viṣṇu. Sūta explains why Vāsudeva is the most appropriate object of worship and discusses the concept of *Avatāra,* how the One can become many.

Chapter four tell of how this *Śrīmad Bhāgavatam* was composed, how Vyāsa (mentioned earlier as the traditional author of most of the scriptures), after compiling the *Vedas,* still felt profoundly dissatisfied, as though his work were not yet complete. Nārada appeared to the distressed sage with the answer. The *Vedas*, he said, though illustrious indeed, do not describe the beautiful *līlā* of the Divine, nor do they impart the philosophy of devotion. "O you who are the master of scriptures! Engage yourself in the description of His unique glories, which alone can satisfy the questionings of spiritual aspirants" (1.6.40).

True, the *Vedas* are largely ritualistic in content, the *Upaniṣads* mystical and abstract. Neither provide sustenance for the *bhakti yogi*, the lover of God. In the *Bhāgavatam*, on the other hand, we have a scripture designed to kindle devotional love. Throughout, the language is deliciously ecstatic and adoring. Tradition has it, then, that Nārada recognized the need in the available spiritual literature and Vyāsa filled it according to his orders. It was then passed on orally from Vyāsa to his son, Śrī Śuka, and from Śuka to Parīkṣit and the assembled holy men.

After a digression recounting the life story of Nārada, we are plopped down into the thick of the lives of Kṛṣṇa, Arjuna, and the rest of the Kuru dynasty, just in the aftermath of the Kurukṣetra war. This will all lead up to the birth of Mahārāja Parīkṣit. In the meantime, we are given our first glimpse of Śrī Kṛṣṇa. He is in His full royal glory, a king, father, and grandfather, nearing the end of His term on earth yet still radiating youthfulness. This first canto contains several important hymns in praise of Him.

The first is the hymn of Queen Kuntī (1.8.17-43). Kuntī was the mother of the five Pāṇḍava princes — Arjuna, Yudhiṣṭhira, Bhīma, Nakula and Sahadeva — and was also the aunt of Śrī Kṛṣṇa. The context of her prayer is Kṛṣṇa's departure from His own kingdom, Dvārakā. His duty to His kinsmen satisfied, the land restored to its proper monarchs, Kṛṣṇa mounted His chariot while a crowd of tearful devotees collected about Him. But it seems the war was not quite finished. Uttarā, the pregnant widow of Arjuna's son Abhimanyu, broke onto the scene in abject terror. She carried in her womb the fetus that would become King Parīkṣit, the last of the Pāṇḍava line, and so Aśvatthāmā, one of their few surviving enemies, dispatched an explosive molten iron weapon in her direction. Responding to the widow's plea for help, Kṛṣṇa, who is the indwelling Soul of everything, protected the fetus from the blast. Thus Parīkṣit is known to have had a special connection to the Divine even before his birth.

"I salute the uncreated original Being, the Supreme Person, the Lord of all, the one transcending *prakṛti*!" Queen Kuntī prayed upon observing Kṛṣṇa's wonderful protection and power.

"Though abiding within and without all beings, none can see You directly" (1.8.18). Her passionate discourse identifies Kṛṣṇa as the Supreme Brahman, indicates that the purpose of His advent was to spiritually liberate the world, and wonders at His marvelous attributes and pastimes. Kuntī sums up the goal of *bhakti yoga* in verse 1.18.42: "O Lord! Just as the river Gaṅgā is a stream flowing towards the ocean, so may my mind, eschewing all other objects, become a continuous stream of love and attachment with You as its sole object."

The next hymn is delivered by Bhīṣma, one of the venerated patriarchs of the clan, who was mortally wounded in the battle and now lay stricken upon the field, waiting to die. Kinsmen, sages and celestials collected around him, and his last words were a beautiful homage to Kṛṣṇa (1.10.20-36).

The text now turns to the story of King Parīkṣit. He ascended the throne at a most inauspicious time; Lord Kṛṣṇa had left the earth and the world shifted into epoch known as *Kali-yuga*, the age of strife and degeneration in which we are now living. (Each cosmic cycle of creation is said to be comprised of four ages, or *yugas* — the *Satya-yuga* [golden age], *Tretā-yuga* [silver age], *Dvāpara-yuga* [copper age] and *Kali-yuga* [iron age], which is characterized by cultural, spiritual and environmental disintegration.) This transition is symbolized by the ghastly sight of a low-born man dressed in royal garb savagely beating a crippled bull and gentle cow. Parīkṣit stumbled upon this scene and drew his sword, subduing the malevolent being. The bull, it turns out, was *dharma*, the cow Mother Earth, and their tormentor Kali (not to be confused with the Divine Mother Kālī). Parīkṣit ordered Kali to leave, but after the creature beseeched him that he must live *somewhere*, the king allowed him five homes: in gambling, intoxicants, debauchery, slaughter, and gold. This last one, we're told, is the source of all *adharma*: deceit, pride, lust, cruelty, and enmity (1.17.1-39). Obviously, the spiritual aspirant must, at some point, renounce these.

Parīkṣit was a good and dutiful king, but one day, while hunting in the forest, he grew thirsty and entered an ascetic's hut to ask for a drink of water. The *brāhmaṇa*, absorbed in deep meditation, could not hear Parīkṣit's repeated requests and didn't move. The king grew a bit piqued and, with the tip of his bow, picked up a dead snake, hung it around the mendicant's neck like a garland, and huffed off. Later, the *brāhmaṇa's* son showed up and flew into a rage. "Within seven days," the child cursed, "the serpent Takṣaka shall, as directed by me, bite this fellow — the persecutor of my father!" (1.18.37). When the ascetic regained external consciousness and learned what his son had done, he was horrified, but a *brāhmaṇa's* curse is irrevocable and the king was doomed.

Parīkṣit then retired to the Ganges to prepare for his death with spiritual disciplines. He is considered very fortunate because the foreknowledge of his own demise allowed him the chance to renounce the world and devote himself entirely to God-realization, something very few people have the courage to do. At the close of the first canto, his spiritual master, Śrī Śukadeva, arrives, and the recitation of *Śrīmad Bhāgavatam* officially begins.

Canto Two: Divine Manifestation

In the first canto we saw the advent of *Kali-yuga*, our own time, characterized by excruciating ordinariness. There will be no more heroes of the calibre of the Pāṇḍavas, no more dynasties as illustrious as the Bhārata line, no more holy men and women as elevated as those of the past. Still, we can revive the power of the past, relive sacred time, by hearing about it and contemplating it. The history of the universe from the undifferentiated Brahman to the *Kali-yuga* will, therefore, be delivered in its entirety to King Parīkṣit. However, before Śuka can begin the Creation narrative, he must establish a clear theological context for it. Before the material creation there was God. But what is God and what is creation? What is the relationship between the two? The second canto explores these questions.

Notice how the Western Creation account as contained in Genesis skips this level of exposition entirely. It begins with God creating the universe, but does not explain why or how, nor does it reveal anything about God's identity and nature. The Hindu sages were far too curious to let these questions go uninvestigated. That an absolute Something somehow "created" what we perceive to be the material world was simply not good enough. They wanted all the details. And what exactly *is* this world, anyway? Their philosophical investigations have a strong proto-scientific bent. What Western scientists eventually came to explain through material biology and physics, Hindu philosophers sought to understand through spiritual formulae. It is fascinating to compare how often their conclusions resemble each other.

This second canto is relatively short, but its significance is broad. According to Swāmī Tapasyānanda, it may be the original nucleus from which the entire *Śrīmad Bhāgavatam* was formed, as it most succinctly expresses the cosmological and theological doctrines held by the *Purāṇas* as a whole.[9] These may be approached in a literal or a figurative sense; the highly mythological material, of course, can be taken as poetic illustrations of abstract concepts. Or they may be taken literally, as many people insist they should. In either case, ultimate Truth need not be confined to the limits of literality.

The ninth chapter contains four verses, 2.9.32-35, which are known collectively as the *catuśloki bhāgavata*[10] ("four-verse *Bhāgavata*"), and which express the essence of the *Purāṇa's* cosmology. Before creation, Brahman, here in the form of Maha-Viṣṇu, alone existed, and at the close of a creationary cycle, Brahman again is the only reality. During the creation, too, Brahman alone exists because the universe itself is Brahman. The appearance of a separateness is due to *māyā*. Objects are combinations of the basic elements of nature. Though appearing to take on new qualities because of these combinations, these elements do not, in fact, lose their elemental quality. Similarly, although Brahman constitutes the universe, It remains completely unaffected by the forms and experiences It seems to have become. Verse 2.9.35 puts it in a nutshell:

> What the seeker after truth has to grasp is that Substance which persists always unaffected through all Its transformations as Its various effects or forms, but suffers no diminution when all these effects or forms are eliminated in the causal condition. The Supreme Spirit is that ultimate Substance.

This is the level of exposition which may be taken literally. The same cosmology, however, is also explained in terms of the play of the gods, where the material creation emerges from the body of the four-armed Viṣṇu. It begins in the subtlest elements which gradually evolve into grosser and grosser ones until material elements are formed. Included in this scheme is the emergence of Lord Brahmā, the creator deity, out of the lotus which grows from Viṣṇu's navel. The details of his appearance and work are examined in the third canto, and it is there we shall look more closely at the actual process of creation.

Chapter Six contains a study of the *Virāṭ-puruṣa*, the same cosmic body we encountered in the *Aitareya* and *Bṛhadāraṇyaka Upaniṣads*. Again, we see that the different elements of the universe are identified with different parts of this Cosmic Person's body. Verses 2.6.22-29 refer to the symbolic dismemberment of *Virāṭ-puruṣa* and the use of the parts as implements of a religious sacrifice, imagery found in the famous *Puruṣa-sūkta* hymn of the *Ṛg Veda*, and the *Bṛhadāraṇyaka Upaniṣad*, Chapter One, section two. God's relationship to the universe is here examined in Vedāntic, Vaiṣṇava, Upaniṣadic, and Vedic modes, and the conclusion of each is identical.

Once God has become the universe, He occasionally projects Himself into it directly in the forms of *Līlāvatāras*, literally "sporting Incarnations", a listing of which is provided in chapter seven.

The one important hymn of the second canto is delivered by Śrī Śuka himself in verses 2.4.11-23. There he praises the Supreme Being and exhorts all to worship Him. The canto comes to a close with a lead-in to the conversation between Maitreya and Vidura, which will span the third canto and which includes the full, detailed Creation account.

Canto Three: Creation; Lord Kapila's Discourse

The third canto covers four particularly important topics, namely the Creation account, the births of the demon brothers Hiraṇyākṣa and Hiraṇyakaśipu, the Varāha (Boar) Incarnation, and the birth and teachings of Lord Kapila. These seemingly divergent themes actually have a connectedness, as we shall see.

The Creation Account

In Hinduism, creation is believed to have taken place in two phases, *sarga* (primary creation) and *visarga* (secondary creation by Lord Brahmā). *Sarga* refers to the manifestation of subtle elements such as time, space, etc., which provide a context for material existence, while *visarga* refers to the origins of the material universe itself, as well as the living beings which inhabit it.

The first four chapters of the third canto deal with the meeting of Vidura, the half-brother of Pāṇḍu and Dhṛtarāṣṭra, and Uddhava, Kṛṣṇa's beloved disciple, and their conversation concerning the fate of the Kuru dynasty. Here Uddhava provides a compact synopsis of Lord Kṛṣṇa's life story. The two part, and Vidura proceeds to the bank of the Ganges at Hardwar, where he visits his spiritual master, Maitreya, and questions him as to how the Supreme Lord Nārāyaṇa creates the world. Maitreya's reply, which spans eight chapters, constitutes the Purāṇic Creation account and is, therefore, one of the most important segments of the *Bhāgavatam.*

Why did God create at all?

> In the beginning the Lord (Bhagavān) alone existed. He was the essence of all, and He was all. He, the pure Spirit, was the master of Himself. All that is called the many was by His will dissolved in Himself. This non-dual and self-revealing Seer saw no object then. When Power (*śakti*) and its manifestations subsided, and the Seer alone remained, the Spirit thought of Himself as non-existent (as the subject has no relevancy without the object) (3.5.23-24).

Significant here is that the "beginning" is only one of innumerable beginnings, for creation and dissolution is an eternally repeating cycle.

Śakti, or the power of Brahman, has withdrawn and become latent, therefore nothing exists. As there is no *māyā* to impose upon Brahman the illusion of duality, Brahman lacks a reference point by which to experience Its own existence. So It creates again.

This highly complex process of primary creation is best approached in steps.

— God is the only seer with nothing to be seen.

— God's consciousness manifests *māyā* (which is characterized by cause, action, and effect).

— God expands Itself as *Puruṣa*; *Puruṣa* imbues *māyā* with *guṇas* (the three subtle qualities or forces: *rajas*, impulse or passion, *tamas*, inertia or ignorance, and *sattva*, balance or goodness).

— *Māyā* + *guṇas* + Time = *Mahat-tattva* (*mahat*, "knowing", *tattva*, "principle"; the all-comprehending entity).

— *Mahat-tattva* is a luminous Intelligence which contains the total cosmic energy. Out of It springs *ahaṃkāra-tattva* (*ahaṃ*, "I", *kāra*, "maker"; consciousness of individuality, the sense of "I am", "I think", "I do", etc.).

— *Ahaṃkāra-tattva* manifests as elements, organs and mind, which form the physical (*adhibhūta*), psychic (*adhyātma*) and spiritual (*adhidaivika*) aspects. Mixed with the *guṇas*, these aspects produce elements such as sound, touch, form, etc.

— The Subtle Elements + Time + the *Will of God* = gross elements. For instance, sound becomes sky, touch becomes air, form becomes fire, taste becomes water, smell becomes earth.

— God differentiates Himself as presiding deities of physical elements. However, these elements, though capable of movement and change, are discordant and cannot combine to form a cohesive material universe. The elements now number twenty-four:

1.) *Mahat-tattva* (Total Material Energy)
2.) *Ahaṃkāra* ("I-ness")
3.) *Buddhi* (Intelligence)
4.) *Manas* (Mind)

The Five Subtle Elements:
5.) Sound
6.) Touch
7.) Form
8.) Taste
9.) Smell

The Five Gross Elements:
10.) Earth
11.) Water
12.) Fire
13.) Air
14.) *Ākāśa* (ether, space)

The Five Organs of Knowledge:
15.) Eye
16.) Ear
17.) Nose
18.) Tongue
19.) Skin

The Five Organs of Action:
20.) Hand
21.) Leg
22.) Anus
23.) Genitals
24.) Speech

— The elemental deities offer God prayers.

— God then enters into the twenty-four elements by assuming the form of Time. Time coheres the elements and God sets them into action.

— Once the elements are set into action, the gigantic universal body, the *Virāṭ-puruṣa*, comes into existence. All beings, all objects, the aggregate of creation, rest within Him.

— *Virāṭ-puruṣa* rests for one thousand celestial years. He is the soul of all beings and is considered the first *Avatāra*.

— Different bodily parts of *Virāṭ-puruṣa* separately manifest, and are entered into by a particular deity — Agni, Varuṇa, the Twin Aśvins, etc. — thus attributing sensations to deities, which allow living entities to experience sensory input (see diagram, page 269).

— The universe is manifested from *Virāṭ-puruṣa's* body parts, as are the social orders.

So completes *sarga*, the primary creation. All the elements required to form the world have come into being; they now need only to be sculpted into something. The celestial artist in this drama is Lord Brahmā, who assumes the role of Creator.

The twenty-four elements, penetrated by the divine will, have combined to form a sense of place, a sort of universal shell within which rages an elemental chaos. This chaos is symbolized by the Cosmic

Empowerment of Deities by Virāṭ-puruṣa and Corresponding Manifestations in Individuals and in Creation

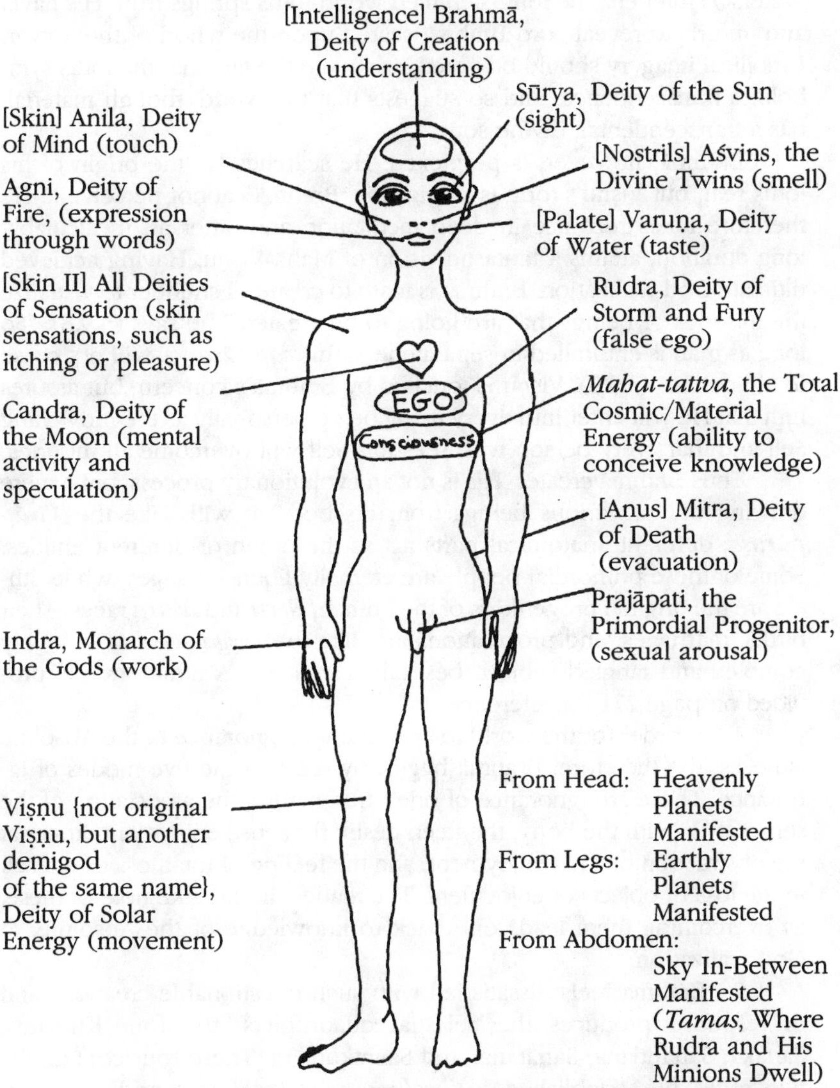

From Head: Heavenly Planets Manifested
From Legs: Earthly Planets Manifested
From Abdomen: Sky In-Between Manifested (*Tamas*, Where Rudra and His Minions Dwell)
From Mouth: *Vedas* and *Brāhmaṇas*
From Arms: *Kṣatriyas*
From Thighs: *Vaiśyas*
From Legs: *Śūdras*

Waters. Now Mahā-Viṣṇu lies down upon the Waters, His thousand-hooded serpent alter-ego, Ananta, supporting Him like a bed. As Nārāyaṇa (another name for Viṣṇu, literally "He Whose Abode is the Waters") slumbers, the long-stemmed world-lotus springs from His navel and unfurls to reveal Lord Brahmā seated upon the whorl of the flower. Umbilical imagery should be noted, as should the fact that the lotus symbolizes transcendence, and so suggests that the world, though material, has a transcendental, divine source.

Brahmā, however, is perplexed. He searches for the origin of his lotus seat, but Viṣṇu's form is so gigantic, Brahmā cannot perceive it. He therefore takes recourse in deep meditation and, after an incalculably long duration, attains a fantastic vision of Mahā-Viṣṇu. Having achieved ultimate God-realization, Brahmā is loath to create. "I shudder to visualize the miseries of beings that are going to be created," he says (3.9.8). "So long as man is enthralled in separateness, this *saṃsāra* . . . will not cease to afflict him" (3.9.9). Viṣṇu is touched by Brahmā's concern, but assures him that He will enter into every living being personally as the indwelling Self and that every person who sees this Self will overcome all miseries.

Thus Brahmā creates. His is not an evolutionary process, but a mere drawing out of various beings from his body at will. Like the *Virāṭ-puruṣa*, different anatomical parts act as the origin of different entities. Some of these primordial people are eternally liberated sages, while others are the original progenitors of the human, *deva* and *asura* races. Their births, marriages, and procreations are, like the *sarga* account, a highly complex and tangled subject, best taken in steps. A family tree is provided on page 271 for reference.

1.) In order for the world to be sustained, ignorance of the Absolute is necessary; therefore, Brahmā begins by creating the five modes of ignorance. These are ignorance of one's true nature, the association of the sense of "I" with the body, the keen desire for sense enjoyment, anger at the obstruction of such enjoyment, and the feeling of total loss of oneself in the loss of objects of enjoyment. The reader should take note of these, as overcoming them leads one back to knowledge of the Absolute, to God realization.

2.) Brahmā feels dissatisfied with such questionable creations and in response produces the celestial quadruplets, the four Kumāras: Sanaka, Sanandana, Sanātana, and Sanatkumāra. These four contemplative sages are established in *brahmacarya* (celibacy) and refuse to procreate. To this effect, they remain children eternally.

3.) The sages' defiance angers Brahmā and the personification of his fury springs from between his eyebrows in the form of Rudra, an aspect of Lord Śiva.

Genealogy of Early Beings

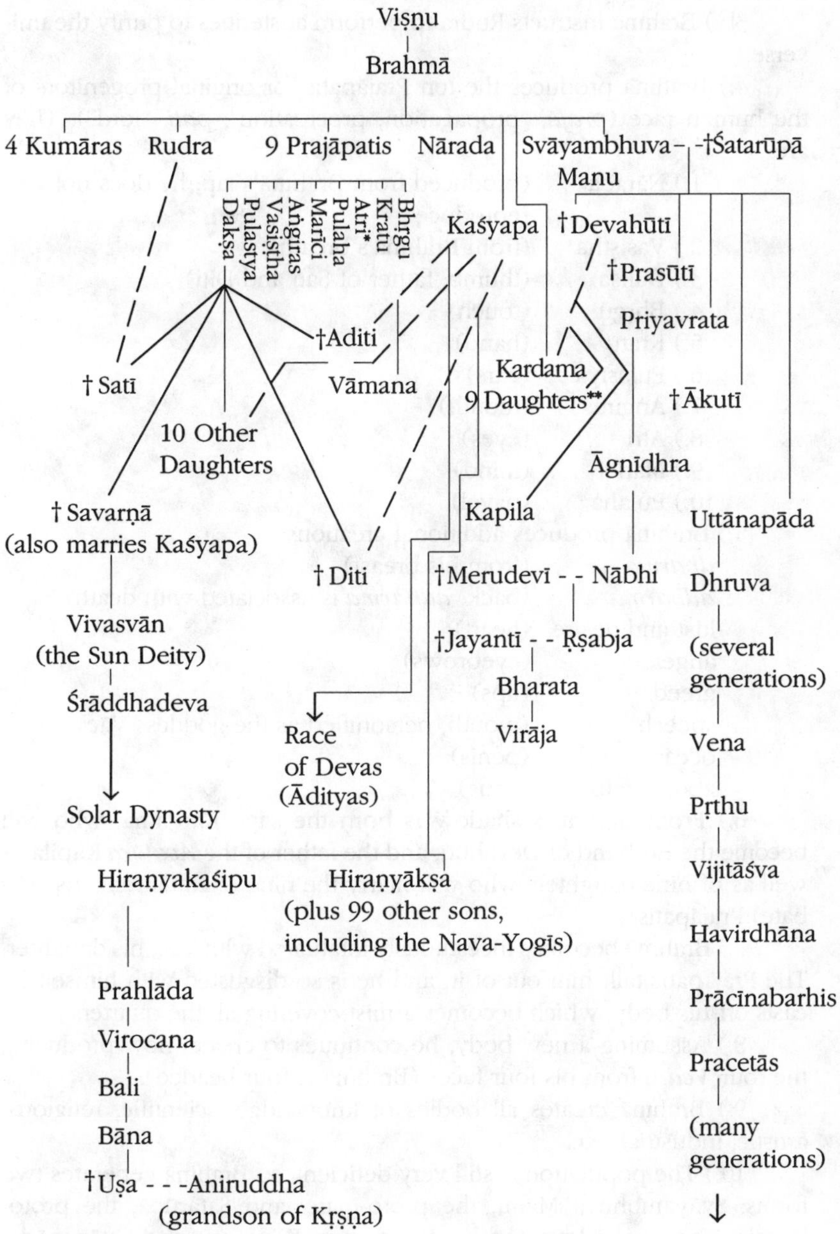

- - - denotes marriage
† denotes a woman

*Atri's Line Becomes the Lunar Dynasty
**married to 9 Prajāpatis

3a.) Rudra produces sons and grandsons of unlimited number; they are fierce and fiery and attempt to devour the universe.

3b.) Brahmā instructs Rudra to perform austerities to purify the universe.

4.) Brahmā produces the ten Prajāpatis, or original progenitors of the human race (*prajā*, "propagation, procreation", *pati*, "lord"). They are:

1.) Nārada	(produced from Brahmā's lap; he does not reproduce)
2.) Vasiṣṭha	(from Brahmā's breath)
3.) Dakṣa	(thumb; father of Sati and Diti)
4.) Bhṛgu	(touch)
5.) Kratu	(hand)
6.) Pulastya	(ears)
7.) Aṅgiras	(mouth)
8.) Atri	(eyes)
9.) Marīci	(mind)
10.) Pulaha	(navel)

5.) Brahmā produces additional creations:

dharma	(from his breast)
adharma	(back; *adharma* is associated with death)
lust and desire	(heart)
anger	(eyebrows)
greed	(lips)
speech	(mouth, personified as the goddess Vāc)
ocean	(penis)
abomination	(anus)

6.) From Brahmā's shadow is born the sage Kardama, who will become the husband of Devahūtī, and the father of the *Avatāra* Kapila as well as of nine daughters who will marry the nine (Nārada remains celibate) Prajāpatis.

7.) Brahmā becomes incestuously infatuated with Vāc, his daughter. The Prajāpatis talk him out of it, and he is so disgusted with himself he casts off his body, which becomes a mist covering all the quarters.

8.) Assuming a new body, he continues to create, now producing the four *Vedas* from his four faces (Brahmā is four-headed).

9.) Brahmā creates all bodies of knowledge: scientific, religious, artistic, industrial, etc.

10.) The population is still very deficient, so Brahmā generates two forms: Svāyambhuva Manu, the proto-male, and Śatarūpā, the proto-female. They make love and have two sons, Priyavrata and Uttānapāda, and three daughters, Ākutī, Prasūtī, and Devahūtī.

11.) Ākutī marries Ruci, Prasūtī marries Dakṣa, and Devahūtī marries Kardama; their issue constitute the population of the world.

The Two Demons and the Boar Incarnation

Varāha, the Boar Incarnation (the word *varāha* means "boar"), is the first to receive a full exposition in the text. His appearance served a twofold purpose: to lift the earth out of the chaos of the Cosmic Waters and set it afloat in the solar system, and to slay the demon Hiraṇyākṣa.

Svāyambhuva and his wife were ready to begin the business of populating, but there was, as yet, no earth upon which the progeny could dwell. It still lay in potential, submerged in the elemental Waters (i.e. the formless chaos). While Brahmā pondered over the means by which to retrieve the earth, a tiny boar, no bigger than a thumb, emerged from his nostril. The divine animal proceeded to grow and grow until it was unimaginably huge. (Two other *Avatāras*, namely Matsya the fish and Vāmanadeva the dwarf, also begin very small and expand to monstrous sizes.) Plunging His snout into the Waters, like a boar looking for truffles, Varāha scooped the earth onto His tusks and set it safely in the sky.

The text now departs from the Varāha episode to give the full account of the backgrounds of the *asura* brothers Hiraṇyākṣa and Hiraṇyakaśipu. Hiraṇyakaśipu will play a significant part in the seventh canto, as he will be the father of the great saint Prahlāda and will be slain by the man-lion *Avatāra* Nṛsiṃhadeva. In this third canto, though, only his previous incarnation and birth are touched upon.

The brothers were not always demons. They began as celestial beings named Jaya and Vijaya (both words meaning "victory") who were the gatekeepers of Mahā-Viṣṇu's heavenly abode, Vaikuṇṭha. One day they presumptuously barred entrance to the four Kumāras who, in turn, cursed them to take birth in the lower regions. "Though we are doomed to a precipitous fall from our present state," the gatekeepers cried, falling to their knees in supplication, "grant that we may not, by virtue of your goodwill, be deprived of our capacity to remember Śrī Hari always" (3.15.36).

The settling of the fate of Jaya and Vijaya sets a precedent which is highly significant to *bhakti* theory. Later in the canto, Śrī Hari Himself says of the two:

> These attendants will soon be born in the species of *asuras*, noted for their antagonism to the *devas*. There they will develop intense antagonism toward Me and as a consequence their minds will get concentrated on Me. They will then have communion with Me

through confrontation, which will help them come back to Me very quickly (3.16.26).

The principles of *bhakti* assert that fixing the mind on God is the surest path to supreme realization, even if the motivation is enmity towards God. Of course, a loving sentiment is preferable, but Brahman is so all-encompassing, even hatred is a part of Him and can be utilized to attain Him. This is in striking contrast to the Western traditions which hold that hatred of God is an unpardonable sin.

It is further understood that anyone who is killed by a divine incarnation achieves instant God-realization, no matter how evil a life they have led. When an *Avatāra* kills, He is exhibiting His causeless love and mercy to both the slain, who is awarded salvation, and to all those beings who might have suffered under the villain's tyranny. Kṛṣṇa and Rāma were both forced to kill demons, and their apparent violence should not be considered acts of brutality, but rather as loving benedictions.

The Pregnancies of Diti and Devahūtī

Jaya and Vijaya, by taking birth as the sons of Kaśyapa and Diti, became the demons Hiraṇyākṣa and Hiraṇyakaśipu. Of great significance are the conditions under which they were conceived, because the story of Diti and Kaśyapa's union is parallel to the story of Devahūtī and Kardama's union, only the former bore demons and the latter bore a divine *Avatāra*. Why?

Diti and Devahūtī were both high-born granddaughters of Lord Brahmā and both married great ascetic sages. The dual conception stories demonstrate that sexuality, while not inherently evil, is a powerful force which has both destructive and creative (or sacred) sides. Which aspect manifests itself depends on the circumstances, motivation, and time. Sex is a good and joyful thing, but if mishandled it can turn ugly. The demon births represent the painful results of reckless sexuality: broken hearts, disease, exploitation, unwanted progeny, what to speak of subtler psychic and karmic entanglements. Lovemaking at the proper time and with the proper person, on the other hand, is beautiful, as is evidenced by the divine birth.

The story is simple. Diti, stricken with erotic passion, seduced her husband during *Sandhyā*, a period in the evening dominated by Lord Śiva in His terrible aspect. This time is set apart for meditation, and sex during *Sandhyā* is an affront to Śiva. The hideous outcome of this indiscretion may seem extreme, after all Diti and Kaśyapa were duly married, but spiritual practitioners of the calibre of Kaśyapa and Diti were expected to live a regulated life with each activity — eating, sleeping, lovemaking — confined to its proper place. If the story also smacks of misogyny, keep in mind that at the time of the text's composition the socioeconomic implications of indiscriminate sexuality were serious enough to threaten a community, and therefore chastity was one of the most highly esteemed traits in a woman. Furthermore, marriage was ideally meant to help restrain the passions, not stir them up.

Like so many of the *Śrīmad Bhāgavatam's* stories, the Diti incident contains several dimensions of significance. More than just a cautionary tale, it illustrates the complex, unseen karmic ties which bring individuals together and unfold their fate. The gatekeepers Jaya and Vijaya, and the errant lovers Diti and Kaśyapa, come together unwittingly in order to play out the karmic results of their individual actions. The story also illustrates the relativity of good and evil, how they are interdependent and, in fact, merely opposite sides of a single reality. Both seem to represent the will of God. Kaśyapa and Diti err, and give birth to demons, but weren't these births ordained by God Himself? In order to combat the demons, Viṣṇu will incarnate twice, as Varāha and the magnificent Nṛsiṃhadeva, thereby blessing the whole world. One of the demons will have a son, Prahlāda, who, despite being a *daitya*, is one of the greatest saints in all Hindu lore. Lastly, the brothers are to be the patriarchs of the demon race, which will play an important part in the ongoing sacred drama. Everything works out in the end; everything has a meaning, a purpose. When viewed in the larger scheme, apparent evil is not so evil after all, for it serves to usher in the ultimate good.

The flip side of the story is the tale of Devahūtī and Kardama. Only after observing strict austerities, and securing a level of spiritual attainment from which they would never fall, did they engage in romantic dalliance. It is significant that they were secure enough in yogic discipline and renunciation that they could enjoy what was their marital right without becoming bound by it. This is the ideal.

After having nine daughters, who went on to marry the nine Prajāpatis, the couple had Lord Kapila, the philosophical discourse of whom spans the last nine chapters of the third canto. Kapila's one disciple was his mother, Devahūtī, and it is to her alone that His extensive lecture was directed.

The Teachings of Kapila

Lord Kapiladeva, the fair-skinned, golden-haired Incarnation, may be based upon a philosopher of the seventh century B.C., also named Kapila, who is said to have authored the *Sāṃkhya* system of thought.[11]

Himself half-mythic, the historical Kapila is so shrouded in legend virtually nothing concrete is known of him, save that references to him appear in Buddhist writings and that connections exist between *Sāṃkhya* and Buddhist philosophies.[12] Many devotees of the *Śrīmad Bhāgavatam* insist, however, that there is no connection between the shadowy "historical" Kapila and the *Avatāra* Kapila depicted in the *Bhāgavatam*.

Sāṃkhya is a system which traces the origin of the material manifestation to the primal causes *puruṣa* and *prakṛti*, and to the disequilibrium of *prakṛti's* constituents, the three *guṇas*. *Puruṣa* is considered a plurality, and each individual represents a *puruṣa* which falsely identifies itself with the evolvents of *prakṛti*.[13] However, Lord Kapila's discourse in the *Śrīmad Bhāgavatam* covers far more than this and, in fact, concentrates not on metaphysics, but on the means and methods of liberation, particularly through the combined paths of *jñāna* and *bhakti*.

Traditional *Sāṃkhya* is non-theistic, while the teachings of this Kapila are richly theistic and devotional. He describes the elements of material manifestation, the causes of bondage to it, and the *jīva's* transmigratory cycle in order that one may, by understanding these things, become free of them. Devotion to Bhagavān, God, is enjoined along with meditation, renunciation, discrimination and total self-surrender. Taken as a self-contained unit, the discourse is a fiery, uncompromising exposition on the necessity of spiritual practice and contains many concrete instructions that are of value to the struggling aspirant.

Canto Four: The Tale of Satī; Saintly Monarchs

The task of human procreation now set into motion by the primordial couple, Svāyambhuva Manu and Śatarūpā, Brahmā's work is done, and in this fourth *skandha* we follow the resulting lineage through the reigns of several important *rājarṣis*, or king-saints. This significance of these narratives is twofold. First, they illustrate how the Divine is constantly expressing Itself through the ongoing stream of time, history, action and human character. Secondly, they demonstrate, through tangible examples, that one can attend to all worldly work and duties while at the same time treading the spiritual path. (This theme was also central to the *Bhagavad-Gītā*.)

The *rājarṣis* of the *Śrīmad Bhāgavatam* administer affairs of state, perhaps the most burdensome of all responsibilities, while their minds are firmly fixed on God. At the end of their terms on the throne, they renounce all and take up ascetic practices full-time, knowing that the only legitimate aim in life is God-realization.

Before the text turns to the *rājarṣis*, however, it relates the strange and disturbing story of Satī. The term *satī*, or "suttee", has come to refer to the now illegal practice of a widow burning herself alive on her husband's funeral pyre as an gesture of devotion to him. If the myth of Satī, as related in the *Śrīmad Bhāgavatam*, is cited as justification for this rite, it shouldn't be, because Satī is not a widow and does not immolate Herself upon a pyre. Her suicide by fire is the result of a spontaneous combustion brought on by intense yogic trance and is a radical expression of religious fervor, as we shall see.

Svāyambhuva Manu and Śatarūpā, you will recall, had three daughters, among them Prasūtī. Prasūtī married the leader of the Prajāpatis, Dakṣa, and together they had sixteen daughters. The youngest was Satī, who was a direct Incarnation of Śrī Devī, the Goddess. She is the eternal *Śakti* of Lord Śiva and thus will later reincarnate as Pārvatī, the gentle aspect of the Goddess, Śiva's permanent consort. In this first manifestation She assumes the form of wife-devotee, much like Sītā was to Rāma or Rādhā to Kṛṣṇa. She is just as much a worshipper of Lord Śiva as She is His wife, and it is in the role of devotee that She executes her dramatic end.

Satī's father, Dakṣa, despised Śiva because he once entered a sacrificial hall where the entire assembly rose to honor him except for Lords Brahmā and Śiva. Dakṣa made obeisances to Brahmā, his own father, but was incensed that his "son-in-law", Lord Śiva, would not stand in deference to him. Dakṣa's preposterous arrogance prevented him from recognizing the divinity in Lord Śiva, and he blustered in front of everyone:

> This Rudra is a blot on the reputation of the deities of the four quarters . . . He covers himself with the ashes of cremated bodies. He wears as his ornaments the bones of dead bodies and garlands of filthy things given by ghosts. He is wrongly called Śiva ("auspicious one"), but he is, in fact, Aśiva ("inauspicious") (4.2.10,15).

He then pronounced a curse on Śiva, declaring that He would cease to receive a share of the ritualistic sacrifice that was actually His due.

Many years later, Dakṣa hosted another massive sacrifice, attended by all of the *devas*, *ṛṣis* and *brāhmaṇas*. Conspicuously absent from the guest list, however, was his daughter, Satī, and son-in-law, Lord Śiva. "I am always welcome in my father's house," Satī said, and She readied herself to go. "There is a type of self-important and worldly-minded man," Śiva told Her, "whose heart aches with jealousy and hatred at great ones established in spiritual consciousness, because he cannot obtain the status and recognition the latter get" (4.3.21). Dakṣa, he explained, cannot understand spirituality beyond outward ceremony and ritual, thus he hates Lord Śiva who, being beyond good and evil, clean and unclean, *dharma* and *adharma*, ignores physical rules and rites. "He will insult you," Śiva lovingly warned, "and he will insult Me."

But Satī took no heed, and went anyway. Upon Her arrival, She was horrified to find that not only would her own father, to whom She used to be the favorite, not deign to recognize Her, but the sacrifice was without the portion allotted to Śiva. This was the most virulent of all insults. She thundered:

> Alas! You are insulting Him, of whose name even the casual utterance by a person would free him from all sins immediately . . . Whose lotus feet are resorted to by great devotees, honey-bees, as it were, in quest of Brahmanic bliss . . . who showers every kind of blessing on those who seek it from Him . . . Therefore I cannot bear to continue in this body born of you, a hater of noble Śiva . . . I shall certainly abandon this body, which I consider a veritable corpse (4.4.14,15,18,23).

Assuming the yellow robes of an ascetic, Satī seated Herself in the meditative posture, took a purificatory sip of water, and entered into yogic concentration. With Her mind fixed on Śiva, Her vital energies controlled, She invoked the element of fire and burst into flames, amidst the shrieks of the assembly.

An effective act of protest, Satī's demise let loose a veritable holocaust. Lord Śiva, usually the gentlest of all the *devas*, exploded in rage and dispatched His legion of ghouls to destroy Dakṣa and his sacrifice. Weapons in hand, they stormed the arena and brought it down, tearing out beams and ripping apart the superstructure. They attacked and dismembered guests and desecrated the articles of sacrifice. Onto the scene came the horrific Vīrabhadra, the embodiment of Śiva's fury, who turned Dakṣa himself into the sacrificial victim. He slaughtered the blasphemer according to ritualistic code, beheaded him, and tossed the severed head into the sacred fire as the offering to Lord Śiva.

Much can be gleaned from this morbid, though powerful, story. The *Śrīmad Bhāgavatam* is a *Vaiṣṇava* text, yet shows that all forms of Brahman are worshippable. To harbor hatred for any of God's manifestations is a mistake. Satī Herself is one of the few real martyrs in Hindu legend. Unwilling to compromise Her devotion to Her chosen God by passively looking on as He was humiliated, She cast off Her body in protest, and not in weakness and submissiveness, but in a blaze of yogic power. The grotesque irony of Dakṣa becoming the sacrificial object to the very deity he so abhorred illustrates the inexorable pull of God, which draws all beings back to Him, as well as the inescapable justice of karmic law.

Tales of the *Rājarṣis*

We now turn to accounts of the primordial royal lineages. Five chapters are devoted to the story of Dhruva, one of the most illustrious of the *Bhāgavatam's* sage-kings. He was the son of Uttānapāda (a grandson of the primordial couple Svāyambhuva and Śatarūpā) and he began his career as a *sādhu* at the age of five. Verbally abused by his stepmother, the child was wounded to the core and retired to the forest in order to devote his life to meditation on Nārāyaṇa. There he met Nārada, who imparted spiritual instruction to him. Nārada's useful discourse in the art of meditation and worship is recounted in verses 4.8.40-4.8.62, and includes disclosure of the great *mantra Oṃ namo bhagavate vāsudevāya* (*Oṃ*, obeisances to God, Vāsudeva). Dhruva observed the most severe austerities for six months, eventually attaining a state of perpetual *samādhi* in which he was granted a vision of Viṣṇu. Due to Viṣṇu's boon, the boy was able to return to the palace, and, in time, ascend the throne. Yet his boyhood vision of God haunted him the rest of his life; though enmeshed in worldly affairs, he longed to recapture that all too brief experience, and it was this sustained passion for another vision which delivered him to ultimate liberation at death.

The rule of king Pṛthu spans a full nine chapters. He is considered a secondary Incarnation and, like Śrī Rāmacandra, a perfect ruler. At the time of his assuming power, the land had been reduced to barrenness, the kingdom to famine, by the misdeeds of his predecessor, Vena. Pṛthu singlehandedly cajoled, worked and even threatened the Earth into releasing Her dormant bounty. He seems to have been the originator of the techniques of agriculture as well as city planning. His greatest achievement, however, was the spread of the gospel of *bhakti*.

The remainder of the *skandha* is devoted to Pṛthu's grandson, Prācīnabarhis, and Prācīnabarhis' ten saintly sons, known collectively as the Pracetās. Śiva again plays an important part, as He assumes the role of *guru* to the Pracetās and delivers the beautiful *Rudra Gītā* (4.24.32-79), a hymn in praise of Mahā-Viṣṇu. Viṣṇu's devotees, He explains, are His devotees, and His devotees are Viṣṇu's. There is no antagonism between them.

The Pracetās' father, King Prācīnabarhis, is a disciple of Nārada and learns from him the allegorical tale of Purañjana ("one who enjoys the body"), a drawn-out parable illustrating the pitfalls of worldly attachments. Nārada also advises the king to forego Vedic ritualism and follow the path of *bhakti.* Swāmī Tapasyānanda indicates that the apparent contradiction — the *Bhāgavatam* extolling the sacrificial performances of Dhruva and Pṛthu then harshly criticizing those of Prācīnabarhis — reflects an historical process taking place, Vedic sacrificial ritualism gradually giving way to *bhāgavata dharma*, the internal path of meditation and devotion.[14]

Canto Five: The Three Lives of Bharata; the Topography of the Universe

A genealogy of the primordial *rājarṣis* continues into *skandha* five, where we meet Priyavrata Mahārāja, one of the sons of Svāyambhuva Manu and Śatarūpā (he is the uncle of Dhruva and a disciple of Nārada). Priyavrata was loath to assume the administrative duties of a king, fearing they would interfere with his spiritual pursuits. Reassured by his grandfather, Lord Brahmā, the sage took the throne and, like the other *rājarṣi* heroes, ruled wisely until his son was grown, then retired to lead the life of a mendicant. We follow the family through Priyavrata's son, Āgnīdhra, Āgnīdhra's son, Nābhi, and then to King Ṛṣabha, a secondary divine Incarnation.

Lord Ṛṣabha is renowned for the holiness of his august offspring and for his practical teachings in the science of *sādhanā.* He was endowed with one hundred sons, the eldest and most important of whom was Bharata. Among the remaining ninety-nine, nine comprised the group known as the Nava-yogīs, famous for their spiritual attainments, who will figure in the eleventh canto. Ṛṣabha's sermon on the need for, and practice of, *sādhanā* is contained in verses 5.5.1-27. He discusses the painful nature of sensual attachments and prescribes a practical plan of action to disentangle oneself from them through renunciation and spiritual inquiry. His recommendations include service to a Self-realized *guru*, equanimity in pain and pleasure, austerity, dedication of works to God, study, hymning, restraint of speech, and so on. The point of all spiritual discipline, he concludes, is to eliminate *ahaṃkāra*, the sense of "I", for freedom from *ahaṃkāra* constitutes spiritual realization.

The Divine Misadventures of Bharata

Chapters seven through fifteen concern the famous story of Bharata. It is after this hero that India, actually called Bhārata or Bhāratavarṣa, is named, and the tale spans three of his incarnations: as a king, as a deer, and as a *brāhmaṇa sādhu*. Bharata's life is both a cautionary tale and a source of inspiration, for it shows the disastrous karmic result of worldly attachment and yet how one can, through honest effort, completely overcome it and attain the ultimate Goal. It also illustrates, in the Goddess Kālī episode, the recurring theme of the universality of the Gods and Goddesses and the universality of the devotees, which we encountered before in the Śiva accounts.

After sufficiently executing the responsibilities of his royal station, Bharata Mahārāja retired to a life of solitude and spiritual contemplation in the forest. He was making excellent progress, until one day he found himself in possession of an orphaned new-born fawn. He took pity on the baby and raised it himself, becoming more and more infatuated with it each day. The greater his obsession grew, the less interested he became in spiritual practice, until he abandoned his *sādhanā* completely. So preoccupied was he with thoughts of the deer, when death caught up with him, he himself took his next birth as a deer. The benefits of *sādhanā*, however, are never lost, and as a result of his, Bharata retained the memory of his former existence. "Alas!" he thought, "The fool that I was, my mind in the end went too far after that deer with the disastrous consequences that have followed!" (5.8.29). Having learned his lesson only too well, he abandoned the herd, frequented the forest hermitages of holy men, and waited out his term in the deer body.

His next, and final, birth was that of the tenth son of a *brāhmaṇa*, and it provides a fine case study of the seemingly mad *paramahaṃsa*, the God-intoxicated soul. In this incarnation he was called Jaḍa-Bharata, or "Crazy Bharata". He had an aversion to the company of others and a mind constantly fixed on God; therefore he appeared senseless, even idiotic. Unwashed, disinterested in study or work, manipulated by others like a puppet, he went about incognito, as it were, for no one could recognize that beneath the layer of dirt and feigned dullness was a luminous sage.

One day a band of Bhadrā Kālī worshippers, searching for an appropriate victim to offer the Mother as human sacrifice, stumbled upon the apparent half-wit and gleefully dragged him back to the temple. Jaḍa Bharata did not resist; so enveloped in God-consciousness was he, death meant nothing to him, save a chance for union with the Divine. After bathing and decorating the victim, the worshippers tied him down before the image of Bhadrā Kālī. The head priest recited the sacrificial *mantras* and took up the ceremonial sword, ready to hack Jaḍa Bharata's head off and offer his blood to the Mother as an intoxicating drink.

Before the blade came down, Kālī Herself suddenly leapt out of the image and, with a ferocious roar, grabbed the sword and sliced off the heads of Her own devotees, thus saving Jaḍa Bharata's life. Clearly, no manifestation of the Divine would ever show preference to His or Her own devotees at the expense of a lover of a different Form. There is only one Universal Spirit, and It loves and protects all spiritual aspirants. Mother Kālī, though ferocious, is the affectionate Benefactress of Her worshippers, but Her actions in this story indicate that allegiance in name only is not sufficient to evoke the Chosen Ideal's favor. While goats are sometimes sacrificed to Kālī, human sacrifices are not enjoined in the *śāstras* and neither Kālī nor any other Divine Manifestation tolerates such a grisly crime. Like Rudra taking the body of Dakṣa as a sacrifice, Mother Kālī took whom She chose, but only the most wicked are punished in such a way, and then only by God personally. Cruelty is never justified.

The last part of the Bharata saga involves his instructions to King Rahūgaṇa, the ruler of Sindhu and Sauvīra. They met one day when the king's palanquin bearers felt the need for an extra hand and, spotting the sage but not recognizing his elevated nature, called him over and set him to work. Because Jaḍa Bharata moved slowly, surveying the path at his feet so as not to trample tiny creatures, the palanquin moved unsteadily and the king hollered at him.

"O bold one," Bharata said calmly, "your ridicule has relevance provided there is a thing called weight for one to bear, provided there is a destination for the traveller to reach, and provided there is corpulence for the *jīva* to be carried. Wise men, however, do not assent to such a proposition" (5.10.9).

All distinctions and modifications of matter, he continued, are unreal; only the Ātman is real. There is no master and no servant, no carried and no carrier, only universal Oneness. Impressed, King Rahūgaṇa hurried down from his palanquin and prostrated before Bharata, whom he now recognized as an illumined soul. Bharata's discourse to the king, which spans three chapters, concentrates on the ultimate unreality of the objective world, the perils of *saṃsāra*, and the uncontrolled mind as the cause of bondage to transmigration. Because of Bharata's wise counsel, the grateful king took to the spiritual path.

The Structure of the Universe

After a brief chapter charting the descendants of Bharata down to Virāja, the last of the line of Priyavrata, the text turns to a schematic description of the universe, geographic and astronomic. The picture it draws bears very little resemblance to the findings of modern science, but a lesson in geography or astronomy is not the point at all. This universe, with oceans of sugarcane juice and mountains beyond which the sun's rays cannot pass, was constructed as an object of meditation. The cosmos is the gross form of Brahman, non-different from It, and by meditating upon its symmetry and grandeur, the spiritual Essence which underlies it is revealed. Swāmī Tapasyānanda compares it to the use of sacred images:

> Just as an image or *yantra* (a ceremonial design) becomes a symbol for worship, and aid for grasping the immaterial Spirit, the whole universe too can be used for such a purpose with great effect by a man endowed with faith.[15]

Worth noting is the lurid description of various hells, and the offenses one has to have committed to be sent there. The point of this chapter (twenty-six) is that our actions have consequences which we are destined to experience personally. In harming others we ultimately bring harm to ourselves. Hindus believe that there are other planetary systems upon which we can take birth besides this one, some delightful, others dreadful, and if our *karma* is too awful, we may temporarily wind up in one of the lower ones. For the spiritually sensitive soul, however, rebirth into this world is painful enough.

Canto Six: On Unexpected Grace

The theme of the sixth *skandha* is divine grace, which is depicted here in the stories of Ajāmila and Indra. Grace is divine favor or intervention which is not dependent on any merit of the receiver, but is given free, for no reason other than that God is infinitely generous and loving. The term "grace" is derived from the Latin *gratis*, given for free. Spiritual life is a mysterious blend of self-effort, self-surrender, and divine grace. Śrī Ramakrishna used to say that the breeze of God's grace is always blowing, and the devotee need merely set his or her sails to catch this breeze. In other words, grace is not something which God metes out here and there, but is a force continuously flowing through everyone, and those who experience it do so because they are receptive to it, while others are not. Even so, sometimes a person who is not normally receptive to it, or is even hostile to it, will have an experience of grace, and then it can only be attributed to divine initiative.

Ajāmila on His Deathbed

One develops receptivity, of course, through regular *sādhanā*, and one of the most important practices is *japa*, or repetition of the divine

Name. The story of Ajāmila, related in the first three chapters of canto six, provides the context for an extensive exposition on the glory of the names of God. Not only does repeating the divine Name sanctify, uplift, enlighten, and engender God-consciousness, but uttering it at the time of death, it is said, instantly delivers one to ultimate liberation. Generally one is incapable of remembering the Lord's name at the moment of death unless he or she has been practicing *japa* throughout their life. But the Name is so potent, even the most heinous sinner *will* attain the highest realization if he somehow remembers it at death. This was the case with Ajāmila.

Once a pious *brāhmaṇa*, Ajāmila somehow slipped into a life of hedonism, cruelty and squalor. Though hard-hearted, he did sustain a love for his youngest son, who happened to be named Nārāyaṇa. When his time to die came, Ajāmila was met by three *Yamadūtas*, hideous emissaries of Yamarāja, the god of death, and in terror he called out the name of his son, Nārāyaṇa. Though he had an entirely different Nārāyaṇa in mind, it didn't matter. The *Viṣṇudūtas*, emissaries of Lord Viṣṇu, instantly appeared to take him to the abode of Śrī Hari. Such is the power of God's name.

An informative conversation between the *Yamadūtas* and *Viṣṇudūtas* ensues. Yamarāja knows well the redemptive power of the Name, and tells his servants, "Even the Lord's name alone, uttered without any knowledge or devotion, constitutes adequate expiation" (6.4.24). How much more effective, then, is the Name meditated upon with reverence and love? Śrī Śukadeva tells King Parīkṣit, "No vow or austerity purifies the heart of man so effectively as devotion engendered easily by hearing and uttering the names of Śrī Hari denoting His sanctifying deeds and excellences" (6.4.32).

Ajāmila was the unwitting, and very undeserving, recipient of divine grace. The story ends with Ajāmila being granted an extension on his earthly life, which he spends wisely in the serious practice of renunciation and *yoga*. When death comes to him a second time, he is safely situated in knowledge of the Ātman and naturally attains the supreme Goal. Ajāmila's commitment to *sādhanā* should remind us that experiences of grace should not be looked upon as attainments in themselves, but as affirmations to motivate us to push farther and harder in our own spiritual efforts.

Indra and Vṛtra: A Tale of Sin and Redemption

In the tale of Indra and Vṛtra we find grace in the form of expiation for the sin of a particular act, in this case the atrocious murder of a *guru*.

The Purāṇic account is a variation on an ancient Vedic myth where Indra slays a great dragon, Vṛtra, to release the element of rain pent up in the creature's body (the word *vṛtra* is derived from the root *vṛ*, "to hold back", "restrain").[16] In this version, Vṛtra is an avenging monster, and not of an archetypal nature.

The account is highly detailed and complex; the essence, however, is that Indra, the leader of the *devas*, on discovering that his *ācārya*, or priest, had sympathies with the *asuras*, murdered him in cold blood. The *ācārya's* father retaliated by creating out of the sacrificial fire the ferocious being Vṛtra, under whose lead the *asura* forces gained dominance over the *devas* and whose very existence was geared to the annihilation of Indra.

Brahmahatya, or the crime of killing a *brāhmaṇa*, is considered the vilest possible sin. By all rights, Indra should have been subject to harsh retribution, but it seems instead as though everything, including his predator, conspired to redeem him. A new *ācārya* arrived and presented him with impenetrable armor; a saint sacrificed his own body so that a magic weapon might be forged from it; Vṛtra, it turned out, was a wise devotee of God and imparted spiritual instruction to Indra during respites in combat:

> O Indra, take up your thunderbolt weapon and kill me, your enemy . . . No warrior fighting with weapons can expect victory always and never defeat . . . The ultimate cause of success and failure of human effort is the Lord . . . Therefore one should remain unperturbed in all situations, whether in fame or in disrepute, in success or in failure, in life or in death (6.12.6,8,14).

Indra slew Vṛtra, thus committing another *brahmahatya* (as Vṛtra was created by a priest, he is considered the priest's son, and therefore a *brāhmaṇa* himself). With the guilt of these sins weighing on him, he fled into hiding amongst the lotuses in the Manas lake, and there experienced the full extent of grace and its redemptive nature. Lord Rudra was the presiding deity of the region where Indra hid, so just by his being there his sin was mitigated through Rudra's grace. Furthermore, lotuses are considered one of the dwelling places of the Goddess Lakṣmī, so by his proximity to them, Indra received Her grace as well. Finally, Indra was purified by his own meditation on Mahā-Viṣṇu. At last the *ṛṣis* approached him with the request that he perform an *aśvamedha*, the horse sacrifice, and with the completion of this rite, Indra was entirely purged of his sin.

Grace, it seems, can take many forms, such as the help and generosity of others, spiritual instruction, or personal redemption. Though the

Divine ultimately bestows Its grace only when and where It pleases, one can encourage this manifestation of grace, as the preceding stories illustrate, by uttering the Divine Name, proximity to sacred places and things, meditation on the Supreme, and religious ritual.

The rest of the *skandha* covers the previous birth of Vṛtra and an account of the additional progeny of Diti, known collectively as the Maruts. After hearing the story of Indra and Vṛtra, King Parīkṣit wanted to know how a being with such a ferocious appearance could have such a devotional temperament. Śrī Śuka then spins the tale of the emperor Citraketu, Vṛtra's former incarnation, which has him develop from a worldly-minded materialist to a renounced aspirant and, finally, to a celestial being. Again, there's a warning against dogmatic exclusivity, because when Citraketu insults Lord Śiva and Mother Pārvatī, the Devī curses him to be demoted to a low birth. That his devotional fervor was not at all decreased by this physical regression, however, is demonstrated by his lofty discourse to Indra.

Vṛtra is significant on several levels. His story shows how one's bodily form and circumstances of birth are a direct result of past *karma*, and a retrograde movement is entirely possible. However, one's outer appearance cannot fully indicate one's inner qualities, particularly one's spirituality, and a horrific appearance may conceal a holy person. Some *sādhus* in India purposely assume a ghoulish appearance, with matted hair, ash-smeared bodies, and so on, to symbolize the illusoriness of the bodily facade. Never judge others by their appearance; you may be taken in by a common egotist dressed in the robes of a holy man, and completely overlook the saint in street clothes.

Canto Seven: Prahlāda and the Man-Lion, Nṛsiṃhadeva

We have arrived at the Prahlāda account, one of the most beloved and most powerful legends in Hinduism. It takes up most of the seventh *skandha*, and rightfully so, for no synopsized version can do this astonishing tale justice. On repeated readings, new layers of meaning continue to reveal themselves, and, like so much Hindu sacred history, the imagery is alternately exquisite and grotesque. The combination of so many disparate elements produces a tale of haunting power. It is a gruesome story, but full of hope and ecstatic devotion.

Hiraṇyakaśipu, remember, was one of the two demon sons of Diti. His twin, Hiraṇyākṣa, was slain by the boar *Avatāra*, and now Hiraṇyakaśipu will face Nṛsiṃhadeva, the man-lion *Avatāra*. These brothers will play the parts of God's adversaries two more times after this, as Rāvaṇa and Kumbhakarṇa during the Rāma incarnation, and as Dakṣa and Śiśupāla during the Kṛṣṇa incarnation. In all six cases, they demonstrate the mode of *vidveṣa bhakti*, or fixing the mind on God in a hateful mood.[17]

The aspirant must read the *Śrīmad Bhāgavatam* itself to experience the full impact of the story, but a hopelessly inadequate synopsis follows.

As a result of hard austerities, the *asura* king, Hiraṇyakaśipu, received a boon from Lord Brahmā which he thought would assure him eternal life. Never could he be slain, the boon stipulated, by day or by night, indoors or outdoors, on the ground or in the air, by man or by beast, nor by any weapon. In the meantime, the *devas* waged war against the *asuras* and plundered Hiraṇyakaśipu's palace. They were about to drag his pregnant wife off, when Nārada appeared and interceded in her defense, knowing that a great future saint was nestled within her. He gave her refuge in his hermitage and imparted spiritual instruction to her which Prahlāda, the child in her womb, overheard and remembered. Because of this, Prahlāda was born already a great devotee.

Prahlāda's devotion was in extreme defiance of his father's values. That he preached *bhakti* to the other *asura* children further threatened the power of his father, who subjected the child to horrible persecution and abuses and ultimately ordered the boy's execution. By the repeated intervention of Lord Viṣṇu, however, Prahlāda emerged from each trial unscathed.

In a psychotic rage, Hiraṇyakaśipu decided to murder the boy himself, but first challenged him verbally. "Where is the Lord of the worlds of whom you speak, if there is any such other than me?" he thundered. "Everywhere," Prahlāda replied." "Is he in this pillar, then?" Hiraṇyakaśipu taunted. "Yes," the child said, "I see Him there too."

"If that be the case," the king sneered, "let him save you now." He drew his sword and struck the pillar, from which a terrible roar suddenly erupted. The world shook, the deities cowered, and out of the pillar leapt gorgeous and terrifying Nṛsiṃhadeva, the half-man half-lion. The golden beast, with gleaming fangs, a quivering tongue, innumerable arms and razor-sharp claws, seized the demon and casually played with him, as a cat plays with a mouse. It was just twilight, and on the threshold of the palace, Lord Nṛsiṃhadeva held the king on His lap and tore him open. He garlanded Himself with the fiend's intestines, tore his heart out, and cast the corpse aside. The demon was dead, yet Nṛsiṃhadeva never violated Brahmā's boon. Hiraṇyakaśipu had been killed neither by man nor beast (but a man-beast), neither inside nor outside (but at the threshold), neither by day or night (but at twilight), neither in the air nor on the ground (but in Nṛsiṃha's lap), and not by any weapon (but by naked claws).

The celestials gathered to honor Him. They beat drums, hymned, danced, showered Him with flowers, but none could pacify Him. His fury continued. Only when Prahlāda, an innocent child with unshakable faith and devotion, approached the Lord, did his tender side emerge. Prahlāda extolled Him in a long hymn (7.9.8-50), the love and wisdom of which melted Nṛsiṃha's heart. After declaring Prahlāda king of the *daityas* and imparting instructions, the *Avatāra* disappeared from sight.

The Prahlāda account exemplifies the protective power of devotion to God. Prahlāda, the perfect renunciate, never cared what evils should befall him. In this sense, he much resembles the sixteenth-century poetess-saint Mirabai, also of royal lineage, whose single-minded love for Kṛṣṇa aroused such hatred in her family members, they abused her and even attempted to murder her by poisoning.[18] Legend has it that Kṛṣṇa transformed the poison into nectar, just as Viṣṇu repeatedly saved Prahlāda from his brushes with death. It is not uncommon for spiritual aspirants to be reviled, even today. The *Bhagavad-Gītā* asserts that what is day for the worldly is night-time for the sage, and what is daylight for the sage is pitch darkness for the rest. The aspirant gradually abandons everything society values most — prestige, fame, money, accomplishment — and this is both bewildering and threatening to ordinary people. Anyone who has made a serious attempt at spiritual development can attest to having lost friends in the process, but what is gained in exchange is immeasurably superior.

The devotee is doubly protected. Through renunciation and detachment, he or she cares very little whether favorable or unfavorable winds blow. Even death is of no consequence, because the devotee is content in the steadiness of the Self. Nevertheless, the devotee is shown special favor by God, is protected and nurtured. Here is where faith comes in, for the devotee trusts the divine Beloved completely and recognizes misfortune as good fortune in disguise; it will, in the long run, reveal itself to have been beneficial. Such is the way of God in ordinary circumstances, but sometimes, in a genuine crisis, the Divine will intercede dramatically, like a lion leaping from a pillar.

Also significant is the Lord's preference of a child's devotion over that of the great and powerful deities'. That childlike purity and simplicity is a necessary element for God-realization is echoed in Jesus' teaching: "Whoever does not receive the kingdom of God like a child shall not enter into it" (Mark 10.15, Luke 18.17). The text does not extol ignorance, of course, but the unencumbered faith of a child not yet colored by arrogance or ambition, disillusionment or bitterness. It is purity and sweetness which takes us to the ultimate Goal; sophistication is of no consequence.

Today, with the grisly reality of child abuse receiving mass attention, myths concerning strong and powerful children are particularly relevant. In the Prahlāda account, as well as the legends of Dhruva and, particularly, Kṛṣṇa, we see the paradigm of a strong child resisting the dangers and abuses inflicted by adults, and his ultimate victory over them. In the case of Prahlāda, it was faith in God which empowered him, for Dhruva, his renunciation and discipline. In Kṛṣṇa's case, the child *is* God, the supremely powerful One. All the children embody the universal Spirit to the same extent as adults, and by internalizing the image of the Supreme Self, Lord Kṛṣṇa, they can reclaim the dignity and security that is their birthright. By identifying with Dhruva or Prahlāda, they learn that healing and strength can be attained through self-mastery.

On a more analytical note, the Nṛsiṃha story deals extensively with the theme of liminality. The tale unfolds layer upon layer of in-betweens. Prahlāda is an *asura*, constitutionally and culturally predisposed to hedonism, but his character is that of a *deva*. He is both and neither, caught in a liminal state. Hiraṇyakaśipu is alternately the super-sensualist and super-ascetic. He is both a depraved demon and singled out for special divine favor. Nṛsiṃha is of partly human form, partly animal. He emerges from a pillar, an inanimate object, thus juxtaposing matter and pure spirit. The conditions of Hiraṇyakaśipu's death are a study of liminal states — twilight, the threshold, etc.

What relevance does the theme of liminality have for the spiritual aspirant? In a sense, every person in the world is in a liminal state. Our true nature is wholly spiritual, pure, deathless and divine. Yet we are embodied, a condition which subjects us to limitedness, to death, to profanity. The deluded, corporeal beings we experience ourselves to be are not our true selves, yet our true, purely spiritual selves evade us. We are not really here, nor are we There. We are not what we think we think ourselves to be, but can't perceive what we are. We are immortal yet experience death. We are pure consciousness yet are embodied. We have absolute knowledge yet are deluded. Our very nature is pure bliss, yet we suffer.

In the Nṛsiṃha episode, even God experiences liminality. Here the Divine is characterized by ambiguity. He is, on the one hand, terrifying, the all-powerful cosmic destroyer against which we are helpless. Yet He is, at the same time, glorious, beautiful, the protector and savior. The occurrence of an *Avatāra* is, in itself, a case of liminality when we consider the paradox of the Absolute in Its entirety taking the form of an embodied person. Because It cannot be divided, the Absolute in Its entirety is contained in a form, yet at the same time is, in Its entirety, pervading and transcending the cosmos. The embodied form is in a liminal state, neither truly embodied nor not embodied.

As we progress on the spiritual path, we enter further and further into a liminal state. Experiencing the functioning of the sense organs and their objects while remaining detached from them is a liminal state. Spiritual perceptions and ecstasies are liminal states.

Varṇāśrama-dharma: The Proper Social Divisions and Stages of Life

The text now departs from the Prahlāda story and launches into a detailed exposition of *varṇāśrama-dharma*, a subject which occupies the remainder of the canto. *Varṇāśrama-dharma* means caste (*varṇa*) and stage of life (*āśrama*) and refers to a social system, at one time strictly upheld in India, but now relaxing somewhat, which determines one's duties, both spiritual and secular. We already encountered the subject in the *Bhagavad-Gītā*, chapter eighteen, but the *Śrīmad Bhāgavatam* provides a far more extensive treatment.

Simply stated, the four *varṇas*, or social divisions, include *brāhmaṇas*, the priestly and scholarly class, *kṣatriyas*, the government administrators and militia, *vaiśyas*, the mercantile and agricultural class, and *śūdras*, the laborers. (Untouchables, or *pariahs*, are not included in the system at all; they are an anomaly, and the cruel treatment they receive is not scripturally sanctioned.) The four *āśramas* are the ideal stages in a man's life, where he begins as a *brahmacarya*, or celibate student, then becomes a *gṛhastha*, a married householder adhering to the spiritual disciplines appropriate to that station, in middle age moves into *vānaprastha*, a gradual withdrawal from the world, and finally accepts *sannyāsa*, complete renunciation. Women, it should be noted, are traditionally not held to the four *āśramas*, but to only two: maidenhood and the married state.

To what extent this is relevant to the Westerner depends on the individual. Clearly, a knowledge of *varṇāśrama-dharma* is extremely helpful in understanding the nuances of the scriptures, myths, lives of the saints, and so on. It is one of the principal features of Indian culture. When we understand the mechanics of *varṇa*, we can see why kings, who are members of the *kṣatriya* class, honor *brāhmaṇas*, or why *brāhmaṇas*, the most esteemed class, are often poor, while members of the lower classes might be rich, and so on.

More importantly, the whole point of *varṇāśrama-dharma* is that wherever in the system one is, by carefully executing the duties of his station and gradually progressing through the *āśramas*, he may achieve the ultimate goal of Self-realization. One's worldly status and/or profession is irrelevant to their spiritual attainment; by performing one's own duty, no matter how humble, as *yoga*, one can make spiritual progress. Some people argue that while not institutionalized, the four *varṇas* exist naturally in all societies. The contributions of all four *varṇas* are necessary in order for a society to survive. Each is equally dependent on the others, therefore a society stratified according to *varṇa* is often compared to a living body, with the *śūdras* as the legs, *vaiśyas* the torso, *kṣatriyas* the arms, and *brāhmaṇas* the head. Without one part, the entire organism is crippled.

In *varṇāśrama-dharma*, society is set up in such a way as to facilitate the smooth operation of mundane life while encouraging spiritual unfoldment. Both are necessary; as Swāmī Vivekānanda said, before a man can concern himself with God, he must have bread in his belly. The *varṇāśrama-dharma* described in *Śrīmad Bhāgavatam* is an ideal. Unfortunately, the caste system as it has actually manifested itself in India is mostly a hierarchical system of etiquette based on standards of symbolic purity and pollution and determined by birth. In the *Bhāgavatam*, heredity is not a factor in determining one's *varṇa*. Though it is most common for an individual to follow the traditions of his family, if his inner nature conforms to the occupations and ideals of a different *varṇa*, then he *is* that *varṇa*. It is a matter of calling, not pedigree.

Furthermore, the standards of morality, discipline, purity and spirituality ascribed to all the *varṇas* are so lofty, the differences between them begin to seem quite irrelevant. Spiritual realization is equally attainable by everyone.

The *āśramas*, or stages in life, similarly allow for one to attend to secular responsibilities and pleasures while progressing spiritually. Not everyone can be a monk, and the married state is considered sacred as well. In fact, all of the *āśramas*, if diligently followed, are sacred. As Ecclesiastes states, "For everything there is a season and a time for every occupation under heaven" (3.1). One can live a normal life, marry, have children, hold a job, and at the same time make sure and steady progress towards God-realization. Human nature is definitely taken into account here; most of us are ordinary people with ordinary emotional needs. It is not evil or gross; everything has its own time and place, that's all.

When the children are grown and retirement age comes, one moves into the *vānaprastha* stage. The beauty of *vānaprastha* is that one withdraws from the world gradually. It is a preparation for *sannyāsa* (total renunciation), where instead of abandoning everything at once and going into shock, one renounces gently. Generally, a man retires from work at this time, turns the family home over to grown children and, with his wife, makes pilgrimages to holy sites. The couple practice *sādhanā* together and begin to observe celibacy. When they have achieved sufficient detachment, they part, and the man wanders alone or resides at a temple, taking the vow of *sannyāsa*, total renunciation of the world.

Obviously, not many people follow this model any more, but it exists as an ideal and an inspiration. It reminds us that whatever stage of life we happen to be in offers the perfect opportunity for spiritual practice, while the future ideal is always complete renunciation. We are all potential *sannyāsins* and are wise to try to cultivate the virtues of *sannyāsa* even while living in the world.

There are certain moral excellences expected of all the *varṇas* and *āśramas*. A glance at them proves that each class and life stage, if carried out beautifully, is indeed sacred. They are: truth, kindness, austerity, purity, forbearance, discrimination, control of the mind and senses, avoiding inflicting pain on others, continence, charity, scriptural study, straightforwardness, contentment, service to holy men, withdrawal from works with selfish motives, preparedness for failures and disappointments, quietude, self-criticism, feeding others, seeing the Lord in all beings, special perception of Divinity in human beings, and practicing the ninefold method of *bhakti yoga*.

Anyone who embodies all of these virtues is already a spiritually advanced soul, a great *yogī*. The reader is advised to study these chapters thoroughly, try to find him or herself in the two schemes, and take to heart as much as is applicable to a Westerner. Women ought to ignore the sexist content, keeping in mind the unflattering position of women in the historical and cultural milieu in which the *Bhāgavatam* was composed. In our day and culture, the general exhortations are directed to both women and men. Students, workers, soldiers, marrieds or singles, renounced *yogīs* or aspirants taking a middle path, all will find their ideal selves described. Whatever our age and occupation, we must strive to perfect ourselves within that context by performing our duties with detachment and intelligence, self-respect and poise, always keeping an eye to the spiritual significance underlying every choice we make.

Canto Eight: The Fish, the Tortoise, and the Dwarf

Three of Viṣṇu's primary *Avatāras* make their appearance in this *skandha*, as does a secondary one, Mohinī the temptress. An overarching theme of the *skandha* as a whole is the chronology of the *manvantaras*, which is one of the ten obligatory subjects of a *Mahāpurāṇa*. The word is *manvantara* derived from *manu*, patriarch, and *antara*, interval, hence an epoch corresponding to a particular world patriarch.

Manvantaras are used as a standard division of history in Purāṇic lore, and there are fourteen *manvantaras* in one *kalpa*, or cycle of cosmic creation, maintenance and dissolution. Each *kalpa* consists of one thousand four-*yuga* cycles. The first Manu was Svāyambhuva, one of the initial beings created by Lord Brahmā. We are currently in the seventh *manvantara* of the cycle.

Chapters two through four relate an incident which occurred during the fourth *manvantara*, the famous story of the Lord's liberation of the elephant king, Gajendra (*gaja*, elephant, and *indra*, lord). In a former life, Gajendra had been a king named Indradyumna and much devoted to Lord Hari. Cursed by the sage Agastya (a well-known Vedic seer whom we find mention of elsewhere in the *Purāṇas*, as well as in the *Mahābhārata* and *Rāmāyaṇa*),[19] Indradyumna took birth among the elephants. Due to his spiritual practices, however, he, much like Bharata in his deer incarnation, remembered his true nature at the last moment.

The tale is a simple one. Gajendra went to the lake to bathe and was attacked by a ferocious crocodile demon. A long struggle ensued, and when it looked as though Gajendra had no hope of surviving, he suddenly overcame his ignorant elephant-consciousness and surrendered utterly to God. His ecstatic and theologically detailed hymn to the Divine in Its impersonal aspect is contained in chapter three, and in response to this outpouring, Viṣṇu Himself appeared on the spot and liberated Gajendra from both the jaws of the crocodile and from his elephant form. The point of the fable is that God comes to the rescue of the devotee who surrenders him or herself completely, no matter how low that devotee may have sunk. Even animals, whose indwelling Ātman is no different from that of humans, are under the Lord's care. The Lord responds to those who cry out to Him. That is a guarantee.

Kūrma, the Tortoise *Avatāra*

The ongoing warring between the *devas* and the *asuras* seems to reflect the fundamental forces responsible for cosmic equilibrium. At different times one side or the other prevails, but the pendulum always swings back again. The losers become the new victors; the strong become weak and fall; back and forth it goes in endless repetition.

The churning of the milk ocean is a figurative tableau which beautifully illustrates how the struggle between opposing forces maintains universal symmetry. It was one of the few times the *devas* and *asuras* cooperated, though their alliance was superficial; both sides secretly wanted to acquire heavenly *amṛta*, the elixir of immortality, for themselves. In the symbolic geography of the cosmos discussed in the fifth canto, there are said to be seven mythological oceans made of water, curd, milk, ghee, wine, sugarcane and salt, respectively.[20] As one churns cream in order to extract butter, so too did the *devas* and *asuras* churn the ocean of milk to extract its many treasures. Though *amṛta* was their chief concern, the ocean yielded a number of items which would prove to be great blessings to the people and the gods. The ocean might be taken to represent the unmanifest cosmos which holds all phenomena in potential.

For a churning rod, they used Mount Mandara, for a churning strap, the divine serpent Vāsuki, and to hold this contraption up, Viṣṇu incarnated Himself as Kūrma, the giant tortoise. He hoisted the mountain onto His massive back, held it in place by hovering above it in another form and pressing down on it with one of His hands, and joined the ranks of both sides by disguising Himself as an *asura* and a *deva*. With the Lord present below, above, and on both sides, the churning began.

The first thing to emerge was a virulent poison called *hālāhala* or *kālakuta*. Its fatal fumes began to spread, and all creatures were doomed. Lord Śiva, in His infinite affection for all, gathered up the poison and swallowed it Himself, which turned His throat blue. Thus He is lovingly called Nīlakaṇṭha, the Blue-Throated One. The few drops which escaped His lips were appropriated by the scorpions, serpents, poisonous plants and other venomous creatures.

Other gifts to emerge from the ocean were:

— Surabhī, the celestial cow of plenty.

— Vāruṇī, goddess of liquor, who went, of course, with the *asuras*.

— Candra, the moon, which Śiva took to adorn His head.

— Kaustubha, the priceless gem which Viṣṇu wears on His chest.

— Rambhā, the heavenly nymph who became the ancestress of the *apsaras*, or celestial dancers.

— Pārijāta, the wish-fulfilling tree, taken by Indra.

— Airāvata, the elephant mount of Indra.

— Dhanus, the magic bow, which eventually found its way to Lord Rāmacandra.

— Ucchaiḥśravas, the seven-headed white stallion, taken by the *asura* Bāli.

— Ramā, or Śrī, an embodiment of Mother Lakṣmī, Viṣṇu's *śakti.*

— Dhanvantari, the primordial physician and partial Incarnation of Viṣṇu who held among his containers of medicine the coveted *amṛta.*

When Dhanvantari emerged with the elixir, the *asuras* snatched it away from Him and dashed off. "Do not be sad," Viṣṇu told the distressed *devas*; "by My *māyā* I shall achieve your end without anyone knowing about it" (8.8.37). He then incarnated Himself as Mohinī, the enchantress, to tease the *amṛta* away from the *asuras* and distribute it, instead, among the *devas.* Later, in chapter twelve, the sight of Mohinī will arouse Lord Śiva's ardor, though He is the Lord of ascetics. This signifies that Lord Viṣṇu is so compelling, so irresistibly attractive, He upsets the calm even of Maheśvara.

Vāmana, the Dwarf *Avatāra*

The Vāmana Incarnation, like Mohinī, came to play a trick. Due to sacrificial rites he had performed, the *asura* king Bāli Mahārāja, Prahlāda's grandson, gained control over both the earthly and heavenly realms. He was not an evil king, but he was proud of his wealth and generosity, and his dictatorship over the universe upset the cosmic balance.

To rectify this situation, Viṣṇu took birth as *brāhmaṇa* of diminutive stature, Vāmana. He was the son of the sage Kaśyapa and his wife, Aditi, who was one of Dakṣa's daughters. Kaśyapa married thirteen of Dakṣa's daughters, including Diti who, you will recall, gave birth to the demons Hiraṇyākṣa and Hiraṇyakaśipu, thus becoming the matriarch of the *asuras.* Aditi, on the other hand, was the mother of the *devas*, and of a divine Incarnation, Vāmana. The word *diti*, by the way, means "limited", while *aditi* means "unlimited". Kaśyapa is the patriarch, then, of both the *devas* and the *asuras.* Bāli and Vāmana are distant cousins. Ultimately, this tangled drama leads back to Lord Brahmā and then to Lord Viṣṇu; God is the source of everything, and everything is interconnected.

In order to wrest control of the worlds from King Bāli, Vāmana, a *brāhmaṇa*, made a visit to his palace. To offer gifts, particularly land or cows, to a *brāhmaṇa* is highly meritorious, so the extravagant Bāli asked the beautiful dwarf what He desired.

"O generous one," Vāmanadeva replied, "all I ask is a small strip of land, as much as is covered by three steps of Mine."

Bāli scoffed at this meager request, but granted it nonetheless. Suddenly, the tiny *brāhmaṇa* began to grow. Before everyone's eyes, He grew to cosmic proportions and with His first step covered the entire universe. With His second, He strode the heavenly realm. His body *was* the universe; Bāli saw the whole of *prakṛti* within the all-pervading, cosmic Being. The king, now stripped of his possessions, his glory, and his dignity, was bound within the serpent-ropes of the deity Varuṇa and brought before Lord Vāmana, who had resumed His dwarf form.

"You promised to give Me earth measured by My three paces," the *Avatāra* said. "Show Me the space for the third."

Bāli, full of devotion, said, "O Divinity, be pleased to take the third step on my head."

Vāmana *was* pleased, and praised Bāli before the whole assembly. "Whomever I particularly wish to bless," the Lord said, "I first take away his wealth" (8.22.24). Bāli's devotion, truthfulness, and unselfishness won him the Lord's favor, and as a reward, Vāmana promoted him to a heavenly realm to wait until the turning of the next *manvantara*, when Bāli was promoted to the post of Indra.

Matsya, the Fish *Avatāra*

The canto closes with the Matsya legend. *Matsya* means "fish", and this *Avatāra* is associated with a deluge myth strongly reminiscent of the Noah story.

The pious king Satyavrata was performing his ablutions one day when he found a tiny fish in the water in his cupped hands. The fish asked him to protect it from predators by taking it home and keeping it in a cup. Satyavrata did this, but overnight the fish grew too big for the cup. The king transferred it to a larger vessel, but soon it was too big for that. He took it to a pond and the same thing happened. The fish grew and grew until only the sea could hold it. "Surely You must be the worshipful Hari, who has assumed the form of a fish for the good of the world!" the king exclaimed (8.24.27).

The fish revealed His identity, and informed the king that a *kalpa*, or day in the life of Lord Brahmā, was soon coming to an end and that when Brahmā lay down to sleep, the cosmic deluge, or *pralaya*, would consume the world. Like Noah, Satyavrata was instructed to collect representatives of all species of animals, as well as the seeds of all species of plant and, accompanied by the Saptarṣis, or seven great seers, board a ship which would magically appear seven days later.

The king consigned himself to meditation on Lord Hari for the interim, and after a week the flood came exactly as foretold, as did the ship. While Brahmā was asleep, the four *Vedas* slipped out of his mouths and were lost in the deluge, only to be snatched up by a certain demon, Hayagrīva (not to be confused with the horse-headed deity of the same name). Matsya's advent served a dual purpose. Using as a rope Vāsuki, the same celestial serpent who served as a cord during the churning of the ocean, the ship was tied to Lord Matsya, who piloted the vessel through the storm. At the same time, He retrieved the sacred *Vedas* and held them in safe-keeping for the next cycle of creation.

According to Swāmī Tapasyānanda, the mystic Fish was Vedic wisdom personified, and that is why He imparted spiritual instruction to Satyavrata during their journey. In his next birth, this Satyavrata became the seventh Manu, named Vaivasvata, of the new *kalpa*. As a matter of fact, his is the *manvantara* in which we are now living.[21] Vaivasvata Manu's descendants comprise the illustrious Solar Dynasty, which is outlined in the next *skandha*.

Canto Nine: Genealogies, Lord Rāmacandra and Paraśurāma

In certain parts the driest *skandha* of all, the ninth concerns itself primarily with *vaṃśānucarita*, or royal genealogies. This, like the *manvantaras* of the preceding canto, is one of the obligatory topics of a *Mahāpurāṇa*, but unfortunately it takes the form of long lists of names and locations with relatively little narrative. Respites come, however, with the story of Lord Rāma, the legend of Paraśurāma, and accounts of several significant saint-kings.

It is enough for the reader to know that the *Śrīmad Bhāgavatam* particularly traces the lineages of two great dynasties: the Solar, descended from Vivasvān, the sun deity, and the Lunar, descended from Soma, the moon deity. Lord Rāma appears in the Solar dynasty, while Lord Kṛṣṇa appears in the Lunar.

King Satyavrata of the Matsya (Fish) *Avatāra* account took his next birth as the Manu of the present age. His name was Śrāddhadeva, or Vaivasvata, which means "Son of Vivasvān, the sun deity". His line can be followed down through Lord Rāma and Paraśurāma, and continued to the last of the race, Bṛhadbala, who fought and died in the battle of Kurukṣetra.

The Devotional *Yoga* of King Ambarīṣa

Among the notables of this dynasty is king Ambarīṣa (Chapters Four and Five), famed for his perfect application of the *bhakti yoga* process. From Ambarīṣa we learn how to spiritualize every aspect of our lives by directing even mundane possessions and activities to the Divine.

The Solar Dynasty

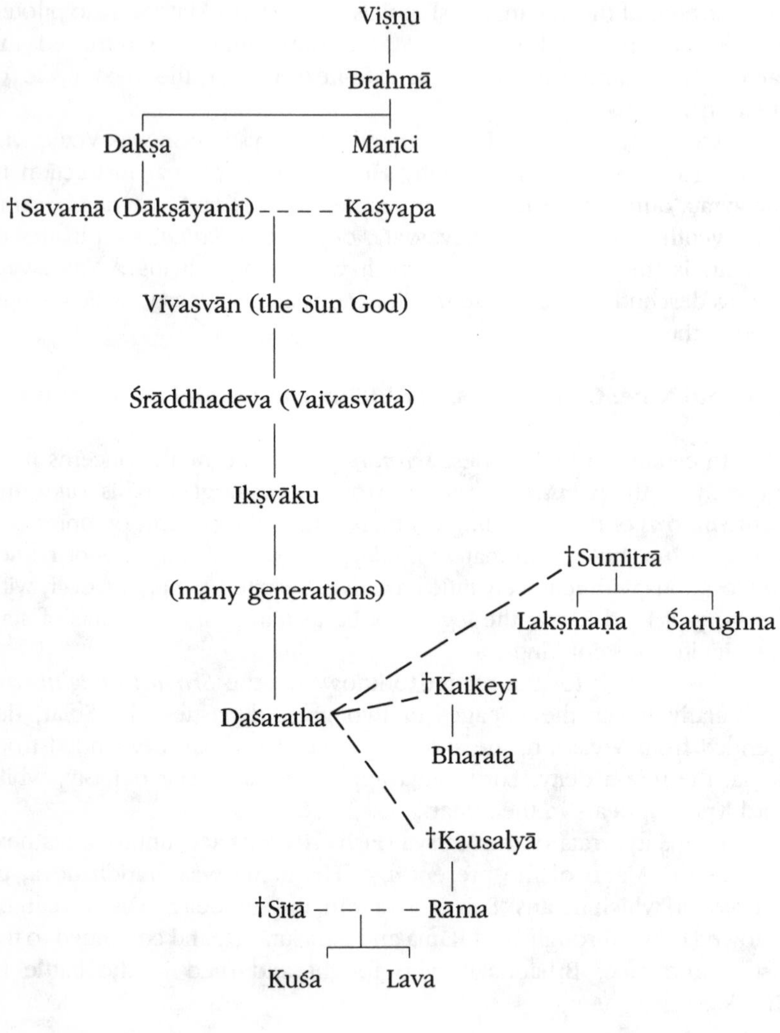

--- denotes marriage
† denotes a woman

Though his wealth and power were incomparable at the time, Ambarīṣa knew that worldly wealth was insubstantial, a fleeting dream, and thus he utilized everything he possessed in the service of Lord Hari and the holy men. With his mind, he concentrated unceasingly on Kṛṣṇa; with his mouth, he praised Him; with his ears he listened to accounts of sacred *līlā.* He engaged his eyes in seeing the consecrated image, his senses of smell and touch in partaking of temple offerings, his head in bowing to the Lord present everywhere, his feet in circumambulating the temple. With his wealth he adored the Supreme Being by sponsoring religious rituals and giving generously to holy people (9.4.15-28). Thus we have another example of the graceful blending of worldly and spiritual life. Clearly, King Ambarīṣa's *yoga* was action oriented; he was not a recluse or contemplative, but rather consecrated his body, actions, and possessions by utilizing them spiritually and, most importantly, cultivating *inner detachment.* One can be surrounded by the world and not a bit affected by it.

Chapters Ten and Eleven contain a condensed *Rāmāyaṇa* which covers the major events in Lord Rāma's life, albeit skeletally. For a full treatment of the Rāma Incarnation, please refer to Chapter Twenty-Six of this volume, where the *Rāmāyaṇa* is examined. Besides Śrī Kṛṣṇa, Rāma is the most widely worshipped Incarnation and the object of some of India's most ecstatic devotional literature.

Heroes of the Lunar Dynasty

The Lunar dynasty can be traced back to Atri, one of the original ten Prajāpatis born from Lord Brahmā. Soma, the moon deity, was born from Atri's tears of bliss, and Soma's son was Budha. Budha married Ilā who, incidentally, was the daughter of Śrāddhadeva, so the Solar and Lunar dynasties had an early historical link, through marriage. Ilā's story is told in the first chapter of this canto, and it's a strange one. Originally born a female, through magic she was turned into a strapping male named Sudyumna. Due to a mishap, Sudyumna was later to have his gender change from male to female and back again each month. He continued to rule, though his subjects were never quite reconciled to him.

Ilā and Budha's son Purūravas married the celestial nymph Urvaśī, and their story is somewhat reminiscent of the Greek myth of Cupid and Psyche. In both cases, the marriage between a human and a supernatural being is dependent on a promise — in the Greek case, that the wife never see the husband, and in the Indian, that she never see him naked. In both cases, meddlesome others cause the promise to be broken while the couple are in bed at night, and the lovers part.

Thirteen generations later, the *Avatāra* Paraśurāma ("Rāma with an Axe") appeared. Like several other *Avatāras,* such as Nṛsiṃhadeva and Kalki, His principal purpose was to purge the world of evil through apparently violent means. In fact, the Paraśurāma account is one of the most gruesome bloodbaths in Hindu legend. He certainly personifies the destructive power of the Divine, as His twenty-one campaigns against the entire *kṣatriya* caste brought them to the brink of extinction. They had become corrupt, persecuting and murdering holy men, plundering the celestial realms and generally becoming a burden on the world. Only a very few survived to repopulate the caste. It was the *kṣatriya's* collective *karma* that brought them to this curious fate, and God's inconceivable mercy that He would liberate them all by delivering the blows Himself. When He finished, Paraśurāma at once abandoned His fighting propensities and retired to Mount Mahendra to live as a gentle, peaceful contemplative. It's said that He exists there still.

The rest of the canto traces the descent of the Lunar dynasty down to the advent of Lord Kṛṣṇa. The race split into two clans, the Yādavas, or descendants of Yadu, and the Pauravas, the descendants of Puru. Yadu and Puru were brothers, the sons of Yayāti. The two clans combined again, through the marriage of Kuntī and Pāṇḍu, during the last phases of the dynasty's existence, when the cast of characters of the *Mahābhārata* saga appeared. Queen Kuntī, remember, delivered the famous prayers to Śrī Kṛṣṇa in the first canto.

Before we get to this divine drama, however, the reader should be aware of a couple of important stories concerning earlier figures in the line. The tale of the patriarch Yayāti is often invoked to illustrate how sensual indulgence always leads to frustration. Like so many Americans of today who are infatuated with youth, this king had no intention of growing old. He wanted to continue wallowing in the sort of pleasures which require youthful vigor, and because no one can stop the onset of age, he attempted to cheat it by swapping his old age for the youth of one of his sons. After approaching his four eldest sons and being flatly refused, he approached Puru, his youngest, and secured his assent. Thus the young man became aged and the selfish father threw himself into hedonistic fun.

After about a thousand years, Yayāti suddenly came to an awareness of the stupidity of his condition. No matter how luxuriantly he fed his senses, he never found satisfaction, only futility. He told his wife:

> All the foods in the world, all animals, all wealth, and all women cannot bring satiety to a man whose mind is victim to inordinate desire. Desire is never satisfied by enjoyment of its objects. Like fire

The Lunar Dynasty

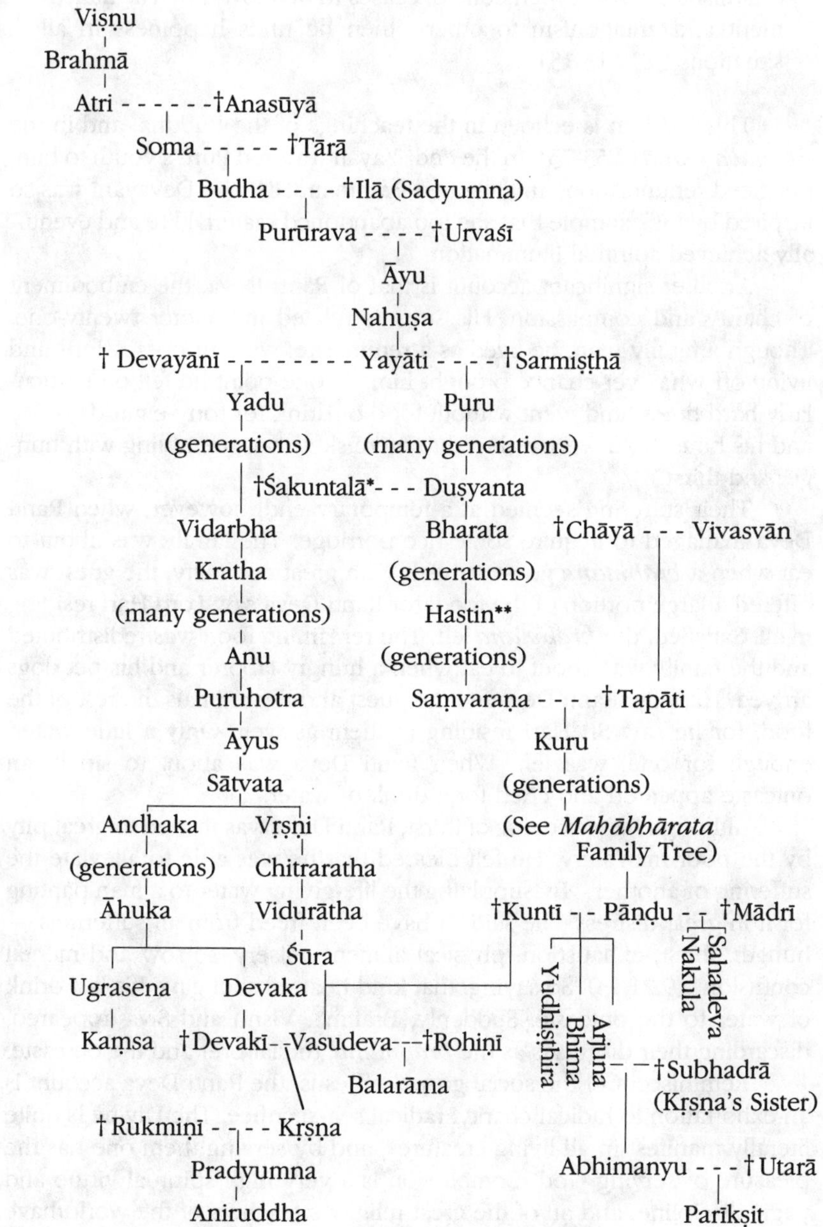

- - - denotes marriage
† denotes a woman

*(as in Kalidāsa's play)
**(as in Hastināpura)

> fed by ghee, it only flames up all the more. When a man's mind, established in same-sightedness, ceases to be moved by vile attachment and antagonism to others, then he finds happiness in all situations (9.19.13-15).

This wisdom is echoed in the teachings of the Buddha, and in the *Bhagavad-Gītā* (2.53-73). In the end, Yayāti restored Puru's youth to him, practiced renunciation, and attained Brahman. His wife Devayānī was so inspired by his example that she too abandoned material life and eventually achieved spiritual illumination.

Another significant account is that of Ranti Deva, the embodiment of charity and compassion. His story is related in chapter twenty-one. Though a family man, he lived as a renunciate, without possessions and living off whatever chance brought him. At one point he fell on particularly hard times, and went without food or drink for forty-eight days. He and his household were reduced to mere skeletons, trembling with hunger and thirst.

Their suffering seemed at a temporary end, however, when Ranti Deva managed to acquire some rice porridge. The family was about to eat when a *brāhmaṇa* guest arrived. With great cordiality, the guest was offered a large portion of the food, for Ranti Deva saw Lord Hari residing in all. Satisfied, the *brāhmaṇa* left. The remaining food was redistributed and the family was about to eat when a hungry laborer and his pet dogs arrived. Happily, Ranti Deva fed the guest and the animals the rest of the food, for he saw Śrī Hari residing in them as well. Only a little water, enough for one, was left. When Ranti Deva was about to sip it, an outcaste appeared and cried for a drink of water.

Although he was dying of thirst, Ranti Deva was moved to great pity by the poor man's cry. He felt blessed that he was able to alleviate the suffering of another. "By supplying the life-giving water to a man panting for it in great distress," he said, "I have been freed from all sufferings — hunger, thirst, exhaustion, physical ailment, misery, sorrow and mental confusion" (9.21.13). So saying, that kind-hearted soul gave his last drink of water to the outcaste. Suddenly, Brahmā, Viṣṇu and Śiva appeared, discarding their disguises as the *brāhmaṇa*, the laborer and the outcaste.

Reminiscent of the social gospel of Jesus, the Ranti Deva account is an exhortation to radical charity, radical self-sacrifice. The Divine is quite literally manifest in all living creatures, and by serving them one has the pleasure of serving God. Compassion is a very high spiritual virtue and yogic discipline, and all of the great religious teachers of the world have made it central to their message. Buddha, it's said, was prepared to sacrifice his own life to save the life of a goat. Jesus said, "Be compassionate as your Father is compassionate . . . because the amount you measure out is the amount you will be given back (Luke, 16.36.38). Says the Qur'an: "Those who spend their wealth in the cause of God (i.e. in charity) by night and day, secretly and openly, have their reward with their Lord; on them shall come no fear, nor shall they grieve" (2.275).[22] To treat everyone with love and compassion is a very difficult *sādhanā*, but one which everyone must master if they expect to reach the highest Goal.

Preamble to the Birth of Lord Kṛṣṇa

As we near the end of the ninth canto, the individuals who will figure in the life of Lord Kṛṣṇa begin to be born. These genealogies serve as an introduction to the spectacular tenth canto which will relate the story of Kṛṣṇa in painstaking and loving detail. The *Śrīmad Bhāgavatam* only gives an outline of the family web, a full account being contained already in the *Mahābhārata.* It is assumed, too, that the audience is already familiar with all of these characters, so deeply do they weave in and out of the fabric of Indian cultural life. The object is to provide a context for the advent of this unique *Avatāra.* The canto closes with a beautiful preamble to the most blessed of stories:

> As the eighth son of Vasudeva and Devakī, the supreme Hari Himself appeared as the perfect incarnation Śrī Kṛṣṇa . . . Whenever there is a decline in *dharma* and an ascendancy of *adharma* the supreme Lord embodies Himself . . . His sportive activity has a twofold aspect — to maintain the order of creation, sustenance and dissolution on the one hand and, on the other, to redeem the *jīvas* from this cycle of worldly existence caused by Himself, and establish them in the bliss of their Ātmanhood . . . Man overcomes the bondage of tendencies generated by *karma* if he but once imbibes with his ears even a handful of the waters of the rivers of His holy fame, which is a veritable ambrosia . . . The Lord delighted the whole world with that form of His — of which every limb was a piece of thrilling beauty — with His charming smile and looks and gracious speech and with His sportive actions which were cast in a heroic mould (9.24.55,56,58,62,64).

Assuming the form of a human being, the canto concludes, He departed to Vraja and fulfilled the deepest longings of the inhabitants there, destroyed enemies, married many wives and fathered many children, performed sacred rites (in which He actually worshipped Himself) in order to exemplify the dharmic way of life, relieved the earth's burden (which had taken the form of the Kauravas) by conferring victory in war on Yudhiṣṭhira, and revealed the Supreme Truth to Uddhava, His beloved disciple. In these acts He fully accomplished the object of His Incarnation, and once done He resumed His transcendental, all-pervading state.

Canto Ten: The Life of Śrī Kṛṣṇa

At last we come to the marvelous tenth *skandha*, the very heart and soul of the *Śrīmad Bhāgavatam.* One could almost say that the first nine cantos serve as a lengthy introduction to or, more specifically, a preparatory course of study for, the tenth canto. Throughout the text so far, God has been referred to by many names — Nārāyaṇa, Hari, Viṣṇu, and sometimes Kṛṣṇa — yet there has been a sense of Kṛṣṇa suggested in all of them. Viṣṇu and Kṛṣṇa are non-different, but there has been an implicit feeling of incompleteness in the world up to this point. Though the Divine is constantly acting in and through the world, a full revelation has not yet occurred. Kṛṣṇa's advent is this full revelation, the purest, most powerful, and most complete manifestation of *Sat-Cit-Ānanda Parabrahman.*

The tenth *skandha* feels different from the rest of the book. It has a magic about it. There is nothing you will ever read which quite resembles it, for it is unique in all world literature, sacred or secular. From a strictly aesthetic standpoint it is gloriously beautiful, but from a philosophical and religious standpoint it accomplishes something more amazing: it describes that which is indescribable, captures in time and space that which is eternal and infinite, makes understandable that which is inconceivable. The eternal Reality which the *Upaniṣads* suggest through abstraction and metaphor is made tangible in the person Kṛṣṇa. We can, without performing a single meditation or making one inch worth of spiritual progress see, hear, feel and come to intimately know the Ultimate Truth.

As soon as one begins to study the tenth canto, the importance of having methodically moved through the first nine becomes apparent. In order to fully experience the effects of the tenth, the mind must be adequately in tune and receptive. It must be primed. This is true of any book, in a way; one might attempt a reading one year and fail to get caught up in it, then pick it up again another year and, because one is now receptive to it, be deeply moved by the same words. In the case of the *Śrīmad Bhāgavatam*, or any sacred text, this receptivity may mean the difference between leaps in spiritual progress and inching along. Kṛṣṇa lives in the text. It is believed to be a theophany, a tangible manifestation of Himself which He left behind so that we can always reach Him. If one is receptive to it, the tenth *skandha* will bring one face to face with the actual, living Deity, Kṛṣṇa.

Kṛṣṇa's life is far too long and detailed to adequately synopsize here. The tenth canto is ninety chapters long, nearly four thousand verses. It makes for fairly quick reading, though, because the subject is so fascinating and the style so exhilarating. The life is broken down into three main segments: infancy and childhood; adolescence, when He romances the *gopīs*; and adulthood, when He assumes the duties of a statesman, family man and spiritual teacher. We will examine the relevance of these periods in turn.

One of the most brilliant features of Lord Kṛṣṇa is that the scope of His life allows ample opportunity for the aspirant to enter into a personal, loving relationship with Him in whatever earthly relationship the devotee finds most relishable. His life sets a precedent in this way, unmatched in any other religious tradition, or even within Hinduism itself. Instead of being subdued, our most powerful emotions are utilized in the struggle for God-realization.

According to *bhakti* theory, we can assume any of a number of *rasas*, or sentiments, in our devotional life. We can take the role of parent to the baby or child Deity, as Mother Yaśodā did to the infant Kṛṣṇa (or the Holy Virgin to the Christ Child). This *rasa* is known as *vātsalya.* If we approach God as friend, as did Arjuna, Uddhava, or the cowherd boys, this is *sakhya rasa.* Considering ourselves servants of an adored Master, like Kaṃsa's messenger Akrūra, is known as *dāsya.* God and devotee can enter into the relationship of passionate lovers, as did Kṛṣṇa and the *gopīs* (*madhura*) or as lovers suffering the pangs of separation, also exhibited by the *gopīs.* Finally, there is the attitude of complete absorption, which was experienced by many devotees who heard of Kṛṣṇa but never had the chance to meet Him in the flesh and therefore availed themselves to meditation on His image in their hearts, which brought them God-realization (*tanmaya*).[23]

Kṛṣṇa's life story is a primer on the theory and execution of *bhakti yoga.* Everything He does is ripe with meaning, and every relationship, loving or antagonistic, exemplifies a spiritual path. One may love God in any fashion one likes by emulating and intimately identifying with the figures that played key roles in this sacred drama. They are not ordinary people, but mystics of the highest order acting the parts of ordinary people for the benefit of the world. The canto opens with Lord Brahmā announcing to the *devas* that the Supreme Being will soon advent Himself and that He commands the celestials to take birth as human beings in order to help Him play out His divine *līlā* (10.1.21-25). Whenever an Incarnation comes, He brings His heavenly entourage with Him.

The Birth of Kṛṣṇa

On the day of Vasudeva and Devakī's (Kṛṣṇa's parents) wedding, Kṛṣṇa's maternal uncle Kaṃsa heard a disembodied voice tell of Kaṃsa's death at the hands of Devakī's eighth child. Without a moment's delay, he grabbed his sister by the hair and raised his sword to decapitate her. Vasudeva frantically intercepted. He talked Kaṃsa out of killing her, but Kaṃsa promptly imprisoned them both and, over the course of some years, seized and murdered every baby Devakī bore. The only child to survive was her seventh, who was miraculously transferred to the womb of Vasudeva's other wife, Rohiṇī. This was Balarāma, Kṛṣṇa's constant companion and Co-*Avatāra.*

In his bloated pride, Kaṃsa thought he could cheat both death and *karma,* but one can easily foresee the outcome of his desperate efforts. Kaṃsa, remember, is the final reincarnation of Jaya, the heavenly gatekeeper cursed by the Kumāras in the seventh canto, and whom we have also seen before as Prahlāda's demoniac father, Hiraṇyakaśipu. Fate decreed that he would be redeemed through mortal combat with Kṛṣṇa. God's compassion is such that even the most wretched of beings is granted spiritual liberation by His touch.

The event of Śrī Kṛṣṇa's birth is extraordinary in every respect. While up in heaven the celestials rejoiced with songs and drums, the earth was still and silent. At exactly midnight, the Lord was born, "like the full moon rising on the eastern horizon" (10.3.8). At the same time, out in the countryside, the simple cowherd's wife, Yaśodā, gave birth to a daughter. But this was no ordinary daughter; she was Yogamāyā Herself, an incarnation of the Divine Mother. Back in Mathurā, Vasudeva and Devakī praised the incarnate Lord with Hymns. Assuming His Viṣṇu form, the Lord imparted instructions, including the *bhakti yoga* method of *vātsalya rasa* mentioned before: "Thinking of Me again and again as both Brahman and your son, you will rise to higher and higher stages of divine love and attain to My state" (10.3.45). Viṣṇu disappeared and only the baby Kṛṣṇa was left. Suddenly, the heavily-chained doors of the prison opened by themselves and the guards fell into a deep sleep. With Kṛṣṇa in his arms, Vasudeva stole away and headed for Vraja.

A storm blew in, but the wonderful snake deity Ādiśeṣa appeared and protected the father and child by sheltering them under his raised hoods. The river Yamunā, which Vasudeva had to cross, parted her waters for him. When Vasudeva arrived in Vraja, he found Yaśodā asleep; she knew only that she had delivered, but had lost consciousness before learning the gender of her child. Vasudeva switched the babies and returned to the prison in Mathurā with the girl.

As soon as he heard the news that Devakī had borne another child, Kaṃsa ran to the spot, snatched the tiny thing out of Devakī's arms and dashed her brains out against a stone slab. Suddenly the baby leapt into the air and assumed Her real form as the radiant, eight-armed Goddess, Yogamāyā. "Fool!" She screamed. "Infant killer! Your enemy is safe, far from here!" (10.4.12). Kaṃsa released Devakī and Vasudeva from prison, but ordered a slaughter of all infants within his jurisdiction.

Śrī Kṛṣṇa's birth story bears striking resemblance to the birth stories of Moses, Oedipus, Siegfried and Jesus. This may be due to the exchanges of ideas between civilizations, or to the existence of an archetypal hero myth rooted deep in the human psyche. Another possibility is that whenever and wherever the Divine manifests Itself, certain predictable patterns follow.

Gopāla, or Kṛṣṇa in His Infancy and Childhood

Gopāla, the boy Kṛṣṇa, is characterized by both playful mischievousness and tremendous power. He gracefully slips back and forth between the two aspects and in a few cases combines them. His charm and naughtiness are characteristic of the divine "trickster", a universal religious archetype. It reflects the inscrutable, unpredictable nature of reality and the way the God, or the gods, appear to take pleasure in playing games with us. Life is incredibly funny most of the time, and no one is laughing more merrily than God.

Naughty Kṛṣṇa, though exasperating, brings supreme joy to His elders. Their anger never lasts long. He bats His lotus-like eyes, pouts His pretty lips, sheds a few counterfeit tears and before you know it the adult is overcome with love and sweeps the child up in her arms. The naughtiness is also partly a guise designed to obscure His Godhood from them. Were His contemporaries aware of His true identity, they would be too overawed to exchange the natural, loving intimacies for which He incarnated Himself. They must mistake Him for an ordinary boy and so, like a regular boy, Kṛṣṇa is sometimes a pest. This is all the effect of *māyā*, which Kṛṣṇa has spun like a veil over the perceptions of His devotees. For a brief time, these great souls were as addled as the rest of us and, just like us, failed to recognize the Divine when It was right in front of them. Occasionally they would have a glimpse, or even a revelation, but would soon forget it and revert back to their common perceptions. This, again, resembles the experience of the ordinary, struggling aspirant.

Among Kṛṣṇa's many pranks, the most significant is His thiefdom. He and His brother Balarāma slipped from house to house in the cowherd settlement, stealing curds and butter. Often they broke the earthenware pots in which the edibles were stored, or poked holes in the bottom of hanging pots and licked up what dripped out. So beloved is this aspect of Kṛṣṇa, many *Vaiṣṇavas* worship images of Kṛṣṇa crawling on hands and knees and holding up a ball of butter. Kṛṣṇa's preoccupation with milk and butter is tied in to His close connection to cows and to the rural idyll in which they are raised.

Cows, of course, are revered in India, being a universal Mother Goddess symbol. This is not strictly a psychological phenomenon; cattle are the mainstay of Indian rural life and, as far as we know, always have been. Milk and milk products are a staple element of the Indian diet, and dung is used as fuel for cooking and heating. Bulls are work animals which pull plows and grindstones. In the Indian economy the cow is literally life itself. Dead cows mean dead humans. The bull is a father who works the land while the cow is a mother who feeds her hungry human children along with her calves. In mythology, the earth is personified as a cow. In the *Śrīmad Bhāgavatam's* first canto, King Parīkṣit discovered the earth, in the form of a cow, being tortured by the personification of *Kali Yuga*.

That Lord Kṛṣṇa, the most complete Incarnation, should be so closely associated with the Mother Earth Goddess in the form of the cow demonstrates the genius of Hinduism. There are no disparate elements in the Divine; all aspects are necessary, beautiful and harmonious. All forms of worship are true, all Gods and Goddesses are true; the simple, provincial religion of the Cow Deity is one with the manifestation of the Upaniṣadic Brahman. There is no such thing as primitive religion; all religious conceptions are one. In Kṛṣṇa as cowherd, the Earth, which is sacred in its own right, and Heaven, in other words *prakṛti* and *Puruṣa*, Yin and Yang, Spirit and Matter, join and find completion.

More than just a thief of butter, Kṛṣṇa is the thief of love. The pots of butter represent the hearts of devotees. He breaks through the hard outer shell (ego, desire, ignorance, etc.) and releases the soft, sweet Self within, the Ātman. This He "devours"; the soul attains union with God and is subsumed into the Universal Soul. It is often a painful process. The women of Vraja and the pots of butter are doubles; Kṛṣṇa's breaking the pots corresponds to His breaking their hearts by prolonging the agony of the soul's yearning for Him, and the ladies' anger reflects the frustration of the soul struggling for Him. But like the butter inside which He devours, the women soften to Him, are overcome with love for Him, and surrender gladly to this love.

The women are helpless against Him, just as the *jīva* is helpless against the irresistible lure of Brahman. Nor can the *jīva* affect Brahman in any way. This is illustrated in a simple incident (recounted in Chapter Nine) where Yaśodā, unable to control Kṛṣṇa's antics, attempted to tie Him to a mortar. Though she started out with plenty of rope, when she tried to tie the knot, it came up short. She added another length of rope and again it came up too short. More and more she added, never able to bring the two ends together. "He who has neither inside nor outside, who has neither before nor after . . . nay, who is the universe itself — Him, the Unmanifest and Supreme . . . Him, the *gopī*, taking for her child, tried to fasten to the mortar" (10.9.13-14).

God cannot be measured, cannot be manipulated. Yet by virtue of the devotees' love, God *allows* Himself to be "confined", that is directly perceived, even within the limited framework of human cognition. He becomes bound to and by His own devotee. Kṛṣṇa took pity on His poor mother, who was by now perspiring and dishevelled, and allowed Himself to be bound to the mortar. This is a very significant incident, illustrating the closeness between the Beloved and the lover and how the Absolute, by the power of love, subordinates Itself to the aspirant. In honor of this pastime, Kṛṣṇa is referred to as Dāmodara, the one with the rope (*dāma*) around His belly (*udara*).

Kṛṣṇa's magnificent powers are displayed in the effortless conquest of many demons sent by Kaṃsa, and by occasional one-upmanship games with the gods. The most celebrated confrontation with a demon was His subduing of the multi-hooded cobra monster Kāliya (Chapters Sixteen and Seventeen). In this incident, the horribly poisonous creature took up residence in the Yamunā river, along the banks of which the cowherd community lived. So potent was his venom that everything which touched the water died, and fumes rose from the surface and struck birds right out of the air. Never had the village been ravaged by such a wave of deaths. Young Kṛṣṇa came to the rescue. After resurrecting all of the victims, He plunged into the poisonous waters and wrestled with the serpent. Climbing onto the creature's hoods, the comely hero performed a dance and stomped the beast into submission. The image of lovely Kṛṣṇa dancing atop the many-hooded serpent is a favorite subject of painting and sculpture. Kṛṣṇa makes even killing beautiful.

Kṛṣṇa subdued gods as well, at least those arrogant enough to challenge Him. Scholars suggest that His overpowering Indra, a once-worshipped but now largely ignored Vedic deity, and Brahmā, also a deity no longer accorded worship, signifies the shift away from Vedic ritualism and its elemental pantheon to the religion embodied in the *Purāṇas.* In the episode concerning Brahmā (Chapters Thirteen and Fourteen), Kṛṣṇa and Balarāma, now old enough to have taken on chores, went out into the countryside with the other *gopas*, or cowherd boys, to graze the calves. Wanting to test Kṛṣṇa's powers, Brahmā spirited the boys and calves away and hid them in his abode, where they were kept perpetually asleep. To spare the village folk grief, Kṛṣṇa expanded Himself into perfect replicas, exact in every physical and personality detail, of each boy and calf. A year went by and the parents and cows never suspected a thing, only their love for their young ones was inexplicably more intense and achingly sweet. Brahmā arrived to inspect the scene and found, to his consternation and amazement, another set of boys and calves. As he looked on, he saw them all turn into radiant Viṣṇu forms, and then into the Supreme Parabrahman. Thrilled to the bone, he offered Kṛṣṇa one of the most exalted hymns in the *Śrīmad Bhāgavatam* (Chapter Fourteen). It extols the glories of *bhakti*, the infinitude and exquisiteness of the Lord, and the mystery of divine Incarnation. Even if you skip over other sections of the *Bhagavatam*, this part is not to be missed.

The obstruction of the *Indra Yajña* and subsequent lifting of Mt. Govardhana (Chapters Twenty-Four and Twenty-Five) is another oft-recounted incident, from which Kṛṣṇa derives the epithet Lala Giridhāra, "One Who Lifts the Mountain". The Vṛndāvana community were preparing for a large *Indra Yajña*, or sacrifice to Lord Indra thanking him for the rain he sends. Kṛṣṇa, in His typical trickster fashion, talked them out of it. Indra was so infuriated by this slight, he sent forth a torrent so ferocious everyone's lives were in danger. Again, Kṛṣṇa came to the rescue, this time by lifting Mt. Govardhana, a very long, low mountain, and holding it over the settlement like a giant umbrella. For seven days He stood motionless, balancing the mountain on the tip of His little finger. Indra was dumbfounded. So were the *gopas*, who finally began to suspect Kṛṣṇa's true identity.

The most significant incidents in Kṛṣṇa's life are not the awe-inspiring demonstrations of power, but precisely the opposite. It is the quieter moments which strike a chord in the hearts of spiritual aspirants. Not so much what He does but what He *is* makes the difference. His gentleness, His playfulness, His sweetness and affection, His tender concern for everyone, His bewitching smile, melting eyes and graceful movements, His genius and humor, everything together amounts to a Being ultimately worshipable as the Absolute Truth and yet infinitely lovable and approachable. His irresistible physical beauty and mesmerizing charm are far more indicative of His divinity than supernatural deeds because these are what grip the hearts of devotees and, in mystics, inspire ecstacy, *samādhi* and, eventually, God-realization.

One day some of Kṛṣṇa's playmates approached Yaśodā with the complaint that Kṛṣṇa was eating dirt. She went to the spot, scolded the child, and looked into his mouth. Within His body she saw the entire universe, the heavens, the deities, Time, Nature, the *guṇas*, the twenty-four cosmic elements, all things in all possible configurations. The theological implications of the vision are important, but equally important is her reaction. She did not relish the vision at all. With awe and reverence she accepted it, but she much preferred the Kṛṣṇa she could know and love as a person, her own cuddly boy. In other words, she adored Kṛṣṇa not because He is the omnipotent, omnipresent, sovereign Godhead, but because He is so sweet. She loved Him because He was lovable, and for no other reason. This is the ideal of *bhakti*, a very high level of spiritual attainment. Knowing Yaśodā's deepest feelings, Kṛṣṇa not only removed the vision, but also erased any memory Yaśodā had of the experience. Once again, she knew Him only as her beloved child.

Govinda, the Lover of the Gopīs

If the tenth *skandha* is the heart of the *Śrīmad Bhāgavatam*, the five chapters describing the *rāsa-līlā*, Kṛṣṇa's love affairs with the *gopīs* (Chapters Twenty-Nine through Thirty-Three), are the heart of the tenth *skandha*. Nothing quite compares to the *rāsa-līlā* in all religious literature, though the Biblical Song of Songs resembles it in its use of romantic love as a metaphor. The *rāsa-līlā* is not exactly erotic because no sexual intercourse takes place. There is much passionate gazing and sighing, fully clothed hugging and kissing, caresses, love talk, but that's where it stops. What we have is the most delicious intensity of *emotion*. Emotion is the point — explosive, excruciating, delectable, sublime — and the *gopīs* embody the highest love of God to be found anywhere. Their bodily sensations are irrelevant because they are merely physical responses to the *gopīs'* acute emotional states. Rare is the person whose passion for God reaches the level of the *gopīs'*; that is why the *rāsa-līlā* is so difficult to understand.

In dazzlingly pristine detail, the text describes the balmy, fragrant nights which set the scene for this very rare event. A cool breeze blew through the lush woods, the moon twinkled on the lotus-dotted waters and the bewitching sound of Kṛṣṇa's flute wafted to the ears of the *gopīs* in their homes. Abandoning whatever they were doing, throwing all thought of social propriety and reputation to the wind, the young ladies slipped away and followed the music into the privacy of the forest. There they met Kṛṣṇa, to whom their entire beings — minds, hearts, bodies, souls — were devoted. There is nothing which compares to the love they felt; it was all-consuming, unknown in the conditioned world except to mystics, who even then only realize a fraction of it.

After talking to them awhile, allowing them to bask in His unimaginable beauty and thus intensify their already excruciating ardor, Kṛṣṇa suddenly disappeared, throwing the poor supplicants into a frenzy of grief. This incident, which may seem cruel, is extremely important because it accurately portrays a phenomenon all serious spiritual aspirants experience, what St. John of the Cross called "the dark night of the soul". After making some tangible spiritual progress and experiencing the closeness and grace of God, an aspirant will undoubtedly be thrown into a "dry period", that is, a sense of God suddenly withdrawing. It is a ghastly experience, where one feels suddenly submerged in the profane, abandoned by God, spiritually dry and brittle as a bone. St. John suggests, as does the *Śrīmad Bhāgavatam*, that these periods are actually brought on by God Himself with the intent of forcing the aspirant to a new stage of development.

The abandonment accomplishes two things. It deflates the devotee's subtle egotism ("Look how spiritual I am"), while forcing him or her to think even more about God ("Why has God gone silent? Where did He go? How can I go on living when I've been cut off from the only thing that has meaning?") and yearn for Him more intensely. In their separation, the *gopīs* were so stricken with despair they could think of nothing but Kṛṣṇa. Thus their minds were fixed on Him as solidly as the *yogī's* mind is fixed in meditation. They plaintively sang out their feelings:

> O Dear Lover, Your assuming of a form is verily for the erasing of the miseries of all . . . How then are You so miserly in administering that medicine, held in such abundance by You, to cure the heart's ailment of us, who are Your own? O Lord! Tarry not to come before our vision (10.32.18).

Chapter Thirty-Three marks the climax of the *rāsa-līlā* in the *rāsa* dance, or circle dance. It is the zenith of spiritual experience, the ecstatic union of God and *jīva*. Back in the *gopīs'* midst, Śrī Kṛṣṇa initiated the collective dance, expanding Himself into as many Kṛṣṇas as there were *gopīs*, so that each girl had her own, personal Kṛṣṇa to love. In a group they sang joyously and danced in a circle like a living *maṇḍala* (a circular sacred diagram used in meditation and ritual) while individually, each *gopī* exchanged intimate caresses with her divine Partner. "Just like an emerald between two golden beads, Kṛṣṇa shone between the *gopīs* on both His sides" (10.33.7).

The celestials in their aerial chariots arrived to watch from the sky and shower blossoms onto the auspicious scene. *Gandharvas*, the heavenly musicians, sang and played. From the air, Kṛṣṇa's dancing forms resembled turbulent dark storm clouds and the *gopīs* brilliant flashes of lightning. One girl held her cheek against Kṛṣṇa's; another held His sanctifying hands against her breasts; another kissed His fingers resting on her shoulders. All abandoned themselves completely to Him, and He reciprocated utterly. Though God is ultimately independent and eternally unaffected, we must remember too that He is Love Itself. The *gopīs* could not love Kṛṣṇa more than He loved them. Kṛṣṇa returned their love in infinitely greater degree, endowing them with *ānanda*, inconceivable bliss. Such an exchange of mutual passion resulted in the highest mystical union.

In the circle we have a symbol of completeness, eternality, perfection. That Kṛṣṇa assumed a form particular to each individual *gopī* reflects that principle of *Iṣṭa-devatā*, the Chosen Ideal, where the Divine, though indivisible and One, assumes innumerable forms for the sake of aspirants and devotees. Each person must approach God in his or her own way, and therefore Brahman assumes a personality uniquely suited to each aspirant. Though two people may worship Śiva, for instance, the Śiva one imagines is, of course, somewhat different than the Śiva the other imagines. Because Śiva is all-encompassing, though, they are both right.

The spiritual experience here takes the form of a dance. The whole cosmic manifestation is a sort of dance — the dance of Brahman expressing Itself — and there are dances within the dance. The galaxies and solar systems whirl perpetually in a dance of the universe; the seasons turn in a cyclical dance of nature; the ocean tides dance in and out. The world also dances in a free form: water dancing as it splashes through a creek bed, bees dancing to communicate the location of pollen, whales leaping into the air for no apparent reason other than the sheer joy of being alive. The unfolding of the *jīva's* consciousness through evolution and the return to the divine Source through involution is the most extraordinary dance of all.

In a sense, the *gopīs* were prophetesses of the highest order, for they paved the way for a new and improved form of spirituality. It is a radical *yoga*, still shocking to some people. In it, God is known so intimately the aspirant's sense of awe, or smallness, or constitutional difference gradually disappears and the Deity is experienced as the most precious Beloved. It is more intimate, even, than the closest human relationship, for God and devotee can blend their very beings, move in and out of the hearts and minds of one another. The Beloved and the lover are ultimately One already, it is simply a matter of realizing it. To affect this intimate love, the aspirant must let go of reverential awe as well as personal shame. This is more difficult than it sounds. The *gopīs*, however, represent the perfection of this mode of spirituality, the absolute summit of *bhakti*.

Dvārakādīśa: Kṛṣṇa the King of Dvārakā

The remainder of the tenth *skandha* reads like a swashbuckling action novel. It is great fun, full of violence and romance. Kṛṣṇa is a *kṣatriya*, a member of the warrior caste, and it is His *dharma* to rule a kingdom, marry many women, and wage war against enemies. In the eleventh canto He will assume the role of spiritual teacher, but until that point His is an action-oriented life. He is the great deliverer, freeing populations from tyrants, swooping into assemblies and carrying off damsels about to marry against their wishes (they get to marry Him instead), lavishing wealth and success on anyone who loves Him, purging the world of evil, ministering to the poor and helpless, and rewarding the good. He is every inch the messianic king, the spiritual *and material* savior.

When Kṛṣṇa reached His early teens, the time came for Him to enter public life and fulfill His destiny. He had to leave forever the pastoral idyll of Vṛndāvana and the residents there who loved Him as their very life. The departure is a heartbreaking scene, with disconsolate *gopīs* obstructing the wheels of His chariot with their own bodies, and everyone weeping helplessly. But Kṛṣṇa had an appointment with fate in the city of Mathurā. Kaṃsa, at last discovering Kṛṣṇa's whereabouts, had challenged Him to a wrestling match, where he intended to kill the boy once and for all. In the arena, before the assembled eyes of the whole city, Kṛṣṇa easily slew His nemesis. After installing Ugrasena as the king of Mathurā, Kṛṣṇa established His own kingdom, Dvārakā, on the western seashore.

The adult Kṛṣṇa of the *Mahābhārata* epic now emerges, as do the key characters of that drama: the Pāṇḍava princes, the tragic Draupadī, the courageous Queen Kuntī, blind Dhṛtarāṣṭra and his hundred sons led by the homicidal maniac Duryodhana, and so many others. We are nearing the close of a full circle, for this is the family into which King Parīkṣit will be born, the family whose story opened the *Śrīmad Bhāgavatam*.

Kṛṣṇa is reputed to have married 16,108 wives, but eight are considered preeminent: Satyabhāmā, Jāmbhavatī, Kalindī, Mitravindā, Satyā,

Lakṣmanā, Bhadrā, and Rukmiṇī, His principal queen. Rukmiṇī is the mother of Kṛṣṇa's foremost heir, Pradyumna, who is the incarnation of the god Kāma, the Hindu Cupid. Pradyumna and his son, Aniruddha, play important roles in the story, both of them being superexcellent warriors and legendary lovers, like their divine forebear. Like His multiple expansions in the *rāsa* dance, Kṛṣṇa expanded Himself into 16,108 Kṛṣṇas and maintained 16,108 separate palaces, one for each queen. In this way, He unstintingly gave of Himself, fulfilling the desires, spiritual and secular, of all who approached Him.

Kṛṣṇa's activities during this period are various and wonderful, but far too copious to discuss in fairness here. The reader should avail him or herself to the *Śrīmad Bhāgavatam* itself and enjoy the pageantry. Though aspirants generally concentrate on the Kṛṣṇa of Vṛndāvana in their devotional lives, the royal Kṛṣṇa is every bit as much the *Avatāra*, only now His opulence and glory are fully manifest. In Vṛndāvana, they were partly hidden; He was as if wearing a partial disguise, and this made Him more approachable. He was the darling of one's heart, not the gracious king to which one pays obeisances. Yet, He hasn't actually changed at all, only exchanged one role for another. He now more resembles His former Incarnation, Lord Rāma, at least in regard to His royal bearing and station. Śrī Rāma certainly commands the intense devotion of many, many Hindus; so should the princely Kṛṣṇa who, as we shall see, completes His earthly mission by imparting direct spiritual instruction. He is the original *guru*, the source and embodiment of all wisdom, and He came to earth to grant liberation to sincere souls.

Not to be missed is chapter eighty-seven, the Hymn of the *Vedas*, or *Śrutigītā*. Here a past incident is recalled, where the personified *Vedas* roused the Lord from His cosmic slumber during the universal dissolution by reciting His majesties. Rich with theological and metaphysical cogitations, it exhorts the *jīva* to renunciation and *bhakti*. It is a beautifully conceived piece, sometimes published alone, in a separate volume.

Canto Eleven: Kṛṣṇa's Last Days

The eleventh canto marks the beginning of the end. It opens with an account of the holy men's curse on the Yādava clan which would ultimately lead to the family's extinction. Śrī Kṛṣṇa's term on earth was nearing its close, and as He and His retinue were due to return to their unmanifest state, He did not interfere with the tragic events unfolding. Yet He had one more duty to perform, and on the last night of His life He delivered His final spiritual discourse, which is known as the *Uddhava Gītā*, after its recipient, Kṛṣṇa's friend and disciple Uddhava.

Teachings of the Navayogīs

Before this, however, four chapters are devoted to the sermon of the *Navayogīs* ("nine *yogīs*"). The *Navayogīs*, remember, were among the hundred sons of King Ṛṣabha, whom we met in the fifth *skandha*. These nine are mentioned again here when Kṛṣṇa's father, Vasudeva, approached Nārada for spiritual instruction. Nārada responded by recalling a dialogue between King Nimi and the liberated *Navayogīs*. Each *yogī* lectured on a different topic, and together the discourses form a marvelously concise overview of spiritual truth and practice. All the basics are here: theology, metaphysics, philosophy and *yoga* according to the *bhāgavata dharma*. If one were to read only this part of the *Śrīmad Bhāgavatam* and nothing else, one would have a decent understanding of its whole teachings.

Kavi speaks on *bhāgavata dharma*, which consists of dedicating all actions and thoughts to the Lord, chanting God's names constantly, and trying to see the Divine in everything and everyone (11.2.33-43). Hari describes what the saintly person practicing *bhāgavata dharma* is like, namely desireless, egoless, renounced, and cognizant of the Ātman in all creatures and of Śrī Hari everywhere (11.2.45-55). Antarikṣa lectures on the many aspects and manifestations of *māyā* and how *māyā* is responsible for creation, preservation and dissolution (11.3.3-16). Prabuddha discusses in detail practical methods for overcoming *māyā*. These include accepting a *guru*, renunciation of sense objects, seeking holy company, cultivating kindness, humility, purity, economy of speech, non-injury, and vision of the Supreme everywhere. Scriptural study is enjoined, as is austerity, charity, *japa*, and so on. Verses 11.3.18-30, in fact, comprise a good synopsis of the techniques of spiritual practice as a whole. Prabuddha concludes that advanced stages of *bhakti* practice result in *parabhakti*, the highest state of pure love, where one experiences the thrill of bliss and a variety of superconscious states, including *samādhi* (11.3.31-33).

Pippalāyana describes the glories of God and of the Ātman in a particularly expansive, Upaniṣadic sense (11.3.35-40). Āvihotra explains that the rituals prescribed by the Vedic texts have an indirect, mystical meaning not understood by worldly folk, who consider them mere formulae for invoking heavenly felicities. Actually, they lead one away from common sense-indulgence towards the state of Ātman-consciousness. He also briefly describes the method of image worship according to the Tantric tradition (11.3.43-55).

The whole of chapter four is given to Drumila's discussion of the divine Incarnations. Included is an account of the Nara-Nārāyaṇa Incarnation, whom Kāma (the god of romantic desire), on the order of Indra, tried to rouse from meditation by sending a company of heavenly beauties. Merely amused by this silly gesture, the Lord generated His own band of glorious women, all as spectacular as Śrī Devī Herself. This story reminds us that the beauty of beautiful people is merely a reflection of the beauty of God. Instead of succumbing to desire or envy, we can think of God whenever we see physical beauty, knowing that it is a special manifestation of His splendor. In this way we can be liberated from its lure.

In Chapter Five, Camasa denounces worldly-mindedness and sense-indulgence as these give way to cruelty and lead the individual to darkness and suffering. Particularly abhorrent are those who justify their indulgences by referring to Vedic passages (11.4.2-18). Though this reference to the Vedic tradition has little relevance to the Westerner, one should nevertheless recognize a strong correlation, namely unscrupulous Christians using the Bible as justification for their misdeeds. War, slaughter, oppression, tyranny, bigotry, persecution and most insane greed have all been justified through Biblical misinterpretation. This is on the big scale. On the small scale, ordinary individuals support their materialism, arrogance, judgementalism and hate through what they mistakenly think are Bible teachings. Ironic though it is, religion has always been a handy justification for all sorts of evil and vice. Certainly this isn't confined to Christianity; we have militant Islam serving as an excuse for violence, fraudulent famous *gurus* amassing millions of dollars, racial hatred disguised as Zionism, and so on. If there's one thing our *Bhāgavatam* teaches us, in fact all of the Hindu scriptures teach us, it is that religion is a path to complete freedom, universality, and oceanic love, not a facade behind which to hide our vices. Eventually, even the religion *itself* is to be transcended in favor of the pure Truth beyond all opposites and conditions. As Kṛṣṇa says in the *Bhagavad-Gītā*: "Abandoning all religion, take refuge in Me alone" (18.66).

The final lesson comes from Karabhājana who describes how the Lord is worshipped in different forms throughout the different *yugas*. In this *Kali-yuga*, He is to be adored in a form with a radiant black complexion (as Śrī Kṛṣṇa) and primarily by chanting His name and reciting His excellences. While we usually think of this *Kali-yuga* as an age of abject degradation, Karabhājana sees it in a different light:

> Great men who see into the heart of things and understand their good sides look upon this age of *Kali* with greater favor than the other ages. For in this age, man attains to his goal merely by extolling God's names and excellences (11.5.36).

God-realization was never so easy, God's grace never so abundant.

Kṛṣṇa's Last Discourse and Exit from the World

The celestials, headed by Lord Brahmā, appeared in Dvārakā to offer hymns to Śrī Kṛṣṇa and to remind Him that His sojourn on earth had come to an end. The Lord promised to depart as soon as the Yādava clan, as directed by the curse, had been annihilated. On the eve of this disaster, Kṛṣṇa's beloved disciple Uddhava approached Him in solitude and said, "O Keśava, my Lord! To remain even a minute without You is impossible for me. Therefore deign to take me also to Your realm with You" (11.6.43).

So Śrī Kṛṣṇa began His final discourse in the art of spiritual realization. His first exhortation: renounce. Give up all attachments, control the mind and senses, and see the whole world in the Ātman and the all-pervading Ātman as one with the Supreme (11.7.6-12). Very well, Uddhava replied, but how? As there are many paths to the Supreme and many different strategies and practices within each path, the answer to this question is necessarily voluminous and detailed. Just as the *Bhagavad-Gītā*, while part of the *Mahābhārata*, is a complete, separate unit unto itself, so too is the *Uddhava Gītā* an independent book, often published alone. For this reason, it is afforded its own chapter in this volume, where texts that are derivations of the *Purāṇas* are examined closely. The reader is therefore directed to chapter twenty-two for a full treatment of the *Uddhava Gītā*.

The *Uddhava Gītā* runs from Chapter Six through Chapter Twenty-Nine, and covers the most astonishing range of subjects while holding fast to its core themes of *bhakti*, renunciation, the oneness of everything and the eternal freedom of the Ātman. It is literally Kṛṣṇa's last word on the subject of spiritual practice. After delivering this timeless message meant for the whole world, Śrī Kṛṣṇa gave Uddhava specific, personal instructions. This is the way a genuine *guru* teaches, imparting general instructions which are applicable and open to all, and also private instructions directed only to the individual disciple. In this regard it is interesting to note that while Kṛṣṇa instructed Arjuna to go out and fight, to act in the world with a detached mind, His instructions to Uddhava were exactly the opposite. He told him to accept the life of a mendicant:

> I direct you to go to the place of pilgrimage known as Badaryāśrama . . . Wearing tree bark as clothing, subsisting on roots and fruits, and free from all desire for enjoyments . . . think deeply in solitude over what I have taught you (11.29.41-44).

Different people have different paths marked out for them and a legitimate teacher will recognize this fact and instruct accordingly.

Poor Uddhava, though, was grief-stricken at the thought of parting from Kṛṣṇa. He clung to the Lord's feet and bathed them in tears. Somehow he pried himself away and embarked on his journey. Kṛṣṇa would soon cast off his physical form anyway, and devotees like Uddhava would be forced to take recourse to the Lord in their own hearts, an Incarnation which is never diminished and is always close at hand.

The eve of *Kali-yuga*, the great shifting of cosmic epochs, was upon them, heralded by evil portents in the sky and land. Dvārakā would soon be submerged in the swelling tide and the Yādavas were fated to obliterate themselves in a drunken frenzy. The destruction parallels the fratricidal holocaust of the Kurukṣetra battle, which wiped out the Kaurava dynasty. Why did these great civilizations have to end and why in such a shattering, apocalyptic blaze?

"If I go away leaving behind this powerful and overbearing clan of the Yādavas," Kṛṣṇa explained, "they will ruin society by their unrestrained excesses" (11.6.30). That is the simple explanation; what it really signifies is the final purge which ushers in the universal cataclysm. It is at once redemptive and tragic, for it indicates the death of the old order, the end of sacred time. Reminiscent of the apocalyptic ending of Wagner's *The Ring*, we have here a Hindu *Götterdämmerung*, "Twilight of the Gods". Kṛṣṇa, Balarāma and their vast retinue disappear; the gods recede and their presence is no longer felt; the world is plunged into profanity and baseness.

It is no accident that God's most glorious and complete Incarnation should come at the crossroads, the moment before the cosmic Fall. He is the culmination of all that sacred time was leading up to, the Super Hero that generations of sacred lineage produced. It is as if the rush of divine power through history collected at this point, like water behind a dam, and like the dam bursting, swelled to its greatest extent then dissipated. His power is still acting in the world, but in a much reduced form.

Kṛṣṇa's death is as elegant as it is supernatural. Like Wagner's cursed ring, which brings destruction wherever it ends up, a cursed mace was fated to destroy the Yādavas. In an attempt to avert the disaster, King Ugrasena had it ground to a powder and thrown into the sea. One bit of iron remained and was swallowed by a fish. When the fish was caught, the fisherman found the piece of iron in its stomach and gave it to a hunter who forged it into an arrowhead. This was the weapon which would kill Śrī Kṛṣṇa. The rest of the filings washed ashore and magically grew into reeds. These the Yādavas used to beat each other to death.

After Balarāma gave up his body in meditation and the Yādavas extinguished their race, Lord Kṛṣṇa took to the forest and sat peacefully under a tree. A hunter, into whose hand the cursed arrow had fallen, mistook the Lord's foot for an animal and shot Him. By a mere prick in the foot the Lord fell. The hunter was horrified, but Kṛṣṇa told him, "What you have executed is only due to My resolve. By My will you shall gain heaven, the realm where men who do good works go" (11.30.39). In a rush of heavenly glory, surrounded by *devas* singing His praises, He burned His physical body in a yogic fire and resumed His all-pervading, Brahmic state.

Canto Twelve: The *Kali-Yuga*

Śrī Kṛṣṇa's disappearance from the earth marked the shift into the last phase of history before the cosmic dissolution and renewal sets the cycle of *yugas* in motion again. It is the *Kali-yuga*, the age of darkness and entropy in which we are now living. This concluding *skandha* explores the many dimensions of *Kali-yuga*, including its characteristics, the spiritual practice appropriate for this epoch, and the last scheduled Incarnation, Lord Kalki.

The first chapter prophesies the royal genealogies that will appear and describes their degraded character and reigns of cruelty. Chapter two provides a fascinating description of *Kali-yuga's* characteristics, a chillingly accurate picture of life today. Wealth, it says, will take the place of virtuous conduct or good character in estimating someone's worth (12.2.2). Courts of law will rule in favor of the rich, poverty being looked upon as sufficient proof of guilt (12.2.4-5). One who is the master of abusive vocabulary will be considered a scholar (notice our "humorists", critics, columnists, etc.) (12.2.4). We will live to eat, not eat to live (12.2.6). Rulers, now merely glorified robbers, will tax the population to the point of misery, which drives the common people to crime (12.2.10,13). Skill in lovemaking will be recognized as the chief excellence in a man or woman (observe our film idols, rock stars, "sex symbols", etc.) (12.2.3).

In the final hours, into this darkness and mayhem will ride the last Incarnation, Lord Kalki. Just as Śrī Kṛṣṇa's advent marked the crossroads of the *Dvārapa* and *Kali-yugas*, so will Kalki's appearance mark the end of the world as we know it and usher in the cosmic renewal. Kalki is a violent and avenging figure, shadowy except for the fact that He will ride horseback, be endowed with the eight yogic powers, and purge the earth.

Chapter Three continues to catalogue the abominations characteristic of *Kali-yuga*. In the later stages people will atrophy physically, becoming dwarfish and emaciated, will have severely decreased life spans, and will live in filth and pestilence. But the malignities of *Kali-yuga* can be overcome, if not on a societal level, at least by the individual. "When the worshipful Lord, the Supreme Person, enters into the hearts of people, He destroys all the evil wrought in the minds by *Kali* . . ." (12.3.45). This is the secret; this is the culmination of all the *Bhāgavatam's* teachings. Śrī Śuka tells King Parīkṣit, "O King! Strive your best to install Keśava in your heart. If you, whose death is near at hand, make your mind concentrated on the Lord now, you can gain the Supreme State" (12.3.46). This is the recommended path to enlightenment in this *Kali-yuga*. What in former *Yugas* had to be accomplished through prolonged meditation, severe austerities, or massive ritualistic worship can now be accomplished by the mere repetition of God's name.

Chapter Four provides a minutely detailed description of cosmic dissolution. After furious natural cataclysms reduce the universe to its elements, these elements will be systematically absorbed into their source in the same step-by-step fashion by which they unfolded Creation.

The Death of King Parīkṣit

The final words of Śuka are contained in a short Chapter Five, where he reminds King Parīkṣit that the real Self is the Ātman and the Ātman is eternal. For one who realizes oneness with Brahman, death does not exist. All his questions finally answered, the King worshipped the sage, expressed his gratitude, and took leave of the place, eager to meet his fate. Retiring to the banks of the Ganges, he sat with his mind and senses ingathered and became absorbed in the unity of the Self with Brahman. The serpent Takṣaka approached the meditating king and inflicted the fatal bite; at once Parīkṣit's body crumbled into ashes.

Mārkaṇḍeya and the Baby

From here on out, our original narrator, Sūta, carries the discourse. The origin, development and oral transmission of the *Vedas* is chronicled in Chapter Six, while the characteristics of the *Purāṇas* are enumerated in Chapter Seven. The next three chapters relate the last story of the *Śrīmad Bhāgavatam*, that of Mārkaṇḍeya and the divine Baby. After practicing austerities for an inconceivable length of time, the great sage Mārkaṇḍeya had a vision of Nara-Nārāyaṇa who offered him a boon. Mārkaṇḍeya asked to see the Lord's *yogamāyā* and was swept up in a hideous deluge in which he suffered for thousands of years. While being tossed about aimlessly, he caught sight of a banyan tree atop a high level of earth and on a leaf of that tree a wondrous, divine infant. He was at once relieved; the sight of the beautiful baby filled him with heavenly joy. With the infant's inward breath, Mārkaṇḍeya was drawn into the boy's body where he found the whole universe exactly as it had been before the deluge. With the child's outward breath, he was expelled back into the deluge. Suddenly the whole vision — deluge, baby and all — disappeared, and Mārkaṇḍeya found himself in his own hermitage again.

It is appropriate that this incident should come at the end of the *Śrīmad Bhāgavatam*, for it bespeaks of the universal dissolution and, in the image of the divine baby, universal renewal. The deluge outside of the child's body represents the formless state of non-manifestation, while the universe inside the baby represents the cosmic manifestation which has its existence within the Existence of God. Both creation and dissolution, Mārkaṇḍeya discovers, are illusory, the mysterious play of *māyā.*

The eleventh chapter has Sūta explain the symbolic elements of the forms which Brahman takes, particularly the *Virāṭ-puruṣa* and Mahā-Viṣṇu, whose various features and weapons carry metaphorical significance. For ritualistic reference, a discussion of the movements of the sun, which is identified as one with Viṣṇu, and of the *devas*, which preside over the months, finishes the chapter.

Conclusion: The *Śrīmad Bhāgavatam* Synopsized and Praised

An overview of the entire *Śrīmad Bhāgavatam* is provided in the penultimate chapter, where each *skandha* is synopsized. While supplying its own loose index, the text here praises itself by recalling the staggering breadth of its subject matter. After having faithfully worked through the whole *Śrīmad Bhāgavatam*, the reader will surely feel a sense of accomplishment contemplating the list of names, stories and teachings, and will realize just how much they've learned and how much richer their inner world has become.

The greatness of the *Bhāgavatam* itself is extolled, as is the spiritual gratification gained by its study. Rightfully, the text points out that other sacred scriptures, while pointing to the Supreme, do not so exuberantly describe again and again the marvelous attributes of God. "Through innumerable stories, anecdotes, in fact through every word of it, the one topic highlighted in this text is the Bhagavān, the one embracing all that exists" (12.13.65). This is true; the *Śrīmad Bhāgavatam* is unmatched in its sheer joy, color and vibrancy. The wondrous, loving God it promotes leaps from the pages. He is splendid, bursting with happiness, and accessible to all.

In the concluding chapter, the *Śrīmad Bhāgavatam* is once again praised and salutations are offered to its speaker, Śrī Śuka, and to Lord Vāsudeva, the Supreme Spirit, by whom this miraculous book was given to the world. The last verse of this gigantic masterpiece succinctly sums up its teachings:

> I offer my salutations to that Hari, by chanting whose Name man is freed from all sins, by surrendering to whom by prostration, he is freed from all misery (12.13.23).

NOTES

1. Tapasyānanda, vol. 1, p. xxiii.
2. Tapasyānanda, p. xxiii; Organ, p. 276.
3. Organ, p. 275.
4. Tapasyānanda, vol. 1, p. xxxiii.
5. Alain Danielou, *Hindu Polytheism* (New York: Bollingen Foundation, 1964), p. 170.
6. Stutley and Stutley, p. 71.
7. Tapasyānanda, vol. 1, p. 301.
8. Stutley and Stutley, p. 341.
9. Tapasyānanda, vol. 1, p. 92.
10. Tapasyānanda, vol. 1, p. 91.
11. Organ, pp. 217-218.
12. Stutley and Stutley, p. 142.
13. Organ, pp. 218-220.
14. Tapasyānanda, vol. 1, p. 301.
15. Tapasyānanda, vol. 2, p. 2.
16. Stutley and Stutley, p. 341.
17. Tapasyānanda, vol. 2, p. 203.
18. A. J. Alston, trnsl., *The Devotional Poems of Mirabai* (Delhi: Motilal Banarsidass, 1980); many of Mirabai's poems refer to this incident.
19. Stutley and Stutley, p. 4.
20. Tapasyānanda, Vol. II, p. 63.
21. Tapasyānanda, Vol. II, p. 296.
22. Zafrulla Khan, trnsl., *The Koran* (New York: Praeger Publishers, 1971).
23. Swāmī Tyāgīśānanda, *Narada Bhakti Sutras* (Madras: Sri Ramakrishna Math, 1983, p. 23.

CHAPTER TWENTY

Other Popular Purāṇas

Of the remaining Purāṇic literature, far too gigantic a corpus for nearly anyone to tackle in its entirety, there are three texts I think deserve a look, and they happen to correspond to the three major thrusts of Hindu sectarianism: Vaiṣṇava (Viṣṇu worship), Śaivite (Śiva worship) and Śākta (worship of the Divine Mother). These are, respectively, the *Viṣṇu Purāṇa*, *Śiva Purāṇa*, and *Śrīmad Devī Bhāgavatam*.

Viṣṇu Purāṇa

One of the earliest of the *Purāṇas* (perhaps the first century B.C.)[1], the *Viṣṇu Purāṇa* is an elegant, relatively terse piece which diligently attends to all of the necessary features of a *Mahāpurāṇa* (creation, genealogies, etc.). The reader who has completed a study of the *Śrīmad Bhāgavatam* will at once be struck by the similarity of its contents to those of the *Viṣṇu Purāṇa*.

Both contain accounts of the Incarnations of Lord Viṣṇu, full creation and dissolution narratives, and a long, detailed study of the life of Śrī Kṛṣṇa, which takes up and entire *skandha*. Many more stories will be familiar: those of Dhruva, Pṛthu, Bharata and the fawn, Dakṣa and his daughters, the Solar and Lunar dynasties, including the Pāṇḍava and Kaurava families, Purūravas and the nymph Urvaśī, and so on. It is only six cantos long, as opposed the *Śrīmad Bhāgavatam's* twelve, but it covers a great deal. It has descriptions of the divisions of the *Veda*, of the four *varṇas* and *āśramas* and the duties associated with them, instructions for spiritual practice, methods of worship, the form, meaning and lore of Viṣṇu, and so on. It almost serves as a summary of the *Śrīmad Bhāgavatam*, but has a feel of its own. Its context, too, is different; this time the dialogue takes place between the student Maitreya and Parāśara, his *guru*. Parāśara heard the *Viṣṇu Purāṇa* from the great Vedic *ṛṣi* Vasiṣṭha, who was his grandfather. A certain non-canonical text, the *Yoga Vāsiṣṭha*, bears his name and teachings; there he acts as the *guru* to Lord Rāmacandra. Vasiṣṭha also figures prominently in the *Ṛg Veda*, parts of which he is believed to have composed.

Śiva Purāṇa

The *Śiva Purāṇa* also conforms to the specifications of a *Mahā-Purāṇa* only it is devoted entirely to Lord Śiva. It is one of the richest sources of Śaivite mythology, hymns, theology, ritual and practical advice, with particular attention paid to Śiva *mantras* and their various complex meanings. Many of the stories, such as the immolation of Satī, are already known to the reader of the *Śrīmad Bhāgavatam.* Others are new. All are beautifully rendered and fascinating.

The text is divided into seven *saṃhitās.* The first, called the *Vidyeśvara-saṃhitā*, is concerned entirely with the supremacy and glory of Lord Śiva and everything associated with Him — the *liṅgam* (phallic emblem), the *Oṃkāra* (*mantra Oṃ*), the *tripuṇḍraka* (three-lined mark on the forehead made from holy ashes), *rudrākṣa* beads (used in Śaivite *japa mālās*, i.e. rosaries), etc.

The second *saṃhitā*, the *Rudra-saṃhitā* (Rudra being another name for Śiva), is divided into five sections. The first deals with creation, and includes the important story of the *Śiva-tattva.* Viṣṇu and Brahmā got into an argument one day over which of them was superior. Suddenly Siva assumed the *Śiva-tattva* form, a giant *liṅgam* without beginning or end. Brahmā turned himself into a swan and searched for the top of this bewildering image, while Viṣṇu assumed the form of a boar and dove down in search of the bottom. For a thousand years they continued to search, but discovered that the *liṅgam* was infinite. At last the weary gods made obeisances to It. "That form can't be directly expressed," Brahmā said. "It is without action and name. Without any sex distinction It has become a *liṅga* (literally, "sign, mark, symbol")[2]. It is beyond the path of meditation" (2.1.7.66).[3] The cosmic sound *Oṃ* radiated from the Form, and Śiva revealed Himself. In this way He demonstrated that He is the Supreme and all other divine manifestations are subordinate to Him.

The second section of the *Rudra-saṃhitā* recounts the sad tale of Satī, Śiva's first *śakti*, or consort, who committed suicide by burning Herself in a yogic fire when Her Lord, Śiva, was slighted. This story was included in the fourth canto of the *Śrīmad Bhāgavatam.* Satī reincarnated Herself as Pārvatī, the incarnation of the Devī as the daughter of the Himalayas and Śiva's eternal *śakti.* Her story is recounted in the third section of the *Rudra-saṃhitā*, which describes the seven austerities She had to perform in order to win Her divine husband.

Next comes the *Kumārakāṇḍa* section. *Kumāra* means "son" or "prince", and this part describes the births of Śiva and Pārvatī's two sons, Kārttikeya and Gaṇeśa. After being suspended in a yogic, trance-like sexual embrace for an inestimable length of time, Śiva and Pārvatī were disturbed by the entreaties of the *devas*, who implored Them to cease. They complied, and Śiva, in order not to offend Pārvatī, held His semen within. Pārvatī, enraged that the gods had caused Her to be barren, cursed them to be barren themselves. Thus none of the other gods have ever sired offspring. Śiva deposited the semen in *Agni*, the cosmic element of fire, who passed it on to the Ganges, who laid it in a thicket, where it sprang up as a magnificent boy. With six heads and twelve arms (though sometimes he is depicted with a single head and two arms), clad in red and bearing weapons, he was Kārttikeya, the radiant, virile, yet ever-bachelor god of war. He went on to slay the demon Tāraka, a tormentor of the gods whom only a celestial hero could vanquish.

The divine couple's other son cut a very different figure. While Kārttikeya was born without the aid of a female, Gaṇeśa was born without the participation of a male. Pārvatī created a son for Herself, handsome, husky and loyal. She positioned him outside Her door as a guard, and when Śiva arrived there, neither recognized the other. Gaṇeśa barred the Lord's entrance. They fought, and Śiva lopped off His own son's head, much to Pārvatī's fury. Śiva ordered the *devas* to travel north and take the head from the first person they met. It so happened they met and elephant, and it was this head they attached to Gaṇeśa's body. Śiva resuscitated the boy and he was born a second time, only now more beautiful than before because he possessed the magnificent head of an elephant.

Gaṇeśa is a gentle and approachable deity, the remover of obstacles and granter of boons. He is invoked at the outset of ceremonies and important undertakings so that no ill fate should occur, and supplicants seek his favor in material matters, for he embodies prosperity, success, peace, and a comfortable life.

The fifth and last section of the *Rudra-saṃhitā* describes the ongoing battles between the *asuras* and the *devas* and Śiva's interventions in them. This theme of opposing forces maintaining the cosmic balance runs throughout the Purāṇic literature.

The *Śatarudra-saṃhitā* follows; *śatarudra* means "one hundred Rudras", and this marvelous section describes one hundred of Śiva's forms, manifestations and Incarnations, including the half-male half-female form, Ardhanārīśvara, which represents the oneness of Śiva and Śakti, or the cosmic principles of *Puruṣa* and *Prakṛti*.

The *Koṭirudra-saṃhitā*, which comes next, is mainly concerned with the saving grace of Lord Śiva and how easy it is to attain. Lord Śiva is the very embodiment of mercy and love; He showers His favor on even the least deserving. This is His unique trait. Among the stories is that of an outcaste woman. Because of her bad conduct in a previous life, she'd been born under the most unfortunate circumstances — blind, lame, and untouchable, orphaned at an early age. Her wretched life was characterized by ignorance and starvation. She happened to be begging on a day auspicious for the worship of Śiva. A wise traveller tossed a bunch of *bilva* leaves, sacred to Lord Śiva, in her outstretched hand and she, upon realizing they were not edible, tossed them away dejectedly. By sheer luck, the leaves fell upon the *liṅgam* image of Lord Śiva. Due to hunger, the woman sat up awake the whole night through. In this way, she unwittingly observed the worship, fasting, and vigil associated with the festival of Śiva. When she died a couple of days later she attained to His blessed state. Such is the efficacy of even the simplest gesture in Śiva's honor, and such is His incalculable compassion.

The *saṃhitā* contains several more salvation stories, chapters describing the wonderful traits and glories of Śiva in His many forms, and a discussion of meaning and observance of Śivarātri, the most important holiday for Śiva's devotees. In Chapter Thirty-Five, Viṣṇu Himself worships Śiva by reciting the celebrated *Śiva Sahasranāma*, or "Thousand Names of Śiva". Here Śiva's every conceivable attribute and activity is given praise as His thousand epithets are recited one after another. It is an awe-inspiring piece, and in reading or chanting it one experiences a hint of the unlimited, all-encompassing grandeur of God. It was after delivering the *Sahasranāma* that Viṣṇu was endowed with His characteristic discus, *sudarśana*, a gift from Lord Śiva as a token of His pleasure.

The *Umā-saṃhitā* deals largely with universal cosmography. The layout of the universe, the planets, the earth and the nether regions are all examined, with particular attention paid to the many horrible hells. Chapter after chapter unfolds as we wallow in lists of every possible sin, shudder to gruesome descriptions of perverse tortures awaiting us as punishment in hell, and sigh in relief as the way of escape through devotion, *yoga* and virtue is revealed. Wonderful stuff. The *Umā-saṃhitā* also includes accounts of creation, of the primordial generations, and of the manifestations of the different forms of the Goddess as Mahākālī, Mahālakṣmī, Sarasvatī, Śatākṣi (Durga) and Umā.

The *Kailāsa-saṃhitā* (Mt. Kailasa is the abode of Lord Śiva) contains practical instructions for spiritual life, including rules for worship, methods of renunciation, proper conduct and habits, and principles of *sannyāsa*. It is a relatively short section.

The *Purāṇa* ends with the *Vāyavīya-saṃhitā*, which continues the theme of creation, only putting special emphasis on Śiva as the cause and Lord of creation. One might say that this *saṃhitā* is the last word on Purāṇic Śivology. Theological issues are explored, as are the bases of spiritual knowledge and practice. Rituals and *mantras* are discussed at length, techniques of *yoga* are enjoined, and the unwavering conviction that Lord Śiva is the Absolute, the Supreme, the original divine Truth is constantly stressed.

Anyone attracted to Lord Śiva, either devotionally or intellectually, will find the *Śiva Purāṇa* a limitless mine of knowledge. Its dimensions are infinite, its stories a sheer delight.

Śrīmad Devī Bhāgavatam

For those devoted to God as the Divine Mother, the most significant *Purāṇa* is the *Śrīmad Devī Bhāgavatam*. More and more Westerners are finding meaning in the feminine conception of the Divine, and the *Devī Bhāgavatam* fills a need by providing an encyclopedic wealth of information about the Goddess and methods for Her realization.

Though not considered a *Mahāpurāṇa*, the *Devī Bhāgavatam* is much revered and cherished by *śāktas* and thus has an importance all its own. It was most likely composed in the eleventh or twelfth century and influenced by the *Tantras*. It resembles the other *Purāṇas* in style, content and format, only the Ultimate Truth is here conceived of as Śrī Bhuvaneśvarī ("Ruler of Existence"), the Great Goddess. She is Brahman, and She assumes different Goddess-forms to achieve different purposes. Viṣṇu, Śiva and the other Gods are subordinate to Her. She is the Creator, Nurturer and Destroyer of the material manifestation. She is the ultimate Goal.

Devotion is the recommended method of realizing Her, and the *Purāṇa* provides the means of developing this devotion through stories, hymns, *mantras*, instructions for meditation and worship, and so on. This is another massive *Purāṇa*, twelve cantos long, but devotees of the Divine Mother are advised to have a go at it, for She is truly embodied in it.

A rather more accessible Purāṇic exposition on the Divine Mother is the extraordinary *Devī Māhātmyam*, also known as the *Caṇḍi*, and it is to this text that we now turn.

NOTES

1. Stutley and Stutley, p. 336.
2. Stutley and Stutley, p. 162.
3. J. L. Shastri, ed., *The Śiva Purāṇa* (Delhi: Motilal Banarsidass, 1981), vol. I, p. 204.

Part VI

Shorter Scriptures Derived From the *Purāṇas*

CHAPTER TWENTY-ONE

The Devī-Māhātmyam (or Caṇḍi)

The beautiful *Devī-Māhātmyam* ("Glory to the Divine Mother"), also known as the *Durgā-saptaśatī* ("Seven Hundred Verses on Śrī Durgā") or *Caṇḍi* (a name of the Goddess denoting Her fearsome aspect) is derived from the *Mārkaṇḍeya Purāṇa.* It is a most venerated, as well as practical, scripture, chanted daily by many devotees and utilized extensively on sacred occasions, particularly the festival of Durgā Pūjā. Its verses are dazzlingly dramatic, at times lofty and sublime, at others alive with action as skillfully rendered as a good novel. Though a variety of forms of the Mother are introduced, they represent aspects of a single Being, and by the end, the *Caṇḍi* has drawn a detailed portrait of Her.

The central theme is the dual nature of the Mother as both supreme Illusion (*Māyā*) and as the bestower of spiritual liberation. The apparent contradiction is resolved if we consider Her not as an adjunct to, or secondary part of, a masculine Deity or Brahman, but as the Supreme Itself. Brahman and *Śakti* are nondifferent; She is everything, both the transcendent Divine and the very world which She has created. It is She who ensnares the *jīvas* in *Māyā* (which is none other than Herself, in Her Incarnation as Illusion) and disentangles them as well. There is no escaping the Mother, and the *Caṇḍi* illustrates this through an allegorical battle between the Devī and the forces of evil and decay, here personified as *asuras* (the race of demons). They cannot avoid Her, and She always wins.

The Quandary of King Suratha

Divided into thirteen brief chapters, the piece opens in the Purāṇic fashion of spinning a short tale in order to secure a narrative context. King Suratha, once a benign ruler of the whole world, is conquered by his enemies, robbed of his treasury and army by his own vicious ministers, and deprived of his sovereignty. In despair, he takes to the forest alone, and finds himself in the hermitage of the great sage, Medhas. There he meets a merchant, also driven from his home, whose wife and kinsmen, crazed by greed, have misappropriated his wealth and thrown him out. This sorry pair discover they are alike in that they continue to pine away affectionately for the same people who robbed and disowned them. How, they wonder, can this be? Why, if they realize the defects of the objects of their attachment, are they unable to let go of them? How can they be aware of their ignorance, yet unable to overcome it (1.1-45)?[1]

They approach the sage with this query. Medhas replies that we are "hurled into the whirlpool of attachment, the pit of delusion, through the power of Mahāmāyā (the Great Illusion), who makes the existence of this world possible (1.53). She creates the entire universe and forcibly draws the minds of men into delusion (1.54-55). Were the living beings not bound by *Māyā*, all would be Self-realized and the universe would serve no purpose. If, then, we are entangled in the inscrutable powers of *Māyā*, despite our better judgement, it is due to the will of Bhagavatī (the All-Powerful).

The king wants to know more about this resplendent Devī (1.59-62). Replies the *ṛṣi*: "She is eternal, embodied as the universe. By Her all this is pervaded. Nevertheless, She incarnates in manifold ways; hear it from me" (1.63-64). Herein is the secret of the Devī's nature. The universe is a projection of Herself, nondifferent from Her. Seen in this light, the world is not evil, profane or separate from the Divine. It is absolutely saturated in the Divine. There is no such thing as mundaneness or profanity because the whole universe is the worshipable Deity.

The Divine Mother as Yoganidrā

Though She pervades creation, she can also be known through anthropomorphic manifestations, the many Goddesses. The *Caṇḍi* describes the principal ones, beginning with Yoganidrā (Meditation-Sleep), the aspect which exists during the intervals between creationary cycles. In other words, when the universe is not, the Devī still is, and Her nature is tranquil, akin to the states of meditation or sleep. This interval of cosmic repose is traditionally symbolized by the image of sleeping Viṣṇu, who reclines upon the serpent Ananta in the midst of the primordial, undifferentiated ocean. The *ṛṣi* Medhas here describes one such cycle of mystic slumber, wherein two demons emerge from the unconscious Viṣṇu's ears and Lord Brahmā, sitting upon the lotus sprung from the sleeping God's navel, implores the Goddess Yoganidrā to manifest Herself and thereby rouse the God from His passive state.

This dynamic, namely the God as static and the Goddess as active, is a basic principle of Hindu metaphysics, found in a nontheistic form in the *Sāṃkhya* categories of *puruṣa* and *prakṛti*, as well as in many theistic forms, such as the image of Mother Kālī dancing atop the prone body of the unconscious Lord Śiva. The point is that Brahman is passive, static, eternally still, while Its aspect of *Śakti* is expressive, full, active, etc. Mother has the power. Father is as if asleep.

Verses 1.72-1.87 comprise the first important hymn-within-the-hymn (there are four in all), Brahmā's prayer to the Devī. Like the *Bhagavad-Gītā* verse 4.24, which identifies God with the very sacrifice performed *to* God, an image which suggests an *advaitic*, or non-dualistic, world-view, Brahmā's prayer begins by identifying the Mother with the propitiatory *mantras* chanted during the sacrifice (*svāhā* and *svadhā*) as well as the sacrifice itself (1.73). She is *Oṃ*, which, according to the *Upaniṣads*, is nondifferent from Brahman. She is the power which creates, maintains and dissolves the universe. She is the supreme knowledge and the supreme nescience, the power of good and the power of evil, the cause of the three *guṇas* (of which all material objects are composed) and the dark night of cosmic dissolution (1.74-78).

Who can extol She, Brahmā concludes, Who not only is the soul of everything, but gives Himself, Viṣṇu and Śiva their forms and causes them to wake or sleep, according to Her will? He beseeches Her to therefore rouse the great, static divinity.

How She accomplishes this is very interesting. She emerges from Viṣṇu's body, where She had been dwelling, and being quitted by Her, He awakes. As Yoganidrā She enters Viṣṇu's body and forces Him into passivity during the dissolutionary period. Thus She controls not only the manifest universe, but the nonmanifest state as well. Freed from His mystic coma, Viṣṇu arises and slays the two *asuras*. So ends the first chapter.

Chapter Two through Four tell the story of the Divine Mother's battle with, and slaying of, the demon Mahiṣāsura. One of the most popular icons of the Devī depicts Her, in the form of Durgā, piercing this demon's buffalo-shaped body (the name Mahiṣāsura means "buffalo demon") with Her long spear while Her lion mount takes a chomp out of one of the *asura's* limbs. This is one of Her most lovely forms, and at the same time most fierce and powerful. Clad in red, multi-armed, adorned with opulent jewelry, She represents the ultimate in feminine beauty and feminine strength. Most importantly, She represents all of the gods blended into One, as the story of Her manifestation illustrates.

The Devī Appears

As a result of the defeat of the *devas* in war with the *asuras*, Mahiṣāsura, at the time chief of the demons, assumed the post of Indra, king of heaven, and thus forced the *devas* to walk the earth like ordinary mortals. The *devas*, headed by Brahmā, approached Śiva and Viṣṇu to elicit their help (2.1-8). What then occurred demonstrates the supremacy of the Goddess over all other conceptions of the Divine, for suddenly a great light issued from the face of Viṣṇu, and one from Śiva, from Brahmā, and all of the gods in turn. This light converged and, pervading the entire universe with its luster, became a female form (2.9-18). The many gods are all but parts of the Devī; together they *are* Her, fragmented, they are individuals.

The implements She carries in Her many hands signify the various deities She represents. Śiva presents Her with a trident drawn from the very one He holds; Viṣṇu brings forth a discus from His own discus and gives it to Her; Indra gives Her a thunderbolt, Brahmā a rosary of *japa* beads and a water pot, Kāla (Time) a sword and shield, etc. She is presented with divine jewelry and armor as well as Her wonderful lion (2.20-30). Possessing the cumulative power of all divine forms, the Mother is omnipotent. Her roar causes all the worlds to reverberate (2.33).

The monumental battle which now ensues between the Goddess and the armies of Mahiṣāsura is described so vividly, the reader can practically hear the sound of metal crashing against metal and feel the impact of exchanged blows. The Mother is never in peril; She can, in fact, destroy the whole universe by a mere glance. She fights for the sport of it, like a cat plays with a mouse prior to eating it. When She tires of the *līlā*, She effortlessly puts an end to it: "As fire consumes a huge heap of straw and wood, so did Ambikā ("Mother") destroy that vast army of *asuras* in no time" (2.67).

Chapter Three is devoted to describing the one-on-one combat between Mahiṣāsura and the Goddess. She easily slays him, as well as the remaining *asura* forces, and the jubilant *devas* dance, sing and offer praises, which are recorded as the whole of Chapter Four. This is the second of the important hymns of the *Caṇḍi*, and concentrates on the Mother's resplendent attributes, Her identity as supreme knowledge and liberation, and Her absolute power. Again and again the *devas* beseech the Mother to offer them protection and grace. They worship Her with celestial flowers and perfumes. Pleased, the Devī tells them to ask of Her a boon, and the two they choose are highly significant. First, they request that whenever She is availed to in a time of calamity, She be bound to respond. In the next chapter She will be called upon to fulfill Her promise, but more importantly, this promise of grace is extended to all of us. She is our vigilant protectress, our refuge in times of trouble or despair.

The second boon requested by the gods is that whenever mortals praise Her with hymns, She must be gracious to them and see to their needs. Thus the potency of the *Caṇḍi* text is established. "Be it so," says the magnificent Bhadrākālī ("Gentle Kālī"), and at once She vanishes.

We are now introduced to two more fiendish *asuras*, the brothers Śumbha and Niśumbha, who, like Mahiṣāsura, have seized control of the three worlds. So arrogant are these two, Śumbha will even have the gall to proposition the Devī Herself! He will, however, pay dearly for it.

The Hymn to Aparājitā

As the *devas* approach the Mother to fulfill Her promise to them, they deliver the dazzling prayer known as the hymn to Aparājitā ("the Unvanquished"). It spans verses 5.8 to 5.81 and concentrates on the Mother's aspect as the indwelling Spirit in all beings. Beginning with the recognition of Her identity as the transcendent Divine, the *devas* praise Her as the "primordial cause and sustaining power" (5.9). In this manifestation, Her complexion will be blue-black (5.12), an attribute reminiscent of the sky at night, in other words of infinity and all-pervasiveness. She is at once the most gentle and the most terrible (5.13). Verses 5.17-5.76 enumerate the forms which the Devī, as the indwelling Spirit, the consciousness of all beings, can be known. "To the Devī who abides in all beings in the form of intelligence," the *devas* pray (5.20- 22); "to the Devī who abides in all beings in the form of sleep . . ." (5.23-25). The repetitions of the verse have Her assume the forms of hunger, reflection, power, thirst, forgiveness, genius, modesty, peace, faith, loveliness, good fortune, activity, memory, compassion, contentment, error and the mother (5.26-76). Notice how the list includes not only spiritual qualities (modesty, peace, faith, etc.), but also sensual drives, cognitive faculties, and the propensity to error. She is also our indwelling Mother. We are never alone in the world, no matter how much it may seem like it at times. Our Mother is always with us. She is the Devī who governs the material elements yet also dwells within them as the all-pervading consciousness (5.77-80).

Thus praised, and invoked to appear, the Mother this time manifests Herself as Pārvatī, the consort of Lord Śiva and presiding deity of the Himālayas. Pārvatī, hearing the *devas'* prayers, casts a Goddess form out from Her physical sheath. Because She came out of the sheath, or *kośa*, She is known as Kauśikī ("From the Sheath").

The *asura* Śambha hears tell of the Devī's exquisite beauty and desires Her for a wife, so he sends a messenger to woo Her on his behalf. She tells the messenger, "He who conquers Me in battle, removes My pride and is My match in strength shall be my husband" (5.120). No one, of course, can overcome the Mother, but the haughty demon, enraged by the rejection, is determined to try. First he dispatches an army, headed by his general, Dhūmralocana. Chapter Six describes their swift demise. Next, in Chapter Seven, he sends armies headed by the demons Caṇḍa and Muṇḍa.

Kālī Appears

As the *asuras* charge at Her, the Mother's countenance darkens with wrath, and borne from Her forehead is Her terrible form as Kālī. Kālī is described as

> . . . armed with a sword and noose, bearing the strange skull-topped staff, decorated with a garland of skulls, clad in a tiger's skin, very appalling owing to Her emaciated flesh, with gaping mouth, fearful with Her tongue lolling out, having deep-sunk reddish eyes and filling the regions of the sky with Her roars . . . (7.6-8).

This horrifying vision falls upon Her foes and flings them, along with their elephants, horses and chariots, into Her blood-dripping mouth (7.9-11). She is death personified, the destructive power of unstoppable Time (Her name is the feminine form of the word *kāla*, "Time"), eternal darkness which suggests both primal terror and the blissful, liberated state beyond pairs of opposites. Kālī is the most widely worshipped of all manifestations of the Goddess. If She strikes terror in us, it is because She embodies that state beyond manifestation which is characterized by nothingness, an idea nightmarish to those attached to finite existence. To the Self-realized soul, however, this is a state of absolute joy, and Mother Kālī a source of comfort.

She easily kills Caṇḍa and Muṇḍa so, in Chapter Eight, Śumbha dispatches additional forces, this time headed by Raktabīja, a menace whose special power is that from each drop of blood which falls from his body, hundreds of full-grown *asura* soldiers are instantly materialized.

The Birth of the *Śaktis*

Chapter Eight contains the marvelous account of the Mother's manifestation as the various *Śaktis*, or embodied powers, of the respective deities. As was mentioned before, the Gods are static without *Śakti*, the power of the Goddess. Chapter Two described a single Devī emanating from the bodies of the *devas*; here, the same principle is at work, only each God projects an individual Goddess bearing identical features and weapons as Himself.

"Whatever was the form of each *deva*, and whatever ornament and vehicle, in that very manner his *Śakti* advanced to fight with the *asuras*" (8.14). Māheśvarī, the *Śakti* of Maheśvara, or Śiva, is seated on a bull, holding a trident, adorned with serpents, and bearing the moon in Her hair, just like Her male counterpart (8.16). So, too, do the *Śaktis* of Brahmā, Viṣṇu, Kumāra (the god of war), Varāha (Viṣṇu's boar Incarnation), Nṛsiṃha (the man-lion), and Indra (8.15-21).

The *Śaktis* join Kālī and Caṇḍikā (the principal manifestation of the Devī) in the fight, but the more wounds they inflict upon Raktabīja, the more *asuras* appear. Here Kālī's identity as the drinker of blood takes a benign turn, for She alone devours the *asura* army and then swallows all of Raktabīja's blood, thus rendering him dry and ending his life (8.56-62). Clearly, the blood on the lips of Mother Kālī is the blood of the wretched and the evil; to Her devotees, whom She loves as Her own children, She gives all protection and care.

The *Śaktis* are Absorbed into the Devī, Their True Source

Now the demon princes, Śumbha and Niśumbha, enter the field of battle themselves. Chapter Nine describes the combat of Niśumbha and the Devī and his inevitable demise. Chapter Ten has the Goddess battling Śumbha alone. "O Durgā," the arrogant demon sneers, "You are puffed up with pride of strength . . . (but) You fight resorting to the strength of others" (10.3).]

This comment betrays his ignorance, for all of these *Śakti* warrioresses are, of course, nondifferent from the Mother Herself. "I am alone in this world here," the Mother replies. "Who else is there beside Me? See, O vile one, these Goddesses, who are my own powers, entering into My own Self." (10.5). At once, the team of *Śaktis* and the Goddess Kālī are absorbed into the body of the Mother, who alone remains. The numerous forms, She explains, were projected by Her power and are now withdrawn back into their source (10.7-8). This incident illustrates how the Mother's power is unlimited, absolute, and complete. She only appears to be fragmented; in fact, Her power is never depreciated. By projecting Herself outward She does not decrease Her original form in the least, nor by drawing Her projections back does She increase Herself. She is changeless and unlimited.

This idea is echoed in the invocatory verse of the *Īśā Upaniṣad*:

> The invisible is the Infinite, the visible too is the Infinite. From the Infinite, the visible universe of infinite extension has come out. The Infinite remains the same, even though the infinite universe has come out of it.[2]

The dreadful battle between the Mother and Her foe ensues, and when She finally destroys him, the universe achieves a state of perfect peace, balance and clarity (10.28-32). The joyful denizens of heaven now praise the beloved Savior in the *Caṇḍi's* longest and most important prayer, the Hymn to Nārāyaṇī.

The Hymn to Nārāyaṇī

Most of Chapter Eleven is devoted to this hymn, which is widely used for liturgical purposes and expresses the most sophisticated theological and devotional developments in the *Śākta* tradition. The name Nārāyaṇī is a feminine form of Nārāyaṇa, a common epithet of Lord Viṣṇu meaning, broadly, "the One Whose Abode is the Primordial Waters".

The Gods beg the Mother of the world to be gracious to Her supplicants, to protect the universe, to remove suffering and to offer Herself as a refuge. Throughout the poem She is addressed in ways which suggest metaphysical truths about Her nature and the nature of Reality in general.

She is the sole substratum of the world because She exists in the form of Earth. She is also the water. She is the primeval *Māyā*, which is the source of the universe (11.4-5). She is the cause of emancipation, all branches of knowledge, and is embodied in all women of the world. She is the bestower of earthly enjoyments as well as spiritual liberation (11.5-8). She is Time and its physical expression in minutes, moments and similar divisions, as well as its expression in constant change which, ultimately, leads the universe to its destruction (11.9). As our true Selves are eternal, however, this is not to be feared.

The Devī is the creator, maintainer and destroyer of the cosmos (11.11). Though these functions are generally attributed to Brahmā, Viṣṇu and Śiva, these Gods have no active volition without the Mother. They can be thought of as, perhaps, the abstract idea behind the function, while the Devī actually conjures it into reality.

She is the substratum of all creation and the embodiment of the three *guṇas* (11.11). Intent on saving the dejected and distressed who take refuge in Her, Mother lifts the sufferings of all (11.12). She is embodied in all of the Goddesses (11.13-21), is the Great Illusion (Mahāmāyā) and the Great Night (Mahārātri). She is the ruler of all things, moving and unmoving (11.3), yet exists within everything (11.24) as the very Self of the universe (11.33).

"*Nārāyaṇī namo'stu te*", the *devas* sing again and again, "O Nārāyaṇī, salutations to You!" The chapter ends with the Devī's disclosure of some of Her future appearances (11.40-55).

The benefits derived from hearing the preceding *Devī-Māhātmyam* are enumerated by the Mother Herself in Chapter Twelve. These include freedom from all misfortune (12.4-5), freedom from fear (12.6), the removal of suffering (12.8), the transformation of bad dreams into good (12.17), peacefulness, friendship among people, and the destruction of evil (12.18-19). Most of all, it draws the devotee nearer to the Goddess Herself (12.20), which is, of course, the most glorious of all benefits. The Mother also gives general instructions on the most auspicious times for reciting or hearing the *Caṇḍi*, as well as for ritual worship.

After imparting this information, She vanishes even as the *devas* are still gazing upon Her. This concludes the *ṛṣi's* narrative of the deeds of the Goddess.

King Suratha and the Merchant are Granted a Vision

The sage Medhas concludes his discourse by reminding his two pupils of the original point of his talk — that it is the Mother who envelops us in delusion and the Mother who liberates us from it. "O great King," the *ṛṣi* says, "take refuge in Her, the supreme Īśvarī. When worshipped She, indeed, bestows on men enjoyment, heaven and final release" (12.5).

Our two heroes therefore retire to the bank of a river to practice austerity, image worship, meditation, and chanting of the hymn to the Devī (13.9-11). After three years the Mother, pleased with their devotion, appears before them and offers them each a boon. The king desires to recover his domain, while the merchant, apparently the wiser of the two, desires that knowledge which eradicates worldly attachment and the false consciousness of "I" and "mine" (13.12-18).

She is more than happy to fulfill their desires and does the king one better, promising that in his next birth he shall be a *Manu* (the progenitor of a race). The merchant she endows with the knowledge that will lead him to Self-realization (13.19-24). With that, She again vanishes, and the *Devī-Māhātmyam* has come to a close.

For aspirants whose Chosen Ideal is the Divine Mother, the *Devī-Māhātmyam* is indispensable. For others, it is still extremely helpful in understanding and contemplating the nature of the seen and unseen realms. The universe is not just dull matter, not alien and impersonal; it is our jubilant, loving Mother. Nature is positively bursting with the Divine Presence. We are never separated from It. Even inanimate objects are incarnations of the Mother. Meditating on this, one discovers a universal oneness, the perception that the multiplicity is an illusion, and that everything is merely the undifferentiated body of the Divine Mother.

NOTES

1. Swāmī Jagadīśvarānanda, *The Devī Māhātmyam or Śrī Durgā-Saptaśatī* (Madras: Sri Ramakrishna Math, 1972), pp. 3-11.
2. Śarvānanda, p. xxi.

CHAPTER TWENTY-TWO

The Uddhava-Gītā

Śrī Kṛṣṇa delivered two major discourses during His earthly lifetime, the *Bhagavad-Gītā* and the *Uddhava-Gītā*. While the *Bhagavad-Gītā* is part of the larger *Mahābhārata*, the *Uddhava-Gītā* appears in the eleventh canto of the *Śrīmad Bhāgavatam*. Its content does not contradict that of the *Bhagavad-Gītā*, but much of it is different. In many cases, it supplements the teachings of the *Gītā* by providing details to or illustrations of basic tenets proposed by the latter. Like all of the *Śrīmad Bhāgavatam*, the *Uddhava-Gītā's* central theme is *bhakti*, devotion to God.

Its setting is the last night of Lord Kṛṣṇa's life. He is fated to depart from this world at a given time, and His devoted servant Uddhava, who loves Kṛṣṇa dearly, approaches the *Avatāra* in time to appeal to Him. "O Keśava," he cries, "my Lord! To remain even a minute without You is impossible for me. Therefore deign to take me also to Your realm with You" (1.43).[1]

Kṛṣṇa's "realm", of course, is Himself, the indivisible Oneness of God. It is as much a state of consciousness, as a place. The Lord is all too happy to bring Uddhava along, but first the disciple must be endowed with knowledge, and this is learned from a qualified *guru* and diligent spiritual practice. As was His style in the *Gītā*, Kṛṣṇa doesn't mince words. "Abandoning all attachment for your own people and relatives," He tells Uddhava, "resign yourself to Me and wander all over the world, recognizing My presence in everything" (2.6).

Control of the Mind

The world, He continues, is insubstantial and transitory; only for the uncontrolled mind does it appear as a multiplicity. Nothing exists which is not the Ātman, and the Ātman is nothing other than the Supreme (2.7,8,9). But how, Uddhava asks, does one control the mind and renounce attachments? It seems almost impossible (2.15-16).

Human beings are uniquely suited for this task, Kṛṣṇa explains, because they are endowed with the discriminative faculty (*buddhi*, also translated as "intellect") with which they can seek Truth through observation and inference. The *buddhi*, as well as all knowledge-gathering instruments (the senses, the mind, etc.) are mere mechanisms, and have no consciousness themselves. There must be a consciousness behind them, an intelligent agent which is the perceiver (2.23). This truth ought to be so obvious one can conclude it for oneself, without the help of a *guru*. To illustrate this point, Kṛṣṇa relates the story of the *avadhūta* (illumined renunciate) and his twenty-four teachers. This narrative spans Chapters Two through Four.

The *Avadhūta's* Twenty-Four Teachers

One day the virtuous King Yadu (from whom the Yādava clan, to which Kṛṣṇa belongs, is descended) met a very young *avadhūta*. Though he bore all the signs of God-realization, he seemed too young to have spent the requisite amount of time studying under a *guru*. "O holy one," the king said, "kindly tell me what it is that always fills your heart with joy, though you are without any object of sense enjoyment and are companionless and alone" (2.30).

"Many *gurus*," the *avadhūta* replied, "have I had, and from them I became free from desires and bondages." Freedom from desire is the secret of the *avadhūta's* happiness, and he learned this lesson not from a spiritual master, but by merely observing the natural world and drawing reasonable conclusions from it. That the tenets of spiritual life are rational and practical, not esoteric and obscure, is indicated by this tale.

The *avadhūta's* twenty-four *gurus* were the earth, air, sky, water, fire, sun, moon, dove, python, ocean, river, moth, honey-bee, elephant, honey gatherer, deer, fish, courtesan, osprey, maiden, arrow-smith, snake, spider and wasp (2.33-35). For example, from the air he learned that if he should happen to come into contact with sense objects he may remain ever unaffected by them, just as the air touches everything but is untouched by anything. Just as the sky is never affected by clouds, so is the Ātman never affected by its proximity to the body. Always in communion with Brahman, the sage remains ever unpolluted, like fire, and contact with him or her is purifying, like water. Like the python, the sage should accept whatever food comes along by chance. Like the ocean, he or she should be deep, profound, boundless and unperturbed. The sage should avoid vulgar music for it pulls one into the snares of sense bondage, just like the hunter's imitative cry of the doe seduces the deer into his net. Just as the fish perishes by swallowing the baited hook, so does an uncontrolled palate ensnare one in sense craving. So go the *avadhūta's* analogies, all of them clever and true. His observations of animals and their perishing through ignorance and blind sense indulgence are particularly keen. The endless search for flavors, sex, and various raw pleasures draw animals into their bondage and deaths. It is equally so with humans, ensnared by *māyā* and going from death to death. Yet humans can avoid such dangers by renunciation. Only we possess that power.

Renunciation is not a matter of puritanism or piety, not a means of self-punishment or life-denial. It is the pursuit of freedom. The spiritual aspirant is uncomfortable with bondage of any kind, and craving, egotism, selfishness, disdain for others, etc. are all forms of bondage. They keep us trapped to the phenomenal world with all its predictability and emptiness. The world is very small, its allurements very petty. Whatever worldly attachments one renounces (not just *things*, but subtle attachments, like the desire for fame or prestige or achievement) is compensated for a millionfold by the yet-unimagined joy and vigor that comes from freedom. Freedom, in fact, is its own reward. There is no such thing as happy bondage.

Bondage and Freedom

In the fifth chapter, Śrī Kṛṣṇa discusses the entangling nature of *karma*. Actions, good, bad or neutral, bind us because as long as we perform reaction-generating action, we must remain embodied so as to suffer or enjoy the karmic results. Even religious rituals, if performed with some expectation of benefit in mind, generate *karma*. However, Kṛṣṇa instructs us to always attend to our responsibilities and duties. It is selfishness, not action per se, which binds us.

How can the Ātman be ever-free, Uddhava asks, if it is trapped within a body which engages in action? If the Ātman cannot be bound, why do we feel as though it is? Kṛṣṇa addresses these questions in Chapter Six. Bondage and liberation, He explains, apply only to the body and mind, which are a product of the *guṇas*. The *guṇas*, in turn, are based on *māyā*, and are not factual. Bondage and liberation are aspects of *māyā*. They do not in any real sense exist. The Ātman, being one with Kṛṣṇa (Brahman) is not affected by *māyā*, just as Brahman is never affected by *māyā* (6.1-4). This is a repetition of Kṛṣṇa's teachings in the *Bhagavad-Gītā*.

Next He describes the being who is free, though living in a body. Always steeped in the bliss of the Ātman, he or she remains a mere witness, and rejects all concern for manifoldness, what to speak of praise or insult, fortune or ruin (8.5-17). The easiest way to reach this state of sublime detachment is by following the path of devotion, which is described in detail in verses 8.29-48. Here Kṛṣṇa lists the qualities a devotee should strive to cultivate, the practical methods of *bhakti yoga* (hearing, worshipping, hymning, offering everything to God, etc.), and in what forms He may be worshipped. If one accepts each form mentioned here as a worshipable divine image, the whole world will appear pervaded by God, an ecstatic, sacred realm where everything is endowed with consciousness. We can worship Kṛṣṇa in the sun, fire, holy people, the cow, the devotee, the sky, air, water, earth, our own Ātman, and the collectivity of living beings (6.42). Try this yourself and you'll soon begin to feel very different.

In Chapter Seven Kṛṣṇa explains that of all spiritual practices, association with holy people is the most efficacious, and He gives examples of devotees who achieved the highest realization from this one practice alone. The supreme example, of course, are the *gopīs.* He goes on, in Chapter Eight, to explain that while the body and mind are a product of the *guṇas,* spiritual disciplines practiced by the body and mind in the mode of *sattva* (purity and goodness) destroy the same body and mind (8.7). One should cultivate *sattva* by associating with sattvic things. These aren't specified in the text, but in their translations, Swāmīs Tapasyānanda and Mādhavānanda list the ten objects classified according to their sattvic, rajasic and tamasic forms. These are presented in the diagram on p. 347.[2]

One clearly sees that sattvic things deal with the Divine and its attainment, rajasic things with worldly gain and its attainment, and tamasic things with evil, ghosts and the occult. Rajasic and tamasic elements are to be strictly avoided because they draw the mind away from the Divine. Concentrating the mind firmly on God is the highest *yoga;* Kṛṣṇa (Viṣṇu) taught this to Sanaka and his group of sages in an incident which is recounted in Chapter Eight.

Brahmā, the Divine Swan, and the Conquest of the Mind

The mind-born sons of Brahmā approached their father with a question: how can the aspirant wean the mind away from sense objects? This is the same question posed by Uddhava at the start of the dialogue. Brahmā was at a loss, and appealed to Viṣṇu for an answer. The Lord appeared in the form of a swan and removed his doubts.

The conquest of the mind, He taught, is effected by a twofold understanding. First, sense objects act upon the mind and intellect, but the mind and intellect are mere organs, not one's conscious, witnessing Self, which is pure Ātman. Second, all sense objects are comprised of the five elements which have their source in, and are non-different from, Brahman. Everything is Brahman and at the same time the true Self, the

The Ten Objects in Their Sattvic, Rajasic and Tamasic Classifications

	SATTVIC	RAJASIC	TAMASIC
1.) Scripture:	those that teach renunciation and the journey back to Brahman	those that deal with worldly benefits	those that are atheistic or injurious
2.) Water:	holy water	fragrant water	liquor
3.) People:	spiritual people	worldly-minded people	evil people
4.) Places:	solitude	public thorough-fares	gambling houses
5.) Times:	*brahmamuhurta* (4:00 a.m. through dawn)	twilight	midnight
6.) Actions:	obligatory rites and unselfish action	profit-motivated action	dreadful or occult action
7.) Initiation:	*Vaiṣṇava* or any pure religion	*Śākta*, or burden-some with rite and detail	any religion involving spirits or evil
8.) Meditation:	on God	on worldly objects	on enemies with a view to revenge
9.) *Mantras*:	*Oṃ* or others for spiritual enlightenment	those for worldly gain	those relating to spirits or the occult
10.) Purification:	of the mind	of the body	of unholy places

Ātman, is ever unaffected by this Brahmic phantasmagoria. Keeping these truths always in mind brings gradual detachment from objects because one begins to see no thing as substantially different from any other thing. What is there, then, to desire or revile?

The three states of consciousness — wakefulness, sleep and deep, dreamless sleep — are presented as an example of the unity of the true Self through any and all modifications of consciousness. This is true, too, of *turīya*, the "fourth state", or supreme Realization. There is only one Consciousness and it resides in all *jīvas* and all modifications of conditioned consciousness as the witnessing Self. (For more on the four states see *Māṇḍūkya Upaniṣad*.)

Bhakti and Related Spiritual Practices

Many different spiritual paths have been advocated by different teachers, Uddhava says; which one is the best? The supreme path, Kṛṣṇa replies, is *bhakti*, the path of devotion. The gradual growth of devotion to God by itself destroys sense attachments, and one who is free of sensual fetters and fixes the consciousness on God in the heart will attain liberation. This very simple premise is the key to spiritual advancement. Renunciation and devotion develop together; devotion naturally gives rise to renunciation because God is so much more delectable than any worldly object or experience, and renunciation clears away any obstacles to the spontaneous growth of devotion.

Devotion, Kṛṣṇa explains, purifies the mind, and the more one's mind is purified, the more one can comprehend the subtle truth of the Ātman. From verse thirty-two to the end of Chapter Nine, Kṛṣṇa provides directions for meditation. These are in keeping with the methods prescribed by Patañjali in his *Yoga Sūtras*, the standard textbook on the art of meditation. They are suitable for everyone. Briefly,

1.) Sit on a level seat with the spine straight and eyes half closed.

2.) Perform a few *prāṇāyāmas*, or rhythmic breathing exercises. These involve inhaling (*pūraka*), retaining (*kumbhaka*), and exhaling (*recaka*) smoothly and easily. Though it is not specified in the text, the usual practice is to execute each step while mentally repeating *Oṃ* a fixed number of times.

3.) Meditate on the mystic sound *Oṃ*, imagining it as the fine thread of a lotus stalk extending from the base of the spine (the *mūlādhāra cakra*) to the region of the heart.

4.) Imagine the lotus of the heart drooping, with the tip down. Make it bloom beautifully, raising it up and opening its eight petals.

5.) On the pericarp in the center imagine the sun. Within the sun, the moon. Within the moon, fire. In the middle of the fire, the form of God.

6.) Hold the mind steadily on God's form, seeing the Supreme Self in the Self, and the Self in the Supreme Self. Try to eliminate all distinction between the seer, the seen and the act of seeing.

In this case, the form of Viṣṇu is recommended as the appropriate subject of meditation. However, the aspirant may meditate on any Divine Form he or she chooses. This could be Jesus Christ, any of the Hindu Gods, Goddesses or *Avatāras*, the formless Brahman, Buddha, or whomever. One can imagine the sky, and ocean, a bright light or any image signifying the Absolute, though it is usually easier to fix the mind on God with a human-like form. The purpose behind the sun-moon-fire progression is to systematically draw the scattered mental energies inward and, step-by-step, fix the concentration deep within. It is not strictly necessary. The important thing is to meditate on God in the heart.

Chapter Ten involves *siddhis*, or occult powers resulting from yogic practices. There are eighteen in all, such as mind reading, assuming any form one likes, unobstructed movement anywhere, the ability to control others and so on. The methods for attaining each of these *siddhis* is openly described, and that advancement in general spiritual practice also results in the spontaneous emergence of *siddhis* without the *yogī* pursuing them. ("To the *yogī* who has thus conquered the senses, controlled the vital forces, attained steadiness of mind, and concentrated it on Me, many psychic powers accrue" (10.1).)

However, *siddhis* are not at all desirable. They will not aid in one's attaining Self-realization; in fact, they can be a hindrance. Rooted in *prakṛti*, serving no reasonable purpose, they can cause delay in spiritual progress because the aspirant becomes infatuated with them. God is the source of all *siddhis*, and they are just so much ephemera. One should ignore them and keep going until the real Goal is reached.

Chapter Eleven is almost identical to Chapter Ten of the *Bhagavad-Gītā*, where Kṛṣṇa describes to Arjuna His many manifestations and glories. This does not escape the Lord's attention, for when Uddhava requests that He list His divine attributes and manifestations for the sake of the devotees' contemplation, He replies, "O Uddhava! You are a clever questioner! This very question was put to Me at the battlefield of Kurukṣetra by Arjuna . . ." (11.6). Like its counterpart in the *Bhagavad-Gītā*, Chapter Eleven is one of the most splendid of this text. It includes a few references that are not included in the *Gītā* (among jewels He is the ruby, among flowers, the lotus, etc.) and the items are listed in different order, but otherwise it is the same. The reader is therefore directed to the chapter on the *Bhagavad-Gītā* for a fuller exposition on this subject.

The system of *varṇāśrama dharma* is elucidated in the next two chapters. *Varṇa* literally means "color", but refers to caste. *Āśrama* means dwelling place, but in this context refers to the four stages of life which men are expected to pass through. Briefly, the four *varṇas* are *brāhmaṇa*, the priestly and intellectual class, *kṣatriya*, the military and government class, *vaiśya*, the mercantile class, and *śūdra*, the laboring class. Each *varṇa* has different responsibilities, sacred and secular, and different personal characteristics, all of which Kṛṣṇa describes in detail.

The four *āśramas* are *brahmacarya*, or celibate student, *gṛhastha*, or married householder, *vānaprastha*, or retired spiritual seeker, and *sannyāsa*, the complete renunciate. Only men are bound to the *āśrama* system; women are considered to have two *āśramas* only, maidenhood and marriage. The point of the *āśramas* is to allow the ordinary man an opportunity to achieve spiritual realization. One need not lead a life of monasticism in order to reach the ultimate Goal; every aspect of life, including sex, career, possessions, pleasure, has its own time and place. Attended to soberly and at the right time, the regular phases of life need not prove an obstacle to Self-realization. At the stage of *vānaprastha*, or retirement, one gradually lets go of possessions and responsibilities and, if possible, visits important pilgrimage sites. Renunciation comes gradually, not as a sudden, shocking leap into the abyss. When one is perfectly ready for that final severing with the world, and not a moment sooner, one takes the vow of *sannyāsa* and becomes a wandering *sādhu*.

While few of us, particularly Westerners, will ever go that far, a thorough study of Chapter Thirteen, the *sannyāsin's* way of life, is extremely beneficial. We must strive for this ideal, even if we know we will not attain it in this lifetime, for most of the rules of *sannyāsa* — renunciation, humility, non-injury, sweetness, purity, devotion, poise, etc. — are applicable to all people at all stages.

Kṛṣṇa has spoken much of devotion, and we know that it involves the cultivation of feeling, but what of devotional practice? What are the specifics of *bhakti yoga*? These are laid out in Chapter Fourteen, verses 19-23. They include reverence for accounts of divine pastimes and excellences, constant repetition of the divine Name, worship, offering hymns and prayers, prostrating, service to devotees, memory of God's presence in all beings, devoting one's speech to describing the Lord and one's mind to renouncing desires, giving up wealth and enjoyment for God's sake, performing the sacred duties of one's station such as rituals, sacrifices, charity, austerity, repetition of *mantras* and so on.

Devotees who have followed these disciplines, Kṛṣṇa says, have attained complete self-surrender and pure, loving devotion. The mind is thus purified, and when such a pure mind is offered to God, all spiritual excellences result. The very same mind, if allowed to linger in the world of multiplicity and to fix itself to sense enjoyment, becomes engrossed in falsehood (14.25-26). That the same mind is both friend and foe is mentioned also in the *Bhagavad-Gītā* (6.6). One should always consider the mind merely another sense organ and not confuse it with the Self. The fact that we can disinterestedly observe the movements of our own minds and pass judgement on what we see there proves that the mind is separate from the Self. While it takes practice, this chattering monkey can be controlled. Because the mind is an object, it can be surrendered to God, as one might surrender any possession. One does not lose anything thereby; quite to the contrary, the purified mind offered completely to God becomes a finely-tuned, highly efficient instrument. The controlled mind is stripped of its superficialities, no longer cluttered with trivia, irrelevancies, and noise. It is tranquil, perceptive, reasonable and endowed with exceptional powers of concentration. One can go so far as to say that the spiritual aspirant practicing mental control becomes more intelligent than he or she was before. And with the mind turned over to God, the aspirant develops a unique dispassion and poise. When God controls this object, it cannot make a false move.

Kṛṣṇa continues to offer specific instructions, now in response to a slew of rapid questions involving the real meaning of various terms, disciplines, sacrifices, and so on. "What is charity?" Uddhava asks; "What is austerity? What is valor? What is truthfulness? What is renunciation?" (14.29). Basic to the practice of any *yoga* are the observance of *yama*, universal moral principles, and *niyama*, particular moral acts. *Yama* consists of non-injury, truthfulness, non-covetousness, non-attachment, conscientiousness, non-hoarding, faith in the scriptures, chastity, moderation in speech, constancy, forgiveness, and fearlessness. Truly universal and inarguable, these principles would be embraced by any major religion. *Niyama* is slightly more Hindu-oriented. It is comprised of cleanliness, purity of mind, repetition of the holy Names, austerity, fire-sacrifice, faith (in God, *guru* and one's self), hospitality, worship, visiting holy places, contentment, service to others, and service to the *guru*. A contemporary Western aspirant probably couldn't stage a fire sacrifice and, unless they planned to visit India, would have to limit pilgrimage to churches and temples, but the remaining elements of *niyama* are certainly manageable. These are the basics upon which all *yogas* — *jñāna, bhakti, rāja, karma, krīya, siddha, etc.*— depend.

From this foundation we can progress to greater specifics. Kṛṣṇa outlines the behavior conducive to spiritual advancement by answering Uddhava's questions in both the positive and the negative. It is a wonderful literary device in that it simultaneously teaches spiritual virtues while exposing the emptiness of both mechanical observances and working for selfish gain. He says:

> The highest charity is the abandonment of the tendency to harm other living beings and not mere doling out of alms . . . Heroism lies in the conquest of one's animal nature and not in mere combativeness . . . Truth is seeing God in everything, and not mere factual speech . . . Real profit is the attainment of devotion to Me, and not the gain of wealth . . . True beauty comes from desirelessness and austerity, and not by mere decorations and jewelry. True happiness consists in seeking neither happiness nor misery, but remaining detached and unconcerned in all situations (14.37,40,41).

Good and bad, it seems, are not fixed polar opposites, but merely different ways of looking at the world. That which helps lead one to God is considered good, while that which poses an obstacle to God-realization is not so good. Yet ultimately the aspirant must pass beyond both of them, recognizing the difference as so much more dualism and so much more *māyā*. Just as Jesus instructed his audience to "resist not evil", Lord Kṛṣṇa says, "What is the use of too long of a description (of good and bad)? To transcend the feeling of distinction between the two is real virtue" (14.45).

But, Uddhava asks, if this is so, why do the *Vedas* contain injunctions and prohibitions? Duties and demerits described in the *Vedas*, Kṛṣṇa replies, have their place, particularly for the worldly-minded, but the spiritual aspirant, the practitioner of *yoga*, is beyond them. There are three principal yogas — *karma yoga, bhakti yoga* and *jñāna yoga* — and one may, according to his temperament, choose one or practice all three simultaneously (15.6-11).

How can a person be beyond good and evil? For a genuine spiritual aspirant, there is no possibility of evil conduct; he or she cannot help but act ethically. As for goodness, Kṛṣṇa explains how the *yogī* passes beyond that too:

> When a person has become adverse to worldly duties because of a true abhorrence to worldly values, and when as a consequence he has gained mastery over the senses, he should strive to make his mind recollected and steady by repeated practice of inward contemplation (15.18).

The point stressed so many times throughout the *Bhagavad-Gītā* and throughout the *Uddhava-Gītā* is stressed yet again: fix the mind on

God. Gather it in, bring it under control, lock out all other thoughts, and hold it securely on the Divine (15.19-24). In this way the Supreme can be known; it is the root of all yogic paths and the goal of all yogic paths. It doesn't matter whether one steadies the concentration by means of disciplined action (*karma*), philosophical reflection (*jñāna*) or image worship (*bhakti*), so long as one steadies that mind (15.24). However, Kṛṣṇa reminds Uddhava that all yogic paths, and their results, are included in *bhakti yoga*.

Continuing on the subject of right and wrong and Vedic injunctions to these effects, Kṛṣṇa spends the whole of Chapter Sixteen discussing the intricacies of these issues. The Westerner may find this section of academic interest only as much of it simply does not apply to Western culture. At length He describes, for instance, the principles of ritualistic purity and pollution as well as the correct way to interpret the *karma-kāṇḍa*, or ritualistic section, of the *Vedas*. Deeply rooted in South Asian culture and psychology, these issues are relevant to Indians, but not to Westerners. However, the tone of the chapter is very important, for throughout it the Lord stresses the *relative* nature of vice and virtue, morality, purity, scriptural interpretation and so on. What may be wrong in one situation is perfectly acceptable in another. For instance, a *sannyāsin's* succumbing to a sexual liaison is considered a heinous degradation, while for an ordinary husband it is perfectly natural and good.

The greater one's personal and spiritual development, the greater is one's responsibility to maintain a high level of conduct. For a man at a lesser stage of evolution, drunkenness and carousing are not that harmful, but for an elevated individual such behavior represents a decline. "A man who is already lying on the ground cannot have a further fall," Kṛṣṇa says. "It is the man who is high or erect that is liable to fall" (16.17). Correct conduct, then, is to be understood as relative to one's circumstances, a point to certainly keep in mind before passing judgement on anyone.

This is not to say that Kṛṣṇa condones sloppy morality or conduct in any way; to the contrary, He expects everyone to gradually improve in character. The one who slides into craving, wrath and moral degeneration, He says, ". . . becomes a zero as far as his humanity is concerned. He is as good as dead. He loses all the great values obtainable through human life" (16.21). Know your station, know your *dharma*, be sensitive to circumstances and behave accordingly. Sensible advice for anyone.

A beautiful revelation concludes the chapter, as Kṛṣṇa discloses the true import of the *Vedas*. Though the *Vedas* may appear archaic in places or preoccupied with material gain or lesser deities, these are superficial characteristics only. The *Vedas* proceeded directly from Brahman and are a tangible manifestation of Brahman. In the *karma-kāṇḍa* section, the part containing instructions for ritual, "What I enjoin as injunctions is Myself in the form of *yajña* (sacrifice)," Kṛṣṇa says. "In the *upāsanā-kāṇḍa* (hymns to the gods) it is Myself that I describe in the form of various deities." And in the *jñāna-kanda*, or the *Upaniṣads*, the Ultimate Negative identified with the Supreme is also Him (16.42- 43). One may interpret this passage to refer to all the world's sacred scriptures.

The Material World and the Ever-Free Ātman

In the third canto of the *Śrīmad Bhāgavatam* we were given a complex creation account which included the evolution of the primary and secondary elements which comprise the material universe. Here Uddhava inquires into the elemental categories. Some schools of thought, he says, claim there are twenty-six elements, others only four, still others claim seven, nine, sixteen, thirteen, etc.. Which school is correct?

They are all correct, Kṛṣṇa replies. Different views occur because some schools consider the resulting elements implicit in their causal elements and therefore do not list them, while others list them all (17.4). But it is not that important. The point of analyzing the natural elements and categorizing them is simply to see their hollow, ultimately unreal nature and thus recognize the Ātman's independence of them. This is the basis of the *Sāṃkhya* philosophy, reputedly first codified by the sage Kapila in the 7th Century B.C.

Briefly, the two primordial elements are *Puruṣa* (Consciousness, the Supreme Soul, Spirit, Śiva) and *prakṛti* (Nature, unmanifest matter, Energy, *Śakti*, the Divine Mother). Both are originally static. *Prakṛti*, however, is activated by the *guṇas* (qualities or "strands"), namely *rajas*, or impulse, *tamas*, or inertia, and *sattva*, or harmony. When *prakṛti* is aroused, she evolves the *tattvas*, or cosmic principles, which include *ahaṃkāra* (ego, or "I-ness"), *buddhi* (intelligence), *manas* (mind), the five gross elements (earth, air, fire, water and ether), the five subtle elements (sound, touch, form, taste, smell), and ten organs of knowledge and action (the sense organs, the bodily limbs, etc.). All together, these comprise the material universe. While *Puruṣa*, the Divine Consciousness, is the source of all life and animation and imbues the *tattvas* with the living spark, it is always separate from them, always unaffected by them. The spiritual aspirant should always strive to identify with *Puruṣa* and not with *prakṛti*, who is personified in the Goddess Mahāmāyā (Grand Illusion). The dichotomy which hits us closest to home is that of the Ātman and the body. As Uddhava points out (17.26), though *Puruṣa* and *prakṛti* are separate, they always appear together and are difficult to distinguish. Nowhere is this more acute than in the Ātman-body problem.

"No doubt *Puruṣa* and *prakṛti* are absolutely separate," Kṛṣṇa states. "This body, which is a series of changes, is the result of permutations and combinations of the *guṇas*" (17.29). So, too, is the whole multiplicity of objects in the universe. No thing is different in substance from any other thing. The divisiveness of objects is an illusion. Neither is one Ātman different from any other; the experience of divisiveness is produced by *ahaṃkāra*, "I-ness", which can be overcome (17.32).

We experience ourselves as individuals, instead of as undifferentiated Brahman, because of the existence of what is known as the *liṅga-śarīra*, or subtle body. The *liṅga-śarīra* is comprised of the five *indriyas* (sense organs, that is, those faculties *by which* the physical organs, which are themselves inert, perceive objects and sensations), the mind, and the tendencies derived from *karma*. It is this subtle body which transmigrates into new bodies following death, *not the Ātman* (17.36). The Ātman cannot transmigrate because it is undifferentiated Brahman and is never affected by matter. It is never one place and not another. It does not move; it is all-pervading. It only *seems* to transmigrate along with the subtle body. This is in keeping with the Buddhist philosophy, which holds that it is not an individual soul which transmigrates, but mental impressions, desires, etc., and they can be snuffed out (hence the term *Nirvāṇa*, "extinguished").

Bodies change, the *liṅga-śarīra* stubbornly holds itself together while undergoing constant transformation, but the Spirit is never born, never dies, never undergoes changes, is never conditioned in any way. The continuity of personhood, even from body to body, is a perceptual illusion. Kṛṣṇa illustrates it well:

> In the light, though the flame is constantly changing, men say it is the same light. Water is continuously flowing away in a river, but men speak of it as the same river. In these cases, resemblance is mistaken for identity. So also ignorant men think and speak of a man of today as the same as of yesterday, though he has long ceased to be (17.44).

This is the most subtle Truth which the *Upaniṣads*, *Bhagavad-Gītā* and *Purāṇas* have to impart. Anyone who enters into this understanding, even intellectually, had graduated to an entirely different level of experience from the common run of humanity.

"Until one is awakened unto Truth," Kṛṣṇa declares, "the experience of *saṃsāra* (embodiment, death, reembodiment) will continue" (17.55). It is want of awareness of the Ātman which keeps one identifying with the illusory *liṅga-śarīra*. One who has successfully severed identification with the subtle body, however, is the liberated saint. He or she can withstand any adversity, any abuse, any persecution with perfect calmness (17.57-58).

But, Uddhava argues, this seems contrary to nature. Is it not instinctual for one, however wise, to recoil from persecution and insult (17.59-60)? Indeed, Śrī Kṛṣṇa replies, "The sharp arrows struck at vital parts of the body do not mortify a man to the same extent as the arrows of filthy abuse which evil men release at you" (18.3). However, we can learn to be strong enough to withstand insult, and as inspiration we can look to the *brāhmaṇa* of Avanti, whose story Kṛṣṇa recounts in chapter eighteen.

The Despised *Brāhmaṇa* of Avanti

He began as a miserly businessman. Cold, perverse, devoid of love, he hoarded money but failed to maintain his family members with even the barest necessities, what to speak of attending to his duties to the gods, who expect a share of a rich man's wealth in the form of ritualistic performance. His sons hated him, his wife and daughters were oppressed by him, the gods were furious at him, and as a result, bad *karma* steadily accrued. It fructified swiftly and horribly. His wealth dissipated suddenly, fire and accident visited his house and his family deserted him completely. He was penniless, friendless, destitute.

By the grace of God, the *brāhmaṇa* was seized by the spirit of renunciation. Hoarding money, he realized, brings no happiness. It gives birth to pettiness and fear, greed and callousness. So he took up the wandering mendicant's way of life which was, for him, particularly harsh because he was persecuted wherever he went. Passersby spat on him, cursed him, beat him, urinated in his begging bowl. Yet he bore it all calmly, without a word in self-defense or a single negative thought about his tormentors.

His steadiness was due to correct understanding, which in this case was twofold. First, he realized that it was not his persecutors who were responsible for his pain, but his own mind. The mind is what makes distinctions between pleasure and pain, vice and virtue, insult and praise. For the mind which is one-pointed, injury does not exist because everything is seen in its Oneness. Secondly, the Ātman, the true Self, is never affected by insult. What's more, the Ātman in others is identical to one's own Ātman. Who, then, is the insulter, who the insulted? The phenomenon of insult or injury is an absurdity, an impossibility. Happiness and misery, birth and death, friend and foe are all products of ignorance. The experience of these has its source within ourselves, not from any outside factor. To control the mind, then, is the sum and substance of spiritual practice.

Sāṃkhya* Philosophy and the Three *Guṇas

In the next chapter, Kṛṣṇa elaborates on the *Sāṃkhya* system expounded in brief in Chapter Seventeen, including a quick creation account and explanation of universal dissolution (*pralaya*) at the close of each cosmic cycle. Again, He stresses that the import of such cogitations is to impress upon one the unreality of the manifest world. "How can there occur the delusion of difference in the mind of one who constantly thinks over this process?" He remarks. "It will take to wings as darkness before the sun . . ." (19.28).

Chapter Twenty is also an elaboration on an earlier theme, the three *guṇas*. Every phenomenon is predominated by one or another *guṇa*, and the ability to recognize this is an important tool for spiritual growth because it fosters detachment and *viveka* (discrimination between the Real and the unreal). Chapter Fourteen of the *Bhagavad-Gītā* is also devoted to the study of the *guṇas*. After a careful reading of that text one should have a firm grasp of the subject, and this section of the *Uddhava-Gītā* can be viewed as an elaboration. Here Kṛṣṇa describes in great detail the many manifestations of the *guṇas* and stresses constantly that while *sattva* (purity, goodness, light, calmness) is to be favored, spiritual realities, moods, and practices are beyond the *guṇas* entirely. The aspirant should seek to transcend them for they are strictly of a material nature, rooted in *prakṛti*.

Understanding how the *guṇas* operate is extremely helpful in developing spiritual perception. For instance, when finding oneself flying into a fit of anger, one can examine the inner phenomenon in a detached way. Instead of thinking, "I am angry", the witnessing self can think, "The rajasic element within me is now predominating." Similarly, finding oneself in a unpleasant environment, or confronting an unpleasant person, one can remain unaffected by discerning the predominating *guṇa*, or combination of *guṇas*, and understanding them to be unreal. The reader may refer to the accompanying chart, which shows how the *guṇas* manifest themselves in different contexts.

The aspirant, Kṛṣṇa says, should always cultivate *sattva* in order to overcome *rajas* and *tamas*. Then, by cultivating tranquility, desireless-

Further Signs of *Sattva, Rajas, and Tamas* Drawn from *Uddhava-Gītā*, Chapter Twenty (and Other Sources)

	SATTVA	RAJAS	TAMAS
General Category:	knowledge	passion	ignorance
Personal Characteristics:	mental control, sense control, forbearance, discrimination, austerity, truthfulness, compassion, memory, contentment, self-sacrifice, desirelessness, faith, aversion to evil, charity, absorption in the Self	desire, pride, activity, greed, haughtiness, longing for selfish ends, sense of multi-plicity, sensuality, enthusiasm arising from excitement, craving for name and fame, ridicule of others, demonstrativeness, aggression	anger, greed, treachery, cruelty, beggar-liness, hypocrisy, languor, quarrelsomeness, depression, delusion, despondency, wretchedness, lassitude, vain expectations, fear, lack of initiative or vigor
State of Consciousness:	wakefulness	dreaming	dreamless deep sleep
State of Mind:	serene, happy, unattached	excited, restless, extroverted	inert, drowsy, depressed
Body Consciousness:	knows Ātman and body as unconnected	knows Ātman as inhabiting the body	believes Ātman and body to be the same
Food:	pure, healthy, easily obtainable	exciting to the senses	impure and unhealthy
Happiness:	from spiritual contemplation	from sense contacts	from delusion (drinking, drugs, sexual depen-dency etc.)
Mood:	peace	excitation/action	inertia
Function:*	balance	impulse	inertia
Color:	white	red	black
Deity:	Viṣṇu	Brahmā	Śiva

*According to *Sāṃkhya.*

ness, and oneness with the Divine, *sattva* can be overcome as well. Completely free from *prakṛti*, one attains Brahman.

Avoiding Low Company

In the ninth canto of the *Śrīmad Bhāgavatam*, fourteenth chapter, we met King Purūravas who married, and was abandoned by, the celestial nymph Urvaśī. As an example of how the company one keeps influences one's spiritual progress or retardation, Kṛṣṇa refers to this story. "One should never associate with people whose ideal in life is mere satisfaction of hunger and sex. One who follows such a person is consigned to the dense darkness of ignorance, just as a blind man led by another blind man" (21.3). King Purūravas's infatuation is a case in point, however the text makes very clear that the company is not to be blamed. If one should be frightened at the sight of a rope, mistaking it for a snake, the rope is not to blame, but the person. Similarly, Urvaśī was not the cause of Purūravas's losing his head; Purūravas was (21.17).

Kṛṣṇa advises us to avoid those people who arouse our sexual ardor, for mingling with them enslaves our minds and senses. Instead, we should seek out the company of holy men and women, whose influence is calming, ennobling, and enlightening. For those of us struggling to overcome our lower natures, holy men and women are our sole refuge in this world.

Pūjā, the Art of Ceremonial Worship

For those interested in performing *pūjā*, or worship of divine images, Chapter Twenty-Two gives some basic instructions. These would be difficult to actually follow without the help of a competent teacher, but the reader will gain a sense of the mood and method of ritualistic worship as well as the theory behind it.

Worship can be performed mentally, so even if the paraphernalia is difficult or impossible to obtain, the aspirant attracted to this discipline need not be hindered. Also, worship can be done in part. One can set up an altar at home and offer the *Iṣṭa* (Chosen Ideal) some flowers, incense, water and food, much to the joy of both the Beloved and the devotee. The elaborateness of the ritual is not important. Devotion is the sole point, and the offerings merely represent concrete expressions of devotion, like giving a gift to someone you love even when there's no occasion for it.

> What is most important is *śraddhā* (sincere faith), and when an offering is made by a devotee with faith, be it only water, I accept it

with great delight. Not to speak of My delight when I am worshipped by a devoted man with flowers, incense, sandal paste and food offering. But offerings, however rich, do not please Me if they are not backed by devotion" (22.17-18).

One may worship God in an image, in a *yantra* (symbolic diagram), in the sun, in the water, in a holy person, or in one's own heart. Meditation is the most important element of worship, so despite the limitation of one's knowledge of ritual, or one's means, one can freely perform a *pūjā* to the best of one's ability.

The climax of the *Uddhava-Gītā's* teachings is contained in its penultimate chapter, where Śrī Kṛṣṇa grandly and yet succinctly sums it up in the concept of *advaita*, or non-dualism.

"All this world," Kṛṣṇa says, "is nothing but the Ātman . . . Therefore great seers have not accepted any existent entity other than the uninvolved and unaffected Ātman. It is He, the Supreme Cause, that shines as the many" (23.6-7). There is no multiplicity, only God, the Ātman. Superimposed on Ātman, by the deluding magic of *māyā*, is the *ahaṃkāra* ("I-ness"), the *buddhi* (intelligence), the *indriyas* (senses), the *manas* (mind), the *vṛttis* (mental waves and images), the *prāṇa* (life force), the body, and the *karma*. All together these unreal, dreamlike influences create the illusion of embodiment.

Jñāna, knowledge, severs the connection between the superimposed mind-body complex and the ever-free Ātman. *Jñāna* is like the sun. When the sun rises, it merely removes the obstacle of darkness, allowing the eyes to see what is already there. It has not created anything new to be seen. Similarly, when ignorance is removed, the Ātman shines as it has always been shining (23.34). Kṛṣṇa describes the Ātman superbly:

> He is self-luminous Consciousness, unoriginated and unfathomable. He is limitless Self-Consciousness without the polarity of subject and object, including in Himself all self-conscious centers and their experiences. He is the absolute One without a second, intuited when thought and words retreat, unable to go further . . . (23.35).

Concluding Instructions to Uddhava

Kṛṣṇa has imparted the greatest knowledge to Uddhava, and to us. The highest Truth has been explained as has the practical means for its attainment. In this concluding chapter, Śrī Kṛṣṇa puts special emphasis on two points: try to see the Divine Ātman everywhere and in everything and everyone, and dedicate all actions and the fruits of such actions ("action" includes thoughts, feelings, and words) to God. This twofold discipline frees one from the bondage of *karma* and gradually develops the perception of ultimate Truth, the divine Oneness of everything. Anyone who embraces the teachings of the *Uddhava-Gītā* becomes sanctified, dear to God, and eligible for oneness with Brahman. Greater still is the person who passes this wisdom on to others (24.25-27).

Finally, Kṛṣṇa instructs his disciple Uddhava to renounce the world completely and accept the life of a saintly mendicant at the place of pilgrimage called Badaryāśrama. Notice that this advice is the opposite of what Kṛṣṇa instructed Arjuna to do. In the *Bhagavad-Gītā*, He told his disciple to "get out there and fight," in other words, to live in the world and attend to his responsibilities, but in a detached manner, dedicating his work to God, and renouncing attachment to the fruits. Is Kṛṣṇa contradicting Himself? Not at all. Every aspirant is unique, and has a unique path to follow. No one discipline, or even belief, is right for everyone. We all have our own temperaments, our own strengths and weaknesses, our own level of development, and a genuine *guru* will take such diversity into account when imparting instructions.

Like the *Bhagavad-Gītā*, the *Uddhava-Gītā* is astonishing in the breadth of subjects it covers and the completeness of its treatment of both spiritual theory and practice. It also resembles the *Bhagavad-Gītā* in that it synthesizes many divergent traditions and extracts the common core of meaning among them, while maintaining respect for their differences. It is an intense text, a dense condensation of the very best of the best. The final verse expresses this sweetly:

> . . . The great Being Kṛṣṇa, from whom the *Vedas* originated, has herein gathered from the extensive garden of *Vedic* thought, this concentrated honey of knowledge and realization of the Supreme. As He collected the *amṛta* (nectar) from the ocean for being distributed among the *devas* (gods), so has He placed this teaching before all devotees for their benefit. I salute that Supreme Person Kṛṣṇa, the greatest of all beings (24.49).

NOTES

1. Tapasyānanda, *Srimad Bhāgavata*, vol. IV.
2. Tapasyānanda, vol. IV, p. 66 and Swāmī Mādhavānanda, *Uddhava Gītā* (Calcutta: Advaita Asrama, 1978), p. 112.

CHAPTER TWENTY-THREE

Other Well-Known Purāṇic Excerpts

There are three additional scriptures derived from the *Purāṇas* of which the reader ought to be aware, for they are in general use among Western aspirants and students at this time.

Bhakti-Ratnāvali

Bhakti-Ratnāvali means "A String of Devotional Gems", and tradition has it that in the Sixteenth Century, Śrī Kṛṣṇa Caitanya Mahāprabhu, a Bengali saint believed by many to be the *Avatāra* of this age, requested his devotee Viṣṇu Purī to fashion him a garland of gems. Viṣṇu Purī immediately understood Śrī Caitanya's meaning, and combed the voluminous *Śrīmad Bhāgavatam* for those passages which most powerfully, concisely and sweetly convey the essence of *bhakti*. Śrī Caitanya offered the compendium at the feet of Lord Jagannātha, the celebrated Kṛṣṇa deity at Purī, and then to all humanity.

With the exception of a very few explanatory verses by the compiler, this text is comprised entirely of *Śrīmad Bhāgavatam* verses arranged around the nine devotional processes of *bhakti yoga*: hearing, hymning, remembering, serving, worshiping, making obeisances, befriending, dedicating oneself, and taking shelter.

The purpose of the *Bhakti-Ratnāvali* is explained best by Viṣṇu Purī himself:

> There are many who, though not apathetic, cannot study or hear the full original *Bhāgavatam* owing to their preoccupation with the various affairs of life. Let this effort of Viṣṇu Purī to bring together the gems of verses from various sections of the *Bhāgavatam* and string them together into a consistent whole become useful to such devotees (1.9).[1]

Śrī Lalitā-Sahasranāma or Śrī Lalithāmbikā Sahasranāma Stotram

Lalitā is one of the names of the Divine Mother. *Sahasra* means "thousand" and *nāma* "names", hence the title, "The Thousand Names of the Divine Mother". An excerpt from the *Brahmāṇḍa Purāṇa*, these verses, while praising the many aspects of the Divine Mother, provide an extensive exposition on the theology and metaphysics of the Great Goddess. Particularly interesting is the discussion of the seven *Ḍākinīs*, or manifestations of the Goddess, located in the *cakra* centers of the body (verses 475-534). It is a powerful text.

Śrī Guru Gītā

This hymn from the *Skandha Purāṇa* extols the *guru* as a manifestation of the Absolute Truth, a theme echoed throughout the *Purāṇas*. Many aspirants utilize this text in liturgical chanting and personal meditation.

NOTES

1. Swāmī Tapasyānanda, *Bhakti Ratnavali or a Necklace of Devotional Gems* (Madras: Sri Ramakrishna Math, 1979), p. 88.

Part VII

The *Itihāsas*

CHAPTER TWENTY-FOUR

Introduction

The *Itihāsas* are a special branch of Hindu literature indelibly and deeply ingrained into the collective consciousness of India. Every Hindu knows these stories by heart, having heard them first in the cradle, later at their mother's knee, and still later as an integral part of their cultural education. The *Itihāsas* are India; India has been molded by them, is always informed by them, and will forever reflect them. They are the very stuff of the Hindu consciousness.

Yet as the world further assumes its new identity as a global village, where religions and cultures are no longer contained within geographic borders, the stories of the great epics are penetrating the lives of non-Indians, and the world is finding that the themes and characters are universal. Something about them touches the depths of everyone; they are rooted in our collective humanity, and in the spiritual truths which undergird all of our lives.

The word *Itihāsa* means "so indeed it was". There are two texts in this genre, the *Mahābhārata* and the *Rāmāyaṇa.* Both are long epic poems, rendered in Sanskrit, which tell the tales of ancient royal families. While the *Rāmāyaṇa,* the shorter of the two, spins the story of the divine *Avatāra* Rāma of the solar dynasty, the *Mahābhārata* tells of the lunar dynasty, which culminates in the birth of the five Pāṇḍava brothers (of whom Arjuna of the *Bhagavad-Gītā* is one), the divine Incarnation Kṛṣṇa, and the apocalyptic Kurukṣetra war. The *Bhagavad-Gītā* is a part of the *Mahābhārata.*

In both cases, the action takes place in a remote past where the line that separates the spiritual and material realms is blurred or missing entirely. The Divine is a constant presence on earth, interacting with mortals, guiding them, leading them to success or ruination according to Its plan. The period before the onslaught of this present cosmic epoch, or *Kali-yuga,* is a sacred time, when the actions of the primordial divine beings fixed themselves forever as legends to educate and inspire us, and made the world what it is. When the universe shifted into profane time, the gods receded, the sacred dried up, and we were left in world absent of meaning, not entirely real.

Yet we may revive sacred time whenever we wish, invoke the Divine whenever we desire, simply by recalling the stories. By reading, reciting, listening to, or even remembering the events of sacred history, the barrier between the celestial and the mundane is again obliterated and *Satya-yuga*, the spiritual golden age, exists again.

CHAPTER TWENTY-FIVE

The Mahābhārata

Mahā means "great", and *bhārata* refers to the descendants of the patriarchal king, Bharata. It is the story of ancient India and of the principal figures who shaped its destiny, and is most likely based on historical people and events, perhaps a tribal war fought in northern India during the first millennia B.C. or earlier. The *Mahābhārata* is the longest poem in the world, one hundred thousand verses long. Divided into eighteen chapters and further into subdivisions, it covers a vast array of subjects, for while the continuity of the central story is maintained, the text includes endless digressions into mythology, spiritual teaching, folklore, morality tales, expositions on statecraft and martial art, and so on. It is said that one who reads the entirety of the *Mahābhārata* need read no other book, because everything of importance is contained in it somewhere. Translated in its entirety, it fills approximately twelve volumes, so a full reading would be an impressive achievement. Most readers should avail themselves of a synopsized version, of which there are many excellent choices in English. These usually stick closely to the principal story line and, if well-rendered, convey the nuances of character and theme.

While attributed to the sage Kṛṣṇa Dvaipāyana, also known as Vyāsa (literally, "the arranger"), to whom the *Vedas* and *Śrīmad Bhāgavatam* are also attributed, the *Mahābhārata* might be a compendium many centuries in the making. Definite dates are unknown, but estimates include as early as 400 B.C. and as late as 400 A.D..[1] The many hands that went into its making account for the breadth of its contents; apparently the text acted like a magnet, drawing to itself all the best ideas of its culture as it wound its way through the centuries. The general reader ought to at least have a look at the *Mahābhārata* in its original to gain a sense of how it feels, sounds and hangs together, and of how fascinating and edifying its digressions actually are. Yet don't be discouraged if the thought of a full reading is too daunting. After a taste of the full text, a synopsis is sufficient.

Even then, the web of characters is so dense, a reader may still find him or herself getting lost. This is no cause for alarm; in time the characters will become clear in one's mind, and in the meantime one can become immersed in what must be one of the greatest soap operas of all time. Passions, romances, loyalties, hatreds, jealousies, deceptions, all sorts of sex and violence, demons, angels, deities, an Incarnation of God, magic, heartache, curses, secret shames, families in chaos, and the highest religious truths all blend together perfectly against a backdrop of the ever-present theme of *dharma*, or the divinely designed right order of things. *Dharma* is a concept, or force, which flows through creation and holds it together; individuals must fulfill their *dharma*, or attend to their natural duty in such a way as to fulfill the purpose chosen for them in life. The characters are often torn as to what is the correct action, the decision most in harmony with *dharma*. They find that *dharma*, like the God among them, Kṛṣṇa, is a trickster, ephemeral, hard to fathom. Yet *dharma*, it turns out, compels them; every twist and turn of their drama is an unfolding of their inexorable destiny. They are not free to determine the course of their own futures or even their own decisions because these are predestined, both by the driving force of *karma* and by the supreme will of God. Nothing happens except by express will of the Divine; free will is, ultimately, an illusion. This is the deeper message of the *Mahābhārata*.

To help the reader sort through the characters, a family tree has been provided. Although no brief synopsis can hope to capture the complexity of the story line, a very bare outline is given below to aid the reader in picking out the essential elements. Once these are understood, the details can be added with confidence.

The Patriarchs

It all begins with Vyāsa, the composer of the *Mahābhārata*, himself. He is both its author and a principal character in it, particularly in the beginning. Born to King Śaṃtanu under miraculous circumstances, he is a perfect forest sage with a wild, frightening outer appearance, but spiritual illumination within. He has composed the *Mahābhārata* in his head and needs a scribe to commit it to paper. Who should appear but the elephant-headed god Gaṇeśa, who agrees to be his scribe on the condition that there be no pause in his recitation. So the work begins.

King Śaṃtanu married the mysterious goddess Gaṅgā (the river Ganges) and with her had a son, Bhīṣma. Because he broke a vow to her, Gaṅgā left him, but Śaṃtanu took a second wife, Satyavatī, who agreed to the marriage only if her son could become king someday. Śaṃtanu was so smitten, Bhīṣma agreed to relinquish the throne and to this end took a vow of lifelong celibacy. This discipline endowed him with immense

Mahābhārata Family Tree

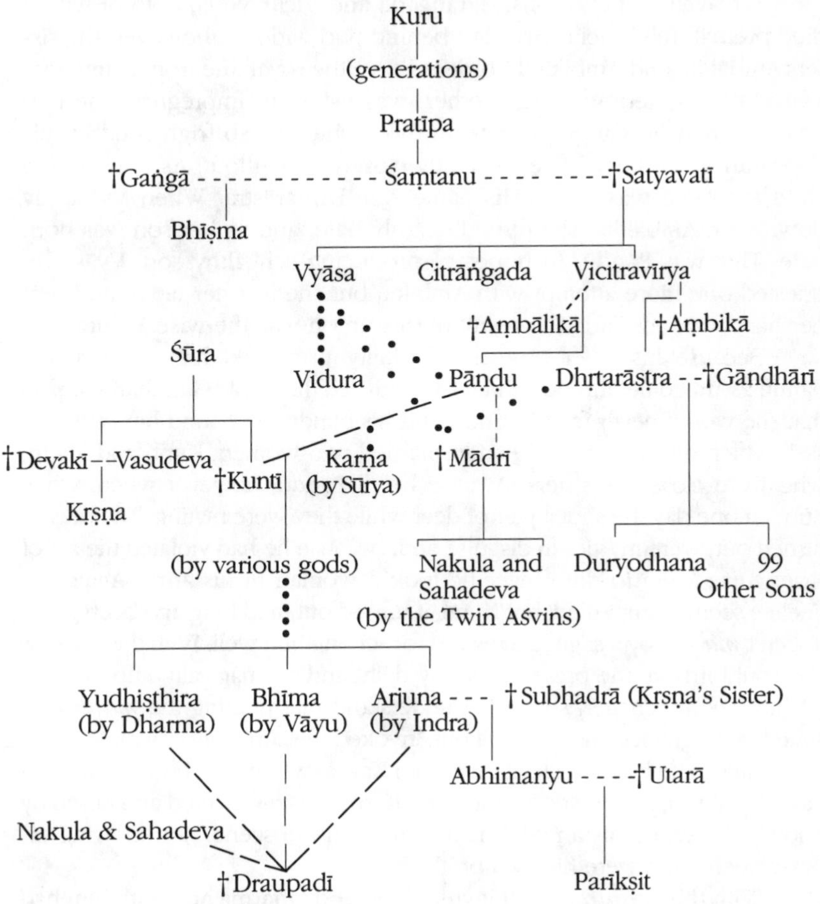

- - - - - denotes marriage

• • • • denotes biological parenting

† denotes a woman

power, and all looked upon him with reverent awe. He played a crucial role in the events to come.

Satyavatī had two sons, Citrāṅgada and Vicitravīrya, both of whom died prematurely. Vicitravīrya left behind two widows, however, the sisters Aṃbālikā and Aṃbikā. In order to save the royal line from extinction, Vyāsa, the mysterious third brother, was asked to impregnate the two sisters. When he lay down with Aṃbikā, she was so frightened by his appearance she kept her eyes tightly closed throughout. As a result, the child she bore was blind. His name was Dhṛtarāṣṭra. When Vyāsa lay down with Aṃbālikā, she turned deathly pale, and so her son was born pale. This was Pāṇḍu. In hopes of producing a healthy son, Vyāsa requested one more attempt with Aṃbikā, but she lost her nerve and sent her handmaid instead. The result of this union was the wise Vidura.

Because his elder brother's disability prevented him from ruling, Pāṇḍu assumed the throne. Dhṛtarāṣṭra married the noble Gāndhārī who, so that she would never fault her husband his blindness, bound her eyes in a sash which never came off. Pāṇḍu married two women, Kuntī and Mādrī, who were close like sisters. A curse befell Pāṇḍu, however when, while hunting one day, he shot a pair of deer while they were mating. The deer, it turned out, were mystics in disguise and, because he had violated the act of love, cursed him to die if ever he took a woman in his arms. Again the lineage seemed imperiled, but Kuntī, it turned out, had long ago been given a secret *mantra* by a sage as a reward for serving him well. With this *mantra* she could invoke the presence of any deity and be magically impregnated by him. As a teenager, she didn't understand that uttering the *mantra* resulted in pregnancy and, to test it out, invoked the sun deity, Sūrya. Much to her dismay, she bore an illegitimate son, Karṇa, whom she bundled up in a basket and sent floating down the river. Karṇa was discovered and raised by a lowly driver, but as an adult reappeared on the scene, not knowing his bitterest enemies were his own brothers.

With this *mantra*, Kuntī invoked the god Dharma and with him had a son, Yudhiṣṭhira, who himself embodied moral and philosophical perfection. With Vāyu, the wind god, she had Bhīma, the strongest man in the world. With Indra, the monarch of the gods, she had Arjuna, the great hero. She disclosed the *mantra* to Mādrī who invoked the celestial twins, the Aśvins, and bore twin sons, Nakula, the embodiment of patience, and Sahadeva, the embodiment of wisdom. These five brothers are the great Pāṇḍavas ("descendants of Pāṇḍu"), the heroes of the *Mahābhārata.* They represent the ideal of Indian manhood.

In the meantime, Gāndhārī, Dhṛtarāṣṭra's wife, became pregnant, but a hard ball grew within her, a ball which would not come out. In desperation, she ordered her handmaid to strike her belly, and out came an amorphous ball of flesh. She divided it into one hundred pieces and placed each piece in separate urns. Miraculously, these grew into one hundred handsome, powerful sons. These are the Kauravas ("descendants of Kuru", an ancestor from some generations back), who would eventually become the Pāṇḍavas fiercest enemies.

Sure enough, one balmy spring day Pāṇḍu got carried away with amorous feeling and, despite her protests, took Mādrī into his arms. He died on the spot. The fatherless Pāṇḍavas were taken in by Dhṛtarāṣṭra and raised alongside his own sons. All the boys were brought up by Bhīṣma and, being of the *kṣatriya*, or warrior, caste, were trained in the military arts by Droṇa, the world's greatest master of arms. Although they were raised in the same household and taught by the same teachers, the Kauravas were always jealous and resentful of the Pāṇḍavas. This was particularly true of Duryodhana, the eldest of the Kauravas, whose jealousy was inflamed to pathological proportions. Karṇa reentered the scene at this point, determined to become a pupil of the famous Droṇa. Not realizing that the Pāṇḍavas were his own brothers, he was drawn over to the Kauravas, to whom he swore allegiance.

The Crisis

One day, while on a journey, Arjuna won the hand of the magnificent Draupadī, and brought her home to meet his family. "Mother," he told Kuntī excitedly, "I've brought something."

"Be sure to share it with your brothers," Kuntī replied absentmindedly. As it is a *kṣatriya's dharma* to unquestioningly obey his parents' orders, it came about that Draupadī married all five of the Pāṇḍavas.

At about this juncture, the divine *Avatāra* Kṛṣṇa entered the picture, being a cousin on the maternal side of the family, the son of Kuntī's brother, Vasudeva. He was close to the Pāṇḍavas, particularly to Arjuna, who was His best friend. Now the Divine was more than merely directing events, He was personally present in them.

Duryodhana's hatred of the Pāṇḍavas steadily mounted. He made several attempts on their lives, all futile, which merely intensified his frustration. He was determined to destroy them, but had to find their weak spot. They seemed invincible, superhuman. Except, that is, for Yudhiṣṭhira's one weakness: he was a compulsive gambler. Seizing upon this, the Kauravas challenged him to a game of dice. The game was, of course, rigged in the Kaurava's favor.

In an assembly of both families, the game commenced, and Yudhiṣṭhira gradually gambled away his vast wealth. Driven by a compulsion he could not control, he gambled away his family's fortune and domain. He gambled away his right to the throne. He gambled away the clothes off his back. He gambled away the clothes off his brothers' backs, then gambled away his brothers themselves, turning them into slaves. He gambled away his own self and, in the final moment, gambled away the one thing left to him — Draupadī.

Surrendering the strong and regal Draupadī to the degenerate Kauravas was the ultimate demoralization. The Pāṇḍavas watched in impotent horror as Draupadī was dragged by the hair into the assembly and Duḥśāsana, one of the Kauravas, began to pull her clothing off before the eyes of everyone. With no one else to turn to, Draupadī raised her voice to God, and called upon Lord Kṛṣṇa to save her. In one of the most celebrated incidents in all Hindu sacred history, Kṛṣṇa heeded his devotee's call and miraculously her sari became endless. No matter how much fabric Duḥśāsana pulled, more and more arose, until he abandoned his intent. Draupadī's honor had been saved.

The Kauravas posed one more throw of the dice, and the Pāṇḍavas were exiled to the forest for thirteen years, at the end of which they could return and claim their territory. Along with Draupadī, the brothers withdrew to the forest, outcasts. There they had many important experiences and adventures, including the cultivation of special, magical weapons to be used in the war which would inevitably ensue when they returned.

Before the thirteen years were up, the Pāṇḍavas returned to the world in disguises. They were successful in hiding their identities until Arjuna agreed to assist a royal ally in battle against Duryodhana's army, which had attacked them. When the Pāṇḍavas' identities were revealed, Duryodhana refused to relinquish their kingdom because they had transgressed the terms of their exile. The Pāṇḍavas begged for a mere five villages. Duryodhana said he would not give them enough earth in which to drive a pin. Kṛṣṇa intervened with diplomatic proposals, which the Kauravas flatly rejected. All peaceful avenues exhausted, the situation had escalated to its most dreaded conclusion: war.

The Kuruksetra War

The two sides of this momentous battle do not represent good and evil so much as they represent cosmic order and chaos, *dharma* and *adharma*. The Kauravas are not wholly evil, rather they lack a sense of harmony with the divine will, a sense of right purpose, a commitment to *dharma*. They are the sons of a blind man, and they suffer from their own form of blindness. Greed, anger, violence, arrogance all obscure one's view of his or her higher purpose. There is no question but that they will lose the battle; we know this all along. We see in history that negative forces — bad governments, institutionalized oppression, cruelty, tyranny — never last. They can't. They are doomed to fail because they are in opposition to the natural order of things (*dharma*). While people can't stand to live under such conditions, the regimes themselves sow the seeds of their own destruction from within.

On the other hand, positive forces always endure. They may, at times, appear to be buried, like the Pāṇḍavas disappearing into the forest, but they inevitably reemerge because they represent the natural state of things, which is order and balance (*dharma*). Good prevails in the end because it is our true, essential nature. Underneath the frenetic mass of *guṇas* which comprise our limited personas is the pure, changeless, blissful Ātman, the Divine Itself. This perfection is the underlying reality of each person and the underlying reality of the world.

The battle, then, can be viewed as an historical event, which it most likely was, as sacred mythology, and also as a metaphor for the constant tug-of-war between *dharma* and *adharma* in the world and within ourselves. The noble aspects of our personalities always struggle against the brutish ones, and while in the short run the lower self may appear to prevail, in the long run it will be vanquished.

In the story, the war has apocalyptic dimensions. It will be a massacre, with pitifully few survivors, which marks the end of the *Dvāpara-yuga* and heralds the coming *Kali-yuga*, the age of degeneration, darkness and quarrel. The opposing armies are massive, comprised of the militias from all over the world, their heads of state having taken sides, like a prototype of the twentieth-century world wars. It is a tragic event, where mass destruction leaves nothing in its wake, and the palpable presence of the Divine departs from the world. Nothing good ever comes from fighting, only desolation and waste. For this reason, many, including Mahatma Gandhi, feel that the *Mahābhārata* is a denunciation of violence, an anti-war statement.

Of interest today is the strict rules of martial etiquette endorsed by the text and observed by its characters. While war was always a brutal affair, warriors were expected to fight it like gentlemen. No fighting would commence until both sides agreed upon a time and a signal was made. Fighting at night was prohibited. Never was one to strike a fallen man, an unarmed man, or a man who had left the field. And never, never were civilians involved. How different this view of war is from the "total war" of today, where any sort of atrocity is perpetrated in the pursuit of victory. The former view of war is an example of military *dharma*, the latter, of *adharma*, which, it seems, is the prevailing condition of nearly every aspect of our lives today.

Before the battle, Kṛṣṇa, intending to remain neutral, stated that He would officially endorse neither side. One side, He said, could have His army, the other, Himself. The Pāṇḍavas gladly chose Kṛṣṇa, while Duryodhana, on behalf of the Kauravas, snatched up the militia. He figured this would put him firmly in the superior position, his forces outnumbering his enemies', but, on the contrary, it was his fatal mistake. The philosophical implication of his choice — matter vs. spirit — is profound.

The armies assembled and lay poised for battle. Arjuna, who had requested Kṛṣṇa to act as his charioteer, asked the divine driver to direct his chariot between the two forces, so that he might have a look at them. Seeing his skilled and regal cousins, his own teacher, Droṇa, his great-uncle Bhīṣma, and other relatives and friends for whom he had a deep regard, ready to fight against him, he was filled with sudden despair. This grisly spectacle, he thought, must be *adharma.* How can killing people for whom he has reverence be right? What satisfaction can come from a victory when the price in lives is so high? He didn't even want the kingdom. With that, he threw down his arms and announced, "I will not fight." So launched the *Bhagavad-Gītā*, the sacred dialogue between the world-teacher, Śrī Kṛṣṇa, and his warrior disciple, Arjuna.

Then the war began. The *Mahābhārata* describes each phase of the battle in exacting detail. Now swashbuckling, now gruesome, other times heartbreaking, it is a fascinating and somewhat upsetting study in the confusion and futility of war. We see how Bhīṣma, who long ago received a boon that he could choose the moment of his death, allowed himself to be slain, for were he to live, the war would go on until the end of the world. He died upon a bed of upright arrows.

Abhimanyu, Arjuna's adolescent son, died tragically in the line of duty and Arjuna was disconsolate. He swore to kill himself if he did not avenge his son's death by sunset the following day, and Kṛṣṇa stalled for time by causing a solar miracle until the deed was accomplished.

Droṇa was killed by a dirty trick. Bhīma slew the man who disrobed Draupadī back at the dice tournament and, to fulfill a curse she lay upon her assailant, drank blood from the fallen body. Karṇa died when Kṛṣṇa urged Arjuna to attack in a way which was clearly *adharma*, which suggests that the will of the Divine determines *dharma*, and that *dharma* is not merely a rigid set of rules. All the sons of the Pāṇḍavas were killed in their sleep, an act which everyone condemned as cowardly and heinous. Duryodhana was satisfied, however, knowing that his enemies' bloodline had been severed. What he didn't know was that Abhimanyu's widow was pregnant with Parīkṣit (the figure to whom the *Śrīmad Bhāgavatam* was spoken). And so the tale twists in and out.

The Final Days

In the end, the Kauravas were vanquished and Yudhiṣṭhira took the throne. His was a good reign, but death comes to everyone, and the story follows each of the remaining characters to their deaths. Dhṛtarāṣṭra, Gāndhārī and Kuntī all took to the forest, where they practiced religious austerities until they calmly allowed themselves to be consumed by a forest fire. Acting according to a curse, Kṛṣṇa's clan obliterated themselves in a bizarre drunken brawl, and Kṛṣṇa, walking in the forest and contemplating the completion of His advent, died in a hunting accident of His own design. After turning the kingdom over to Parīkṣit, the Pāṇḍavas, along with Draupadī, assumed the lives of wandering spiritual aspirants. They visited places of pilgrimage, then began the long ascent up the Himālayas. Somewhere along the line a friendly dog joined the band. One by one each of them died, until only Yudhiṣṭhira and the dog were left. They arrived at the summit of the Himālayas, the entrance into heaven. There Indra appeared in his chariot, ready to sweep Yudhiṣṭhira up to paradise. However, the dog, he said, must stay. There's no room for dogs in heaven. Yudhiṣṭhira could not leave his faithful companion behind, and refused to go.

Then the dog's true identity was revealed — it was the god Dharma, Yudhiṣṭhira's own father, disguising himself to test Yudhiṣṭhira's loyalty. At once the dog vanished, and Yudhiṣṭhira entered heaven. But who should he find there but Duryodhana, the homicidal wretch. His own saintly family was nowhere to be found. He was then taken to hell, where, in the darkness, he heard the suffering voices of his loved ones. Bewildered, enraged, cursing the gods and cursing *dharma* for delivering a beast to paradise and consigning the virtuous to torment, he took a seat and vowed to stay there in hell with his family. Love, for him, was far more compelling than pain or pleasure.

At once the vision of hell disappeared. It had been another test. Before him he saw his father, Dharma, and the celestial minstrel, Nārada. Happiness and punishment, family and enemies, in fact all opposites, are illusions. Yudhiṣṭhira achieved that state of peace beyond all duality, and there he saw Karṇa and all of his brothers, Draupadī, Duryodhana and all the sons of Dhṛtarāṣṭra transfigured and serene, for all beings are destined for that ultimate Peace. It is the birthright of all.

NOTES

1. Stutley and Stutley, p. 169.

CHAPTER TWENTY-SIX

The Rāmāyaṇa

Like the *Mahābhārata*, the *Rāmāyaṇa* revolves around the theme of *dharma*. Also like the *Mahābhārata*, it includes a divine *Avatāra*, though while Kṛṣṇa played a secondary role in the former epic, here Lord Rāma is the central character of the story. *Ayana* means "journey", or "career", so the title *Rāmāyaṇa* may be loosely translated as "The Adventure of Rāma".[1] Not so given to digression, and the work of a single author, Vālmīki, the poem holds relatively close to a central storyline, which recounts in detail the thrilling life of Rāma, the greatest king and hero.

Some scholars believe that in its most ancient, perhaps oral, form, the *Rāmāyaṇa* did not portray Rāma as an *Avatāra*, but as a human endowed with divine qualities. His identity as an *Avatāra* of Viṣṇu may have evolved over time, though Rajagopalachari argues that the idea of Rāma's divinity did exist during Vālmīki's day, though would not develop to its fullest extent for some centuries more.[2] In either case, Rāma, unlike Kṛṣṇa, was not always aware of His divine identity. Like Christ before his baptism, Rāma manifested divine attributes, but was not conscious of their full implication. Only near the end, when Brahmā appeared and reminded Him that His advent was nearing completion, did Rāma learn the truth.

Whether *Avatāra* or human, Rāma embodies the prototype of the perfect man. Perfect in wisdom, beauty, talent and *dharma*, He demonstrates the ideal in any relationship. He is the ideal son, brother, citizen, ruler, husband, master, and, ultimately, worshipable deity. At the end, He will have to compromise His husbandhood in order to keep peace in the state. Unfortunate though this may be, it suggests that where a conflict of the two arises, a ruler must put the good of the state before the good of his family. It is a harsh rule, but it is the way of *dharma*. In the *Rāmāyaṇa*, *dharma* is often harsh, and conforming to it sometimes brings unhappiness in the short-run. Nevertheless, the story is meant to extol *dharma* as a transcendent reality, an ultimate good not subject to the permutations of the relative world.

Much misery occurs in the *Rāmāyaṇa*, misery that often could have been avoided had a character made one decision differently, or had not clung so tenaciously to *dharma*. These are divine beings, the reader might think, so why do they let such terrible things happen? The explanation lies in the concept of *līlā*, divine sport. God takes form as a human in order to generate sacred events, which both uplift the world as they are occurring and become fixed in time as a story. Whenever the story is remembered, the sacred is invoked and the devotee is inspired, expanded, delighted. In divine *līlā*, even sorrowful events are delightful, because they are imbued with the sacred. They are rich with both meaning and powerful spiritual presence. As the *Rāmāyaṇa* is *līlā*, Rāma must, for instance, refuse to usurp the throne from His brother Bharata, though Bharata begs Him to. Had Rāma taken the throne, everyone's troubles would have been over, nothing else would have happened, and there would have been no *Rāmāyaṇa*. Keep in mind, too, that for the Divine, all actions in this world are mere play, frolic, a dance. What seems tragic or grotesque to us is merely so because of our ignorance, the strange veil of *māyā*. For the Divine, everything is *ānanda*, sheer bliss.

The characters of Sītā, Rāma, and Lakṣmaṇa, Rama's younger brother and constant companion, correspond exactly to Rādhā, Kṛṣṇa and Balarāma. They are, in fact, earlier incarnations of this holy trinity, identified in the spiritual realm as Lakṣmī, Viṣṇu and Ananta-Śeṣa, the serpent deity associated with Viṣṇu. More so than any other earthly manifestation of the Divine Mother, Sītā fully embodies the qualities of *prakṛti*. She is truly an Earth Goddess. The name Sītā means "furrow", which suggests the fertility, nourishing properties, and depth of the earth. Because they receive seed and give forth new life, furrows can be viewed as the earth's female generative organs.[3] In the Chinese *I Ching*, the trigram K'un, which represents the feminine aspect of the cosmos, resembles a furrow. Indeed, Sītā was not even born of a human, but of the earth itself. While performing a ceremonial spring plowing, King Janaka discovered the babe in the overturned earth and adopted Her. Sītā lives much of Her life deep in Nature, in the forest, first with Rāma and Lakṣmaṇa, and later in the hermitage of the sage Vālmīki. At the end of the epic, Rāma assumes His original Viṣṇu form and ascends to the heavens while Sītā is engulfed by the earth and descends into its protective, feminine depths. These upward and downward motions accurately symbolize the couple's identities as the primordial *Puruṣa* and *Prakṛti*.

Sītā is supremely beautiful and regal, golden complected, and often depicted in a green sari. Rāma, Her counterpart, is depicted as green-skinned and dressed in gold attire. Thus, like the images of Rādhā-Kṛṣṇa, or the counter-balance of the Chinese Yin-Yang symbol, we see each half of the cosmic polarity including within itself the other in potential. Isolated, *Puruṣa* and *Prakṛti* are entirely static. Without *Prakṛti*, *Puruṣa* is nothing but undifferentiated consciousness, a Subject without an object to experience. Without *Puruṣa, Prakṛti* is undifferentiated substance, inert matter. Only in combination do they manifest their powers; only when they unite is the universe created. In the *Rāmāyaṇa,* Rāma and Sītā are separated, and the central action involves Rāma's elaborate adventure to reunite with Her. Even when He loses Her a second time, Rāma has a golden image of Her installed on the throne beside Him, because without *Śakti,* Divine Power, Brahman can do nothing. They must be together, for they are, in truth, one.

Rāma is depicted as green because He is described as having the dark complexion of a beautiful emerald. He holds a bow and, depending on the period in His life, is either dressed in the garb of a forest ascetic or in the crown and garland of a king. He is cool-headed yet deeply feeling, gentle yet an expert warrior, romantic yet entirely self-controlled. He treats all superiors with the humility of a servant and all subordinates with compassion and respect. He adapts gracefully and humbly to any situation, for He is egoless. In Rāma we have the ideal role model for anyone in any station.

Lakṣmaṇa, like his later incarnation, Balarāma, is pale-complected and hot-tempered, though his passion is not derived from ignorance or egotism but from extraordinary devotion to Rāma and Sītā, neither of whom he can stand to see slighted. He is surrendered entirely to their service.

Yet even Lakṣmaṇa's devotion can't match that of Hanumān's. Hanumān is, perhaps with the exception of the *gopīs,* the greatest example of self-surrendered devotion in all of Hinduism. His love takes the form of *dāsya,* servitude, and Rāma is his whole life. Popular iconography shows him tearing open his chest to reveal Rāma and Sītā dwelling in his heart. He wants nothing whatsoever except to serve Rāma, can think of nothing except Rāma, can see nothing except Rāma. Though he is a mere monkey, his total abandonment in Rāma makes him the highest mystic and saint.

Rāvaṇa, Rāma's arch-enemy, is a *rākṣasa,* a type of demon that can assume any form. He is the king of the island country Laṅkā, now Sri Lanka. More contemporary renderings depict him as merely a cruel, decadent tyrant, though traditionally he is believed to have possessed multiple heads and arms — a grotesque sight, yet fearsomely powerful. We have met this soul before, as Kṛṣṇa's heinous uncle Kaṃsa, and as Prahlāda's demonic father, Hiraṇyakaśipu. His story is told in the *Śrīmad Bhāgavatam,* where the one-time gatekeeper of heaven was cursed to assume demonic forms, though would be blessed when God incarnate slew him personally each time. He is the eternal adversary, the same person come again and again, working out his salvation through *vidveṣa bhakti*, or fixing the mind on God in a hateful mood. The distressing scene of his abduction of Sītā reduces many Indians to tears, so real is the event for them.

In India, the *Rāmāyaṇa* is honored and cherished, recited publicly and meditated upon privately. Countless plays, movies, dances, paintings, sculptures, picture books and even comic books have been based on it. It is one of the great stories of all time, at once both intimate and sweeping. While it is alive with exciting action, intrigue and profound emotions, it is sublimely spiritual as well. It has lent itself to scholarly analysis as a literary piece, philosophical treatise, and an anthropological and sociological document. Its depth is fathomless.

Prologue: The Origin of the *Śloka* Meter

Vālmīki, the poet who set the story of Rāma to verse, was a contemporary of Rāma's. One day the celestial sage Nārada visited Vālmīki in his forest *āśrama*. Vālmīki asked him, "Who among the heroes of this world is highest in virtue and wisdom?" Nārada replied, "Rāma is the hero of whom you inquire."[4] With that, Nārada narrated to Vālmīki the full story of Śrī Rāma. Vālmīki was so moved by this story, it haunted him continuously thereafter.

One day, as he was walking by the river bank, he saw two birds sporting in a tree. A nearby hunter shot the male bird and killed him, causing the female to lament. Witnessing this piteous scene, Vālmīki cursed the hunter, saying, "O hunter, because you have killed one of these love-intoxicated birds, you will wander without rest all your long years."

In a moment, Vālmīki constrained himself, and wondered why he had been given to such an uncontrolled outburst. Then he noticed that in his curse he had invented a new form of poetry. His utterance was four lines long, each line of eight syllables, with some rhymes. He dubbed this new stanza a *śloka*, because it reminded him of *śoka*, the Sanskrit word for "grief". It was by witnessing this terrible sorrow that Vālmīki had been moved to invent the *śloka* meter, and it was by means of the *śloka* that he decided to tell another story of sorrow and separation, the story or Rāma.

Bāla-kāṇḍa: Rāma's Childhood and Marriage

Bāla means "child", or "young", and this first section deals with the life of Śrī Rāma up through His marriage to Sītā, which marks His transition to adulthood.

Before the divine advent, the gods approached Viṣṇu, distressed over the uncontrolled power of the *rākṣasa* monarch, Rāvaṇa. Due to his having practiced severe austerities, Rāvaṇa had won a boon from Lord Brahmā that he may be killed by neither gods nor demons. He never considered including humans in the boon, assuming them too inconsequential to pose a threat. If this scenario sounds suspiciously like the story of Hiraṇyakaśipu in the seventh canto of the *Śrīmad Bhāgavatam*, keep in mind that Rāvaṇa is the reincarnation of Hiraṇyakaśipu, and that when divine events unfold on earth, certain patterns inevitably follow. Implored by the gods, Viṣṇu then and there decided to take birth as a human being and deliver the world from the tyrant. He was accompanied by His *Śakti*, the goddess Lakṣmī, who took birth as Sītā.

Like Sītā's, Rāma's birth was miraculous. The childless King Daśaratha of Ayodhyā performed a complicated royal rite designed to produce a son. Out of the sacred fire arose a deity bearing a golden bowl of rice pudding, which Daśaratha divided among his three queens. In due time, Queen Kausalyā bore Rāma, Queen Kaikeyī gave birth to Bharata, and Queen Sumitrā had twins, Lakṣmaṇa and Śatrughna.

Rāma's childhood was full of heroic feats and wonders, culminating in His winning of Sītā's hand in marriage. Travelling North with Lakṣmaṇa and their teacher, Viśvāmitra, Rāma entered the kingdom of Videha, where King Janaka was holding a *svayaṃvara,* a ceremony in which a princess chooses a husband among an assembly of suitors. As in most *svayaṃvaras*, the hopeful princes, after reciting their lineages,[5] had to pass a test of skill, in this case stringing the celestial bow of Lord Śiva. None of the gentlemen who tried could even lift it, what to speak of stringing it. However, Rāma lifted it easily and strung it so tightly it snapped in two, emitting a roar that shook the earth. Enchanted, Sītā placed a garland of white flowers around Rāma's neck, indicating Him to be Her new husband.

On the same day that they were married, Lakṣmaṇa married Sītā's sister and Bharata and Śatrughna married Her two cousins.

Ayodhyā-kāṇḍa: Rāma is Banished

Ayodhyā is the capital city of the kingdom of Kosala, where Rāma was to reign, hence the name of this second section. Rāma and Sītā lived happily in Ayodhyā for many years, and when King Daśaratha grew ready to retire, preparations began for the lavish festivities of Rāma's coronation. Rāma was well-known and fervently loved by the population, as well as by Kausalyā's co-wives, who were thrilled by the prospect of Him becoming king.

Enter into the picture Mantharā, the hunchbacked maidservant of Queen Kaikeyī. Twisted as much in mind as in body, this sinister old woman nagged Kaikeyī incessantly, filling her head with false fears, until she had the confused queen convinced that her own son, Bharata, ought to rule and Rāma be banished for fourteen years. She also reminded Kaikeyī that Daśaratha owed the queen a favor. Many years earlier she had rescued him in battle, and hence he had offered to grant her any wish. She could think of nothing at the time, and had subsequently forgotten the incident. Now Mantharā convinced her to demand her due.

Kaikeyī's request horrified the king so deeply he fell down into an illness from which he would never recover. Rāma, on the other hand, took the news calmly and immediately made preparations to depart. He cared nothing for Himself, only to fulfill His *dharma* by adhering to His father's words will cheerfulness and poise. His is an example to emulate in times of disappointment.

Despite Rāma's protestations, Sītā insisted She accompany Him to His banishment in the forest. Finally He relented. Lakṣmaṇa also accompanied Him. As the threesome made their way to the outskirts of the city, crowds of sorrowing subjects followed on foot. They all preferred to join Rāma in His exile rather than bear the pain of separation from Him. He managed to slip away, though, and the trio began their trek southward, on a journey which would take them to the farthest tip of the subcontinent and beyond.

In the meantime, Daśaratha died in grief, and Bharata, who had been away on an errand all this time, returned to an Ayodhyā he didn't recognize. Angered by the turn of events, he lingered only long enough to perform his father's funeral rites, then left in search of Rāma.

Bharata managed to catch up with the party and begged Rāma to return and rule the kingdom. Rāma refused, explaining that it is a son's duty to honor the words of his father and mother. He hadn't the *right* to disobey them. This was *dharma*. Bharata's assuming the throne, then, was only correct and good, as was Rāma's living in the forest. Most people today don't take such a strict stance on obeying their parents' every word, though it is considered a son or daughter's *dharma* to do so. Confucianism also holds reverence for, and obedience to, one's parents (*hsiao*) as an ultimate societal and religious value.

Bharata agreed to return and carry out the functions of a ruler, but only as Rāma's regent. He begged Rāma's sandals from Him and made his way back to Ayodhyā holding them, as a sign of reverence, on his head. Once back, he installed them in a shrine as a symbol of Rāma's sovereignty, and bowed before them every day. He never for an instant forgot who the true king was and that he was merely the king's servant.

Araṇya-kāṇḍa: The Abduction of Sītā

Araṇya means "forest", and this third section recounts the trio's adventures during their exile there. For about ten years, their lives were peaceful and happy. They enjoyed the idyll of Nature in her beauty, met many forest sages, and occasionally had run-ins with demons and the like.

Their joy was shattered, however, when a lewd female *rākṣasī*, Śūrpaṇakhā, came upon their camp one day. She made lascivious advances to Rāma, who merely laughed at her and told her to have a try at Lakṣmaṇa. Lakṣmaṇa found nothing funny about the scene and ignored her. Enraged by this rejection, Śūrpaṇakhā, moved to attack Sītā. Lakṣmaṇa interceded and cut off the demoness' nose and ears. Howling in pain and humiliation, she flew at once to her brother, Rāvaṇa, who vowed to avenge the insult. He would kidnap Sītā.

Rākṣasas can assume any form at will, so first Rāvaṇa sent his minister Mārīca disguised as a golden deer of unearthly beauty. Seeing this creature grazing nearby, Sītā fell in love with it and begged Rāma to go fetch it. Reluctantly, he followed it into the forest, where it suddenly called out in an impersonation of Rāma, "Sītā! Lakṣmaṇa! Help!"

Lakṣmaṇa was incredulous, but Sītā was frightened, and insisted he go. Now She was vulnerable to Rāvaṇa's attack. He took the form of a wandering holy man and came upon Her for alms. As She trustingly approached him, Rāvaṇa grabbed Her roughly, assumed his true form and flew away with Her. As they whisked through the sky, over the mountains, Sītā screamed and struggled; Her jewelry loosened and fell from Her body, some of it landing among a tribe of monkeys, who gathered it to show their leader. A valiant old vulture named Jaṭāyu tried to rescue Her, but he was aged, and no match for Rāvaṇa. Rāvaṇa cut off his wings, and the poor soul fell to the ground to die. Eventually Rāvaṇa and Sītā arrived in Laṅkā, and Rāvaṇa deposited Her in an enclosed garden where She was guarded over by *rākṣasīs*. Luxurious though it was, Sītā was disconsolate.

Meanwhile, Rāma and Lakṣmaṇa searched for Her. They came upon Jaṭāyu who, with his dying breath, disclosed the identity of Sītā's abductor. They performed last rites for the courageous animal.

Sītā's whereabouts were still unknown, though, so they began to search for clues. The first came in the form of a celestial being named Danu, whom Rāma released from a demon body. Someone who could help Rāma in his search, Danu said, was the deposed monkey king, Sugrīva.

***Kiṣkindhā-kāṇḍa*: Rāma is Joined by the Monkeys and Bears**

Kiṣkindhā was the cavern city wherein dwelled Vāli (also called Vālin, or Bāli), the brother of the deposed Sugrīva. This section deals largely with Rāma's adventures among the monkeys and bears, hence its name.

Rāma and Lakṣmaṇa were spotted by Sugrīva from a nearby hill, so he sent his aide, Hanumān, to find out who they were. Escorted back to Sugrīva, they discovered that Sugrīva and Rāma had much in common. Sugrīva, too, had lost a kingdom to his brother, as well as his wife, who was now with Vāli. The two became firm friends and made a pact: Rāma would help Sugrīva vanquish Vāli and regain his kingdom, and in return Sugrīva would enlist the aid of his armies to help find and liberate Sītā.

In a telling incident, the jewelry which had fallen from Sītā's body and been collected by the monkeys was brought out. Rāma recognized the earrings, necklace, bracelets and so on, but as Lakṣmaṇa examined each piece he failed to recognize any of it. Until, that is, he was shown her anklets. "Yes," he said, "*these* are definitely Sītā's." So chaste was his attitude toward his brothers's wife, Lakṣmaṇa's gaze had never risen above Her ankles.

Rāma advised Sugrīva to take Vāli on in one-on-one combat. Hiding in a nearby cluster of foliage, Rāma watched the two battle. Both were extraordinarily strong and brave. At the critical instant, however, Rāma shot and mortally wounded Vāli, thus returning the kingdom and its forces to Sugrīva. True to his word, Sugrīva dispatched search parties in all directions in hopes of locating Sītā. A month later, the parties sent to the North, East, and West returned, but not the Southern party.

Having reached the bottommost tip of India, the party, which included Hanumān, encountered another old vulture, named Sampāti. He was Jaṭāyu's brother, and told them that he had seen Rāvaṇa and Sītā pass overhead on their way to Laṅkā, across the sea. Without boat or bridge, the party had to rely on someone who could leap across the great expanse of water. Hanumān was the son of Vāyu, the wind god, and so could make the jump. He made himself grow and grow until he was as large as a mountain, then braced himself for the leap.

***Sundara-kāṇḍa*: Hanumān Gives Sītā a Message**

Sundara means "beautiful", and according to H. Daniel Smith, some say it refers to the beautiful nature of Hanumān, without whom Sītā's rescue would have been impossible, while others believe it is a reference to the beautiful sights of Laṅkā: palaces, gardens and natural wonders. Still others insist is has to do with the beauty of Sītā's strength, Her maintaining Her dignity, chastity and poise throughout Her ordeal. Yet others say if refers to the beautiful message Hanumān delivered to Sītā from Rāma, and the message Sītā sent back to Rāma. Whatever the meaning, it is one of the most poignant sections of the epic.

Hanumān soared across the sea in a single bound. Landing in Laṅkā, he searched for Sītā everywhere, at last finding Her in one of the royal gardens. Perching himself in a tree, he saw Her, now pale and thin, yet shining with an inner radiance, approached by Rāvaṇa. As he did at every visit, the *rākṣasa* urged Her to forget Rāma and learn to love him instead. If She didn't he would make Her into a stew and eat Her. Throughout the captivity, Rāvaṇa never laid a hand on Sītā, but Her unwavering devotion to Rāma infuriated him.

As soon as Rāvaṇa left, Hanumān crept closer to Sītā and introduced himself. He showed Her Rāma's ring to prove that he had been sent by Rāma personally, and he assured Her that Her husband would soon come for Her.

Sītā was overjoyed, and gave Hanumān a jewel from Her hair to deliver to Rāma. If He didn't come and rescue Her, Sītā said, She would surely die. Hanumān assured Her with comforting words, and departed.

Before leaving Laṅkā, Hanumān decided to give some trouble to the *rākṣasas* and to confront Rāvaṇa face to face. He got into a scuffle with some *rākṣasa* soldiers and was dragged before the king, whom he gleefully badgered. Rāvaṇa ordered him shackled and his tail set on fire, which was just what Hanumān secretly wanted. As he was capable of altering his size, he easily slipped out of his bonds, then raced through Laṅkā, setting the entire city ablaze with his flaming tail. With a single leap he flew across the sea and landed again among his companions in India. The *rākṣasas* would not soon forget him.

Yuddha-kāṇḍa: The Battle and Its Aftermath

Yuddha means "war" and this section is so named because Rāma and his rival meet at last.

As soon as word of Sītā's whereabouts reached Rāma, His forces, which were comprised of monkeys, bears and other creatures, immediately reacted. They advanced to the southernmost tip of the continent, only to be obstructed by the sea. At once they began to build a bridge by hurling large stones into the water. For seven days and nights they toiled without respite until a solid causeway stretching to Laṅkā had been built. They crossed, and invaded Laṅkā.

The *Yuddha-kāṇḍa* is the longest section of the *Rāmāyaṇa*, containing blow-by-blow details of the various phases of combat, individual battles, supernatural weapons and their effects, and the many characters that take part. One of the most gripping incidents is that of the snake-darts — darts which upon impact become large serpents which encircle and paralyze their victims. Rāma and Lakṣmaṇa were hit by two such darts and lay on the battlefield, virtually lifeless. They appeared done for. Suddenly an enormous celestial bird descended from the sky and chased the snakes away. It was none other than Garuḍa, Viṣṇu's bird-mount.

In another incident, Lakṣmaṇa lay critically wounded and only a particular herbal remedy could save him. It grew high in the Himālayas, and Hanumān, riding on the wind, vaulted to their peaks in search of it. He looked and looked for the medicinal plant, but could not locate it. Knowing that Lakṣmaṇa was a breath away from death, he tore off an entire mountain and carried it back with him.

At the climax of the battle, Rāma and Rāvaṇa fought face to face. Their combat was fierce, long, and bloody, but Rāma possessed a special arrow given to Him by the Vedic seer Agastya (a character who also appears in the *Mahābhārata*[6]). This sparkling arrow held all the power in the universe, and Rāvaṇa was felled in one shot.

Forthwith, the victor Rāma installed Rāvaṇa's virtuous brother Vibhīṣaṇa on the throne of Laṅkā and instructed him in the art of statecraft. Vibhīṣaṇa ordered Sītā's release.

She was bathed, dressed and adorned in jewelry befitting a queen. Surrounded by His allies, Rāma waited. Sītā then appeared, as regal and breathtaking as the moon. But strangely, Rāma seemed not to notice Her. The closer She came to Him, the more he withdrew, until He turned away from Her completely. Lakṣmaṇa could scarcely believe his eyes; others were aghast and dismayed. Rāma's face darkened.

"*Āryaputra*," Sītā whispered. Meaning "beloved", or "noble one", it is an intimate address of a wife to her husband.[7]

"I have killed the enemy," Rāma said coldly. "I have seen to your release. I have done my duty as a *kṣatriya*. My vow is now fulfilled."

Rāma went on to explain to the crowd that as this woman had lived in another man's house, Her virtue was violated, and He could no longer consider Her His wife.

This ghastly scene calls up images, still true even in Western culture, of women being blamed and punished for their own rapes. In orthodox Indian tradition, a woman's most valued possession was her chastity. Were that compromised — even in the case of rape — the father or husband of the woman was expected to banish her.[8] Rāma was acting in accordance to the dictates of formal *dharma*. Today, we can view the case of Sītā and the terrible injustice She was forced to endure as a reflection of all of the oppression women are subjected to, and the fact that they themselves are often blamed for their mistreatment. Even when the Mother of the Universe advents Herself, She is subject to mistreatment by men. But despite Her oppression, Sītā never surrendered Her dignity or Her sense of self-worth. She was infinitely strong, and clung tenaciously to what she knew to be the truth.

She spoke out in Her defense, "If I have not been true to You, let the fire consume Me." The trial by fire would prove Her innocence. A pyre was built, the gods invoked, and Sītā walked into the flames. A great wail arose from the crowd as She disappeared into the blaze.

With a mighty flash, the gods appeared in the firmament. Unseen by the crowd, Brahmā descended to Rāma's side and reminded Him of His true identity as the Incarnation of Nārāyaṇa and Sītā's as the Divine Mother Lakṣmī. Then he vanished.

Out of the flames arose Agni, the god of fire himself, and accompanying him, Sītā — pure, unscathed, vindicated.

"This woman is innocent," Agni declared. "Accept Her as Your own."

Rāma had known Her innocence all along, but wanted to prove it before the eyes of the people. Suddenly His whole demeanor changed, and He accepted His beloved back again. The fourteen years of His exile were at an end, and He, Sītā and Lakṣmaṇa returned to Ayodhyā, triumphant.

The most popular image of Rāma in Hindu iconography is His coronation. Flanked on either side by Sītā and Lakṣmaṇa, Hanumān kneeling humbly at His feet, Rāma stands glorified, the crown of Ayodhyā adorning His handsome head.

While Rāma ruled, the land was fertile, the people prosperous, and no enemies threatened the peaceful state.

***Uttara-kāṇḍa*: The Sad Ending**

Uttara means "later," "subsequent" or "concluding", indicating both that it is the final section of the *Rāmāyaṇa*, and that it narrates events subsequent to Rāma's coronation. Many scholars question Vālmīki's authorship of this section and, according to Smith, there is a widespread tendency in India to ignore this last part.[9] This may be due to the fact that the story takes such painful turns. Rajagopalachari rejects it entirely, and leaves it out of his translation, considering Rāma's actions completely out of character and the entire *kāṇḍa* a literary outgrowth and expression of the endless suffering of India's women.[10] Authentic or not, the events are provocative and powerful, worthy of consideration.

Before leaving Ayodhyā, Hanumān begged from Rāma two boons. "Stay always in my heart, O Lord," he said, "and let me live as long as Your story is told." Rāma was pleased to grant these boons, so we can assume that Hanumān is still alive, either in the flesh, in spirit, or in the sense that his memory and example still inspire devotees of God.

One day Sītā consulted Rāma about Her wish to take a pilgrimage to the banks of the holy Ganges. Rāma readily agreed. As Sītā prepared to leave, Rāma held court and asked His ministers about the people's opinion of His rule. One counselor came forward and revealed that the people were murmuring about Sītā. A ruler sets an example which the people imitate, and husbands were worried that Rāma's willingness to take Sītā back encouraged men to accept back wayward wives.

Rāma deliberated carefully. While He knew Sītā was blameless, peace in the state took priority. He instructed Lakṣmaṇa to see Her as far as the pilgrimage site, but to return alone. Then He retired to His chambers and lamented. Lakṣmaṇa did as he was told, and sorrowfully abandoned Sītā by the river.

About a dozen years passed. As was a king's duty, to assure the well-being of the state Rāma arranged for a year-long ceremonial sacrifice. The ritual required that the queen participate, so Rāma ordered a golden statue of Sītā to be installed on the throne next to Him. Saints and sages from all over arrived to assist in the ceremony, and towards the end of the year great throngs of spectators gathered, including fellow monarchs. The ceremonial hall was packed.

Among the guests was the sage Vālmīki and his two boy disciples, the twins Kuśa and Lava. The word *kuśalava* means "wandering minstrel/poet"[11], and the boys were, in fact, bards. With Rāma's permission, Vālmīki ordered his two charges to chant a long poem set to music that he had taught them. Guests remarked to one another that the children bore a curious resemblance to King Rāma.

What should the children sing, but the *Rāmāyaṇa*! The crowd was enthralled. Rāma was deeply stirred. For several nights in succession the boys sang the woeful tale, and when they reached the point of Sītā's banishment, Rāma suddenly realized who these boys were: His and Sītā's own sons.

Acting on a change of heart, He ordered Sītā's return. The crowd roared in assent. The next day, Vālmīki brought Sītā before the assembly. Her eyes were downcast, Her face sorrowful. Rāma publicly claimed Kuśa and Lava as His own sons, and was ready to accept Sītā back, pending Her own testimony. A hush fell over the crowd. Sītā's eyes were fixed to the floor. The humiliation She had been forced to endure was outrageous.

"If Rāma has always been foremost in my heart," She said, "then may Mother Earth herself deliver Me. If I have been wholly His, body and soul, then may Mother Earth herself deliver Me. If I have loved none but Him, then may Mother Earth herself deliver Me."

A rumbling arose; the earth began to tremble and shake. It suddenly erupted in a deafening sound and split wide open. From the dark chasm arose a gleaming throne atop which sat the Earth Goddess Herself. "My child," She said lovingly, extending Her arms to her daughter, Sītā. Aglow, Sītā embraced Her mother, and the two descended into the earth's depths. The ground shifted, the chasm closed. Sītā was gone forever.

The world of men had certainly failed Sītā. In the tradition which produced the *Rāmāyaṇa*, the measure of a woman's greatness was her loyalty to her husband, and even in the very end it is to this which Sītā testified as proof of her virtue. From a feminist perspective, this is deeply disturbing. However, it is significant that She appealed not to a transcendent male deity, but to an aspect of the Divine Mother. Rejected by a world dominated by men (She was kidnapped, imprisoned, accused, reviled and banished), She was lovingly accepted and protected by the Cosmic Female. This was Her true element, a spiritual reality of which She, in fact, was an Incarnation. This is a very powerful and positive image.

Rāma never remarried. He always kept the golden image of Sītā enthroned by His side. One by one His family members passed away until His time to depart came as well. Surrounded by well-wishers, He proceeded to the river Sarayū where, after performing ceremonial ablutions, He slipped under the surface of the water. At once, He reemerged in His eternal Viṣṇu form. Seated upon the coils of the celestial serpent, Ananta-Śeṣa, radiant with spiritual effulgence, He ascended skyward and disappeared.

All *Avatāras* perform several functions. They purify the world by their presence and quicken the spiritual progress of all living entities, as well that of subsequent generations. The *Avatāra* injects new *śakti* into the stream of humanity, *śakti* which will continue to spiritually animate long after the *Avatāra* has departed. When this *śakti* is depleted, the *Avatāra* comes again. Rāma fulfilled this function, then came again in the form of Śrī Kṛṣṇa.

Avatāras also teach. Although this synopsis did not include Rāma's discourses, the *Rāmāyaṇa* does recount His teaching, not only on spiritual topics, but also on *dharma* and statecraft as well. Yet, Rāma primarily taught by example. Keeping in mind that His banishment of Sītā is most likely an interpolation, Rāma's conduct stands as a unique ideal to study and emulate.

The most important function of an *Avatāra*, however, is to deliver to the world a tangible form of God to love. By cultivating devotion to a chosen divine form (an *Iṣṭa-devatā*), a spiritual aspirant attains intimacy with the Divine and hence renunciation, knowledge and spiritual realization. Everyone is different, therefore God must assume different forms in order to attract everyone. Śrī Rāma is one of the most beloved *Avatāras*. Like Jesus, His humanness makes Him accessible. He loves, jokes, cries, just like us. He understands what it is like to experience loss. He shows us that it is possible to observe self-control and spiritual practices while married and engaged in work.

Most of all, His personality and physical form are irresistible. This is how the Divine "tricks" us into spiritual aspiring. By dwelling upon the delightful features of Lord Rāma, we are inadvertently meditating on the Absolute Truth.

NOTES

1. Daniel H. Smith, ed., *The Picturebook Rāmāyaṇa* (Syracuse: Maxwell School of Citizenship and Public Affairs, Syracuse University, 1981).
2. C. Rajagopalachari, *The Ramayana* (Bombay: Bharata Vidya Bhavan, 1957, renewed 1975), p. 15.
3. Stutley and Stutley, p. 278.
4. Quotations in this chapter are culled from Smith and Rajagopalachari.
5. Stutley and Stutley, p. 295.
6. Stutley and Stutley, p. 4.
7. Rajagopalachari, p. 306.
8. Smith, p. xxxii.
9. Smith, p. xxxvi.
10. Rajagopalachari, p. 311.
11. Smith, p. 167.

Part VIII

Scriptures of *Yoga*, *Bhakti* and *Vedānta*

CHAPTER TWENTY-SEVEN

Scriptures of Yoga, Bhakti and Vedānta

The focus of this book has been the official sacred canon of Hinduism, those books which all Hindus deem religiously authoritative. However, a few texts standing outside the high canon are important enough to warrant mention here. All of these titles are greatly esteemed and, while not bearing the stamp of sacredness, are powerful conveyors of truth and wisdom. Each is the product of a purely human literary effort, the authors writing from their own experiences of spiritual realization.

A Word on the *Sūtra* Verse Form

A number of Hindu texts are written in a verse form called the *sūtra*. *Sūtra* means "thread" and is a cognate with the English word suture. Back before the invention of the printing press, books had to be copied by hand or, as was often the case in India, committed to memory. The *sūtra* verse is designed for just this purpose, and therefore each verse is composed of the fewest possible words. Like a bare thread with only a single bead, the *sūtra* verse includes only the minimum essentials, often to the point of lacking complete sentence structure.[1] They are meant to be elaborated upon by a teacher or commentator and English translations generally provide commentaries. The books included in this section are all composed in the *sūtra* verse, as is indicated by their titles.

The *Yoga Sūtras* of Patañjali

Patañjali, who lived during the second century B.C., was not the originator of *yoga*, only its systematizer. In his masterpiece, the *Yoga Sūtras*, we have a concise, yet thorough exposition on the theory and practice of *yoga*, or the technique for realization of the Supreme. It is not a sectarian work; it adheres to no particular theology or doctrine. Here *yoga* does not refer to either *karma*, *bhakti* or *jñāna yoga*. Known in some circles as *rāja yoga*, or the "king of *yogas*", this is the pure, unencumbered practice of mental control in meditation which leads to direct perception of the Ultimate Truth. Because it deals with realities that can be known through experience, it is applicable to all spiritual aspirants, whatever their philosophy.

The first three chapters are undoubtedly Patañjali's, while the fourth may be a later interpolation.[2] There is no break in continuity, however. Chapter One addresses how and why mental control, that is, restraining the basic substance of the mind, or "mind-stuff" (*citta*), from taking forms (*vṛttis*, literally "whirlpools") reveals one's true state as the unmodified Absolute, here called *Puruṣa*. The second chapter continues the discussion on theory, which is quite sophisticated, and then describes the actual techniques of meditation. Chapter Three describes the various tangible results of *rāja yoga*, including psychic ability and other occult powers, and Chapter Four explains the final goal of *yoga*: pure knowledge and freedom.

The *Yoga Sūtras* are direct, intense, and highly intellectual. They read almost like a course in psychology. Any good translation, therefore, will include a thorough commentary.

Nārada Bhakti Sūtras

This wonderful manual on divine love is attributed to the celestial sage Nārada, who figures prominently in the *Purāṇas*. Cursed to wander homeless in the universe forever, he turned his misfortune into a boon and became the prototypical wandering *sādhu*. Accompanying himself on the stringed *vīṇā*, he constantly sings hymns in praise of God and instructs earnest spiritual seekers who need him. His *guru* was his father, Brahmā himself. The quintessential *bhakta* and heavenly minstrel, who better to write the book on *bhakti yoga*? Whether or not you believe Nārada to be the author, or believe in the existence of Nārada at all, these eighty-four verses are so lovely, certainly the author was someone who resembled Nārada very much.

A major theme in the *Nārada Bhakti Sūtras* is that *jñāna* and *bhakti* are not in opposition to one another but, in fact, compliment one another. While *bhakti* and *jñāna* lead to the same goal, the *Bhakti Sūtras*, like all *bhakti* literature, see *bhakti*, love for God, as a goal in itself. The sweetness of *bhakti*, the preeminence of *bhakti* among other spiritual disciplines, the different moods of *bhakti*, and the actual practice of *bhakti* are all explored in a tone of genuine tenderness and reverence. Nārada supports his assertions with examples from the lives of ancient devotees and sages. This is a marvelous text, beautifully rendered and easy to follow.

Brahma Sūtras (or *Vedānta Sūtras*)

Vedānta is the philosophy of the *Upaniṣads.* The word itself can mean "the end of the *Vedas*", in the sense that the *Upaniṣads* are the final portion of the Vedic literature. It can also mean "the end-point of all knowledge", or the ultimate philosophy, leading to realization of Brahman.

The *Brahma Sūtras,* also called the *Vedānta Sūtras,* comprise one-third of the *prasthāna-traya,* or triple canon of *Vedānta*[3], the other parts being the *Upaniṣads* and the *Bhagavad-Gītā.* Written by Bādarāyaṇa some time between the third and fifth centuries[4], it attempts to systematize the teachings of the *Upaniṣads.*

The *sūtra* verse form is necessarily short and abrupt, and Bādarāyaṇa's are so reduced, a commentary is needed to understand them. Śaṅkarācārya's commentary is the most famous, and it was upon the *Brahma Sūtras* that he based his theory of *Advaita* (non-dualistic) *Vedānta.* On the other hand, Rāmānuja's commentary sees in the same text support for a more dualistic, theistic and devotional view. The *Sūtras* cover a vast array of subjects and make for difficult reading, but a familiarity with the principal *Upaniṣads* will prepare one for the task.

NOTES

1. Swami Prabhavananda and Christopher Isherwood, *How to Know God* (New York: New American Library, 1968), pp. vii-viii.
2. Organ, p. 227.
3. Swāmī Gambhīrānanda, trnsl., *Brahma-Sūtra Bhāṣya of Śaṅkarācārya* (Calcutta: Advaita Ashrama, 1977), p. v.
4. Stutley and Stutley, p. 53.

Glossary

adharma — ("non-dharma") Actions which are contrary to *dharma*, lack of virtue, actions which are contrary to the divinely designed right order of things. See **dharma**.
ādheya-ādhāra — The ground of Being and that which stands upon the ground, both of which are Brahman.
adhibhūta — ("supreme being") According to the eighth chapter of the *Bhagavad-Gītā*, worldly ephemera, that which is changeable and perishable.
adhidaiva — ("supreme God") According to the eighth chapter of the *Bhagavad-Gītā*, *Puruṣa*, or pure spirit, pure consciousness. Can also refer to the personal aspect of God, such as Śiva or Kṛṣṇa.
adhiyajña — ("supreme object of sacrifice") According to the eighth chapter of the *Bhagavad-Gītā*, Kṛṣṇa or God.
adhvarya or **adhvaryu** — A type of priest, a functionary in the Vedic *soma* sacrifice.
adhyātman — ("supreme Self") According to the eighth chapter of the *Bhagavad-Gītā*, the aspect of Brahman which is localized in the individual.
Aditi — ("not limited") 1.) The Vedic goddess of limitless space, as opposed to her sister, Diti ("limited"), the goddess of earthly phenomena. 2.) A primordial progenitrix, the mother of the race of *devas* and wife of the sage Kaśyapa. Her sister Diti is the mother of the races of demons.
Ādityas — A category of Vedic atmospheric deities, sons of Aditi. They include Mitra, Varuṇa, Dhātar, Aryaman, Aṃśa, Bhaga, Vivasvat and Āditya.
advaita — ("non-dualism") The philosophy that Brahman, God, is the only Reality and that nothing exists apart from It. The philosophy of the oneness of Brahman and Ātman. Also called *Vedānta*, it is the opposite of *dvaita*, or dualism.
Āgamas — ("that which has come down") Non-Vedic sectarian works associated with Śaivism, Vaiṣṇavism and Śaktism.
Agastya — A Vedic seer to whom many hymns of the *Ṛg Veda* are attributed.
Agni — ("fire") Vedic god of fire, intermediary between the gods and humans, who conveyed the essence of worshippers' sacrifices to the gods.

agnidhra — A type of Vedic priest, a functionary in the Vedic *soma* sacrifice.

agnihotra — ("fire offering") The Vedic fire sacrifice consisting of the pouring of oblations into the sacred fire.

ahaṃkāra — ("I-maker") The ego. One of the four "internal organs", the others being mind *(manas)*, mind-stuff or mental waves *(citta)*, and intellect *(buddhi)*.

ahiṃsā — Non-violence.

Aitareya Upaniṣad — One of the principal *Upaniṣads* which deals chiefly with the subject of creation.

Ajāmila — A worldly sensualist who, by calling out the name of God with his dying breath, was granted spiritual liberation. His story is contained in the sixth canto of the *Śrīmad Bhāgavatam.*

ājña cakra — The sixth of the seven yogic *cakras*, or energy centers, located above and between the eyes, or in the area of the psychic "third eye". See **cakras**.

ākāśa — ("ether") Ether, the subtlest of the five elements, which was the first material evolvent of Brahman. It pervades the universe and is the conductor of vibration and sound.

Ambarīṣa — A *rājarṣi,* or saintly king, whose devotional practices are chronicled in the ninth canto of the *Śrīmad Bhāgavatam.*

amṛta — ("immortal") The heavenly nectar of immortality, produced from the primordial ocean when it was churned by the *devas* and *asuras.*

anāhata cakra — The fourth of the seven yogic *cakras*, or energy centers, located at the heart. See **cakras**.

Ānanda — ("bliss") Infinite Bliss, an aspect of Brahman, along with Existence (*sat*) and Consciousness (*cit*).

ānandamaya kośa — The bliss sheath; of the five *kośas,* or subtle and material layers which cover the Ātman, that closest to the Ātman. See **kośa(s)**.

Ananta-Śeṣa — ("infinite serpent") The multihooded, divine serpent companion of Viṣṇu. When Viṣṇu lies down in mystic slumber on the primordial waters during the period of cosmic dissolution, Ananta-Śeṣa serves as His bed. Balarāma, Kṛṣṇa's brother, is considered an incarnation of Ananta-Śeṣa.

Aṅgiras — 1.) Agni. 2.) One of the nine *prajāpatis,* or primordial progenitors sired by Brahmā. He was the initiator and first performer of the sacred fire ritual.

annamayakośa — Physical sheath; of the five *kośas*, or subtle and material layers which cover the Ātman, the physical body.

anuvāka(s) — Lessons, or thematic divisions, of the *Taittirīya Upaniṣad.*

āpaḥ — ("waters") 1.) The all-pervading, primordial "waters" which represent the formless, undifferentiated state before creation. 2.) One of the gross primordial elements, or evolvents, of the material manifestation.

apāna — The *prāṇa*, or vital air, responsible for excretion and sexual generation. See **prāṇa(s)**.

Aparājitā — ("The Invincible") An epithet of the Divine Mother; Durgā.

apsarasas — Celestial nymphs.

Āraṇyakas — ("forest texts") A portion of the Vedic literature presenting philosophical and allegorical interpretations of the Vedic rituals.

Arjuna — Warrior-disciple of Lord Kṛṣṇa in the *Bhagavad-Gītā*; one of the five Pāṇḍavas; a principal figure in the *Mahābhārata*.

Āryans — ("nobles") Nomadic race of proto-European stock who, at approximately 1500 B.C., migrated into India and gradually infused it with their culture and religion. The Vedas were a part of their oral tradition.

āsana — ("seat", "posture", "position") 1.) A yogic posture. 2.) Posture for meditation. 3.) Place or mat where one sits for meditation.

āśrama — 1.) Hermitage or dwelling place of spiritual practitioners. 2.) Any one of the four stages into which the ideally-lived life is divided: celibate student (*brahmacarya*), married householder (*gṛhastha*), retirement and contemplation (*vānaprastha*) and complete renunciation or monastic vows (*sannyāsa*).

asura(s) — A race of demons, or, more accurately, celestial beings whose personality is characterized by anger, avarice and a lust for power. They constitute a force ever in opposition to the *devas*, or gods.

aśva — Horse.

aśvamedha — The ancient Vedic horse sacrifice performed by kings. The opening verses of the *Bṛhadāraṇyaka Upaniṣad* employ it as a metaphor for the creation of the cosmos from the universal body of God.

aśvattha — The Indian fig tree or banyan tree.

Aśvatthāmā — In the *Mahābhārata*, the son of Droṇa and Kṛpi; the Kaurava warrior who slew the five sleeping sons of the Pāṇḍavas and hurled the *brahmāstra* weapon at the unborn Parīkṣit.

Aśvins — ("possessed of horses") The celestial Twins. Their name is derived from the fact that their parents, the goddess Saṃjñā and the sun-god Sūrya, assumed the form of a mare and stallion when they conceived them.

atharvan — A class of Vedic priest whose duties were primarily pastoral, and associated with the use of the *Atharva Veda*.

Atharva Veda — One of the four Vedas, containing rituals and *mantras* for domestic use, such as protection, good fortune, medicine, etc.

Ātman — The Self, the Soul, the Supreme Soul, the immanent aspect of Brahman.

Auṃ — See **Oṃ**.

Avatāra — ("descent") An incarnation of God, such as Kṛṣṇa, Rāma or Jesus.
avadhūta — A religious mendicant.
avidyā — ("non-knowledge") 1.) Ignorance. 2.) "Lower" knowledge comprised of all arts, letters and sciences not connected to the attainment of Brahman.
Ayodhyā — The birthplace and kingdom of Lord Rāma.

Bādarāyaṇa — (C. 200 - 450 A.D.) Author of *Brahma Sūtra* or *Vedānta Sūtra*, the standard commentary on the *Upaniṣads*.
Balarāma — Brother of Lord Kṛṣṇa.
Bali — The *rākṣasa* king from whom the dwarf *avatāra*, Vāmana, begged three steps of land; grandfather of Prahlāda Mahārāja. His story is recounted in the eighth canto of the *Śrīmad Bhāgavatam.*
Bāli — Monkey king of the *Rāmāyaṇa*, who usurped the throne from his elder brother, Sugrīva. Rāma helped depose him and reinstate Sugrīva.
Bhagavad-Gītā — ("the Song of God") The most popular and influential scripture of Hinduism, taking the form of a dialogue between the incarnate God, Kṛṣṇa, and His warrior disciple, Arjuna, on the field of battle. An excerpt from the larger *Mahābhārata*, it describes the nature of Ultimate Truth and the many means of Its attainment.
Bhagavān — ("one endowed with six attributes") God; the Lord; the Personal God of the Devotee; God endowed with six attributes: infinite treasures, splendor or beauty, power, knowledge, glory or fame, and detachment.
Bhāgavata Purāṇa — See *Śrīmad Bhāgavatam.*
bhakta — Practitioner or *bhakti yoga*, the path of love and devotion to God.
bhakti — Love and devotion to God.
bhakti-yoga — The path to union with God through the cultivation of intense, ecstatic love. This is achieved through the practice of any of nine disciplines: hearing, chanting, remembering, worshiping, praying, serving, surrendering, establishing intimacy, and taking refuge.
Bharadvāja — A Vedic *ṛṣi* and teacher.
Bharata — An ancient king after whom India (Bhāratavarṣa) was named. Son of Śakuntalā and Duṣyanta.
Bharata or **Jaḍa** ("Insentient") **Bharata** — A saintly king of the *Śrīmad Bhāgavatam*, three of whose births are recounted in the fifth canto. Being too attached to his pet deer, he took a birth as a deer. His next birth was that of a *jaḍa*, a holy man in so high a spiritual consciousness, he appeared insensate to the common observer.
Bharata — The elder brother of Lord Rāma, who ruled Ayodhyā during

Rāma and Sītā's exile.

Bhīma — In the *Mahābhārata*, the second eldest of the five Pāṇḍava princes. See *Pāṇḍavas.*

Bhīṣma — In the *Mahābhārata*, a brilliant and chivalrous warrior, son of the goddess Gaṅgā (the Ganges) and King Śaṃtanu. He derived his power from a vow of lifelong celibacy and died upon a bed of arrows on the battlefield of Kurukṣetra.

Bhūḥ or **Bhūr** — First of the three *vyāhṛtis*, or mystical utterances, comprising the invocation of the holy *Gāyatrī mantra* and spoken at the commencement of sacred rituals. *Bhūḥ* refers to the terrestrial realm, the physical plane, as opposed to the atmospheric or celestial plane (*Bhuvaḥ*) and the spiritual (*Svaḥ*). See *Gāyatrī.*

Bhuvaḥ — Second of the three *vyāhṛtis*, or mystical utterances, comprising the invocation of the holy *Gāyatrī mantra* and spoken at the commencement of rituals. *Bhuvaḥ* refers to the realm of space, the subtle realm, or celestial realm, as opposed to the terrestrial plane (*Bhūr*) and the spiritual (*Svaḥ*).

Brahmā — The god of creation, or personification of God's creative aspect, a dimension of the Hindu *trimūrti* ("three forms") or divine trinity, the other two aspects being Viṣṇu, the sustainer, and Śiva, the dissolver.

brahmacārī — 1.) A celibate student, first of the four *āśramas*, or stages in life. 2.) A novice monk.

brahmacarya — 1.) First of the four *āśramas*, or stages in life, that of the celibate student. 2.) Celibacy.

brāhmaṇas — One of the four castes or *varṇas*, traditionally comprised of priests, religious leaders, scholars and intellectuals.

Brāhmaṇas — The portion of the Vedic literatures dealing with directions for the performance of sacrifices.

Brahmapuram — ("City of Brahman") The human heart, which is the dwelling place of God, or Ātman/Brahman.

Brahmā Purāṇa — One of the eighteen *Mahā-Purāṇas*, or principal Purāṇas. See *Purāṇa(s).*

Brahma Sūtras or **Vedānta Sūtras** — Classic commentary on the *Upaniṣads* by Bādarāyaṇa, laying down the foundations of the *Vedānta* philosophy. Composed sometime between 200 and 450 A.D..

Bṛhadāraṇyaka Upaniṣad — The longest and most illustrious of the principal *Upaniṣads*. See *Upaniṣad(s).*

Bṛhaspati — ("Lord of Prayer") Vedic god of righteousness, morality and sanctity.

Buddha — ("the Awakened One") Prince Siddhārtha Gautama (6th century B.C.) who achieved Nirvāṇa, or enlightenment, by his own efforts and whose highly rational, empirical and practical teachings posed a challenge to the ritualistic Hinduism of his day. Hindus consider him to be an *Avatāra*, or incarnation, of Viṣṇu.

buddhi — The intellectual or discriminative faculty; one of the four "internal organs", the others being mind (*manas*), the mind-stuff, or mental waves (*citta)*, and ego (*ahaṃkāra*).

cakra(s) — ("wheel") 1.) Any of seven energy centers, or centers of consciousness, located at points along the spine, or, more specifically, along the *suśumnā*, or subtle nerve channel which runs along the spine. As each *cakra* is "awakened" or "opened" successively higher states of consciousness are experienced. The *cakras* are said to resemble lotuses, and may be visualized as such. They are located at the base of the spine (*mūlādhāra cakra*), at the sexual organ (*svādiṣṭhāna cakra*), at the navel (*maṇipūra cakra*), at the heart (*anāhata cakra*), at the throat (*viśuddha cakra*), between and slightly above the eyebrows (*ājña cakra*) and at the crown (*sahasrāra cakra*). 2.) The fiery discus carried by Viṣṇu.

caṇḍāla — An outcaste, a lowborn person.

Caṇḍi — Also called *Devī Māhātmyam* and *Śrī Durgā Saptaśatī*, a text extolling the glories of the Great Goddess, or Divine Mother. Excerpted from the *Mārkaṇḍeya Purāṇa*, it includes exciting narratives of Her heroic exploits as well as several hymns of praise.

Candra — The deity of the moon.

Chāndogya Upaniṣad — One of the principal *Upaniṣads*. See *Upaniṣads*.

cintāmaṇi — 1.) A mythical touchstone that turns base metals into gold. 2.) The name of a prostitute whose influence initially directed the saint Bilvamaṅgala Thakur to spiritual life.

Cit — ("consciousness") Infinite Consciousness; one of the aspects of Brahman, along with Existence (*Sat*) and Bliss (*Ānanda*).

citta — Mind-stuff, mental waves or whirlpools, one of the four "internal organs", the others being mind (*manas*), intellect (*buddhi*), and ego (*ahaṃkāra*).

Citraketu — A king, whose spiritual advancements and pitfalls are recounted in the sixth canto of *Śrīmad Bhāgavatam*.

Dadhyac — A Vedic *ṛṣi* who is mentioned in the *Bṛhadāraṇyaka Upaniṣad* in reference to the famous *madhu-vidyā* or "honey wisdom". After teaching this science to Indra, the *deva* threatened to lop off Dadhyac's head if he should reveal it to anyone else. The Twin Aśvins, however, removed his head and replaced it with a horse's head. When he taught the twins the secret wisdom, it was this equine head that Indra cut off, and the Aśvins quickly replaced Dadhyac's human head to his body. See **Aśvins**.

daitya(s) — ("descendants of Diti") One of the demon races of Hindu mythology.

ḍākinī(s) — 1.) Quasi-divine attendants of the Goddess Kālī 2.) A type of seductive demoness. 3.) In tantric Buddhism, benign goddesses, though often of deceptively frightening appearance.

Dakṣa — One of the nine primordial *prajāpatis,* or progenitors of the human race, born of Lord Brahmā. He is the father of many illustrious daughters, including Diti (the mother of the demoniac races), Aditi (the mother of the *devas*), Savarṇā (mother of the sun god) and Satī, the incarnation of the Divine Mother and consort of Lord Śiva.

ḍamaru — Śiva's hourglass-shaped drum, with which He beats out the inexorable rhythm of time, the destroyer of everything.

Dāmodara — ("rope around the belly") An epithet of the child Kṛṣṇa when, after catching Him stealing butter, His foster-mother Yaśodā attempted to tie him back with a rope, only to discover that no matter how much rope she added to the length, it always turned up too short.

darśana(s)— ("seeing") 1.) The spiritually uplifting act of viewing the sacred image in a temple or of being in the presence of the *guru.* 2.) Collective term for the six orthodox philosophical schools in Hinduism: *Vaiśeṣika, Nyāya, Sāṃkhya, Yoga, Pūrva-Mīmāṃsā* and *Vedānta.*

Daśaratha — The father of Rāma and His brothers.

dāsya — The mood of a servant toward his or her master, one of the *rasas,* or devotional relationships the *bhakti yogi* can have with God.

Dattātreya — A partial incarnation of Viṣṇu; the son of one of the primordial *ṛṣis,* Atri; the spiritual preceptor of non-Āryan beings, such as Prahlāda; sometimes portrayed as a combination of Brahmā, Viṣṇu and Śiva in a single person.

deva(s) — ("shining one") 1.) A god. 2.) The atmospheric deities of the Vedic pantheon, now primarily relegated to the status of demigods. 3.) The race of celestials, ever at odds with the *asuras,* or demons. 4.) Suffix attached to the name of a God-man, such as Kapiladeva.

Devahūtī — Mother and disciple of the *Avatāra* Kapila; wife of Kardama Muni and mother of nine daughters who marry the nine *prajāpatis,* or primordial progenitors.

Devakī — The natural mother of Lord Kṛṣṇa; wife of Vasudeva; cousin of Kaṃsa, Kṛṣṇa's nemesis.

devanāgarī — ("script of the gods") The Sanskrit script.

devatā — See **Iṣṭa-devatā**.

devī — 1.) Goddess, feminine of *deva.* 2.) Suffix attached to the name of a married woman, such as Sarada Devi.

Devī — The Goddess, The Divine Mother.

Devī Māhātmyam — See **Caṇḍi**.

Dhanvantari — A partial incarnation of Viṣṇu; the lord of the arts of medicine, which he introduced to the world. Dhanvantari was manifested from the churning of the primordial ocean.

dhāraṇā — Fixing the mind on a single point; sixth of the eight steps of *rāja yoga*, or formal meditation.

dharma — Duty; one's prescribed work; the duties assigned to one's caste; one's calling; virtue; righteousness; goodness; the pattern of right living; living in accord with the order of the universe; the divinely designed right order of things.

Dharma Śāstras — The general name for a genre of law books which include civil, moral and religious codes. The most famous is that by Manu, *Manu-smṛti*.

Dhenu — A mythological cow who represents the Earth. She is a form of the goddess of speech, Vāc.

Dhṛtarāṣṭra: In the *Mahābhārata*, the royal father of the hundred Kuru princes, the enemies of the five Pāṇḍavas, or sons of Pāṇḍu, Dhṛtarāṣṭra's brother. Born blind, Dhṛtarāṣṭra, though the elder, was unfit to rule, thus Pāṇḍu ruled in his stead. Upon Pāṇḍu's death, controversy over whose descendants were heirs to the throne resulted in the devastating Kurukṣetra war. Dhṛtarāṣṭra's wife, Gāndhārī, voluntarily bound her eyes, so that she could share in her husband's affliction.

Dhruva — A saintly king of the *Śrīmad Bhāgavatam*; as a small child he was slighted by his stepmother, and took to the life of a solitary mendicant in the forest, where he received a vision of Viṣṇu. His story is recounted in the fourth canto.

dhyāna — Meditation, holding the mind in steady concentration, the seventh step of *rāja yoga*, or formal meditation.

Diti — ("limited") 1.) Vedic goddess of earthly phenomenon, as opposed to her sister, Aditi ("limitless"), the goddess of limitless space. 2.) A primordial progenitrix, the mother of the demonic races, wife of the sage Kaśyapa.

Draupadī — In the *Mahābhārata*, wife of the five Pāṇḍava princes. Hers is the only case of polyandry known in Hindu lore. In the gambling tournament episode, one of the most dramatic in the epic, she is saved the disgrace of being disrobed before the assembly by the divine intervention of Lord Kṛṣṇa, who made her *sari* endless.

Droṇa — In the *Mahābhārata*, the revered teacher of military arts to the Kaurava and Pāṇḍava princes.

Durgā — ("the unreachable") The Divine Mother in the form of Protectress, Guardian and absolute *Śakti*, or Power.

Duryodhana — In the *Mahābhārata*, the eldest of the Kaurava princes and greatest nemesis to the Pāṇḍavas, the destruction of whom he worked for ceaselessly.

Dvāpara-Yuga — Of the four *yugas*, or epochs in the duration of the world, the third.

Dvārakā — The kingdom over which Śrī Kṛṣṇa ruled during His earthly life.

Dyaus — 1.) The sky. 2.) Ancient Vedic sky god. Also known as "the father of light" (*dyu-pitar*), he corresponds to the Greek Zeus and Roman Jupiter.

Gajendra — ("elephant lord") King of the elephants who, when seized by an alligator who would not free him, prayed devoutly to Viṣṇu and was saved by Him. His story is recounted in the *Śrīmad Bhāgavatam.*

Gaṇapati — See **Gaṇeśa**.

Gandharvas — A race of winged, celestial musicians.

Gāndīva — Arjuna's magical bow, which had the power of a thousand bows.

Gaṇeśa or **Gaṇapati** — Elephant-headed god, the son of Śiva and Pārvatī. Gaṇeśa is the remover of obstacles and bestower of the good life. He is invoked at the commencement of worship to remove all obstructions between the worshipper and the deity being adored.

Gaṅgā — 1.) The river Ganges. 2.) The personification of the Ganges as a goddess.

Gārgī — A celebrated woman *ṛṣi* whose philosophical dialogue with Yājñavalkya in the assembly of sages is a high point of the *Bṛhadāraṇyaka Upaniṣad.*

Garuḍa — The carrier of Viṣṇu, a celestial bird, often depicted as part bird, part man.

Gāyatrī — 1.) One of the most revered and powerful of the Vedic *mantras*, recited daily by devout *brāhmaṇas.* Ostensibly an invocation to the sun, its deeper meaning suggests a meditation on the physical, subtle and spiritual realms and on the effulgent God which is their source. It goes:

Oṃ Bhūr Bhuvaḥ Svaḥ
Tat Savitur Vareṇyam
Bhargo Devasya Dhīmahi
Dhiyo Yo Naḥ Pracodayāt

"Oṃ. Salutations to the terrestrial sphere. Salutations to the sphere of space. Salutations to the celestial sphere. May we meditate on the effulgent light of Him who is worshipful and has given birth to all worlds. May He direct the rays of our intelligence towards the path of good."

2.) The Goddess Gāyatrī, presiding deity of the *mantra.*

Gokula — The pastoral district along the Yamunā river where Śrī Kṛṣṇa passed His childhood.
gopa(s) — ("cowherd") 1.) The cowherd boys who were playmates of Kṛṣṇa. 2.) Men of the Vṛndāvana settlement where Kṛṣṇa had His childhood pastimes. They were cowherds by profession.
Gopāla — ("cowherd") Śrī Kṛṣṇa as a cowherd boy.
gopī(s) — ("cowherdess") The milkmaids of Vṛndāvana, lovers and playmates of the young Kṛṣṇa. Their romantic dalliances with Kṛṣṇa in the forest correspond to the highest stages of spiritual realization and mystical union attained through the path of *bhakti yoga*, or devotional love.
Gotama — Third century B.C. founder of the *Nyāya*, or logic, school of Hindu philosophy.
Govardhana — A mountain in Vṛndāvana which Śrī Kṛṣṇa lifted and held over the village like an umbrella to shield the residents from torrential storms sent by Indra. To this day it is revered as extremely sacred. An epithet of Kṛṣṇa is Govardhanadhara, "lifter of Mount Govardhana".
Govinda — ("delighter of the senses", "delighter of the cows") A name for Śrī Kṛṣṇa.
gṛhastha — Second of the four *āśramas*, or stages of life, that of the married householder.
guṇa(s) — ("cord", "thread") According to the Sāṃkhya philosophy, the three modes of material nature, the interaction of which gives rise to all worldly phenomena. The predominance of one of the *guṇas* over the others, or a mixture of two dominant *guṇas*, can be observed in any place, person, object or event. The *guṇas* are *rajas*, or impulse, action, heat, passion; *tamas*, or resistance, inertia, heaviness, ignorance; and *sattva*, or harmony, purity, lightness, goodness.
guru — The spiritual teacher, preceptor, guide.
Guru Gītā or **Śrī Guru Gītā** — A hymn to the greatness of the *guru*, excerpted from the *Skanda Purāṇa*.

hālāhala — A deadly poison produced when the *devas* and *asuras* churned the primordial ocean. To save the world from its effects, Lord Śiva drank the poison and held it in His throat; the few drops which escaped His lips became the poisonous plants, insects and reptiles of the earth.
haṃsa — 1.) A swan or, more accurately, a species of Himalayan goose known for its beauty and grace. 2.) A term denoting a spiritually elevated individual who, like a swan on the surface of a lake, is unaffected by the "waters" of the material world, or, like the swan in flight, has raised his or her consciousness to the heights of Brahman. There is also an Indian legend that the *haṃsa* is capable of extracting the pure milk from a

mixture of milk and water; similarly, the human "*haṃsa*" can discern Truth from illusion, the spiritual from the material.

Hanumān — From the *Rāmāyaṇa*, the heroic monkey devotee of Lord Rāma. Hanumān is considered one of the great role models for *bhaktas*, as his life is a study in single-minded devotion and perfect service to his Chosen Ideal.

Hari — ("fair", "golden yellow") An epithet of Viṣṇu.

haṭha-yoga — The *yoga* of physical exercises and breath control, aimed at maintaining health and fitness, preparing the body for long-term meditation, and inducing refined states of consciousness through *āsanas*, or physical postures.

Hayagrīva — ("horse-necked") 1.) An *Avatāra* of Viṣṇu. 2.) One of the names of the Cosmic Person spoken of in the *Upaniṣads*, Whose primordial dismemberment gave rise to the material cosmos. He is thematically linked to the sacrificial horse of the Vedic *aśvamedha* sacrifice, whose dismemberment ceremonially recreates the universe.

Hiraṇyagarbha — ("golden womb", "golden egg") 1.) God as creator, the source of all manifestations, spiritual and material. The amorphous Hiraṇyagarbha represents the first step of Brahman's expression of Itself as manifest Reality, or Brahman with attributes. 2.) An epithet of Brahmā.

Hiraṇyakaśipu — King of the demonic *daitya* race, father of the saintly Prahlāda. Viṣṇu incarnated as Nṛsiṃhadeva, the man-lion, in order to vanquish him. His story is recounted in the seventh canto of the *Śrīmad Bhāgavatam*.

Hiraṇyākṣa — The *daitya* brother of Hiraṇyakaśipu; he battled, and was vanquished by, Viṣṇu's Varāha, or boar, Incarnation.

hotā or **hotṛ** — A variety of priest, a functionary in the Vedic *soma* sacrifice.

īḍā — One of two subtle nerve channels, or *nāḍīs*, running along the spinal cord. The *īḍā* is situated to the left of the spine while the other channel, the *piṅgalā*, is situated on the right.

Indra — The chief of the *devas*, the Vedic deity of sky, rain, and lightning. Often compared to Zeus, he figures prominently in the hymns of the *Ṛg Veda* and in the mythologies of the *Purāṇas*.

indriyas — The interior sense organs, in other words the subtle sensory faculties which perceive objects through the medium of the physical sense organs. They include the five organs of perception (sight, hearing, smell, taste, touch), the five organs of action (tongue, hands, feet, organs of excretion and genitals), and the mind.

Īśā Upaniṣad — One of the principal *Upaniṣads*, dealing primarily with reconciling knowledge and action.

Iṣṭa or **Iṣṭa-devatā** — The Chosen Ideal; of the many forms of God, the one which the devotee loves most and feels the greatest affinity with.
Īśvara — ("Lord", "Controller") God in His personal aspect.
Itihāsas — ("so indeed it was") The genre of sacred scripture which includes the epic poems, namely the *Mahābhārata* and the *Rāmāyaṇa.*

jaḍa — ("insentient") The highest state of yogic concentration, in which the *yogī* is so absorbed in divine consciousness he or she appears to be insensate to the outside world.
Jaḍa Bharata — ("insensate Bharata") An ancient king whose spiritual journey, with its pitfalls and successes, is recounted in the fifth canto of *Śrīmad Bhāgavatam.* His lives include that of a king, a deer, and a *jaḍa.*
Jagannātha — ("Lord of the Universe") The famous deities of Kṛṣṇa, His sister Subhadrā, and brother Balarāma housed at the temple in Purī, Orissa. The charming, saucer-eyed faces of the statues are of a curiously aboriginal quality; the deities' origin remains mysterious and the subject of debate.
Janaka — 1.) A saintly king, well-known for his ability to carry out the administrative duties of his station while remaining completely detached from them as well as from the world. 2.) The father of Sītā.
japa — The repetition of a *mantra*, often the name, or names, of God. *Japa* can be performed vocally or mentally, and is often performed with the aid of a strand of meditation beads, known as a *japa mālā.*
Jaṭāyu — From the *Rāmāyaṇa*, a courageous vulture who attempted to intercept Rāvaṇa's journey to Laṅkā with the kidnapped Sītā. Jaṭāyu was mortally wounded but, with his dying breath, directed Rāma and Lakṣmaṇa in the direction where Sītā had been carried.
Jaya — One of Viṣṇu's doorkeepers. When he and his brother, Vijaya, barred the four Kumāras from entering Viṣṇu's abode, they cursed him to take birth as a demon, and he subsequently became Hiraṇyakaśipu.
jaya — ("victory", "glory") A salutary invocation, as in "*Jaya* Śrī Kṛṣṇa" ("All glories to Lord Kṛṣṇa").
jīva — The soul; the semblance of the individual; the Ātman still ignorant of Its divine identity and thus laboring under the misconception that It is an individual and subject to rebirth.
jñāna — ("knowledge") Knowledge, or direct perception, of the Ultimate Truth; discrimination between the Real and the unreal.
jñāna-yoga — The *yoga* of knowledge, wherein the aspirant strives to realize Brahman without attributes by discriminating between that which is Real, i.e. Brahman, and that which is unreal, *māyā.* Through the process of elimination (a practice known as *neti neti* — "this is not Brahman,

nor is that Brahman"), the *yogī* comes to perceive the oneness behind everything.
jñānī — A practitioner of *jñāna-yoga.*

Kaikeyī — From the *Rāmāyaṇa,* one of the wives of Daśaratha, Lord Rāma's father, and the mother of Bharata, Rāma's half-brother. It was she who had Rāma banished and Bharata enthroned in His place.
kāla — Time, the force that destroys all earthly things.
Kālī — ("time") The Divine Mother in Her terrible aspect, the Dark Mother, the Devourer, the Destroyer. Kālī represents all phenomena — earthly, cosmic and spiritual — and thus Her appearance is terrifying, but Her appearance, like the *māyā* She personifies, is an illusion. One of the most widely-adored forms of the Goddess, She is in fact our affectionate, loving Mother. Time, as Her name implies, can only destroy physical matter; it cannot destroy our true Selves, which are spiritual and eternal.
Kāliya — In the Kṛṣṇa account, a giant, poisonous serpent who took residence in the Yamunā river. The child Kṛṣṇa wrestled with and subdued him.
Kali-yuga — Of the four *yugas,* or epochs in the duration of the world, the last, and the one in which we are living. It is characterized by degeneration, quarrel, irreligion and darkness.
Kalki — The future *Avatāra* of Viṣṇu, Who will appear before the dissolution of the world at the close of this cycle of earthly time. Riding a white horse, He will assume the role of the divine Destroyer and purge the earth of its evil elements.
kalpa — The period of universal manifestation, comprised of 1,000 *yugas,* or 4,320,000,000 years. Each *kalpa* comprises one "day" of Brahmā, who lives the span of one *mahākalpa,* or a hundred "days" and "nights" of the above period of time. This constitutes the period of cosmic manifestation of which our universe is merely a fragment.
kalpataru — The wish-fulfilling tree of Hindu mythology; it symbolizes the world which, in time, fulfills all of our desires but which we eventually find empty and must abandon.
Kāma — 1.) Sensual passion; romantic love; physical desire; pleasure. 2.) The Hindu god of romantic love and desire; Eros; Cupid.
Kaṃsa — The wicked fraternal uncle of Śrī Kṛṣṇa who plotted His murder and was eventually slain by Him.
Kapila — 1.) An *Avatāra* of Viṣṇu, the son of Devahūtī and Kardama Muni, who expounded the *Sāṃkhya* philosophy to His mother. His life and teachings are contained in the third canto of *Śrīmad Bhāgavatam.* 2.) Seventh century B.C. founder of the *Sāṃkhya* philosophy, considered a different person from the *Avatāra* Kapila.

Kardama — A primordial progenitor and one of the mind-born sons of Lord Brahmā. The husband of Devahūtī and father of the *Avatāra* Kapila.
karma — 1.) Action; work; doing. 2.) The results or fruits of our actions. 3.) The cosmic law of cause and effect whereby all of our actions create reactions which we are destined to experience later in this or a future life.
karma-yoga — The *yoga* of action or work, whereby the *yogī* performs all of his or her duties sacramentally, as service to God, and renounces attachment to the fruits of work.
karmi — An individual who has not yet taken to the spiritual path, and therefore is working in the world for his or her personal gain.
Karṇa — Of the *Mahābhārata*, a fierce and talented warrior. The long-lost brother of the Pāṇḍavas, he was given at birth to a low-born couple to raise and, not knowing of his familial tie, swore allegiance to the Kauravas, their enemies, and fought against his brothers in the Kurukṣetra war.
Kārttikeya — The god of war, son of Śiva and Pārvatī.
Kaśyapa — A primordial progenitor and mind-born son of Lord Brahmā; with his wife Aditi, he is the father of the race of gods (*devas*) and of the dwarf *Avatāra*, Vāmana, and with his other wife, Diti, he is the father of the races of demons (*asuras* and *daityas*).
Kaṭha Upaniṣad — One of the principal *Upaniṣads*, being the dialogue between the saintly *brāhmaṇa* youth Naciketas and Yama, the god of death.
kaustubha — A magical gem which emerged from the churning of the primordial ocean. Viṣṇu wears it upon His breast.
Kauravas — ("descendants of Kuru") In the *Mahābhārata*, the sons of Dhṛtarāṣṭra, headed by Duryodhana; the foes of the Pāṇḍava princes.
Kena Upaniṣad — One of the principal *Upaniṣads*, a meditation on Brahman as the inner Perceiver, not that which is perceived.
Keśava — ("handsome-haired") A name of Kṛṣṇa and/or Viṣṇu.
kīrtana — The congregational singing of hymns and/or chanting of God's names.
kośa(s) — ("sheath(s)") Any of the five sheaths, or subtle and material layers, which enclose the Ātman and give rise to one's sense of individuality and limited self. They are the *annamayakośa*, or physical sheath, the *prāṇamayakośa*, or vital energy sheath, the *manomayakośa*, or mental sheath, the *vijñānamayakośa*, or intellectual sheath, and the *ānandamayakośa* or bliss sheath.
Kṛṣṇa — One of the principal manifestations of God in the Hindu religion. An *Avatāra* of Viṣṇu, tradition sets His advent at approximately 3,000 B.C., though secular scholars place Him somewhat later. Gauḍīya Vaiṣṇavas take Him to be the Supreme Personality of Godhead, superior

and original to both Viṣṇu and impersonal Brahman. Of unearthly beauty, ravishing sweetness and extraordinary wisdom and power, He is adored as the Divine Child, Divine Lover, and Supreme *Guru*. He is the speaker of the *Bhagavad-Gītā* and the subject of some of Hinduism's most sublime mythology, sacred music and devotional poetry.

Kṛṣṇa Dvaipāyana — See **Vyāsa**.

kṣatriya — Of the four *varṇas*, or castes, that of government administration and military. Royalty and police are also members of this *varṇa*.

kumāras — ("boys") Saintly quadruplets, among the first generation of primordial beings born directly from the mind of Lord Brahmā. Given entirely to spiritual life, they refused to grow to sexual maturity, and remained children eternally.

kuṇḍalinī — ("coiled up", i.e. like a serpent) The spiritual energy which normally lies dormant at the base of the spine, like a sleeping, coiled serpent. Certain yogic exercises (*kuṇḍalinī yoga*) can "awaken" this energy and draw it, in steps, up the spinal column, thus opening the *cakras*, or seven energy centers located along the spine. As each of the *cakras* is opened, increasingly higher states of consciousness are achieved. See **cakras**.

Kuntī — In the *Mahābhārata*, wife of Pāṇḍu, mother of the five Pāṇḍava princes, and paternal aunt of Śrī Kṛṣṇa.

Kūrma — ("tortoise") Lord Viṣṇu's tortoise incarnation.

Kurukṣetra — Site of the momentous, fratricidal war depicted in the *Mahābhārata*. It was on this battlefield that Śrī Kṛṣṇa spoke the *Bhagavad-Gītā* to Arjuna.

kuśa — A type of sacred grass used in Vedic ceremonies and by *yogīs* as seat for meditation.

Lakṣmaṇa — In the *Rāmāyaṇa*, the brother and constant companion of Lord Rāma.

Lakṣmī — The Goddess of Fortune; a principal manifestation of the Divine Mother; the *Śakti*, or female counterpart, of Lord Viṣṇu.

Lalitā — A manifestation of the Divine Mother as a dear, playful young girl of whom the universe is a toy.

Lava — In the *Rāmāyaṇa*, one of the twin sons of Śrī Rāma, the other being *Kuśa*.

līlā — 1.) The divine play, or sport, of God. 2.) The cosmic manifestation, which is God's joyful frolic with Himself as Player, playmate(s) and field of play. 3.) God's activities and pastimes on earth when He takes birth as an *Avatāra*, for example, *Kṛṣṇa-līlā*.

liṅgam — ("symbol", "sign", "mark") The representative form of Lord Śiva as a pillar or phallic symbol. The *liṅgam* represents both Śiva's creative power and His being the axis, fulcrum, or center of all Reality.

liṅgaśarīra — The subtle body, or that which transmigrates with the soul to another body. It includes the inner sense organs (see *indriyas*), the mind, and the *saṃskāras* (impressions, tendencies, memories).

Madhu — 1.) A demon killed by Lord Kṛṣṇa.
madhu — "Honey", "sweetness" symbolic of the bliss of Brahman and the sweetness of the love exchanged between the aspirant and God.
madhu-vidyā — ("honey knowledge") A portion of the *Bṛhadāraṇyaka Upaniṣad* which describes, in poetic terms, the oneness of all reality and the ineffable sweetness which underlies it.
Mahābhārata — ("Great Epic of the Descendants of Bharata") — The great sacred epic of ancient India which, with its infinite digressions, philosophical expositions, and forays into religious, social, and cultural instruction, weaves the tale of the royal family descended from King Bharata. It climaxes in the momentous war of Kurukṣetra, where the heroic Pāṇḍava brothers and their cousins, the Kauravas, clash in battle for the throne of India. The longest epic poem in the world, its verses include the *Bhagavad-Gītā.*
Mahādeva — ("Great God") An epithet of Lord Śiva.
Mahādevī — ("Great Goddess") An epithet of the Divine Mother.
Mahāmāyā — ("the great Illusion") The Divine Mother in Her form as *māyā*, i.e. the cosmic manifestation, *prakṛti*, the illusion of earthly reality. The irony of Mahāmāyā is that She is both the Power which ensnares us in illusion, and the means of our liberation from it.
Mahā-Purāṇas — The eighteen principal texts in the Purāṇic corpus, as opposed to the twelve *Upa-Purāṇas*, or lesser *Purāṇas.* They include the *Brahma*, *Brahmāṇḍa, Brahma-vaivarta*, *Mārkaṇḍeya*, *Bhaviṣya*, *Vāmana*, *Viṣṇu*, *Bhāgavata*, *Nārada*, *Garuḍa*, *Padma*, *Varāha*, *Śiva*, *Liṅga*, *Skanda*, *Agni*, *Matsya*, and *Kūrma Purāṇas.* Some devotees include the *Devī Bhāgavata Purāṇa* among the *Mahā-Purāṇas.*
mahārāja — ("great king") 1.) Honorific title for a monarch. 2.) A title of respect used when addressing a *swāmī*, or member of the renounced order of life.
maharṣi — ("great seer") A great mystic or God-realized being.
mahātma — ("great soul") Honorific title for a spiritually advanced individual.
Mahāsaṃhitās — ("great conjunctions") In the *Taittirīya Upaniṣad*, a study of how all phenomena are interconnected, using, as an analogy, conjunctions in Sanskrit grammar.
Mahāvākyas — ("great utterances") The great Upaniṣadic dictums, such as *tat tvam asi* ("That thou art"), *ahaṃ Brahmāsmi* ("I am Brahman"), etc.
mahat — The cosmic Intelligence; the cosmic principle of knowing; the

ocean of awareness.

Mahat-tattva — In the early stages of creation, the sum total of material ingredients, which will evolve into phenomena as we know it.

Maheśvara — ("Great Lord") An epithet of Lord Śiva.

Mahiṣa or **Mahiṣāsura** — ("buffalo"/"buffalo demon") A buffalo demon slain by the Divine Mother Durgā.

Maitreyī — In the *Bṛhadāraṇyaka Upaniṣad*, a *yoginī* who becomes the disciple of her saintly husband, Yājñavalkya, before he retires from the world. The portion of the text containing their dialogue bears her name (*Maitreyī Brāhmaṇa*).

mālā — A garland of beads used in meditation and chanting.

manas — Mind; one of the four internal organs, along with *ahaṃkāra* (ego), *buddhi* (intellect) and *citta* (mind-stuff).

maṇḍala — A sacred, symbolic diagram, often of a circular motif.

Māṇḍūkya Upaniṣad — One of the principal *Upaniṣads*, concerned chiefly with the *mantra Oṃ*.

maṇipūra cakra — The third of the seven yogic *cakras*, or energy centers, located in the area of the navel. See **cakras**.

manomayakośa — The mental sheath; of the five *kośas*, or subtle and material layers which cover the Ātman, the mind.

mantra — A spiritually potent word or phrase, such as the name(s) of God, or *Oṃ*.

Manu — Any of several primordial progenitors of the human race. Each epoch of world history is predominated by one Manu or another.

Marīci — One of the nine *Prajāpatis*, or primordial progenitors born directly from the mind of Lord Brahmā.

Mārkaṇḍeya — An ancient holy man who was given a vision of God in the form of a divine Infant who held the entire cosmos in His body. The Mārkaṇḍeya account is found in the twelfth canto of *Śrīmad Bhāgavatam*.

Maruts — A variety of Vedic storm gods.

Mathurā — The birthplace of Lord Kṛṣṇa.

Matsya — ("fish") Lord Viṣṇu's fish *Avatāra*.

māyā — The cosmic Illusion; the illusion that the One has become many; that which causes us to believe we are separate from Brahman; the illusion that the multiplicity of the material world is real; the play of the Divine as the material manifestation.

Mīmāṃsā or **Pūrva-Mīmāṃsā** — Of the six orthodox philosophical schools of Hinduism, that of the Vedic apologists, founded by Jaimini in the third century B.C..

Mohinī-mūrti — Viṣṇu's Incarnation as a beautiful woman. She charmed the elixir of immortality away from the *asuras* to give to the *devas*, and alone aroused the amorous passion of Lord Śiva, the cosmic ascetic.

mokṣa — Spiritual liberation from the cycle of rebirth. The same as *mukti.*
mukti — Spiritual liberation from the bondage of rebirth.
Muṇḍaka Upaniṣad — One of the principal *Upaniṣads*, chiefly concerned with the realization of Brahman.
muni — A contemplative hermit.

Naciketas — In the *Kaṭha Upaniṣad*, the *brāhmaṇa* boy who journeys to the abode of the god of death and engages in a philosophical dialogue with him.
nāḍīs — Subtle nerve channels, the principle three of which are the *suśumnā* in the spinal cavity, the *iḍā* to its left, and the *piṅgalā* to its right.
nāga(s) — 1.) Snake, serpent. 2.) A race of celestial snakes.
Naimiṣāraṇya — The forest where the sages collected to hear the first recitation of the *Śrīmad Bhāgavatam.*
Nakula — In the *Mahābhārata*, one the five Pāṇḍava brothers. He and his twin, Sahadeva, are the sons of the Aśvins, the celestial twins.
Nanda — Śrī Kṛṣṇa's foster father in Vṛndāvana.
Nandin — Lord Śiva's bull.
Nārada — The celestial minstrel; one of the mind-born sons of Lord Brahmā; the traditional author of the *Nārada Bhakti Sūtras.*
Nārada Bhakti Sūtras — Quasi-canonical text expounding the theory and practice of *bhakti*, the path of devotion. It is traditionally attributed to the celestial sage Nārada.
Nara-Nārāyaṇa — Incarnation of Viṣṇu as twin sages.
Narasiṃha or **Nṛsiṃha** — ("man-lion") Viṣṇu's Incarnation as a half-man half-lion. Because He appeared in order to rescue his devotee, the child Prahlāda, from certain death, Narasiṃha is invoked for protection. His narrative is found in the seventh canto of *Śrīmad Bhāgavatam.*
Nārāyaṇa — ("The One Whose Abode is the Waters") An epithet of Viṣṇu, particularly in reference to His reclining upon the "waters" of cosmic dissolution prior to a new creationary cycle.
Naṭarāja — ("Lord of the Dance") Lord Śiva in His destructive aspect, performing the dance of cosmic dissolution and renewal.
neti neti — ("not this, not this") Associated with *jñāna-yoga*, the discipline of constantly distinguishing between the Real, or Brahman, and the unreal, or *māyā*. Everything one encounters is rejected as not Brahman, and therefore false. Eventually the *yogī* comes to an understanding of the divine Reality which is purely spiritual Existence-Consciousness-Bliss.
Nīlakaṇṭha — ("Blue-throated") An epithet of Lord Śiva. When the churning of the ocean produced the deadly poison *hālāhala*, Śiva, in

order to save the world from its effects, drank it and held it in His throat, which then turned blue.

Nirguṇa — ("without qualities") Brahman in Its impersonal aspect without attributes.

Nirvāṇa — ("extinguished") Spiritual liberation, enlightenment, ultimate bliss. The term "extinguished" refers to the obliteration of individual self, ego, attachment to the world, suffering and rebirth.

niyama — The second of the eight steps of *rāja-yoga*; regular habits and observances. These include austerity, study, contentment, purity and worship of God.

Nṛsiṃha — See *Narasiṃha.*

Nyāya — Of the six orthodox philosophical schools of Hinduism, the school of logic, founded by Gautama.

Oṃ — The *bīja mantra*, or seed *mantra*, representative of Brahman. All sounds, all mantras, all phenomena — natural, supernatural and spiritual — have their source in it, their destination in it and their existence in it. It constitutes the Ultimate Truth in the form of sound. It is Everything. Also spelled *Auṃ.*

pañcaprāṇas — ("five vital airs") The five divisions of *prāṇa*, or vital force, which animates the body and its functions. They include *prāṇa*, which governs breath and respiration, *apāna*, responsible for excretion and reproduction, *vyāna*, the nervous and circulatory systems, *samāna*, digestion and assimilation of food, and *udāna*, the upward-rising energy which conveys the soul out of the body at the time of death.

Pāṇḍavas — ("descents of Pāṇḍu") In the *Mahābhārata*, the five sons of Pāṇḍu: Yudhiṣṭhira, Bhīma, Arjuna, Nakula and Sahadeva.

paṇḍita — A learned scholar, particularly in Sanskrit grammar and religious texts.

Pāṇḍu — In the *Mahābhārata*, husband of Kuntī and Madrī, father of the five Pāṇḍava princes, brother of Dhṛtarāṣṭra.

paramahaṃsa — ("supreme swan") 1.) A monk belonging to a particular sect of the Śaṅkara order. 2.) A God-realized person. See **haṃsa**.

Paramātma — Supreme Ātman.

Paraśurāma — ("Rāma with an axe") An *Avatāra* of Viṣṇu who slew most of the *kṣatriya* caste when they had usurped the religious authority of the *brāhmaṇas.*

Parīkṣit — The saintly king who, learning that he had but a week to live, retired to the banks of the Ganges to fast and meditate and there was met by Śrī Śukadeva, who proceeded to recite to him the *Śrīmad Bhāgavatam.* Parīkṣit is the grandson of Arjuna, and was in power when the turn of the world epoch came and time shifted into the dreaded *Kali-yuga*, the age of quarrel and degeneracy in which we now live.

Pārvatī — The Divine Mother in the form of the Daughter of the Himalayas; the *Śakti*, or divine consort, of Lord Śiva; mother of Gaṇeśa and Kārttikeya.

Patañjali — Second century B.C. codifier of the *rāja-yoga* system; author of the *Yoga Sūtras*.

piṅgalā — One of the two subtle nerve channels, or *nāḍīs*, running along the spinal column. The *piṅgalā* is situated to the right of the spine while the other channel, the *iḍā*, is situated to the left.

pitṛs — Ancestors; manes.

Pradyumna — The chief son of Śrī Kṛṣṇa and Rukmiṇī.

Prahlāda — A saintly child devotee of Lord Viṣṇu. Though born a *daitya*, one of the demoniac races, he was of a devotional temperament and, as a result, was persecuted by his wicked father, Hiraṇyakaśipu. His plight brought forth Viṣṇu's half-man half-lion *Avatāra*, Nṛsiṃhadeva, who saved him.

Prajāpatis — ("fathers of creatures") The primordial progenitors of the human races.

Prakṛti — The active aspect of Brahman; principle of energy/matter/substance from which the world evolves; Nature; material substance; *māyā*; the Goddess; the Divine Mother; the counterpart to *Puruṣa*, the aspect of Brahman which is pure spirit.

pralaya — The period of cosmic dissolution; the universal "sleep" between cycles of creation.

prāṇa — The vital force; the animating life energy. See **pañcaprāṇas**.

prāṇamayakośa — The prāṇic sheath; of the five *kośas*, or subtle and material layers which cover the Ātman, the vital energy layer.

praṇava — The *mantra Oṃ*.

prāṇāyāma — Breath control; breathing exercises; the science of calming the body and inducing certain states of consciousness through manipulation of the breathing; fourth of the eight steps of *rāja-yoga*.

prasāda — ("mercy") Food which has been consecrated by first being offered to God.

Praśna Upaniṣad — One of the principal *Upaniṣads*, concerned primarily with *prāṇa*, the life force within us.

prastāva — A portion of the Vedic *soma* sacrifice.

pratihāra — A portion of the Vedic *soma* sacrifice.

pratihartā — The priest who sings the *pratihāra* portion of the Vedic *soma* sacrifice.

pratyāhāra — Gathering the forces of the mind inward; the fifth of the eight steps of *rāja-yoga*.

prastotā — The priest who sings the *prastāva* portion of the Vedic *soma* sacrifice.
preyaḥ — From the *Kaṭha Upaniṣad*, that which is pleasurable, but not necessarily good for one (as opposed to *śreyaḥ*, that which may not be pleasant, but which helps one advance spiritually).
pūjā — Ritualistic worship performed either at one's home altar or in a temple.
Purāṇa(s) — ("ancient") A genre of sacred literature which illustrates spiritual truths through stories, histories, genealogies, myths and dialogues. Primarily devotional in nature, different *Purāṇas* espouse the worship of a particular Divine Ideal or another, such as Kṛṣṇa, Viṣṇu, or Śiva. See **Mahā-Purāṇas**; **Upa-Purāṇas**.
Puruṣa ("person", "man") 1.) That aspect of Brahman which is pure spirit, pure consciousness (as opposed to *prakṛti*, which is the aspect of Brahman that has become matter). 2.) In creation accounts, the primordial, cosmic Person. 3.) The Ātman or Self.

Rādhā or **Rādhikā** or **Rādhārāṇī** — The *śakti*, or consort, of Śrī Kṛṣṇa. An Incarnation of the Goddess Lakṣmī as a simple, unlettered cowherd damsel, She demonstrates the highest attainment of God-realization through the path of ecstatic love and is a mystic and *yoginī* par excellence.
Rāhu — An *asura* responsible for the eclipses of the sun and moon, which he is said to swallow. He was slain by Viṣṇu's Mohinī-mūrti Incarnation.
rāja — King.
rajas — Of the three *guṇas*, or modes of material nature, that of impulse, action, passion.
rāja-yoga — The *yoga* of meditation.
rākṣasa(s) — A type of demon which can assume any form at will. They kill and eat humans yet may also be sexually attracted to them. Rāma's enemy, Rāvaṇa, was a *rākṣasa*.
rākṣasī(s) — Female *rākṣasa(s)*.
Rāma or **Rāmacandra** — One of the most illustrious and beloved *Avatāras* of Viṣṇu; the ideal king, husband, brother, warrior and savior; the hero of the epic poem *Rāmāyaṇa*.
Rāmāyaṇa — Epic poem recounting the saga of Rāma and Sītā, composed by Vālmīki.
rasa(s) — ("juice", "flavor") Any of seven sweet relationships the devotee can enjoy with their chosen Divine Beloved: neutrality, master-servant, parent-child, child-parent, friend-friend, lovers in separation and lovers in union.

rasa dance — The circular dance Śrī Kṛṣṇa and the *gopīs* (cowherd damsels) performed in the forest of Vṛndāvana.
Rāvaṇa — In the *Rāmāyaṇa*, Lord Rāma's arch-enemy. A *rākṣasa*, he kidnapped Sītā and held Her captive in Laṅkā (now Sri Lanka), of which he was the king.
ṛc — A type of praise stanza, used in the *Ṛg Veda*.
Ṛg Veda — The most important of the four *Vedas*, a collection of devotional and philosophical hymns.
Rohiṇī — The mother of Śrī Balarāma, Kṛṣṇa's brother; the second wife of Vasudeva.
ṛṣi — ("seer") 1.) A saint or seer. 2.) Ancient sages to which the Vedic knowledge was revealed.
Rudra — ("ruddy", "red", "flashing") 1.) Śiva 2.) Red-complected Vedic deity of storms and tempests, a forerunner of Śiva.
Rudras — A category of ancient Vedic storm deities.
Rukmiṇī — Kṛṣṇa's queen at Dvārakā.

sādhanā — Spiritual practices; spiritual disciplines.
sādhu — A holy man; a monk; a wandering holy man.
Saguṇa — ("with qualities") 1.) God with attributes. 2.) The Personal aspect of God. 3.) The aspect of Brahman that has become this material manifestation.
Sahadeva — In the *Mahābhārata*, one of the five Pāṇḍava brothers; the twin of Nakula.
sahasrāra cakra — The seventh, and highest, of the seven yogic *cakras*, or energy centers, located in the crown. It is associated with the experience of superconsciousness. See **cakras**.
Śaiva or **Śaivite** — ("of Śiva") 1.) A devotee of Lord Śiva. 2.) Of or pertaining to Śiva and His worship.
Śākta — ("of Śakti") 1.) A devotee of the Divine Mother. 2.) Of or pertaining to the Divine Mother and Her worship.
Śakti — ("power", "energy") 1.) Primal Power; Divine Energy; the active, dynamic aspect of Brahman which actualizes the principles of creation, preservation and destruction. 2.) The Divine Mother; the Great Goddess. 3.) The feminine counterparts to the male deities, such as Brahmā, Viṣṇu and Śiva. The Goddess constitutes the Power (*Śakti*) which makes the concept represented by the God a reality.
samādhi — Superconsciousness; the eighth, and culminating, step of *rāja-yoga* wherein the meditator experiences him or herself as unlimited, as Ātman, and united with Ultimate Reality.
samāna — The *prāṇa*, or vital air, responsible for digestion and assimilation of food.

sāman(s) — Songs utilized in Vedic ritual.
Sāma Veda — Of the four *Vedas*, a collection of hymns culled from the *Ṛg Veda* and arranged for liturgical purposes.
saṃhitā — 1.) A collection of methodically arranged compositions of a similar theme or character. 2.) The four *Vedas*.
Sāṃkhya — Of the six orthodox philosophical schools of Hinduism, that which explains material phenomena as the interplay of *puruṣa* and *prakṛti* and of the three *guṇas*. Founded by Kapila in the seventh century B.C..
saṃsāra — The perpetual cycle of birth, death and rebirth; transmigration; reincarnation.
sanātana dharma — ("eternal truth") 1.) Truth in its purest form, beyond worldly sectarianism and dogma. 2.) Hinduism.
Śaṅkara or **Śaṅkarācārya** — (A.D. 788-820) One of India's greatest philosopher-saints and the chief exponent of *advaita vedānta*, or theological nondualism. He was the founder of a system of monastic denominations which are still in existence and the author of voluminous scriptural commentaries and original works which form the basis of mainstream Hindu thought.
sannyāsa — 1.) The final of the four *āśramas*, or stages of life, that of the complete renunciate. 2.) The monastic life. 3.) The initiation into the final stage of monastic life, complete renunciation of the world, known commonly as "taking *sannyāsa*".
sannyāsī or **sannyāsin** — 1.) One who has taken vows of *sannyāsa*. 2.) A monk.
śānti — "Peace".
Sarasvatī — The Divine Mother in Her form as the Goddess of Learning, Scholarship, Music, Literature and the Arts. The *Śakti* of Lord Brahmā.
śāstra(s) — 1.) Scriptures. 2.) Treatises and lawbooks of the post-Vedic period, such as the *Dharma-Śāstras*.
Sat — ("existence") Infinite Existence; one of the aspects of Brahman, along with *Cit* (consciousness) and *Ānanda* (bliss).
Sat-Cit-Ānanda or **Saccidānanda** — ("Existence-Consciousness-Bliss") An epithet of Brahman, Who is unlimited, absolute Existence, Consciousness and Bliss.
Satī — The first *Śakti* of Lord Śiva Who, after Her father publicly insulted Śiva, immolated Herself in a mystic fire born of Her meditation. She then reincarnated as Pārvatī.
Śatrughna — In the *Rāmāyaṇa*, the twin brother of Lakṣmaṇa.
sattva — Of the three *guṇas*, or modes of material nature, that of goodness, purity, spirituality, peace. See **guṇas**.
Satya-yuga — Of the four *yugas*, or epochs in the duration of the world, the first; characterized by spirituality and virtue.

Savitar — Deity of the sun. Same as *Savitṛ*, *Savitri*, and *Sūrya.*
Savitṛ or **Savitri** — See **Savitar**.
Śeṣa — Thousand-headed cosmic serpent, associated with Viṣṇu, who reclines on his coils. Also called Ananta.
siddha — ("perfect", "boiled") 1.) A spiritually perfected person. 2.) One who has cultivated *siddhis.* See **siddhi(s)**.
siddhi(s) — Any of eight supernatural powers attained through yogic practice. *Siddhis* are not an indication of spiritual advancement, which may or may not be accompanied by them.
Śiśupāla — A wicked king slain by Śrī Kṛṣṇa.
śiṣya — Disciple.
Sītā — ("furrow") The Divine Mother in Her Incarnation as the *Śakti* of Lord Rāma. Her name is derived from the fact that She is the daughter of the Earth, was discovered in a furrow while the earth was being tilled, and returned to the center of the Earth at the end of Her life.
Śiva — ("auspicious") One of the principal manifestations of the Divine. He is the Cosmic Yogi, the Lord of Meditators, the Great Renunciate, the Supreme Godhead. In His role as the universal destroyer before the commencement of cosmic renewal, He is Naṭarāj, the Lord of the Dance. In His symbolic form as the *liṅgam,* He is the universal Creator and the axis of all Reality. Both violent and peaceful, erotic and ascetic, creative and dissolutive, He is all things to all people.
Śiva Purāṇa — One of the principal *Purāṇas,* devoted to Lord Śiva.
skandha(s) — Divisions of the *Śrīmad Bhāgavatam*; the twelve cantos or books.
śloka — A type of verse or meter used in the Hindu scriptures. May also refer to a specific verse, such as "the third *śloka* of chapter ten".
smaraṇam — ("remembering") Fixing the mind on God at all times; one of the principal disciplines of *bhakti-yoga.*
smṛti — ("remembered") Post-Vedic sacred texts, such as the *Purāṇas, Itihāsas, Tantras,* etc. The name is derived from the fact that their contents were passed down orally before being arranged into specific literary works and committed to writing. Compare to **śruti**.
soma — 1.) An intoxicating sacramental drink offered to the gods in Vedic sacrifice. 2.) The name of the sacrifice in which *soma* is offered into the sacred fire and the remainder drunk by the officiating priests. 3.) A principal Vedic deity, the god of *soma.*
śraddhā — Faith.
śravaṇam — ("hearing") Listening to recitations of scripture, discourses by the *guru,* etc.; one of the principal disciplines of *bhakti-yoga.*
Śrī — ("prosperity", "good fortune" also "revered", "holy") 1.) The Divine Mother in Her form as Lakṣmī. 2.) An honorific title for a revered person,

deity or text. 3.) An honorific title for a respected man, the equivalent of "Sir" or "Mister". The female equivalent is *Śrīmatī*.

Śrī Durgā Saptaśatī — See **Caṇḍi**.

Śrīmad Bhāgavatam — Also called *Bhāgavata Purāṇa*, the most illustrious and popular of the *Purāṇas*. Extraordinarily rich in philosophy, theology, history, myth and practical spiritual instruction of universal applicability, God is here emphasized in His forms of Viṣṇu and Kṛṣṇa. The tenth canto, which is devoted entirely to the pastimes of Kṛṣṇa, is one of the most renowned pieces of religious literature in the world.

Śrīmad Devī Bhāgavatam — The *Purāṇa* devoted to God as Divine Mother. A principal scripture in the *Śākta* tradition.

Śrīmatī — ("revered mother") An honorific title for a woman.

śreyaḥ — In the *Kaṭha Upaniṣad*, that which may not be pleasurable, but is necessary for spiritual advancement. Its opposite is *preyaḥ*, that which is pleasurable, but neither good for you nor conducive to spiritual unfoldment.

śruti — ("heard") The Vedic literatures, specifically the four *Vedas*, the *Brāhmaṇas* and the *Upaniṣads*. The title is derived from the belief that these texts were revealed by the Divine directly to the minds of the Vedic *ṛṣis* (seers). Compare to **smṛti**.

Subhadrā — Kṛṣṇa's sister; the wife of Arjuna; mother of Abhimanyu. Hers is the central image in the famous Jagannātha deities in Purī. See **Jagannātha**.

śūdra — Of the four *varṇas*, or castes, the lowest, that of the laborer.

Sugrīva — In the *Rāmāyaṇa*, the monkey king whose throne was usurped by his brother, Bāli. Sugrīva and his army helped Rāma vanquish Rāvaṇa and rescue Sītā, after which Rāma reinstated Sugrīva as king.

Śuka or **Śukadeva** — The original speaker of the *Śrīmad Bhāgavatam*. After hearing the core of the text from his father, Vyāsa, he expanded upon it to King Parīkṣit and the assembly of sages on the banks of the Ganges.

Surabhī — The celestial wish-fulfilling cow, originally produced from the churning of the ocean.

Sūrya — The sun deity. Same as *Savitṛ*, *Savitri*, and *Savitar*.

suśumnā — The subtle nerve, or *nāḍī*, running up the hollow in the spinal column. It is flanked on either side by the *iḍā* and *piṅgalā* nerves, and passes through the seven *cakras*, or centers of consciousness. As the *kuṇḍalinī*, or spiritual energy lying dormant at the base of the spine, is awakened, it climbs up the *suśumnā* and activates each *cakra* in turn, inducing higher and higher states of consciousness.

Sūta — The narrator of the *Śrīmad Bhāgavatam*. He recited the text from memory to the assembled sages in the forest of Naimiṣāraṇya.

Suvaḥ — See **Svaḥ**.

svādiṣṭhāna cakra — The second of the seven yogic *cakras*, or energy centers, located at the reproductive organs. See **cakras**.
Svaḥ or **Svāhā** — One of the three *vyāhṛtis*, or mystical utterances, comprising the invocation of the holy *Gāyatrī mantra* and spoken at the commencement of rituals. *Svaḥ* refers to the spiritual realm, as opposed to the terrestrial (*Bhūr*) and the celestial (*Bhuvaḥ*).
svāmī — ("master") A monk; one who has mastered his own lower self. The female counterpart is a *pravrājikā* ("woman ascetic").
svayaṃvara — A ceremony in which a princess or noblewoman chooses a husband from among an assembly of suitors.
Śvetāśvatara Upaniṣad — One of the principal *Upaniṣads*, concerned chiefly with the presence of Brahman in all creation.

tamas — Of the three *guṇas*, or modes of material nature, that of inertia, ignorance, darkness.
tapas — ("heat") Austerities and ascetic practices, so named because of their spiritual intensity and the fact that they literally produce a state of heat in the body.
tapasyā — The practice of *tapas*.
tat tvam asi — "That thou art" i.e. "you are Brahman"; one of the *Mahāvākyas* ("Great Utterances") of the *Upaniṣads*.
tattva(s) — Principal elements or evolvents of matter.
Tretā-yuga — Of the four *yugas*, or epochs in the duration of the world, the second.
triloka — ("three abodes") The Vedic conception of the universe as three-tiered, with terrestrial, atmospheric, and celestial realms. Later, the *triloka* came to represent the physical, subtle and spiritual states.
Trimūrti — ("three forms") Brahman in Its personal, threefold aspect of Brahmā, Viṣṇu and Śiva.
turīya — ("the fourth") The state of pure, unlimited God-consciousness. It is so named because we are normally privy to three states of consciousness: wakefulness, dreaming sleep, and deep, dreamless sleep. *Turīya* is the "fourth state", beyond all three.

udāna — The *prāṇa*, or vital air, responsible for conducting the soul out of the body at the time of death.
Uddhava — Beloved disciple of Lord Kṛṣṇa, to whom Kṛṣṇa delivered His final discourse on the last night of His life.
Uddhava Gītā — Śrī Kṛṣṇa's final discourse, delivered on the last night of His life. It is so named because it was spoken to Uddhava, Kṛṣṇa's beloved devotee. The *Uddhava Gītā* is contained in the eleventh canto of the *Śrīmad Bhāgavatam*.

udgātā or **udgātṛ** — The priest who chants the *udgītha* and *upadrava* sections of the *soma* sacrifice.
Udgītha — ("to chant aloud") 1.) *Oṃ*. 2.) The second part of the *Sāma Veda*. 3.) The *Sāma Veda* as a whole.
Upaniṣads — ("come sit near me") The philosophical or mystical portion of the *Vedas*; shorter treatises which espouse the oneness of Brahman and Ātman and the underlying unity of all Reality. Though there are 108 *Upaniṣads*, ten are considered preeminent. The derive their name from the image of the *guru* beckoning the disciple to sit down for instruction. They are also referred to as the *Vedānta*, (*veda*, "knowledge", *anta*, "end") because they come at the end of the Vedic corpus and because they contain the limit of all knowledge, Ultimate Truth.
Upa-Purāṇas — Eighteen lesser *Purāṇas*, that is, texts that hold a lower place than the more revered *Mahā-Purāṇas*. They are the *Sanatkumāra*, *Narasiṃha*, *Nāradīya* or *Vṛhannāradīya*, *Śiva*, *Durvāsasa*, *Kāpila*, *Mānava*, *Auśanasa*, *Vāruṇa*, *Kālikā*, *Śāmba*, *Nandi*, *Saura*, *Pārāśara*, *Āditya*, *Māheśvara*, *Bhārgava*, *Vāsiṣṭha*.
upāsanā — A meditation which draws the mind, in steps, from the mundane to the spiritual. It is a common form of philosophical exposition in the *Upaniṣads*.
Urvaśī — A celestial nymph married to the human king Purūrava of the Lunar dynasty.

Vāc — The Goddess of speech.
vairāgya — Renunciation.
Vaiśeṣika — Of the six orthodox schools of Hindu philosophy, that of proto-science and atomic theory. Founded by Kaṇāda in the third century B.C..
Vaiṣṇava — ("of Viṣṇu") 1.) A devotee of Viṣṇu. 2.) Of or pertaining to Viṣṇu and His worship.
vaiśya — Third of the four *varṇas*, or castes, that of the mercantile class.
Vali — See **Bali**.
Vāli — See **Bāli**.
vallī(s) — Section headings in the *Taittirīya Upaniṣad*.
Vālmīki — The author of the *Rāmāyaṇa*.
Vāmana — ("dwarf") Viṣṇu's dwarf *Avatāra*.
vānaprastha — Of the four *āśramas*, or stages of life, that of the retiree. In this stage, a husband and wife gradually renounce the world while travelling to holy sites of pilgrimage together as a preparation for the final stage, *sannyāsa*.
Varāha — ("boar") Viṣṇu's boar *Avatāra*.
varṇa(s) — ("color") The four social and occupational divisions, or

castes. They include *brāhmaṇas*, the priestly and intellectual class; *kṣatriyas*, the governmental and military class; *vaiśya*, the mercantile class; *śūdra*, the laboring class.

varṇāśrama-dharma — The system by which society is ordered according to the four *varṇas*, or castes, and four *āśramas*, or stages of life.

Varuṇa — The Vedic deity of the waters.

Vasiṣṭha — One of the most prominent of the ancient Vedic *ṛṣis*.

Vasudeva — Kṛṣṇa's biological father.

Vāsudeva — ("descendant of Vasudeva") Kṛṣṇa.

Vāyu — Vedic deity of wind.

Veda(s) — ("knowledge") The most ancient and most revered of the Hindu scriptures. The four *Vedas* include the *Ṛg*, *Sāma*, *Yajur*, and *Atharva*. They are the oldest religious scriptures in the world still in use, and primarily contain devotional and petitionary hymns as well as instructions for ritual. The *Upaniṣads* are considered a part of the Vedic corpus as well, but constitute a philosophical shift away from outward ritual to a more internalized form of spirituality.

Vedāṅgas — ("limbs") Texts auxiliary to the *Vedas* which deal with the correct performance of sacred rituals. They include expositions on pronunciation, meter, etymology, grammar, astronomy and ceremony.

Vedānta — ("end of the Veda") 1.) The *Upaniṣads*. 2.) The philosophical and religious tradition which is derived from the *Upaniṣads*. 3.) One of the six orthodox philosophical schools of Hinduism. 4.) The ultimate conclusion of all knowledge, namely that Brahman is all.

Vedānta Sūtra — Standard treatise on the *Upaniṣads* by Bādarāyaṇa. Composed sometime between the third and fifth centuries, it attempts to systematize and summarize the teachings of the *Upaniṣads* in the form of aphorisms. Also called *Brahma Sūtra*.

Vidura — In the *Mahābhārata*, the saintly half-brother of Pāṇḍu and Dhṛtarāṣṭra.

vidveṣa-bhakti — The path to God through hatred. The reasoning behind *vidveṣa-bhakti* is that fixing the mind on God, in whatever mood and for whatever reason, is a sure path to union with God. Therefore one whose thoughts constantly dwell on God, even because one is obsessed with hatred of God, will make progress towards God.

vidyā — "Knowledge", "wisdom", "science".

Vijaya — One of Viṣṇu's doorkeepers who, because he and his brother, Jaya, barred entrance to the four Kumāras, was cursed to take birth as a demon. He subsequently became Hiraṇyākṣa.

vijñānamayakośa — The intellectual sheath; of the five *kośas*, or subtle and material layers which cover the Ātman, the intellectual/discriminative layer.

vīṇā — A stringed instrument; carried by the celestial devotee-minstrel Nārada as he roams the universe serenading God.
Virāṭ-Puruṣa — God as the Cosmic Person, Whose body is the universe.
Virāṭ-Rūpa — God as the Cosmic Person, Whose body is the universe.
Virocana — ("shining upon", "illuminating") An epithet of the sun deity.
Viṣṇu — ("all-pervading") One of the principal manifestations of the Divine. Beautiful, loving and radiant, He is associated with the preservation of the universe, and periodically takes birth on earth in the form of *Avatāras*, the three most significant of which are Rāma, Kṛṣṇa and Buddha.
Viṣṇudūtas — Order-carriers of Viṣṇu. Resembling Viṣṇu in every respect, these angelic beings appear to liberated souls at the moment of death to usher them to Viṣṇu's abode.
Viṣṇu Purāṇa — One of the principal *Mahā-Purāṇas*, focusing on devotion to Viṣṇu.
viśuddha cakra — The fifth of the seven yogic *cakras*, or energy centers, located at the throat.
Vivasvat or **Vivasvān** — ("brilliant one") Epithet of the sun deity.
viveka — Discrimination, particularly discrimination between the Real and the unreal.
Vṛndāvana — The rural village where Kṛṣṇa spent His childhood pastimes.
Vyāsa or **Vyāsadeva** — ("compiler", "editor") Legendary author/compiler of the *Vedas* and *Purāṇas.* Also called Kṛṣṇa Dvaipāyana.
vyāhṛtis — The three mystical utterances comprising the invocation of the holy *Gāyatrī mantra* and spoken at the commencement of rituals: *Bhūḥ*, *Bhuvaḥ*, *Svaḥ.*

Yādavas — ("of Yadu") The branch of the Lunar dynasty descended from Yadu. Śrī Kṛṣṇa was born into this line.
Yadu — Patriarch of the Yādava line of the Lunar dynasty. The other line descended from his brother, Puru.
yajña — Ritual sacrifice, oblation, worship.
Yajur Veda — Of the four *Vedas*, the manual for performance of ritual sacrifice.
Yājñavalkya — Celebrated sage of the *Upaniṣads.*
yakṣa(s) — Spirits or sprites of the field and jungle; they may be either beneficent or malignant.
yama — Principles of self-restraint; the first of the eight steps of *rāja-yoga.*
Yama or **Yamarāja** — The god of death; ruler of the realm of death.

Yamadūtas — Order-carriers of Yama, the god of death; they appear to sinners at the moment of death to drag them to Yama's abode.
Yamunā — The river upon the banks of which Śrī Kṛṣṇa played as a child.
yantra — A type of mystical diagram used in meditation.
Yaśodā — Śrī Kṛṣṇa's beloved foster-mother.
yoga — ("yoke", "link") 1.) Union with God. 2.) Methods used to unite one with God; spiritual practices.
Yoga Sūtras — Guide to the theory and practice of *rāja-yoga*, the core of which was compiled by Patañjali in the second century B.C..
yogī or **yoginī** (feminine) — A practitioner of *yoga.*
yoni — Vaginal symbol representing the Goddess, or *Prakṛti.* It is joined to the *liṅgam*, which represents Śiva or *Puruṣa.*
Yudhiṣṭhira — The eldest of the Pāṇḍava brothers.
yuga(s) — The four epochs in the duration of the world: *Satya-yuga, Tretā-yuga, Dvāpara-yuga* and *Kali-yuga.* We are presently in the *Kali-yuga.*

Bibliography

Alston, A.J., *The Devotional Poems of Mirabai* (Delhi: Motilal Banarsidass, 1980).

Ashokānanda, Swāmī, *Meditation, Ecstasy and Illumination* (Calcutta: Advaita Ashrama, 1990).

Bhaktivedanta Swami Prabhupāda, A.C., *Bhagavad-Gītā As It Is* (Vaduz, Lichtenstein: The Bhaktivedanta Book Trust, 1983).

Coulson, Michael, *Teach Yourself Sanskrit* (New York: David McKay Company, Inc., 1976).

Danielou, Alain, *Hindu Polytheism* (New York: Bollingen Foundation, 1964).

Easwaran, Eknath, *Dialogue With Death: The Spiritual Psychology of the Kaṭha Upaniṣad* (Petaluma: Nilgiri Press, 1981).

Gambhīrānanda, Swāmī, *Brahma-Sūtra Bhāṣya of Śaṅkārācarya* (Calcutta: Advaita Ashrama, 1977).

Gambhīrānanda, Swāmī, *Chāndogya Upaniṣad* (Calcutta: Advaita Ashrama, 1983).

Gambhīrānanda, Swāmī, *Kaṭha Upaniṣad* (Calcutta: Advaita Ashrama, 1980).

Gambhīrānanda, Swāmī, *Praśna Upaniṣad* (Calcutta: Advaita Ashrama, 1979).

Harshananda, Swami, *A Dictionary of Advaita Vedanta* (Bangalore: Sri Ramakrishna Ashrama, 1990).

Jagadiswarananda, Swami, *The Bṛhadāraṇyaka Upaniṣad* (Mylapore: Sri Ramakrishna Math, 1985).

Jagadīsvarānanda, Swāmī, *The Devī Māhātmyam or Śrī Durgā-Saptaśatī* (Madras: Sri Ramakrishna Math, 1972).

Jung, Carl et. al., *Man and His Symbols* (Garden City: Doubleday and Company, 1964).

Khan, Zafrulla, *The Koran* (New York: Praeger Publishers, 1971).

Krishnānanda, Swāmī, *The Bṛhadāraṇyaka Upaniṣad* (Shivanandanagar: The Divine Life Society, 1984).

Madhavānanda, Swāmī, *The Bṛhadāraṇyaka Upaniṣad* (Calcutta: Advaita Ashrama, 1965).

Madhavānanda, Swāmī, *Uddhava Gītā* (Calcutta: Advaita Ashrama, 1978).

Mukhyananda, Swami, *Oṃ, Gāyatrī and Sandhyā* (Mylapore: Sri Ramakrishna Math, 1989).

Nikhilānanda, Swāmī, *The Upaniṣads, Vol. II* (New York: Harper and Row, 1959).

Noss, David S. and Noss, John B., *A History of the World's Religions* (New York: Macmillan Publishing Company, 1990).

Organ, Troy Wilson, *Hinduism, Its Historical Development* (Woodbury: Barron's Educational Series, Inc., 1974).

Parasharānanda, Swāmī, *Garland of Prayers* (Singapore: Ramakrishna Mission Singapore, 1990).

Prabhavananda, Swami and Isherwood, Christopher, *The Song of God: Bhagavad-Gītā* (New York: New American Library, 1972).

Prabhavananda, Swami and Isherwood, Christopher, *How to Know God* (New York: New American Library, 1968).

Prabhavananda, Swami and Manchester, Frederick, *The Upaniṣads, Breath of the Eternal* (Hollywood: Vedanta Press, 1975).

Rajagopalachari, C., *The Mahābhārata* (Bombay: Bharatiya Vidya Bhavan, 1979).

Rajagopalachari, C., *The Rāmāyaṇa* (Bombay: Bharatiya Vidya Bhavan, 1975).

Ramakrishna-Vedanta Wordbook (Hollywood: Vedanta Press, 1978).

Ranganathananda, Swami, *The Message of the Upaniṣads* (New York: Ramakrishna-Vivekananda Center, 1942).

Sargeant, Winthrop, *The Bhagavad-Gītā* (Albany: State University of New York Press, 1984).

Śarvānanda, Swāmī, *Aitareyopaniṣad* (Mylapore: Sri Ramakrishna Math, 1978).

Śarvānanda, Swāmī, *Īśavāsyopaniṣad* (Mylapore: Sri Ramakrishna Math, 1981).

Śarvānanda, Swāmī, *Kenopaniṣad* (Madras: Sri Ramakrishna Math, 1981).

Śarvānanda, Swāmī, *Māṇḍūkyopaniṣad* (Mylapore: Sri Ramakrishna Math, 1976).

Śarvānanda, Swāmī, *Muṇḍakopaniṣad* (Mylapore: Sri Ramakrishna Math, 1974).

Śarvānanda, Swāmī, *Taittirīyopaniṣad* (Mylapore: Sri Ramakrishna Math, 1977).

Shastri, J. L., ed., *The Śiva Purāṇa* (Delhi: Motilal Banarsidass, 1981).

Smith, Daniel H., *The Picturebook Rāmāyaṇa* (Syracuse: Maxwell School of Citizenship and Public Affairs, Syracuse University, 1981).

Stutley, James and Stutley, Margaret, *Harper's Dictionary of Hinduism* (San Francisco: Harper and Row Publishers, 1977).

Tapasyānanda, Swāmī, *Bhakti Ratnāvali or a Necklace of Devotional Gems* (Madras: Sri Ramakrishna Math, 1979).

Tapasyānanda, Swāmī, *Śrīmad Bhāgavata, The Holy Book of God* (Mylapore: Sri Ramakrishna Math, 1980).

Tyagīśānanda, Swāmī, *Śvetāśvatara Upaniṣad* (Mylapore: Sri Ramakrishna Math, 1979).

Tyagīśānanda, Swāmī, *Nārada Bhakti Sūtras* (Madras: Sri Ramakrishna Math, 1983).

Vijñānānanda, Swāmī, *Śrīmad Devī Bhāgavatam* (Delhi: Munshiram Manoharlal, 1977).

Vimalananda, Swami, *Śrī Lalithāmbikā Sahasranāma Stotram* (Tirupparaitturai: Sri Ramakrishna Tapovanam, 1984).

Vireswarananda, Swami and Adidevananda, Swami, *Brahma-Sūtras: Śrī-Bhāṣya* (Calcutta: Advaita Ashrama, 1986)

Vivekananda, Swami, *Rāja Yoga* (New York: Ramakrishna-Vivekananda Center, 1956).

Wilson, H.H., *Viṣṇu Purāṇa* (Delhi: Nag Publishers, 1980).

Pronunciation of Sanskrit Words

Vowels

a as in b*u*t.
ā as in f*a*ther.
i as in f*i*t.
ī as in f*ee*.
u as in p*u*t.
ū as in b*oo*t.
e as in f*a*te.
ai as in k*i*te.
o as in r*o*pe.
au as in c*ow*.

ṛ is pronounced *ri*, as in p*re*tty, but with a slight trill, like a German r.
ṝ is pronounced *ri* as in *Ri*ta, again with a slight trill.
ḷ as in tab*le*.

Consonants

The Sanskrit consonants pronounced as in English are: *k, g, d, t, j, p, b, l, m, n, y, r, s,* and *h*.

c is pronounced *ch*, as in *ch*at.
ch is *ch-h*, as in pin*ch-h*itter.

ñ is pronounced *nya*, as in ca*ny*on or the Spanish ma*ñ*ana.

v is pronounced as a cross between a *v* and *w*, as in *svami* (swami).

In consonants followed by an *h*, the pronunciation of the primary consonant remains unchanged while the *h* is distinctly vocalized:
kh as in roc*k-h*ard.
gh as in bi*g-h*ead.
jh as in hed*ge-h*og.
th as in si*t-h*ere.
dh as in sa*d-h*eart.
etc.

The letters transliterated with a dot below them — *ṭ, ṭh, ḍ, ḍh, ṇ,* are pronounced as in English, but with the tongue hitting the roof of the mouth as opposed to the hard ridge directly behind the teeth.

ś is pronounced *sh* as in *sh*ine.
ṣ is also pronounced *sh*, but with the tongue against the palate.

Visarga

Some words end with a mark called a *visarga,* which in English transliteration appears as an *h* with a dot below it: *ḥ*. It is pronounced as an *h*, but with a repetition of the vowel sound which preceded it. For instance, *gajaḥ*, elephant, is pronounced *gaja-ha. Devīḥ* is pronounced *Devī-hi.*

Index